FACILITIES MANAGEMENT AND DEVELOPMENT FOR TOURISM, HOSPITALITY AND EVENTS

Edited by

Ahmed Hassanien and **Crispin Dale**

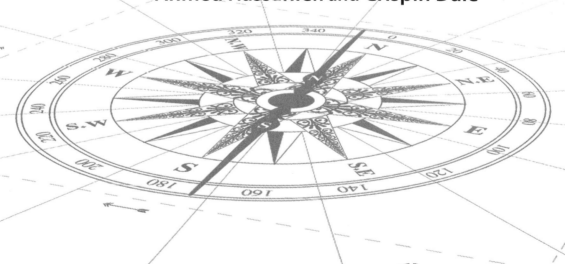

www.cabi.org

CABI is a trading name of CAB International

CABI
Nosworthy Way
Wallingford
Oxfordshire OX10 8DE
UK

CABI
38 Chauncey Street
Suite 1002
Boston, MA 02111
USA

Tel: +44 (0)1491 832111
Fax: +44 (0)1491 833508
E-mail: info@cabi.org
Website: www.cabi.org

Tel: +1 800 552 3083 (toll free)
Tel: +1 (0)617 395 4051
E-mail: cabi-nao@cabi.org

A catalogue record for this book is available from the British Library, London, UK.

Library of Congress Cataloging-in-Publication Data

Facilities management and development for tourism, hospitality and events / edited
by Ahmed Hassanien and Crispin Dale.
    pages cm. -- (CABI tourism texts)
 Includes bibliographical references and index.
 ISBN 978-1-78064-034-1 (alk. paper)
1. Facility management. 2. Tourism--Management. 3. Hospitality industry--Management.
4. Special events--Management. I. Hassanien, Ahmed. II. Dale, Crispin.

 TS155.F222 2013
 658.2--dc23

                     2012046418

ISBN-13: 978 1 78064 034 1

Commissioning editor: Claire Parfitt
Editorial assistant: Alexandra Lainsbury
Production editor: Simon Hill

Typeset by SPi, Pondicherry, India
Printed and bound by Gutenberg Press, Malta.

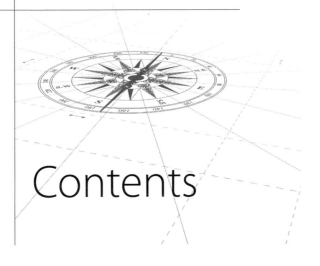

Contents

FACILITIES MANAGEMENT AND DEVELOPMENT FOR TOURISM, HOSPITALITY AND EVENTS

CABI TOURISM TEXTS are an essential resource for students of academic tourism, leisure studies, hospitality, entertainment and events management. The series reflects the growth of tourism-related studies at an academic level and responds to the changes and developments in these rapidly evolving industries, providing up-to-date practical guidance, discussion of the latest theories and concepts, and analysis by world experts. The series is intended to guide students through their academic programmes and remain an essential reference throughout their careers in the tourism sector.

Readers will find the books within the CABI TOURISM TEXTS series to have a uniquely wide scope, covering important elements in leisure and tourism, including management-led topics, practical subject matter and development of conceptual themes and debates. Useful textbook features such as case studies, bullet point summaries and helpful diagrams are employed throughout the series to aid study and encourage understanding of the subject.

Students at all levels of study, workers within tourism and leisure industries, researchers, academics, policy makers and others interested in the field of academic and practical tourism will find these books an invaluable and authoritative resource, useful for academic reference and real world tourism applications.

Titles available

Ecotourism: Principles and Practices
Ralf Buckley

Contemporary Tourist Behaviour: Yourself and Others as Tourists
David Bowen and Jackie Clarke

The Entertainment Industry: an Introduction
Edited by Stuart Moss

Practical Tourism Research
Stephen L.J. Smith

Leisure, Sport and Tourism, Politics, Policy and Planning, 3rd Edition
A.J. Veal

Events Management
Edited by Peter Robinson, Debra Wale and Geoff Dickson

Food and Wine Tourism: Integrating Food, Travel and Territory
Erica Croce and Giovanni Perri

Research Methods for Leisure, Recreation and Tourism
Edited by Ercan Sirakaya-Turk, Muzaffer Usyal, William E. Hammitt, and Jerry J. Vaske

Facilities Management and Development for Tourism, Hospitality and Events
Edited by Ahmed Hassanien and Crispin Dale

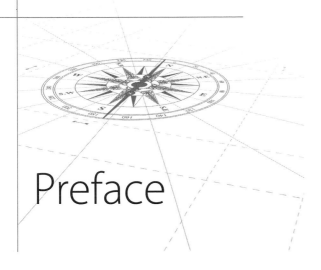

Preface

Facilities management and development for tourism, hospitality and events (THE) are becoming increasingly important, from both theoretical (academic) and applied (practitioner) perspectives. This should not be surprising given that land, property and resources represent major components of the foundation of the industry. Whether it is a restaurant, a hotel, a visitor attraction or an event venue, any such facility is invariably extremely valuable, costs a great deal of money to develop and operate and represents much of the environment in which guest or visitor experiences are generated and delivered. In spite of the importance of facilities within the THE industries, little has been written in the academic literature that focuses on the facilities themselves: the specific operational issues that they encounter; their role within destination development and as the interface between the multi-faceted hospitality, tourism, leisure and events sectors. As future managers in the industry, it is imperative that students have a sound basic knowledge of property, and the various resources, systems and services associated with it, in order to be able to manage and control facilities as efficiently, effectively and sensitively as possible. In other words, it is important that students or future managers gain a basic understanding of the concept of facilities management, of how it has grown and developed rapidly over recent years, of its present and potential scope and, in particular, how it is being increasingly adopted and applied within THE operations. For example, why do many hotels no longer operate their own laundries; why do many visitor attractions and event venues outsource catering and other guest/visitor services?

The book examines the concepts of project management, physical evidence and design, and their application in the context of THE facilities. For example, what factors typically affect the design and layout of a hotel room, or the reception area of a visitor attraction or event venue? How is the industry responding to changes in consumer demand, and what new types and styles of facility are being developed?

The book then considers the various subsequent stages in the property development process, focusing on the key determinants of feasibility that apply to any project, namely site, market, finance and legal considerations. For example, what are the potential sources of funding for THE projects, and how might one assess the potential return on a proposed capital investment? In addition, the book looks at the principles, process and mechanics of the planning system in some detail. For example, on what grounds are planning applications in respect of visitor attractions commonly turned down?

In addition, the book examines the construction phase of any THE project, such as the addition of extra rooms to a hotel or the extensive refurbishment of an existing visitor attraction. In particular, it considers those consultants typically involved in such projects, as well as the role and responsibilities of the client and the project manager. The book also examines the important associated area of maintenance and renovation management in some detail.

Cost and market pressures are increasingly forcing organizations to operate THE facilities more efficiently and effectively than ever before, resulting in a growing trend towards the use of alternative strategies such as contracting out or outsourcing, thereby, theoretically, enabling operators to focus more on their 'core' business. Therefore, the book examines the basic rationale for the adoption of such strategies, including both their potential advantages and disadvantages, and common types of agreement and contract type.

In addition, the book explores the growing imperative for all types of tourism, hospitality and event operation to be able to demonstrate and evidence due diligence in terms of what is now termed sustainability, corporate and social responsibility and environmental management. It discusses the potential components of this wide-ranging and far-reaching concept in the context of THE operations, in particular considering how such operations can easily damage the environment, or, on the other hand, can readily adopt a whole range of policies and initiatives to help achieve development that is sustainable into the future. The book compares and contrasts custom and practice relating to the operation and management of THE facilities within three types of sector: public, private and not-for-profit.

In addition, the book considers the significance of effective and appropriate facilities management competences in facilitating the planning, development and evaluation of THE facilities. It examines key approaches towards addressing leadership, innovation, knowledge management, work process knowledge, entrepreneurship and achieving and sustaining competitive advantage.

Ahmed Hassan n
Edinburgh Napier University

Crispin Dale
Wolverhampton University

Michael Herriott
Edinburgh Napier University

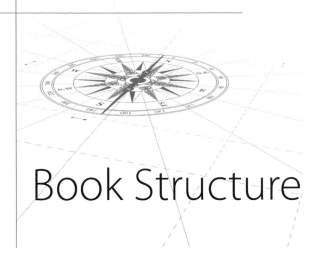

Book Structure

The material in the book is presented in five sections that reflect different perspectives and issues regarding facilities management and development. The first section of the book (Chapters 1–2) provides an initial understanding of what facilities are and their scope in the context of THE. Chapter 1 examines the concept of facilities management within the context of the THE industries. It investigates the scope of facilities management and explores the growing importance and evolution of facilities management with particular emphasis on the motives behind it. Also, it discusses the benefits and objectives of facilities management for THE operations. Chapter 2 outlines what is meant by a THE facility and explores the different levels of facilities. This includes primary, sub and ancillary facilities. This categorization helps in understanding the relationship, management and development of THE facilities. It would not be unusual for facility managers to focus mainly on the primary level; however, it is crucial that they understand how the sub and ancillary facilities can be managed so as generate further value for their business. This chapter also considers the scope and different types of THE facilities. This acknowledges that the scope of facilities management should encompass stakeholder groups and the breadth of THE facilities and attractions. A discussion of the characteristics of services and their influence on facility decision making is also provided.

The second section of the book (Chapters 3–8) explores the different services that facilities management can cover within the context of THE facilities. Chapter 3 focuses on project management in THE facilities. As the chapter explains, this incorporates the key management principles of planning, organizing, leading, coordinating and controlling project resources. The chapter acknowledges the uniqueness of some of the projects that may be carried out in facilities and categorizes these within an uncertainty/complexity typology framework. The chapter also explores how projects should be managed if they are to be carried out successfully. What is key is that customers are central to any project that is being proposed. Chapter 4 discusses the purpose, components and limitations of a feasibility study. The facility manager and operator should use the feasibility study for their decision making on whether to proceed with any development. This can only be accomplished successfully if the respective stages of the feasibility study are addressed comprehensively. Though it can be a time-consuming and costly exercise, if conducted appropriately it will act as an excellent foundation for the future success of the THE facility.

Chapter 5 moves on to explore the physical evidence of a THE facility. As the chapter explains, this is crucial for reducing the sense of intangibility that a customer experiences when purchasing a THE facility service. The chapter recognizes the importance of atmosphere in a THE facility and how this can be generated. This encapsulates the 'servicescape' model for the effective design of the facility and how this can affect the customer experience. This includes the interaction of the facility on the human senses, with different stimuli such as music and colour having a profound impact on the customer experience. In the design and development of THE facilities, managers should be aware of the psychological influence that these aspects can have on human behaviour. This is necessary for understanding not only how customers experience the facility, but also how employees interact within their working domain.

Chapter 6 investigates the role of information technology in THE facilities. The chapter presents a typology of technologies as they relate to THE facilities. The chapter acknowledges developments in technologies as a process of political, economic and social changes that have occurred historically. The authors conclude that technologies have the potential to drive change in facilities to meet day-to-day consumer needs and demands.

Chapter 7 explores the concept of outsourcing in facilities and how this can be used as a means of not only reducing costs but also as a means of generating further value for the customer experience within the facility. The chapter acknowledges the different levels of outsourcing and why it may be used within THE facilities. Facility managers should make a careful appraisal of their non-core activities and assess their viability for outsourcing. The chapter proposes financial, physical, human, operational and strategic factors that should be considered, as well as a range of hard and soft criteria that should be considered when conducting an outsourcing assessment. Central to this is the decision matrix, which could be used as a basis for classifying any outsourcing decision. Facility managers and operators should determine to what extent any outsourcing would affect the development of the facilities resources and core competences. This is crucial when considering the future strategic direction of the facility.

In the final part of this section, Chapter 8 explores the concept of cost management. The chapter notes the importance of costs at both a tangible and intangible level. This includes the cost of physical resources such as equipment and materials, in addition to the opportunity cost of pursuing a particular course of action in the development of a facility. In this respect, the chapter proposes a scenario planning approach to understanding cost management. Key to this is understanding the financial issues of selecting different alternatives. This is in terms of the break-even point and overall projected financial performance.

The third section (Chapters 9–12) focuses on the sustainable development and management of THE facilities. This section explores different sustainable development issues within the context of THE facilities. Chapter 9 explores sustainable facilities design and management. The chapter acknowledges the strategic value of sustainable development for facility developers, owners, operators and managers. It explores the origin and growth of sustainable development in the THE sector, the motivators for developers, owners and operators of THE facilities to adopt sustainable policies and practices, and investigates current issues in sustainable design and management in the THE sector. The chapter highlights the widespread adoption of a sustainable management agenda and the legislative and regulatory environment as key factors for motivating THE facility managers, operators and developers to adopt sustainable practices in their design principles. Certification programmes such as the LEED and Living Building Challenge, which the chapter explains, have engendered these design principles. Such programmes have made it commonplace for facility managers, developers and operators to embed sustainability in their day-to-day working practices.

Chapter 10 continues with the sustainability agenda and explores corporate social responsibility for facilities in THE. The chapter recognizes the growing expectation for organizations to demonstrate transparency in their ethical and social principles. The chapter provides lucid debates surrounding corporate social responsibility and drivers for its growing prevalence. The chapter notes the focus of THE facilities towards goals and objectives that reflect more than just the financial bottom line. This is being empowered by key stakeholder needs and expectations that embrace customers and communities.

Chapter 11 investigates environmental management in THE facilities. The chapter recognizes the essential requirement for facilities to incorporate environmental management practices in light of global demographic and infrastructural pressures. The chapter notes the challenges for THE facilities in embedding environmental practices. This includes the individualistic, fragmented and relatively small-sized composition of facilities in the THE industries. Financial pressures and consumer sensitivity towards balancing environmental concerns with service quality further compound this issue. The authors note the continuous need to enlighten facility managers, operators, developers and users of the benefits and consequences of engaging in environmental management practices.

The concluding part to this section, Chapter 12, addresses more specifically waste and energy management. The chapter notes that waste is one of the key problems for the global population and further acknowledges that the THE industries are a major contributor to waste and energy consumption. The chapter discusses the implementation of energy and waste management in the design, construction and operation of THE facilities with the driver to generate resource and cost efficiencies. This includes a THE waste management programme that requires THE facilities to embrace the preparation, implementation and evaluation phases in their practices. The chapter also provides a range of examples for renewable energy management and efficiency.

The fourth section (Chapters 13–17) explores various key competencies or functions required for effective facilities management and development. Chapter 13 discusses leadership as a key competence for THE facilities. The chapter acknowledges that the area of leadership is complex and encompasses a range of different theories. The central tenet is to engineer innovation and creativity among those responsible for the management, development and operation of the facility. The chapter goes on to discuss leadership in the context of a group process; a personality or behaviour; and as a power, transformational or skills perspective.

Chapter 14 discusses the role of innovation in THE facilities. The chapter looks at various aspects of innovation in the THE industries. It includes discussion on the definition, importance, motives, drivers, types, process and measurement of innovation. Chapter 15 explores entrepreneurship in THE facilities. The chapter discusses the theory of entrepreneurship in the context of THE facilities. As mentioned before, innovation and creativity are central tenets of entrepreneurial thinking. However, in addition to this, the chapter notes that it is also the effective management of resources for exploiting opportunities to fulfil customer needs. The chapter also acknowledges the strategic role of entrepreneurship and opportunities for value creation in THE facilities.

Chapter 16 addresses the issue of work process knowledge in THE facilities. As well as defining the phenomenon, the chapter highlights work process knowledge's importance in THE facilities, recognizing the organization, the individual and customers as the key drivers. An understanding of work process knowledge has the potential to help THE facility managers and employees to provide better customer service. Conversely, the chapter acknowledges how a lack of understanding can ultimately result in service failure. The chapter then explores factors that affect work process knowledge and how facility managers can develop work process knowledge among their staff. In this respect, the chapter noted the importance of work process knowledge issues concerning communication, flexibility, size and complexity of operations, worker attitudes and seasonality to the effective management of the THE facility. Finally, Chapter 17 explores the concept of knowledge management and explains its significance and types within the context of THE facilities. The chapter looks at the internal and external sources of knowledge within organizations. It also examines the processes of knowledge creation/ acquisition; knowledge storage, identification, sharing and retrieval processes; and knowledge sharing, transfer and utilization.

The aim of the fifth section (Chapter 18) is to look at the vital requirements for THE facilities management through summarizing the key messages of previous chapters. Accordingly, Chapter 18 focuses on different essential requirements for successful and efficient facilities planning, development and management in the THE industries.

Acknowledgements

The authors would like to thank a number of colleagues who have given support, suggestions and advice, which assisted in the development of this book. We thank them for taking the time and effort to share their thoughts or support:

- All the contributors, because this book would have never been completed without their help.
- The two referees who reviewed the proposal and provided us with positive and constructive feedback and comments.
- The editors at CABI, especially Claire Parfitt and Alexandra Lainsbury, who have been especially helpful in bringing the book to publication.
- Crispin Dale would like to thank his mum, Mrs Isobel Dale and the immediate family, for their support.
- Mr Michael Herriott for his support in the development of the book idea.
- Finally, colleagues at our respective universities, Edinburgh Napier and Wolverhampton, and our colleagues in the THE industries.

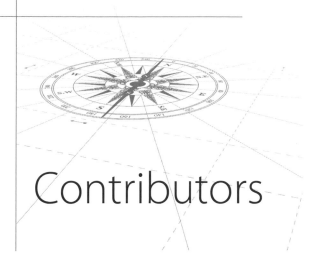

Contributors

Abel Duarte Alonso, PhD, is a Researcher and Lecturer at the University of Western Sydney, School of Business and School of Marketing, Tourism, and Leisure, Edith Cowan University, Western Australia. Alonso's research interests are varied, primarily in small and medium enterprises (SMEs), particularly in rural environments (wineries, farming, food production, value-added products). Other research interests include urban, rural, hospitality and tourism entrepreneurship. Contact information: University of Western Sydney, School of Management, Locked Bag 1797, Penrith South DC, NSW 2571, Australia; e-mail: A.DuarteAlonso@uws.edu.au

Michael Conlin, JD, FIH, is a Professor at the Okanagan School of Business, Okanagan College in Kelowna, BC and holds an appointment in the Faculty of Graduate Studies at the University of Guelph where he teaches in the MBA in Hospitality and Tourism. He also holds an appointment with Royal Roads University in Victoria, where he teaches tourism management in the Faculty of Tourism and Hotel Management. Contact information: Okanagan School of Business, Okanagan College, 1000 KLO Road, Kelowna, British Columbia, Canada V1Y 4X8; e-mail: mconlin@okanagan.bc.ca

Crispin Dale, PhD, is a Principal Lecturer in the School of Sport, Performing Arts and Leisure at the University of Wolverhampton and has taught tourism and hospitality at undergraduate and postgraduate level for a number of years. Crispin Dale has published widely in peer-reviewed journals. His research has focused on strategic management and business development in the tourism, hospitality, sport and events industries. He has also been involved in researching new product development and innovation in events venues. Contact information: School of Sport, Performing Arts and Leisure, University of Wolverhampton, Gorway Road, Walsall, West Midlands WS1 3BD, UK; e-mail: c.dale@wlv.ac.uk

Pauline A. Gordon is Programme Leader of International Hospitality Management at Edinburgh Napier University. She received a BA degree in International Hospitality and Tourism Management and an MSc degree in Tourism Management from Robert Gordon University. Pauline has more than 20 years' experience in industry and academia and her research interests include: investment appraisals in hospitality businesses and teaching, learning and assessment and the transition of international students to higher education in the United Kingdom. Contact information: School of Marketing, Tourism & Languages, Napier University Business School, Napier University – Craiglockhart Campus, Edinburgh EH14 1DJ, UK; e-mail: P.Gordon@napier.ac.uk

Ahmed Hassanien, PhD, is a Lecturer and the Course Leader of Hospitality Management Programmes at Edinburgh Napier University. He has published many articles in international-refereed conferences and periodicals and is a reviewer for a number of international academic periodicals. His research has focused on innovation, repositioning, branding and product development in the tourism, hospitality, sport and events industries. Contact information: School of Marketing, Tourism & Languages, Napier University Business School, Napier University – Craiglockhart Campus, Edinburgh EH14 1DJ, UK; e-mail: a.hassanien@napier.ac.uk

Mohamed F. Hawela, PhD, is a Senior Lecturer at Greenwich School of Management. Before joining Greenwich School of Management, he taught at Ulster Business School, University of Ulster while he was doing his PhD. In addition to this he taught at several Universities in the Middle East. His research interests are in the areas of knowledge management, organizational learning, e-learning in the workplace and innovation. Contact information: Greenwich School of Management, Greenwich Campus, Meridian House, Royal Hill, Greenwich, London SE10 8RD, UK; e-mail: mhawela@greenwich-college.ac.uk

Azilah Kasim is an Associate Professor of Tourism at Universiti Utara Malaysia (UUM). She obtained her undergraduate degree from Brock University, Ontario; Masters degree from Michigan State University and PhD from University of East Anglia, UK. Azilah has been working at UUM for approximately 18 years. Her research interests include: corporate social responsibility in hotels as well as marketing and management issues of tourism products and destinations. She has published extensively in those areas. She has served as a member of the editorial board of the *Malaysian Management Journal* for three years since 2004, and is still active in reviewing manuscripts for a number of international journals including *Annals of Tourism Research*, *Journal of Sustainable Tourism* and *Anatolia: An International Journal of Tourism and Hospitality Research*. Azilah is currently a visiting Associate Professor at the Institute of Asian Research, University of British Columbia, Vancouver. Contact information: Tourism and Hospitality Department, College of Arts and Sciences, Universiti Utara Malaysia, 06010 Sintok, Kedah, Malaysia; e-mail: azilah@uum.edu.my

Vlad Krajsic, is a Lecturer and Researcher at the University of Western Sydney, School of Business. His research interests include hospitality, tourism and organizational/management studies. Contact information: University of Western Sydney, School of Management, Locked Bag 1797, Penrith South DC, NSW 2571, Australia; e-mail: v.krajsic@uws.edu.au

Shuna Marr, PhD, is a Lecturer at Edinburgh Napier University. She is also the undergraduate programme leader in Tourism. She has developed and delivers modules primarily in airline- and airport-related subjects to undergraduate students in Hong Kong as well as the UK, and also lectures and supervises on Masters and DBA programmes. Shuna has been involved in tourism since 1978, working in retail travel and owning three travel agencies over a period of 20 years and lecturing in travel, tourism and hospitality subjects since 1998. She has also undertaken a large number of consultancy projects for the Scottish Qualifications Authority, including educational research projects and writing unit descriptors, assessments, exemplars and teaching material for many travel- and tourism-related subjects. Her main research area focuses on work process knowledge in visitor attractions and events. Contact information: School of Marketing, Tourism & Languages, Napier University Business School, Napier University – Craiglockhart Campus, Edinburgh EH14 1DJ, UK; e-mail: s.marr@napier.ac.uk

Peter Mudie is a Lecturer in Marketing at Edinburgh Napier University. He is the author of *Marketing: An Analytical Perspective* (Prentice Hall) and co-author, with Angela Pirrie, of *Services Marketing Management* (Butterworth-Heinemann). He is published in the *European Journal of Marketing* and the *Service Industries Journal* and was a contributor to *Internal Marketing: Directions for Management*, edited by Richard Varey and Barbara Lewis (Routledge). Contact information: School of Marketing, Tourism & Languages, Napier University Business School, Napier University – Craiglockhart Campus, Edinburgh EH14 1DJ, UK; e-mail: P.Mudie@napier.ac.uk

Michelle O'Shea is a Researcher and Lecturer in sport and hospitality management at University of Western Sydney. Her research interests include organizational/cultural studies in the services sector, and gender and diversity studies within sport organizations and sport contexts. Contact information: University of Western Sydney, School of Management, Locked Bag 1797, Penrith South DC, NSW 2571, Australia; e-mail: m.oshea@uws.edu.au

Işıl Özgen, PhD, is Assistant Professor of Tourism Management at Dokuz Eylül University Faculty of Business, where she has been since 1997. She is also a professional tourist guide. She received her PhD in Tourism Management with her thesis 'Waste Management at Large Scale Hotels' from Dokuz Eylül University in 2005. From 1997 to 2010 she worked at Dokuz Eylül University as research assistant, and since 2010 as Assistant Professor and the head of the food and beverage department. Her research interests are environmental management, food safety and sanitation, organization and management issues related to tourism facilities. She has many published articles and papers about the subjects mentioned above. Contact information: Dokuz Eylül University, Faculty of Business, Izmir, Turkey; e-mail: isil.goksu@deu.edu.tr

Neil Robinson lectures at Salford University Business School, teaching at both undergraduate and postgraduate levels. Neil has research interests in dark tourism, heritage and information technology and has published widely in tourism, hospitality and event management journals. Contact information: University of Salford, Salford Business School, Maxwell Building, Salford M5 4WT, UK; e-mail: n.robinson@salford.ac.uk

Peter Robinson is Principal Lecturer, Head of Leisure and Head of the Arena Theatre at University of Wolverhampton. Peter has a background working in tourism and events management and his research interests include visuality, image, behaviour and business development in tourism and events. Peter has published a number of edited textbooks, together with research papers, trade journals and conference presentations. Peter is the West Midlands Representative for the Tourism Management Institute, a member of the Institute of Travel and Tourism Education and Training Committee and is also a member of the Executive Committee for the Association for Event Management Education. Contact information: School of Sport, Performing Arts and Leisure, University of Wolverhampton, Gorway Road, Walsall, West Midlands WS1 3BD, UK; e-mail: P.Robinson@wlv.ac.uk

Dimitri Tassiopoulos, PhD, is a Chief Research Manager at SAHARA, Human Sciences Research Council, South Africa and a Research Associate of the Tourism Department, Nelson Mandela Metropolitan University, South Africa. Since 1993, he has been involved in various national and international research projects of a multidisciplinary and multi-institutional nature. Dimitri is a board member of a number of international peer-reviewed research journals. He has presented several papers at national and international conferences. Dimitri is the author and editor of multiple edition books, and has written a number of academic articles and chapters on various topics. Contact information: PO Box 210 856, The Fig Tree, 6033, Port Elizabeth, South Africa; e-mail: dtassio@absamail.co.za

J. Stephen Taylor currently lectures at Edinburgh Napier University. He previously held similar positions at the Universities of Strathclyde and Dundee. He has a diverse range of research interests, which range from research philosophy to McDonaldization, website performance measurement through to competitive strategy and more recently to natural area tourism. His contributions have been published in numerous books and journals such as the *International Journal of Hospitality Management*, *Tourism and Hospitality Research*, *Tourism Recreation Research* and the *Journal of Travel and Tourism Marketing*. Beyond academia Stephen is an avid mountaineer (in the UK, the Alps and much further afield) and he attempts to manage a death metal band. Contact information: School of Marketing, Tourism & Languages, Napier University Business School, Napier University – Craiglockhart Campus, Edinburgh EH14 1DJ, UK; e-mail: js.taylor@napier.ac.uk

Anthony Wong is an industry practitioner who has had plenty of experience in the hospitality industry. Anthony started his career as a nature guide and subsequently developed himself to become one of the most successful businessmen in Malaysia. He is currently the owner and managing director of Asia Overland Limited and Frangipani Hotel Resort & Spa. Compassion and love for nature are the driving factors that motivated Anthony to adopt a sustainable approach in managing his companies. He is currently active in sharing some of his environmental management knowledge with other interested hotel managers. Contact information: Managing Director, Frangipani Langkawi Resort & Spa, Langkawi, Malaysia; e-mail: anthony@asiaoverland.com.my

Kamil Yağcı, PhD, is an Assistant Professor in the Department of Tourism and Hotel Management at the University of Giresun (Turkey), where he has been a member since 2010. He graduated from the Faculty of Business, Department of Tourism Management, Dokuz Eylül University, Turkey in 1999. He completed both his MSc in the field of Total Quality Management in 2003 and his PhD in the field of Tourism Management in 2010 at Dokuz Eylül University. His main research interests lie in the area of quality management, ICT in tourism, e-tourism, supply chain management practices in tourism, organization theories and their application in tourism industry. He is also certified as lead auditor for ISO 9001:2000 and ISO 1401:2004 Quality Management Systems. Contact information: Giresun University Bulancak School of Applied Sciences, Department of Tourism and Hotel Management (Dept. Chair), Bulancak, Giresun, Turkey; e-mail: kyagci74@yahoo.com

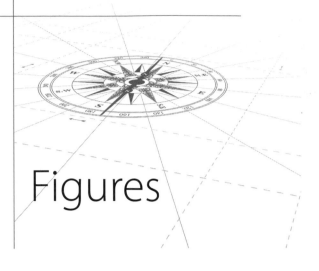

Figures

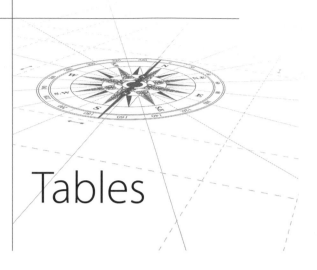

Tables

Case Studies

To my pretty wife Eman and lovely children Mariam, Noor and Yusuf; without their love and attention this book would have been finished in half the time.

Ahmed Hassanien

To my beautiful Rachel and sweet children Saffron and Imogen because of all the wonderful things they do for me and for supporting me all the way.

Crispin Dale

chapter 1

Introduction to Facilities Management

Ahmed Hassanien
Edinburgh Napier University

Crispin Dale
University of Wolverhampton

LEARNING OBJECTIVES

Having completed this chapter, readers should be able to:

- understand the concept of facilities management within the context of the tourism, hospitality and events (THE) industries;
- investigate the scope of facilities management;
- explore the growing importance and evolution of facilities management with particular emphasis on the motives behind it;
- discuss the benefits and objectives of facilities management for THE operations.

INTRODUCTION

The THE industries have metamorphosed over the past three decades. Facilities management is one of the areas of business that can lay claim to a similar 'enlargement'.

There is little argument that facilities management was first used as a term in the USA in 1975 (Maas and Pleunis, 2001). However, the 1980s were responsible for most of the growth in facilities management. In 1980, 40 professional facilities managers met in Michigan, USA and set up the National Facility Management Association. Only two years later, in 1982, the name was changed to the International Facilities Management Association to reflect its international constituency. At the same time, educational establishments began offering courses in the subject. Cornell University, Ithaca, USA first offered a doctoral course in strategic facilities management in 1983. There was considerable debate as to whether this facilities management was a 'real' discipline, in much the same way that THE academics have had to work hard to gain academic credibility. It has been argued that 'managers' have always looked after 'facilities' while producing a product or service. So what has changed? Klee (1997, cited in Maas and Pleunis, 2001) argues that the environment in which management operates has changed in several key respects:

- The energy crisis. The 1970s saw a sudden interest in energy efficiency. Office space utilization often became a part of this review.
- Organizations were evaluating the internal processes, and deciding whether departments 'added value' to the product or service being produced. They also considered whether a particular aspect of their business was what they should be involved in – in other words, was it a core process that they could identify as being responsible for their success? If not, could someone else do it better?
- The product life cycle became ever shorter. This meant that not only were products brought to market faster, but their life 'expectancy' in the marketplace became shorter as businesses sought to adjust to a more demanding and better informed customer. Customization, not mass production, became the goal for many firms.
- Firms changed the way they did business very quickly, whether through mergers and acquisitions, de-layering, management buy-outs, relocations, privatizations or outsourcing. The physical premises and support services needed to adapt equally swiftly.

As a result of the above, a group of managers found themselves searching for an identity around which they could develop professionally. However, while facilities management's origins are clearly in the USA, it has adapted and established itself in Europe, particularly in the UK (after 1986) and The Netherlands (around 1988).

Within the UK a wide range of individuals found they were spending at least part of their working day being de facto facilities managers. Some were in charge of large corporate head offices with hundreds of 'internal customers' (for example, the BBC), while others were private/NHS Trust hospital managers charged with ensuring the medical staff and patients were adequately served. What became clear was that the THE industries employed individuals whose job description read like that of a facilities manager – contract catering, school bursars, university support staff and even hotel general managers.

However, despite its obvious alignment, exploratory research (Jeffries, 2000) found that within the hotel sector, for example, little use is made of the term 'facilities management', with those responsible for the above strategic issues being either hotel general managers or their chief engineers (often referred to, for example, as 'property managers'). These individuals have both a front and back of house responsibility, and must balance the needs and desires of internal and external customers.

Until recently, little detailed consideration has been given to the facilities management subject area within the context of THE operations. As a result, the main goal of this chapter is to look at the concept, significance, evolution and scope of facilities management. Accordingly, this chapter will start by outlining the theoretical framework within which facilities management operates. This is important because it enables the conceptualization of the key principles of facilities management as they apply to the THE industries.

EVOLUTION OF FACILITIES MANAGEMENT: HOW?

Many THE businesses are involved in the development, maintenance, management, marketing and sales of space and facilities for a wide variety of purposes. It is worth thinking about the range of facilities that are managed in the context of THE. The past three decades has seen a significant change in attitude towards facilities in the context of THE. From a historical perspective, businesses may not have maximized their facilities to their full potential. However, competitive pressures have generated the desire for businesses to gain as much value from their facilities as possible. This has seen facilities management evolve in the following ways:

- From a property-based discipline concerned with *reactive*, *operational* aspects of property management, services and maintenance (including cleaning, 'caretaking', waste disposal and catering) into a much more *proactive*, *strategic* role. In this role, it is also concerned with the design of property and the work environment, purchasing, and future management and maintenance of the property – thus, it covers a broad area of 'non-core' activities. Such activities could include IT services, security and even human resources management. From a management perspective, facilities management must consider the needs of all building users, together with the needs of others who may be affected by the management of the building. The needs of different stakeholders (e.g. customers, employees, suppliers, shareholders, community) therefore have to be considered.
- From making do with the physical assets and relying on the existing premises towards opportunity for reinvestment and differentiation. The pace of the competitive environment and new players threatening in the marketplace have resulted in facilities having to rebrand and maximize their offerings. Space utilization has been key to this process, whether this has been by existing staff or the sale and rent of this space to others. This change can be seen in terms of the following examples of change in the use and productivity of space:
  - Airport canteen-style cafeteria with one retail outlet into a multi-outlet food court, making much more intensive use of the same seating area.
  - Hotel lobby public area with guest seating into an area that includes a number of small retail outlets and more limited guest seating.
  - City museum with full display area into a display area with cleared central facility for use as reception or banqueting facility.
  - Hotel with extensive gardens to the location of a large marquee in the garden as an additional meeting/function room for events and banquets.

- From in-house provision to outsourcing or contracting out. On a micro scale, this may include services in the facility itself, such as security, cleaning or IT. On a macro scale, the facilities themselves may be contracted out to operators who have the expertise and resources to operate them more efficiently and effectively. For example, if we consider the hospitality facilities at theme parks, it is not unusual for branded outlets to have a presence.
- From a local or national focus to a global or international focus. In addition, the management and operation of facilities has become multi-national in nature. This is to ensure the most efficient operation of facilities and that brand standards are being maintained.

EVOLUTION OF FACILITIES MANAGEMENT: WHY?

There are many different reasons that explain the role played by facilities management in the success of THE operations. This success depends mainly on the effective management of its component parts. Key authors list many different reasons and factors that make facilities management essential for THE operations (e.g. Cotts and Lee, 1992; Alexander, 1996; Atkin and Brooks, 2009; BIFM, 2013). These can be classified as a combination of internal and external factors, which include the following.

External

Globalization

Facilities operate in a globalized society where there is greater mobility. This results in increased competitive pressures, changing consumer behaviour and the need to maintain facilities in line with global influences. Facility managers therefore have to be receptive to the forces of globalization and understand the impact that these have on the business.

Business continuity and workforce protection in an era of heightened market turbulence and security threats

Facilities management is concerned with focusing on the organization's strategic objectives, adopting the most effective methods for carrying out the core and non-core business and implementing improvements to the current resources. This allows for both short- and long-term threats to the organization to be identified and acted upon accordingly, in order to avoid detrimental effects occurring in the market or external environment.

The THE industries operate in a dynamic and turbulent external environment. Effective management of facilities is vital to an organization's long-term success. Many companies within the industry without a structured and well-developed business plan have gone into administration – Flyglobespan, Zoom, Oasis Hong Kong and Elizabeth Hotels, to name but a few.

Facilities management also encourages the development of security management, a particularly vital aspect of a THE operation. Plans and procedures are created in order to ensure that employees know how to recognize and deal with threats of any kind and that a recovery strategy is in place in order to restore stability to the working environment as quickly as possible. In the context of hotel provision, it is common for managers to liaise with other hotels in order to accommodate guests and employees if an incident does occur.

Security measures at THE facilities

A terrorist attack in India on 26 November 2008 targeted two of Mumbai's exclusive hotels, the Taj Mahal Palace and the Oberoi, killing over 160 people and injuring many more. This resulted in hotels reviewing their security measures for guests staying in their facilities. This included the introduction of car checks and all baggage being put through security scanners upon entry to the hotels.

To ensure traveller safety, airport security facilities have evolved to include naked body scanners. However, it has been acknowledged that such security measures at hotel and airport facilities can impact upon the guest and travelling experience, with additional queuing times and, in the case of naked body scanners, an infringement on civil liberties.

Source: http://www.time.com

Changes in legislation and government policy

To meet the requirements of legislative and governmental policy changes, modifications and/or adaptations by facilities can be required. For example, in the UK the implementation from 2006–7 of the smoking ban in all enclosed public space resulted in facilities having to adapt their premises to cater to new and existing markets. This included providing facilities in the premises for those customers still wanting to smoke. However, it also generated an opportunity for businesses to maximize their food retail income from markets being attracted to a smoke-free atmosphere. Thus, many THE facilities have made adaptations to the physical facility and food and beverage operations to capitalize on this market.

Development of information and communication technologies

Information technologies have a significant impact on the communication of facilities to external audiences, through to the use of technologies as a basis for assisting the day-to-day operation of the facility. Internally, visitor management technologies can be used to monitor customer movements through the facility, thus enabling more efficient and effective guest flows. Externally, social networking and related media have enabled facilities to quickly disseminate their goods and services to target markets. Chapter 6 discusses and illustrates a number of examples where technologies have been used in the management and development of facilities.

Increasingly mature and competitive markets

THE facilities are in an especially sensitive position due to a challenging economic climate. Businesses must not only compete on price, but also on offering their guests something their competitors cannot. Furthermore, those businesses that operate in a saturated or maturing market can find themselves needing to make adaptations and improvements to their facilities. Small independently owned businesses can be seen to be at a disadvantage in this respect because they may not have the money available to put towards refurbishment of their property or adding value to their current products.

Market development at Center Parcs

In a partnership with event theming company Event Prop Hire, Center Parcs has entered the corporate travel market. This has entailed the development of themed team-building packages including espionage, back to school and I'm a High Flyer, Get me Out of Here! Center Parcs is able to maximize its existing facilities in the development of these packages with Event Prop Hire supplying the necessary additional materials. Such packages enable the company to access the growing corporate market for team-building residential events.

Source: http://www.travelmole.com

Fluctuating land and property prices

Arguably, in terms of economic value, the physical premises will be the facility's greatest asset. This will be influenced by land and property prices that can increase or decrease, depending on the economic situation of the regional, national and global economy. The acquisition and development of a facility can be an important strategic manoeuvre for businesses seeking to gain maximum value from rising property prices. However, as values can decrease as well as increase, the assessment of risk is an important part of this process.

Changing consumer demands and expectations

It is important to note that facilities management should consider the influence of human and social factors. These factors determine the overall design, layout and functioning of the facility. Aspects including constrained budgetary resources and the aforementioned rise in social networking have influenced the perceptions and expectations of customers. Customers are able to compare and contrast facilities through ease of comparison and recommendation on social media sites. This has led to greater buyer power, with facilities often lowering their prices or offering promotions in order to fuel demand. Other factors, including greater environmental awareness, have also led consumers to visit organizations that take responsibility for the environment and their surrounding community.

If the organization is not able to meet their guests' increased expectations, this results in unsatisfied consumers, who may complain and/or switch to competitors. The third section of this book (Chapters 8–11) illustrates more examples of how environmental management is introduced into facilities.

Internal

Effective management of an organization's resources

The facility will comprise a number of tangible and intangible resources and assets. These include physical, human, financial and reputational resources. Each of these resources will have a cost implication for the organization and it is not unusual for the physical premises and human resources to incur the highest outgoings for the business. Facilities management enables these resources to be maximized, ensuring as much value as possible can be generated from them and that costs are kept to a minimum.

Enhancing staff skills

Facilities management encompasses the practice of human resource management, because employees are as much of an asset to an organization as the fixtures and fittings. Most large corporations will have a department that solely handles this responsibility, however in smaller operations senior management would be expected to carry out this work.

In the process of trying to make the work as efficient as possible, departments are likely to be merged or new systems introduced. This creates a wider spectrum of training employees in order to carry out their work properly. Therefore by reviewing practices and procedures on a regular basis through facilities management, the skills and knowledge of the workforce are continually being enhanced.

Staff can expect facilities to be fit for purpose and enable them to perform their job effectively. Poorly designed and ill-equipped facilities have the potential to result in poor morale and an inability of senior staff to manage their premises effectively. Effective facilities management is therefore imperative in THE organizations, in order to ensure current operational procedures are carried out successfully, but also constantly reviewing their guest and employee needs and acting accordingly.

Enabling new working styles and processes

Working styles and processes are continuously reviewed to determine if there are ways in which they could be carried out more effectively, save costs or increase revenue. Facilities management encourages the pursuit of continually improving the working environment. Managers use change management techniques in order to ease the introduction of any new developments. A workforce that is supported at every stage of change is more likely to support and feel involved in the decision (By and Dale, 2008).

Helping integration processes associated with change, post-merger and acquisition

It is inevitable that facilities will proceed through transitionary periods in order to be as competitive as possible. These transitionary periods may be precipitated by merger or acquisition activity, where the organization has to review, reduce and/or reposition its facilities. This will involve a process of change and well-managed facilities can enable this transition to occur more easily.

Enhancing an organization's identity and image

A company that has successful power over all aspects of its business will portray a strong sense of togetherness and control. Using facilities management to achieve organizational objectives (Anderson, 1993) ensures that the identity and image of the organization is essentially in their own hands. They are actively managing all core and non-core processes in order to remain proactive to their surrounding internal and external environment rather than reactive to it. This therefore displays strong organizational culture and the ability to be flexible to change.

'Sweat the assets'

An objective of facilities management is to generate as much value from the assets as possible. Facilities management involves reinvention and renovation, which are key to maximizing the potential of the assets of the business. As existing markets either evaporate or potential new ones emerge, the facility has to think creatively how it can use its existing asset base to generate further business.

Cinemas sweat their assets

Over the past 30 years cinemas have evolved from independent outlets to multiplex entertainment centres incorporating 3D technologies. However, cinemas have always been challenged by periods of the day and week when attendances can be low. Therefore, seeking out ways to maximize the existing resources for additional uses has been a strategy for many operators. This has included using the facilities for events, conferences and concerts. For example, New York's Met Opera signed a deal with selected cinema chains to stage live high-definition performances. During the showings, the cinemas would be fitted with opera house interiors to enhance the authenticity of the experience for customers. This was not only profitable but reciprocally increased attendances at the originating base of the opera company.

Source: http://www.leisuremanagement.co.uk

Enabling future change in use of space

Facilities management aims to create an environment that can be changed readily in order to meet the needs of the market the organization is operating in or to create more effective working procedures. For example, in hotels this can include the back or front of house, such as the kitchen, offices, bedrooms, restaurants, bars and receptions.

A recent trend within the industry is the use of facilities for meetings, events and conferences. Areas should be designed in order to be flexible and multi-purpose, for example, hotel bedrooms that can be used as meeting rooms, restaurants or bars that can be used for private parties and conference rooms that can be used for wedding receptions.

Delivering effective and responsive services

Through the practice of facilities management, THE organizations are able to focus on their core business and outsource areas that could be better carried out by those specializing in that area. This may involve the catering, maintenance and security aspects of the facility. THE facilities are then able to solely concentrate on effectively and efficiently delivering their product and service in order to meet their guests' needs and expectations. Service failures can potentially be acted upon quickly by the designated department or operation managing that aspect of the facility.

Providing competitive advantage to the core business

A key objective for facilities management is to gain a competitive advantage. This may be achieved in a number of ways, which will be highlighted throughout this book. What is essential is that this advantage is sustainable and meets VIRUS (Valuable, Inimitable, Rare, UnSubstitutable) criteria to enable this to happen (Haberberg and Rieple, 2008).

Leaner and more efficient organizational structures

Organizations have become less hierarchical in their structure (Phondej *et al.*, 2010), creating the need for employees to operate in more areas than they previously would have had to. For example, fewer organizations continue to employ an operations manager; instead they have spread these responsibilities among senior management such as heads of departments, general managers or team leaders. Tourism Information Centres in towns and cities are often structured around a team leader who will be responsible for the day-to-day management of staff at the facility.

Companies have also looked at ways in which to become more efficient by outsourcing their non-core business to organizations that specialize in that area, therefore allowing time and resources to be concentrated on their core business (Atkin and Brooks, 2009). For example, most large hotels now outsource their laundry to companies rather than operate a laundry department themselves in house. This lowers costs and creates a more efficient working environment for housekeeping departments. These new developments show that organizations have had to consider management of their facilities more than ever, in order to cut costs and utilize the skills available in their workplace.

Need for greater flexibility in use of space and working environments

The THE industries are dynamic and continuously changing and evolving. Therefore organizations must anticipate the changing needs of their consumers along with the development of their competitors and plan for these changes accordingly. There has been a recent trend of, for example, using hotels as event venues. Therefore hotels are required to ensure their facilities are adequate to meet the needs of as many markets as possible. Facilities management allows organizations to plan for any possible changes of consumer needs and to be flexible with their available space, whether this is in guest or staff areas.

Tighter operating margins and cost/revenue-driven strategies

As the operating margins of facilities become increasingly tighter due to resource costs, facilities seek to adopt cost-cutting and ancillary revenue strategies. This may be in the form of additional charges for food and beverages, merchandising and so on, or by providing an additional use for the facility during off-peak periods as the example below illustrates.

Maximizing Racecourse Facilities

Racecourses have traditionally been seen as having a single purpose, namely horse racing. However, there are periods when these facilities are under-utilized because of factors such as seasonality and demand. The acreage and related stadiums and hospitality facilities that they contain have provided opportunities for further revenue generation. Newbury Racecourse, Berkshire, located 40 minutes from London, has developed a brand entitled Newbury LIVE, and are staging live concerts. Other UK Jockey Club racecourses also provide their facilities as concert venues, for example the staging of the Acoustic Music Festival of Great Britain at Uttoxeter Racecourse and the Chester Rocks concert at Chester Racecourse.

Source: http://www.leisuremanagement.co.uk

Questions

1. From the discussion of the internal and external factors, what are of highest priority for THE facilities? Provide a reason for your answer.

2. Are there any further internal or external factors THE facilities should be aware of? Provide a reason for your answer.

THE CONCEPT AND SCOPE OF FACILITIES MANAGEMENT

An examination of the literature uncovers the fact that facilities management means different things to different people because the concept and its scope have been defined and described in a variety of ways. In addition, there have been some claims that facilities management is indefinable and that providing a definition is self defeating, because its main aim is to remain flexible (Anderson, 1993; Parry and Collins, 1993). Some definitions have, however, emerged that are useful for understanding the concept and scope of facilities management (Table 1.1).

Table 1.1. Definitions of facilities management.

Author	Definition
Regterschot (1988)	Facilities management is the integral management (planning and monitoring) and realization of housing, services and means that must contribute to an effective, flexible and creative realization of an organization's objectives in an ever-changing environment.
Becker (1990)	Facilities management is responsible for coordinating all efforts related to planning, designing and managing buildings and their systems, equipment and furniture to enhance the organization's ability to compete successfully in a rapidly changing world.
Nourse (1990)	Facilities management unit is seldom aware of the overall corporate strategic planning, and does not have a bottom-line emphasis.
Cotts and Lee (1992)	The practice of coordinating the physical workplace with the people and work of an organization; integrates the principles of business administration, architecture, and the behavioural and engineering science.
Anderson (1993)	Facilities management is not concerned principally with buildings or the activities that happen inside them. Facilities management should be concerned with 'the achievement of organizational objectives, which may or may not involve premises.' This approach serves to focus on the consumer's demands and requirements rather than the traditional supply-based view of the property industry. Accordingly, the term 'facilities management' frequently relates to the work environment and the physical assets of an organization. This in part shows the depth of facilities management and to what extent it is a large part of modern business as a vocational subject.
Owen (1994)	Facilities management is the active management and coordination of an organization's non-core business services, together with the associated human resources and its buildings, including their systems, plant, IT equipment, fittings and furniture; necessary to assist the organization to achieve its strategic objectives.
Park (1994)	Facilities management is the structuring of building plant and contents to enhance the creation of the end product. As with all systems, it is the generated benefit to the business or activity that matters, not the system itself.

(Continued)

Table 1.1. Continued.

Author	Definition
Barrett (1995)	Facilities management is an integrated approach to operating, maintaining, improving and adapting the buildings and infrastructure of an organization in order to create an environment that strongly supports the primary objectives of that organization.
Alexander (1996)	The process by which an organization ensures that its buildings, systems and services support core operations and processes as well as contribute to achieving its strategic objectives in changing conditions.
Then (1999)	The practice of facilities management is concerned with the delivery of the enabling workplace environment – the optimum functional space that supports the business processes and human resources.
Nutt (2000)	The primary function of facilities management is resource management, at strategic and operational levels of support. Generic types of resource management central to the facilities management function are the management of financial resources, physical resources, human resources, and the management of resources of information and knowledge.
Maas and Pleunis (2001)	The responsibility for coordinating efforts to ensure that buildings, technology, furniture and organizational trends are responded to over time.
Roberts (2001)	Facility management is about: understanding the business; planning and providing for the business; determining levels of space and service provision; budgeting and controlling fixed and variable occupancy costs; managing performance of buildings, budget, people and time; managing change; being invisible; being professional.
IFMA (2003)	Facility management is a profession that encompasses multiple disciplines to ensure functionality of the built environment by integrating people, place, process and technology.
BIFM (2013)	The British Institute of Facilities Management (BIFM) defines facilities management as the integration of processes within an organization to maintain and develop the agreed services that support and improve the effectiveness of its primary activities.

Questions

1. Review the definitions in Table 1.1 What are the key themes that emerge from them?
2. To what extent do these definitions acknowledge the scope of facilities management?
3. To what extent do these definitions acknowledge facilities in the THE industries?

Controversy on the definition of facilities management has caused further confusion regarding identifying its scope. For instance, Cotts and Lee (1992) argue that facilities management can cover 14 various functions including: (i) management of organization; (ii) facility planning and forecasting; (iii) lease administration; (iv) space planning, allocation and management; (v) architectural/engineering planning and design; (vi) workplace planning, allocation and management; (vii) budgeting, accounting and economic justification; (viii) real estate acquisition and disposal; (ix) construction project management; (x) alteration, renovation and workplace installation; (xi) operations, maintenance and repair; (xii) telecommunications, data communications and network management; (xiii) security and life-safety management; and (xiv) general administrative services. Similarly, Atkin and Brooks (2000) suggest different types of facilities management services, including human resources management, financial management, real estate management, health and safety and contract management and change management, in addition to building management, domestic services (such as cleaning and security) and utilities supplies.

Then (1994) identifies six areas of management that facilities management needs to cover: (i) strategic management; (ii) asset management; (iii) service management; (iv) change management; (v) people management; and (vi) information management.

Along the same lines, *Effective Facilities Management: A Good Practice Guide* (FEFC, 1997) lists what the FEFC believes to be the core competencies of facilities management as: (i) property management; (ii) financial management; (iii) organizational management; (iv) innovation and change management; and (v) human resources management.

Alexander (1996) classifies the scope of facilities management into three broad areas: strategic, tactical and operational. At the strategic level, facility managers will be making corporate decisions concerning the future direction of the business. This will involve an understanding of the external competitive environment and the utilization of the facilities resources to gain an advantage. At the tactical level, the facility will require managerial descison making on the functioning of its component parts. This may involve tactical decisions concerning the marketing, human resources, finance and physical aspects of the facility. At the operational level, the facility manager will be engaged in the day-to-day aspects of ensuring the business operates efficiently and effectively.

On the other hand, Barrett (1995) argues that there is no definitive guide to what services the facilities management department should supply, because the objective of facilities management is to supply what is best for the organization.

It could be argued that the various definitions of facilities management have led to confusion and misperception regarding the concept and scope of facilities management. There is confusion regarding the exact meaning of facilities management (e.g. strategic vs operational definitions;

hardware vs software). Indeed, this confusion can be attributed to the gap between academics' and practitioners' use of the term and application of the concept within the context of different industries.

So, what can we understand about facilities management from the above definitions and scope of facilities management? From a general perspective we can deduce the following:

- The range of definitions can be classified into two main groups. The first comprises conceptual definitions that attempt to explain the essential nature of facilities management as a concept. The second covers technical definitions that are used to designate these tools or activities that take part in this activity.
- Facilities management is a multi-disciplinary field that comprises different areas such as built environment, property management, services management and design management.
- The main purpose of facilities management is to help organizations to achieve their goals in terms of competitive advantage, sustainability, profitability and flexibility. Indeed, facilities management plays a supporting role in improving the performance of the organization.
- While most of these definitions may differ, a common thread emerges that includes the function/task (e.g. to coordinate, maintain, develop), the resource focus (e.g. workplace, buildings, equipment) and the purpose/target of facilities management (e.g. operational efficiency and effectiveness). Regarding this latter point, it should be noted that some of these definitions do not look at the impact of effective facilities management on organizations (e.g. Maas and Pleunis, 2001, p. 28; Robert, 2001; IFMA, 2012).
- Facilities management is an integrated approach or process of activities that requires specific management functions such as planning, organizing, control and evaluation.
- Facilities management is mainly concerned with the functionality of the workplace or the physical environment of organizations through integrating people, place and process (Alexander, 1996). This means that facilities management can be applied to all THE organizations because they require space or workplace for their products/services.
- There are different levels of facilities management, namely operational, tactical and strategic. This grouping will help us to further understand the different levels of facilities management.

From a THE perspective, the following can also be considered:

- There is no agreement regarding the different services that facilities management can provide for THE organizations (e.g. accounting, maintenance, design, security).
- There is no agreement regarding the type of services that facilities management can provide for THE organizations (i.e. core/essential activities or non-core/supporting ones). Interestingly, there are fine lines between them because classifying a service as a core or non-core activity for any organization depends on many factors, such as the norms of the industry, culture or category of organization. For example, customers may classify 'housekeeping' as a core service for an international 5-star hotel and a non-core service for a budget hotel. Also, ticketing for events and in-flight catering for an airline organization. Regardless of an organization's focus on its core services, it needs also to concentrate on the supporting services to protect its assets and add value to its products (Atkin and Brooks, 2009).

Based on the above discussion regarding the concept and scope of facilities management, and for the purpose of the present book, facilities management might be seen as a multi-disciplinary field that covers different functions and requires various management skills/ competencies, enabling the facility to further improve the performance of its core or primary business and achieve its operational, tactical and strategic objectives in changing conditions.

Several dimensions of this definition need to be highlighted:

1. Facilities management is a multi-disciplinary field and an umbrella term that covers different functions. These include project management, environmental management, property management, asset management, behavioural management, business administration, strategic management, operations management, construction or architecture management and change management.

2. Facilities management requires various management skills/competencies. This may include planning, organizing, implementing, evaluating, monitoring, coordinating, controlling, leading, innovating and so on.

3. Facilities management is mainly concerned with the design and development of an organization's workplace (i.e. physical facility) or workspace (i.e. online facility) and with the provision and management of support services or activities (e.g. security, maintenance, renovation, environmental management, CSR, and so forth).

4. Facilities management enables organizations to further improve the performance of its core or primary business (e.g. adding value, quality, functionality, flexibility or sustainability).

5. Facilities management enables organizations to achieve their operational, tactical and strategic objectives in changing conditions (i.e. political, economic, social, technological and competitive influences).

The current book will focus on diferent aspects of facilities management within the THE industries. In other words, the book will look at different facilities management-related competencies, services or functions. There are some reasons behind focusing on facilities management in this way. First, facilities management is a very recent phenomenon in all disciplines in general and in the THE industry in particular. Second, there is always a facilities management process going on in THE facilities because of its vital importance. Third, the authors believe that some THE operations do not use the terms 'facilities management' or 'facility manager' and apply other terms for the process and the persons in charge of managing their facilities. This is because facilities management can cover different types of services performed by different types of manager. Therefore, the authors believe the best way to grasp the phenomenon of facilities management is to explore it through more common processes such as sustainability, environmental management, outsourcing, maintenance and refurbishment.

SUMMARY

This chapter deals with various aspects of facilities management in the hospitality industry. It includes discussion of the concept, scope, levels and importance of facilities management within the context of THE facilities. Finally the chapter has concluded with an overview of the structure of the book in terms of its content and context. The next chapter will look at the concept and scope of the THE industries and their different sectors.

REVIEW QUESTIONS

1. Define the concept of facilities management. What is its significance within the context of the THE industries?

2. How has the role of facilities management in THE changed over the past 25 years? Illustrate your answer with industry-related examples.

3. To what extent does the facilities management role vary in scale and significance across different sectors of THE?

4. In recent years, facilities management has emerged as a service sector in its own right, centred around the growing need for organizations to manage their property and working environments as efficiently and effectively as possible. Discuss.

Case Study

Qatar World Cup 2022

Based in the Middle East, Qatar is a peninsula located on the east coast of Saudi Arabia on the Persian Gulf. Qatar has a population of approximately 1.5 million and covers an area of approximately 11.5 square kilometres. The country is predominately low lying, with extensive plains of sand. The climate is hot most of the year around, with temperatures rising to 40°C during June, July and August. Qatar is one of the richest nations in the region, with its economy built on a high dependence on fossil fuels, including oil and gas. Culturally, Islam is the main religion in Qatar, practised by the majority of the population, though other religions such as Christianity, Hinduism, Sikhism and Buddhism are also accepted.

Qatar is governed by Sheikh Hamad bin Khalifah Al Thani, who seized power from his father in a peaceful coup in 1995. Qatar is relatively liberal but draws on Shari'a law to govern aspects of its legal system. Drinking alcohol in public is strictly prohibited. Though alcohol can be consumed in bars and nightclubs, these are few in number and located mainly in the upper range hotels. In line with Islamic tradition, pigs and pork

(Continued)

Case Study. Continued.

produce cannot be imported or sold in the country. The Qatar government also finances the popular Arabic language television channel, Al-Jazeera.

In 2022, Qatar will host the FIFA World Cup. The Qatar government has invested heavily in the staging of sporting events. This has included the Qatar Masters golf tournament and the Qatar ExxonMobil Open tennis tournament, the World Indoor Athletics Championships 2010 and the 2006 Asian Games where US$2.8 billion was spent on the competition and associated facilities. It has also invested in its own training facilities, including the Aspire Academy to develop Qatar's sporting excellence. This investment in sporting events has been as a means to diversify the economy away from fossil fuel industries on which Qatar has a high dependence, though it should be noted that these industries have enabled this inward investment in sporting facilities to occur. Staging mega-events is argued to permanently boost trade by 30% (Rose and Spiegel, 2009).

During the initial stages of the bid, FIFA inspectors expressed concerns about the lack of facilities, including accommodation and transportation. In addition to this are the cultural and climate differences, with restrictions on the drinking of alcohol and the hot temperatures. Staging the 2022 FIFA World Cup will result in excess of US$70 billion of new investment in Qatar; US$3 billion will be spent on stadiums. An additional nine new 'eco-friendly' stadiums will be built. This will include the newly developed Al-Khor, Al-Wakrah and Al-Shamal 45,000 seat capacity stadiums. Three existing stadiums will be redeveloped and all stadiums will be fitted with carbon-neutral solar-powered cooling technology to reduce the temperature during matches. The venues will also be modular or semi modular in construction, so they can be dismantled and used by developing countries following the event.

US$12.4 billion will be spent on accommodation facilities. This includes the construction of 240 mainly 4-star properties, providing 90,000 hotel rooms. Additional retail, hospitality and entertainment facilities will also be generated through small business development and franchising. US$44 billion of related infrastructure developments to the rail, road and air sea networks are also intended. This includes improvements to the New Doha International Airport (NDIA), the New Doha Port and the construction of the Qatar–Bahrain causeway; a Doha metro system is due to be completed in 2021. The key event facilities are all concentrated within a 60-km radius.

An important part of pre-planning when developing these facilities is their legacy once the event has finished. Indeed, with the rapid development of accommodation facilities, it has been noted that this may generate an oversupply both before and after the World Cup (HVS, 2011). The aim is to reuse these as office or residential spaces and develop areas into 'media cities'.

Additional sources: http://www.ukti.gov.uk; http://www.bbc.com

Questions

Compare and contrast the facilities of other countries that have staged mega-events such as the Olympic Games and the World Cup.

1. What facilities have been developed for the event?
2. How much expenditure has gone into these facilities and how has it been generated (i.e. public, public–private partnership, private)?
3. What has been the legacy of these facilities following the event? How have these facilities been re-used or redeveloped?
4. In the context of Qatar, consider how THE facilities will need to be adapted to meet the demands of the international visitor when the World Cup is being staged. What challenges will this present?

GLOSSARY OF TERMS USED IN THIS CHAPTER

Facilities management	A multi-disciplinary field that covers different functions and requires various management skills/competencies, enabling the facility to further improve the performance of its core or primary business and achieve its operational, tactical and strategic objectives in changing conditions.
Mergers and acquisitions	A merger is when two or more organizations agree to become one organization, whereas an acquisition occurs when one organization purchases another.
Organization's resources	THE facilities comprise a number of tangible and intangible resources and assets. This includes physical, human, financial and reputational resources.
Security management	Plans and procedures are created in order to ensure that employees know how to recognize and deal with threats of any kind and that a recovery strategy is in place in order to restore stability to the working environment as quickly as possible.
Sweat the assets	Generating as much value from the assets as possible. Facilities management involves reinvention and renovation, which are key to maximizing the potential of the assets of the business.

REFERENCES AND ADDITIONAL READING

Alexander, K. (1996) *Facilities Management Theory and Practice*. Taylor & Francis, London.
Anderson, C. (1993) *Facilities Management Case Study: Prince Phillip Hospital*. CFM Working Paper 93/08 February. Centre for Facilities Management, Strathclyde University, Scotland.
Atkin, B. and Brooks, A. (2000) *Total Facilities Management*, 1st edn. Blackwell, Oxford.
Atkin, B. and Brooks, A. (2009) *Total Facilities Management*, 3rd edn. Blackwell, Oxford.
Barrett, P. (1995) *Facilities Management: Towards Best Practice*. Blackwell, Oxford.

Becker, F.D. (1990) *The Total Workplace: Facilities Management and the Elastic Organization*. Van Nostrand Reinhold, New York.

British Institute of Facilities Management (BIFM) (2013) Available at: http://www.bifm.org.uk/bifm/about/facilities.

Brujin, H. de, van Wezel, R. and Wood, R.C. (2001) Lessons and issues for defining 'facilities management' from hospitality management. *International Journal of Contemporary Hospitality Management* 19(13/14), 476–483.

By, R. and Dale, C. (2008) Tourism SMEs and the successful management of organisational change. *International Journal of Tourism Research* 10(4), 305–313.

Cotts, D.G. and Lee, M. (1992) *The Facility Management Handbook*. American Management Association, New York.

Crawshaw, J. (1993) A look forward. *International Journal of Contemporary Hospitality Management* 5(2), doi: 10.1108/09596119310036557.

FEFC (1997) *Effective Facilities Management: A Good Practice Guide*. The Further Education Funding Council (FEFC) in collaboration with the National Audit Office (NAO). Stationery Office, London.

Haberberg, A. and Rieple, A. (2008) *Strategic Management: Theory and Application*. Oxford University Press, Oxford.

HVS (2011) *The Race for 2022*. Available at: http://www.hvs.com

IFMA (2013) *What is FM?* Available at: http://www.ifma.org/know-base/browse/what-is-fm-

Jefferies, E.J. (2000) A preliminary investigation into facilities management in hotels. BA dissertation, University of Strathclyde, Glasgow, UK.

Jones, C. and Jowett, V. (1998) *Managing Facilities*. Butterworth-Heinemann, Oxford, Chapters 1 and 3.

Losekoot, E., van Wezel, R. and Wood, R.C. (2001) Conceptualising and operationalising the research interface between facilities management and hospitality management. *Facilities* 19(7/8), 296–303.

Maas, G. and Pleunis, M. (2001) *Facility Management*. Kluwer, Alphen aan den Rijn, The Netherlands.

Nourse, H.O. (1990) *Managerial Real Estate: Corporate Real Estate Asset Management*. Prentice-Hall, Englewood Cliffs, New Jersey.

Nutt, B. (2000) Four competing futures for facility management. *Facilities* 18(3/4), 124–132.

Owen, D. (1994) Contracting out in a facilities management context. Master's thesis. University of Salford, Salford, UK.

Park, A. (1994) *Facilities Management: An Explanation*. Palgrave, New York.

Parry, B. and Collins, B. (1993) Where is FM going? *International Journal of Contemporary Hospitality Management* 5(2), doi: 10.1108/09596119310036638.

Phondej, W., Kittisarn, A. and Neck, P.A. (2010) The conditions and factors with successful female leadership in Thailand: a conceptual framework. *Review of International Comparative Management* 11(1), 52–65.

Ransley, J. and Ingram, H. (eds) (2004) *Developing Hospitality Properties and Facilities*, 2nd edn. Butterworth-Heinemann, Oxford, Chapters 1 and 3.

Regterschot, J. (1988) Facility management: het professioneel besturen van de kantoorhuisvesting. Kluwer, Bedrijfswetenschappen, Deventer, Holland.

Roberts, P. (2001) Corporate competence in FM: current problems and issues. *Facilities* 19(7/8), 269–275.

Rose, A.K. and Spiegel, M.M. (2009) *The Olympic Effect*. National Bureau of Economic Research, October

Swarbrooke, J. (2002) *The Development and Management of Visitor Attractions*, 2nd edn. Butterworth-Heinemann, Oxford, Chapters 3 and 5.

Then, D.S.S. (1994) People, property and technology – managing the interface. *Facilities Management* 2(1), 6–8.

Then, D.S.S. (1999) An integrated resource management view of facilities management. *Facilities* 17(12/13), 462–469.

chapter 2

Tourism, Hospitality and Events Facilities

Crispin Dale
University of Wolverhampton

Ahmed Hassanien
Edinburgh Napier University

LEARNING OBJECTIVES

Having completed this chapter, readers should be able to:

- recognize the concept and environment of tourism, hospitality and events (THE) facilities;
- consider the different levels of THE facilities;
- understand the scope of THE facilities;
- evaluate the characteristics of services and their impact on THE facilities.

INTRODUCTION

The chapter will initially outline what is meant by a THE facility. The chapter will then progress to exploring the different levels of facilities before reviewing their scope. A discussion of the characteristics of services and their influence on facility decision making will then be provided. Finally, the chapter will provide possible solutions for THE facilities to overcome the challenges caused by those characteristics.

WHAT IS A FACILITY?

Facilities come in all shapes and sizes and it is important to initially determine what is understood by this term. Facilities can be fixed, mobile, permanent, semi-permanent or temporary in nature. Their management and operation will be provided by the private, public or voluntary sectors for the purposes of accommodation, catering, sport, recreation, leisure and/or business. The ownership and operation of a facility may be managed by a large, medium or small corporation or enterprise.

Facilities are therefore multifaceted and diverse, but they are created to meet a specific purpose for which they are intended. This timescale may be short, medium or long term in nature and will be influenced by many of the internal and external factors outlined previously in Chapter 1.

LEVELS OF THE FACILITIES

THE facilities can be separated into multiple levels, which can be classified as primary, sub- and ancillary facilities (see Fig. 2.1). It is important to acknowledge this so that we can further refine the context and scope of THE facilities and their management and development.

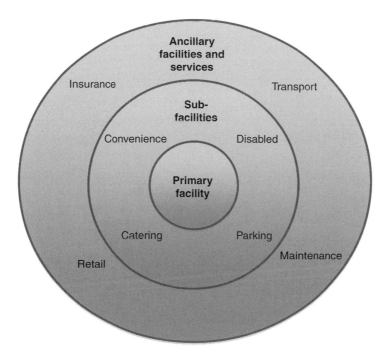

Fig. 2.1. The levels of THE facilities.

- Primary facilities are those facilities that act as the main purpose for use and/or visitation. They fulfil a core benefit for the user (i.e. tourists, residents or visitors), which may be for relaxation, leisure, food, lodging, entertainment and so on.
- Sub-facilities are the supporting elements or services of the primary facility. These may be located and/or housed within the primary facility itself. These sub-facilities may be managed by the primary facility or may be outsourced to a third party through contracting out, which will be explored in more detail in Chapter 7. For example, a conference centre will include parking facilities, catering facilities, disabled facilities and so on.
- Ancillary facilities and services are those that supplement both the primary and sub-facilities. These facilities and services are required for the day-to-day operation and functioning of the primary and the sub-facilities. These ancillary facilities may be outsourced to a third party or be managed by an independent organization. So, they may not be under the direct control of the facility itself, such as transportation facilities for events venues. For example, a theme park requires the services of maintenance providers who may be contracted in to ensure the operation of the rides. Though they may have a base on site, their main facility of operation may be located externally to the primary theme park facility. Finally, it should be noted that it is not always easy to delineate between the sub-facilities and ancillary facilities because they often overlap and are closely interrelated.

Activity

Choose a THE facility. As per Fig. 2.1, identify the different sub- and ancillary components of that primary facility.

SCOPE OF THE FACILITIES

When exploring the scope of facilities in the THE industries it is important to acknowledge the way in which they interrelate with each another. Figure 2.2 illustrates the different connections and relationships between THE facilities and their supporting components. The diagram can be separated into two main parts: stakeholder groups and THE facilities and attractions.

Stakeholder groups represent the first half of the diagram. This includes those stakeholders that generate and influence demand for the facility, including target markets, consumer and interest groups and the media; those stakeholders that are able to facilitate the demand for the facility, including the transport sector and distributors; and finally those stakeholders that govern the facility, including planners, developers and controllers. Each stakeholder/ stakeholder group will have a degree of power and interest that will influence the planning and development of the facility. An understanding of its stakeholders is crucial if the facility

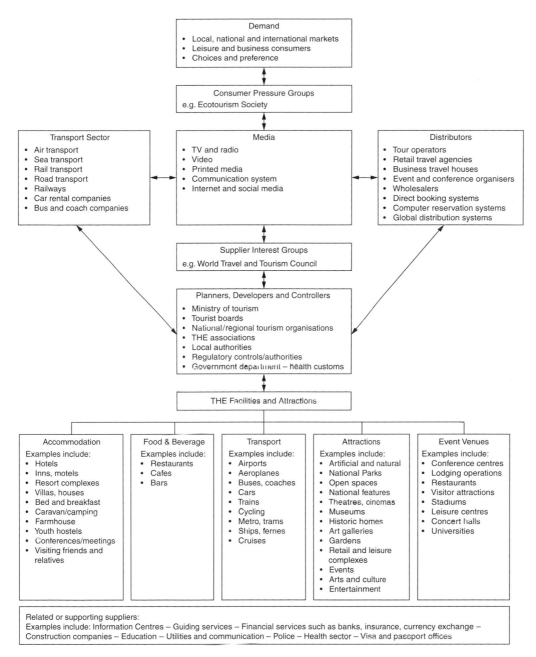

Fig. 2.2. The scope and nature of THE facilities.

is to function and be managed successfully. The stakeholder concept and an explanation of its power and interest, in the context of project management, are given in Chapter 3.

The THE facilities and attractions are represented in the lower part of the diagram by the accommodation, food and beverage, transport attractions and event venues sectors.

Demand

Demand for THE services will be driven by consumer behaviour, preferences and market trends. THE facilities should have strategies in place that target a range of international, national or local markets. These strategies will be influenced by a number of factors including:

- the nature of facility ownership (i.e. corporate chain, independent etc.);
- the type of facility (i.e. leisure or business);
- the size of the facility (i.e. large, medium, small);
- the level of service the facility is offering (i.e. high, mid-range, budget).

Consumer pressure groups

Facilities will have a number of consumer and pressure groups, which will influence their planning and development. Their degree of power and interest will be governed by their ability to exert this on the planning and development of the facility. For example, with climate change being a key influence in society, environmental groups may wish to ensure the sustainable practices of the facility. The degree to which the facility is able or even desires to pursue this as part of its development will depend on its overall strategic intent. Chapters 9–12 of the book provide a number of topics on this subject.

Supplier interest groups

Supplier interest groups may provide information and intelligence informs the management and development of the facility. These may include professional associations such as Association of Event Organizers or the Institute for Hospitality or transnational governance structures such as the World Travel and Tourism Council. Such interest groups offer networking and business development opportunities for facilities.

Media

Media will act as a major stimulus for demand for the facility and will come in many forms. This includes a combination of above and below the line promotional practices, such as traditional printed media (e.g. leaflets, flyers and newspaper/magazine advertising) and internet, television and radio communications. The significance of social media such as Facebook, Twitter and YouTube has enabled facilities to maximize their marketing capabilities. However, at the same time, consumers and consumer groups have facilitated the use of the social media to voice opinion and feedback. This can act positively or negatively for the facility, depending on the nature of the discourse being presented.

Distributors

Distributors will assist in generating demand for the facility. This may include intermediaries that enable the consumer to be directed and gain access to the facility. For example, wholesalers such as tour operators can be used to facilitate supply to the facility; agents such as travel agents and ticketing agents can be used for bookings to the facility. Computer reservation systems and global reservation systems will be the underpinning mechanisms to achieve this distribution. These will be discussed more fully in Chapter 6.

Transport

The transport sector enables the mobility of the consumer to the facility. This will include air, sea, rail and road methods of transportation. It should be noted that different methods of transport would provide facilities in their own right and these will be discussed more fully later in the chapter.

Planners, developers and controllers

Planners, developers and controllers will manage the overriding governance of facilities and the preceding stakeholders. This will embrace local and national government structures including local authorities, national governmental organizations (NGOs) and regulatory boards and commissions. These will provide the legal parameters in which the facility is able to operate.

THE FACILITIES AND ATTRACTIONS

Accommodation

Accommodation facilities are broad and encapsulate a range of different enterprises. It is challenging to delineate between different accommodation types because they often overlap and are closely interrelated. The primary function of accommodation will be to provide a place for rest and recuperation. Hassanien *et al.* (2010) adapt criteria originally developed by Medlik and Ingram (2000) to accommodation. These criteria include the location of accommodation (urban, rural, coastal etc.); the purpose of the visit (leisure, business, health etc.); duration of stay (permanent, semi-permanent, temporary); service provided (full service, self-service etc.); alcohol provision (licensed or unlicensed); size of accommodation (large, medium or small); accommodation class or grade; and ownership and management (private, public, independent, multinational, franchise etc.). Figure 2.3 outlines the different types of accommodation facilities (Hassanien *et al.*, 2010).

As outlined earlier, these accommodation providers will have sub- and ancillary facilities that support their day-to-day operation. For example, upper range hotels may include beauty salons, gift shops, newsagents and so on. The facility manager should consider how these sub-facilities are incorporated into the overall operation of the business so as to add value. This may be in the form of guest experience and satisfaction, or as a means of generating additional revenue for the facility.

Food and beverage

The primary function of food and beverage facilities is the sustenance and refreshment of customers and users. These facilities come in many types and forms and are wide ranging in nature. The scope of food and beverage facilities is outlined by Hassanien *et al.* (2010) in Fig. 2.3.

Transport

The transport sector is unique in that it supports the supply of users to and from facilities while also potentially acting as a primary facility in its own right. For example, cruises offer an on-board experience that includes accommodation, entertainment, dining and so on, while also providing excursions for passengers to destinations en route.

Transport providers have repositioned themselves to embrace the holistic consumer experience. They are no longer a means to an end in getting someone from A to B. They are part of the customers' overall experience and provide the necessary facilities accordingly.

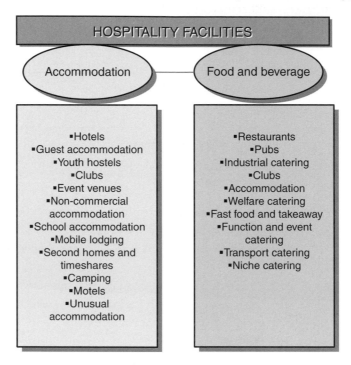

Fig. 2.3. Accommodation and food and beverage facilities.

Terminal 5, Heathrow, London

Terminal 5 at Heathrow, London, opened in March 2008. It is the largest freestanding structure in the UK and covers 640 acres. It is used exclusively by British Airways and is able to manage 30 million passengers a year. The terminal provides accommodation facilities, including Sofitel; eating facilities, including Gordon Ramsey Plane Food; shopping facilities, such as Burberry, Cartier and Gucci. The sub-facilities provided enhance the overall ambience and brand image of the facility.

Attractions

Similar to other facilities, the composition of attractions is wide ranging. Broadly, attractions can be classified as natural; man-made but not built to attract visitors; man-made and purpose built; and special events (Swarbrooke, 2002). Leask (2010) delineates these further into specific categories, as illustrated in Table 2.1.

Table 2.1. Visitor attraction categories. (Adapted from Leask, 2010.)

Attraction type	Examples
Theme parks/ amusement parks	Water parks, amusements, themes
Museums and galleries	Art, cultural, historical, collection-based, virtual, open-air museums
Natural	Gardens, national parks, forests
Animal	Safaris, farms, zoos, aquariums
Visitor centres	Cultural, industrial, transport
Religious sites	Churches, mosques, temples, etc.
Heritage	Castles, forts, historic houses, visitor centres, monuments, industrial, dark, archaeological, military, music

The challenge is to understand the composition of the levels of the facility. For example, a theme park can be classified as a holistic facility; however, it will comprise a number of other facilities that are interrelated with other facility categories. These include accommodation, food and beverage, and transport. The development and management of these facilities will be influenced by a number of factors:

- category of the attraction (man-made, natural etc.)
- ownership and structure
- size and capacity
- theme of the facility.

Activity

1. Select a visitor attraction from the categories in Fig. 2.1.

2. Identify the sub-facilities that make up that attraction. How do they interrelate with the attraction and what it is offering?

3. To what extent can the attraction improve its sub-facility offering?

Events venues

Hassanien and Dale (2011) reviewed the literature on event venues typologies and illustrate this in Table 2.2. In their review of the classifications of events venues they provide a number of conclusions: (i) there is no single universally accepted classification for events venues; (ii) the scope of the sector is difficult to define; (iii) most of the classifications are intuitively, rather than, empirically based; and (iv) events venues mean different things to

Table 2.2. Typologies of events venues. (Adapted from Hassanien and Dale, 2011.)

Weirich (1992, p. 15)	Montgomery and Strick (1995, p. 4)	Seekings (1997, pp. 49–53)	Lawson (2000, p. 57)	McCabe et al. (2000, p. 191)
1 Hotels	1 Hotels	1 Hotels	1 Purpose designed	1 Residential
2 Conference centres	2 Conference centres	2 Universities	a Conference venue	a Resort hotels
3 Resorts	3 Resorts	3 Conference centres	b Multi-use auditoria	b Airport hotels
4 Universities	4 Convention centres	4 Specialist and unusual venues	2 Adapted use	c Suburban hotels
5 Community centres	5 Limited service hotel		a Convention hotels	d Boutique hotels
6 Exhibition halls	6 Non-traditional		b Function rooms	e Residential centres
7 Cruise ships			c Theatres	f Colleges/universities
			d Concert halls	g Cruise ships
			e Public halls	2 Non-residential
			f Universities	a Purpose built
			g Colleges	b Exhibition halls
			h Arenas	c Theatres
			3 Occasionally used	d Arenas and stadiums
			a Libraries	3 Special venues
			b Art galleries	a Historic buildings
			c Museum	b Museums and zoos
			d Stadiums	c Sporting venues

Davidson and Cope (2003, p. 27)	Rogers (2003, p. 97)	Venue Directory (2004, p. 4)	BACD (2007)	Whitefield (2009)
1 Hotels	1 Hotels	1 Hotels	1 Hotel	1 Purpose built conference venues
2 Conference centres	2 Purpose built	2 Purpose built	2 Unusual venue	2 Hotels with conference venues
3 Academic	3 Colleges, universities, academic	3 Universities	3 University or other educational institution	3 Educational establishments with conference venues
4 Residential conference centre	4 Civic	4 Miscellaneous/ unusual	4 Multi-purpose venue	4 Visitor attractions with conference venues
5 Unusual	5 Unusual		5 Conference/training centre	
			6 Purpose built conference centre	

different people. Hassanien and Dale (2011) continue to provide criteria for classifying events venues based on strategic, market, physical, service and activity factors.

Not withstanding these observations, events venues are a key component of the THE industries and will overlap with the aforementioned categories of facilities including accommodation, transport, food and beverage.

CHARACTERISTICS OF THE FACILITIES

In this section we summarize the main characteristics of THE facilities as service organizations and look at the impact of these characteristics on the planning, development and management of THE facilities. The broad characteristics of services are intangibility, inseparability, heterogeneity, perishability and lack of ownership. Table 2.3 outlines the individual service characteristics that can be associated with THE facilities and their possible solutions.

Intangibility

THE services are intangible in that they cannot be seen, touched, smelled or tasted prior to purchase. For example, a venue facility customer will not be able to sample the service experience prior to visiting. Their prior purchase decision making will be influenced by past experiences of using the facility, the image and reputation of the facility, recommendations from referral sources (e.g. relatives, colleagues, social networking sites) and so on. The purchase decision based on the customer's perception of value will have a degree of risk and the facility operator will need to manage customer expectation before, during and after the experience. This may be achieved through ensuring quality of service in order to reinforce customer perceptions of the business. This will convey recommendations to other potential users of the facility and thus enhance the image and reputation of the facility. Social networking sites have had a significant effect in influencing buyer decision making, as the example below illustrates.

Social media and events

Social media have become a significant feature of the event industry. The use of social media sites such as Twitter, Facebook and YouTube has become a profound way of promoting an events offering. A survey of people working in event production by IT supplier Etherlive found that over 90% felt that social media was a key part of their event. This included raising the profile of the event, audience engagement and the sharing of images.

Source: http://www.eventmagazine.co.uk

Table 2.3. THE service characteristics solutions and challenges. (From Hassanien *et al.*, 2010, adapted from Hoffman and Bateson, 2006.)

Characteristic	Challenges	Solutions
Intangibility	• THE service cannot be seen, touched, smelled or tasted • Not easily displayed or sampled prior to purchase • Pricing is difficult	• Make use of tangible clues and physical evidence • Ensure quality of service • Utilize personal sources of information • Utilize social networking technologies • Create a strong organizational image
Inseparability	• Service provider is involved in the production process • Customer is involved in the production process • Other customers are involved in the production process (shared experience)	• Effective selection and training of personnel • Implementing and ensuring brand standards are maintained across multi site operations
Heterogeneity	• Standardization of the THE service experience • Quality control is difficult to achieve • Different customer expectations	• Standardization of the THE service • Customizing the service experience so that it meets the customers' needs
Perishability	• Service is time limited • Matching supply and demand challenges	• Creative pricing and effective reservation systems • Effective yield management • Development of complementary services • Development of non-peak demand strategies
Lack of ownership	• Customer does not own the THE service • Customer only owns memories of the THE service experience	• Ensure quality of the THE service experience • Ensure the customer experiences 'moments of truth'

Inseparability

THE services are inseparable. The service can only be consumed at the point of production. For example, if a festival ticket holder wishes to experience the event, then they have to physically attend. It is accepted that different media such as radio, television and the internet may play a role in conveying the event to different audiences, but this fails to capture the atmosphere, ambience and overall experience of being at the event itself.

This is one of the most challenging aspects for facilities, particularly if the primary facility is large and dependent on a number of sub-facilities. The risk that may be associated with delivering a consistent experience to customers is likely to be greater. The facility provider therefore has to ensure that customer expectations are managed throughout.

Heterogeneity

Service experiences in THE facilities are heterogeneous. Each time the service is delivered the customer experiences it differently. This can be very challenging for facility managers and customers will have different expectations of the service delivery. For branded facilities, which operate multiple operations across regions and nations, this can be compounded further. Facility managers therefore have to discover ways in which they can maintain a level of consistency with the service experience. Standardizing the service offering is one method for achieving this. The use of service scripts in the delivery can ensure consistency among personnel in the facility. Standardizing the design and furnishings of facilities also goes some way to ensuring that the customer will receive an experience that is consistent with their expectations.

Perishability

Services in THE facilities are perishable. They cannot be stored or stockpiled for later use and sale. THE facilities have to maximize their capacity to ensure the optimum level of revenue is achieved for the business. So facilities can be adapted for multiple uses. Hassanien and Dale (2011) found that the flexibility of event venues is a key aspect of design. If a facility can be used in different ways for different markets, then this has the potential to maximize use and capacity.

Appropriate forecasting and yield management are also important strategies for ensuring the optimum use of the facility. It is not unusual for hotels and airlines to adopt over-booking policies in which their occupancy rate on any given day may exceed the number of rooms.

Lack of ownership

Customers using THE facilities will be unable to take away the physical premises in which the service is being delivered. This results in a lack of ownership. The customer will only have the memories of the service experience that have been generated at the facility. Facility managers therefore have to ensure that the experience at the facility is enduring, so as to enable repeat custom and recommendation to other potential users. The maintenance and updating of the facility is important for reinvigorating the experience among target markets.

Activity

Select a THE facility. What is the impact of these characteristics on the facility?

Suggest strategies that facility managers can use in minimizing the negative impacts of these characteristics.

Case Study

Ferrari World Abu Dhabi

Overview

Ferrari World Abu Dhabi is the world's first Ferrari theme park, which was opened in 2010. It recognizes itself as the largest indoor theme park in the world. Abu Dhabi is the capital of the United Arab Emirates (UAE), in the Middle East. Abu Dhabi itself has seen enormous growth and development over the last three decades, with mass construction and urbanization of the landscape. In 2010, Abu Dhabi was ranked by Frommer's Guide and Lonely Planet as one of the top 10 destinations to visit. Abu Dhabi is the perfect location for Ferrari World Abu Dhabi because of its unique location at the crossroads between the three continents Europe, Asia and Africa.

The theme park is located on Yas Island on the north east side of Abu Dhabi's mainland. It is a 10-minute drive from Abu Dhabi International Airport, 30 minutes from the city of Abu Dhabi and 50 minutes from Dubai Marina. Yas Island is designed and developed to be an international tourist destination and leisure centre that comprises different types of tourism, hospitality and events facilities.

The theme park facility

Construction of the park began in 2007 and was completed in 3 years. The theme park provides a wide range of Ferrari-inspired rides and attractions that appeal to children and adults. The concept of the theme park is inspired by the well-known Italian sports car manufacturer Ferrari. So, Ferrari's unique features and innovative technology were mirrored in each aspect of the theme park throughout the various planning and development stages of the project. The park includes the world's fastest roller coaster, Formula Rossa, where goggles have to be worn by those using the ride for their own protection.

The owner of Ferrari World Abu Dhabi is the Abu Dhabi government. Farah Leisure Parks Management LLC, a subsidiary of Aldar Properties PJSC, is responsible for the management and operation of the theme park. The park also collaborates with partners and sponsors including Shell, Mountain Dew, CNN and First Gulf Bank.

The theme park also offers a number of services to add more value to its offerings. Examples of these services include: valet parking, free parking, lockers, ATMs, baby changing and feeding facilities, strollers, smoking areas and prayer rooms.

(Continued)

Case Study. Continued.

For health and safety reasons, guests are not allowed to bring food and drink into the park. However, Ferrari World Abu Dhabi offers their guests a broad array of Italian and international dishes through its different restaurants and food carts. This also includes the provision of Michelin 4 star experienced Italian chefs.

The park can also be used for meetings, incentives, conferences and exhibitions (MICE). The park facility provides a unique location for this activity and is attempting to capitalize on the growth of MICE in the UAE region. The park provides more than 3000 square metres of events space and caters for a range of privatization packages for use of the facility.

Facility design – facts and figures

The theme park has been designed in the style of the Ferrari motorcar and the roof infrastructure mirrors the profile of the Ferrari GT body. The following are some interesting facts and figures about the park:

- The roof covers 200,000 square metres and uses enough aluminium to cover 16,750 Ferraris. If Ferrari World Abu Dhabi was turned upright, it would be one of the tallest man-made structures in the world at over 300 floors.
- The roof houses the largest Ferrari logo. It measures 65 metres in length and covers an area of 3000 square metres.
- The indoor area is 86,000 square metres.
- 100,000 cubic metres of concrete were used for the slabs of Ferrari World Abu Dhabi – 10,000 cubic metres more than was used for Wembley Stadium in London.
- Ferrari World Abu Dhabi has the largest space frame structure ever built, with a total of approximately 172,000 members and 43,100 nodes.
- Ferrari World Abu Dhabi needed 12,370 tons of steel to create its structure; the Eiffel Tower only needed 7000 tons.
- The gross footprint area of the plaza level is equivalent to approximately 15 American football fields.
- A football field needs 8400 square metres of grass coverage; to cover the area around the roller coasters at Ferrari World Abu Dhabi, 4.5 times that amount was used – approximately 39,000 square metres of ground cover.
- The Bell'Italia ride displays more than 40,000 hand-planted miniature trees.
- Ferrari World Abu Dhabi includes 1200 dining seats – enough to feed the entire park at full capacity in 3 hours.

Sources: http://www.viceroyhotelsandresorts.com/en/abudhabi/activities/activities
http://themeparks.about.com/od/middleeastthemeparks/p/ferrari-world-abu-dhabi.htm
http://www.telegraph.co.uk/travel/destinations/middleeast/uae/8125409/Ferrari-World-Abu-Dhabi-Inside-the-worlds-biggest-indoor-theme-park.html
http://en.wikipedia.org/wiki/Ferrari_World
http://www.ferrariworldabudhabi.com/en-gb/about-us/construction.aspx

Questions

1. Profile the different levels of THE facilities at Ferrari World Abu Dhabi (i.e. ancillary, sub and primary).

2. Evaluate the distinctive features of the Ferrari World Abu Dhabi facility. How distinctive are they when compared with competitor offerings?

3. Discuss the present and future impact of Ferrari World Abu Dhabi on Abu Dhabi as an international tourist destination.

4. Search the Internet for further information about Ferrari World Abu Dhabi. What could help Ferrari World Abu Dhabi to further improve its facility offerings in the market?

GLOSSARY OF TERMS USED IN THIS CHAPTER

Ancillary facilities Ancillary facilities and services are those that supplement both the primary and sub-facilities.

Heterogeneity THE services are heterogeneous in that the experience of the service will be different each time it is delivered.

Inseparability The production and consumption of THE products are inseparable as customers have to go to the place where the product is being produced for it to be consumed.

Intangibility The THE products are intangible in that they cannot be seen, touched, smelled or tasted prior to purchase.

Lack of ownership The customer does not own the THE products or services.

Perishability The THE products are perishable and cannot be stored or stockpiled for later use and sale.

Primary facilities Facilities that act as the main purpose for use and or visitation. They fulfil a core benefit for the user (i.e. tourists, residents or visitors), which may be for relaxation, leisure, food, lodging, entertainment etc.

Sub-facilities The supporting elements or services of the primary facility. These may be located and/or housed within the primary facility itself. These sub-facilities may be managed by the primary facility or may be outsourced to a third party through contracting out.

REFERENCES AND ADDITIONAL READING

Airey, D. and Tribe, J. (eds) (2005) *An International Handbook of Tourism Education*. Elsevier, Oxford.

BACD (2007) *British Conference Venues Survey 2008*. Available at: http://www.myvenues.co.uk/news/Industry/BACD-releases-latest-conference-industry-research/966 (accessed 19 June 2010).

Cooper, C.P., Fletcher, J., Gilbert, D.G. and Wanhill, S. (1998) *Tourism: Principles and Practice*, 2nd edn. Pitman, London.

Cooper, C., Fletcher, J., Fyall, A., Gilbert, D. and Wanhill, S. (2005) *Tourism: Principles and Practice*, 3rd edn. Prentice-Hall, Harlow, UK.

Davidson, R. and Cope, B. (2003) *Business Travel: Conferences, Incentive Travel, Exhibitions, Corporate Hospitality and Corporate Travel*. Pearson Education, Harlow, UK.

Gilbert, D.C. (1990) Conceptual issues in the meaning of tourism. In: Cooper, C.P. (ed.) *Progress in Tourism, Recreation and Hospitality Management*, vol. 2. Belhaven, London, pp. 4–27.

Goeldner, C.R., Ritchie, J.R.B. and McIntosh, R.W. (2000) *Tourism: Principles, Practices and Philosophies*. John Wiley, New York.

Hall, C.M. (2003) *Introduction to Tourism: Dimensions and Issues*, 3rd edn. Hospitality Press, Frenchs Forest, Australia.

Hall, C.M. (2005) *Tourism: Rethinking the Social Science of Mobility*. Prentice-Hall, Harlow, UK.

Hall, C.M. and Page, S.J. (2006) *The Geography of Tourism and Recreation*, 3rd edn. Routledge, London.

Hall, C.M., Williams, A. and Lew, A. (eds) (2004) Tourism conceptualisation, institutions and issues. In: Lew, A., Hall, C.M. and Williams, A. (eds) *A Companion to Tourism*. Blackwell, Oxford.

Hassanien, A. and Dale, C. (2011) Toward a typology of event venues. *International Journal of Event and Festival Management* 2, 106–116.

Hassanien, A., Dale, C. and Clarke, A. (2010) *Hospitality Business Development*. Elsevier, Oxford.

Hoffman, K.D. and Bateson, J.E.G. (2006) *Essentials of Services Marketing: Concepts, Strategies and Cases*, 3rd edn. Harcourt College Publishers, London.

Holloway, J.C. (2009) *The Business of Tourism*, 8th edn. FT/Prentice-Hall, Harlow, UK.

Lawson, F. (2000) *Congress, Convention and Exhibition Facilities*. Architectural Press, Oxford.

Leask, A. (2010) Progress in visitor attraction research: towards more effective management. *Tourism Management* 31(2), 155–166.

Lockwood, A. and Medlik, S. (eds) (2001) *Tourism and Hospitality in the 21st Century*. Butterworth-Heinemann, Oxford.

Lumsdon, L. (1997) *Tourism Marketing*. Thomson Learning, London.

McCabe, V., Poole, B., Weeks, P. and Leiber, N. (2000) *The Business and Management of Conventions*. Wiley, Oxford.

Medlik, S. and Ingram, H. (2000) *The Business of Hotels*, 4th edn. Butterworth-Heinemann, Oxford.

Montgomery, R. and Strick, K. (1995) *Meetings, Conventions, and Expositions: An Introduction to the Industry*. Van Nostrand Reinhold, New York.

Page, S. and Connell, J. (2009) *Tourism: A Modern Synthesis*, 3rd edn. Cengage Learning, Andover, UK.

Rogers, T. (2003) *Conferences and Conventions: A Global Industry*. Butterworth-Heinemann, Oxford.

Rogers, T. (2008) *Conferences and Conventions: A Global Industry*, 2nd edn. Elsevier, Oxford.

Seekings, D. (1997) *How to Organise Effective Conferences and Meetings*, 6th edn. Kogan Page, London.

Swarbrooke, J. (2002) *The Development and Management of Visitor Attractions*. Butterworth-Heinemann, Oxford.

Swarbrooke, J. and Horner, S. (2001) *Business Travel and Tourism*. Butterworth-Heinemann, Oxford.

Teboul, J. (2006) *Service is Front Stage: Positioning Services for Value Advantage*. Palgrave Macmillan, Basingstoke, UK.

Timothy, D. and Teye, V. (2009) *Tourism and the Lodging Sector*. Elsevier, Oxford.

Weirich, M.L. (1992) *Meetings and Convention Management*. Delmar Publishing, New York.

Whitfield, J.E. (2005) An analysis and critique of an evolving conference industry within the UK from post war to the present day. PhD thesis, Bournemouth University, UK.

Whitfield, J.E. (2009) Why and how UK visitor attractions diversify their product to offer conference and event facilities. *Journal of Convention and Event Tourism* 10, 72–88.

chapter 3

Project Management

Peter Robinson
University of Wolverhampton

LEARNING OBJECTIVES

Having completed this chapter, readers should be able to:

* introduce the concept and purpose of project management;
* explore project management in the context of the tourism and hospitality sectors;
* evaluate the application of a range of project management tools.

INTRODUCTION

Project management is an essential component of both the strategic and operational activities of a business, and is embedded within the context of operations management as the approach through which facilities, products and services can be designed, improved and implemented.

Project management allows those tasked with projects to understand the entire scope of a project, aligning a range of interlinked factors to deliver the end result on time and on budget. In the tourism and hospitality sector it is made somewhat more complex by the intangible nature of the sector, but within the context of this publication it is also able to become a vehicle through which students can understand the nature of service and product development and the challenges that face managers at all stages of a project.

DEFINING PROJECT MANAGEMENT

Slack *et al.* define a project as 'a set of activities with a start point and a defined end state, which pursues a defined goal and uses a defined set of resources' (2007, p. 497). Kruger *et al.* describe it as 'a unique or one-time endeavour; it entails a series of interdependent tasks each with a starting and completion date; it has a specific objective that needs to be completed at a certain predetermined time and cost; it utilizes resources and entails risk; and it always involves a customer' (2005, p. 493). Kruger *et al.* define project management as 'the planning, organising, leading, co-ordination, and control of the resources of the project to ensure that the project is completed by a certain date and within the quality requirements and cost constraints' (2005, p. 495).

While detailed consideration is given to the different size, scale and scope of projects later in this chapter, it is worth introducing here the varied type and scale of projects that may take place in tourism and hospitality organizations, noting of course that this list is only intended to give a representative sense of the variety of possible projects:

- building a hotel;
- installing a new ride at a theme park;
- planning a sporting event;
- developing and implementing a new destination brand;
- building a new zoo enclosure;
- installing children's play facilities;
- refurbishing a restaurant kitchen;
- installing a new IT system;
- delivering a fund raising campaign;
- managing European funding for business support;
- delivering a lottery-funded project.

As suggested by these definitions, projects are characterized by the fact that they are usually unique activities that are rarely if ever repeated and any repeat would have a new set of goals and a new end point. All projects should have an overall objective and all are temporary activities. This is in contrast to a programme that may be a continuing process of change and development, although some ambiguity may arise around, for example, a programme of refurbishment of hotel bedrooms. For clarification:

- a project has a defined set of resources to be used in a defined period of time;
- a programme shares existing resources over a longer period of time, and may be continual, so, for example, when the 100th hotel bedroom has been refurbished, the first one may need doing again.

The typology of projects model provides a visual system to understand the scale and scope of projects, which are essentially measured by their levels of uncertainty: what may change externally that will affect the project, and by their complexity: the number of people, organizations and/or locations involved. This is illustrated in Fig. 3.1.

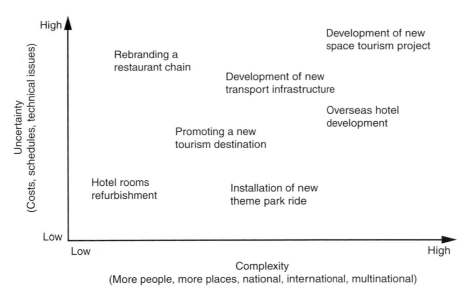

Fig. 3.1. A typology of projects.

PROJECT PURPOSE

There are a number of reasons why an organization may require project management and this could be for anything from developing a new CRM system to building new facilities, but it may also be for changes to an existing facility or a change in the way that the organization operates.

Before embarking on a project it is important for the organization to determine what the project is, and what it is seeking to achieve. A number of matrices have been developed by academics to try to classify projects, but these don't translate well to private sector tourism and hospitality businesses, because they tend to prioritize a number of projects using a format more suited to the public sector, where certain projects need to be selected from a long-term plan. While this may be true of a private sector organization, the likelihood is that any significant project will already be scheduled into the business strategy.

Example: Conservation on display

The heritage tourism sector has long debated the balance between conservation and access, the latter being carried out behind closed doors. By contrast, the visiting public have been confronted with signs stating 'do not touch' and some attempts at explaining the damage that is being done by visitors. In recent years there has been a move to demonstrate conservation in action and the major conservation projects that may have meant the property had to be closed for a season is now carried out in full view of visitors, who are able to find out more about the role of conservators. Such projects rely on safe working principles

(Continued)

> **Example.** Continued.
>
> and effective interpretation, but remove some of the pressure of deadlines for projects to be completed before the start of the season, while also enhancing the quality of the visitor experience for some, and managing it effectively for those who are not so interested but would have been disappointed had they been unable to visit. This project achieved two separate purposes, achieving both education and conservation objectives.

Table 3.1 attempts to classify the types of projects that are most common in this sector, while recognizing that there are also different levels of project management required. The overall project will invariably be linked to the overall strategy of an organization and also to operational strategies.

THE FEASIBILITY STUDY

Before commencing a major project, decisions need to be taken about what the project should be, or which project should be prioritized, and the benefits of the project to the business. For some projects a detailed feasibility assessment will be carried out that will evaluate the scope of the project and identify the conditions under which it is feasible. For example, a period of reduced land prices may be the ideal conditions for acquiring land to build a leisure complex, but if the prices are low because the area is perceived to be undesirable, there needs to be a strategy for mitigating these issues.

A feasibility study seeks to evaluate a range of factors to assess the planned project, and detailed studies may consider a number of different scenarios, giving consideration to marketing, market potential, likely demand and future financial forecasts. It is, in effect, testing the project, as illustrated in Fig. 3.2. Chapter 4 will explain in more details the topic of feasibility studies.

> **Example** – A high-speed project
>
> High Speed 1 (or HS1) was the project name for the development of the high-speed route to France from London, starting at St Pancras station and creating a high-speed link to Stratford International Station (the station for the London 2012 Olympics) on its way to the Channel Tunnel. Although the project focused on both the redevelopment of the historic St Pancras station and the new high-speed line, it is the latter that best exemplifies the feasibility of a project. Planning for the line started in 1989, after the opening of the Channel Tunnel, and planned to reach a terminus at London King's Cross Station. No less than eight different routes were proposed before the final route was chosen. The final choice was based on the feasibility of building the railway line, taking into account the best terminus station (now London St Pancras International) and based on a philosophy of maximizing the regeneration benefits of the project while minimizing the impacts of the project on the environment and on residential areas.

Table 3.1. Types of projects.

Strategic/operational objective	Project purpose (linked to strategy)	Scale of project	Project responsibility
Major capital investment – business growth	Development of new sites – either new build or redevelopment, e.g. new hotel, new theme park, redevelopment of disused sites/buildings.	Major project	An overall project manager will be employed, probably by the main development contractor. The contracting organization may also employ a project manager. Once complete the project management plan may continue internally with recruitment and marketing activity.
Significant capital investment – development of existing facilities	Creation of new markets or generating new business, e.g. building a spa next to an existing hotel, adding a new ride to a theme park.	Major project	An overall project manager will be employed by the main contractor, but the contracting organization will need to keep a closer eye on the project because it could have a direct impact on existing business activities and customers if the site remains oper.
Capital investment – refurbishment of facilities	Such a project may be a one-off full refurbishment, or a gradual phased refurbishment. It may take place over the closed season (tourism attractions), the business may close for a period of time or the project may be phased (a room, wing or floor at a time in a hotel).	Small to large	For a refurbishment at a closed site project management will be carried out by the contractor, with the specific part of the site handed over to them to manage (to keep control of access, health and safety etc.), but for a phased redevelopment, which may even be carried out by an in-house team, project management is likely to be internal to the organization.

(Continued)

Table 3.1. Continued.

Strategic/operational objective	Project purpose (linked to strategy)	Scale of project	Project responsibility
Information technology	Development of new IT systems, CRM systems or online marketing.	Medium	IT project managers are individuals with specific skills for this type of project – often such a project is in two phases: the development of the software, and then the installation and training within the business.
Service and process design	In many tourism and hospitality businesses significant changes can be made in a business by making changes to the way in which processes work and service is delivered – this could be as simple as a training programme or as complex as a full organizational restructure.	Small to medium	Generally managed in-house, or working with a consultant.
Funded projects	The tourism and hospitality sectors often receive business support through the public sector – projects may be delivered through local authorities, universities and similar organizations.	Small to medium	A project manager is employed with both project management skills and knowledge of the sector they are working within.

Minor changes and projects	This may include the use of vacant space for a new purpose, such as a space for education groups, or a reallocation of the use of different spaces.	Small (unless construction work is required)	Managed in-house.
Operational changes	Most organizations have an operational strategy, which may focus on specific areas of development, such as improving quality or increasing revenue generation.	Small	Managed in-house.
Marketing strategy	Although marketing is generally an on-going function, the development of a new brand or service may require a dedicated strategy and action plan that cannot be resourced within the business.	Small to medium (large when major investment is used)	Managed in-house or by a marketing agency with the relevant skills.
Product development	Product and service development is less time-constrained, because the focus is often on getting it right rather than rushing it through.	Small to large	Managed in-house, often by a dedicated group of employees, overseen by senior management as the overall project managers.

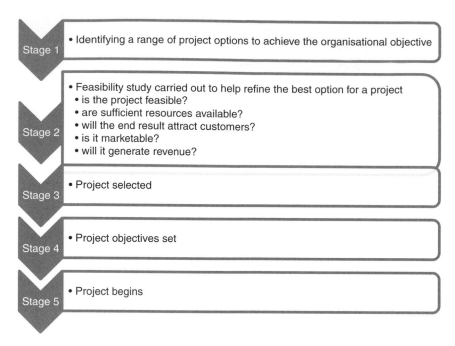

Fig. 3.2. Choosing the right project.

Activity

1. Consider a tourism attraction that you know well, and think of a project to enhance the visitor experience.

2. Carry out a feasibility study to assess the project, and provide a conclusion that states if the project is feasible or not.

INITIATING A PROJECT

Table 3.1 demonstrates that project management will at some time be invaluable to an organization. It is often discussed as a 'skill', but it can also be described as a 'process', or as 'process management', requiring an approach that coordinates varied and complex activities to achieve a set timescale, deadline and budget. Project management is, then, best described as a set of skills including budget management, people management, leadership, negotiation skills and conflict management, among others.

The key principle, however, is that all of the projects an organization pursues require effective project management to bring them to completion on time. Imagine, for example, the problems for a new hotel if it was not ready on time but had taken bookings for its opening week from customers who had paid a premium, or a theme park that had set its annual opening times but was unable to open because a new ride was not complete, or a zoo that planned an event to celebrate a new species of animal but the enclosure was not ready, or a new sports stadium hosting an event but not being complete by the date of the event.

Having identified the purpose of the project, it needs to be formalized. This is achieved through the development of specific project objectives, defining the scope of the project – that is, what it should achieve and how – and then developing a strategy for it. In other words, what is the end point of the project? how will we know when it has been achieved? what are the range of responsibilities for the project manager? and how will project management meet its objectives? Some of these elements can also be plotted within the project plan as milestones (see Gantt charts, critical path method (CPM) and programme evaluation and review technique (PERT) later in this chapter).

A number of writers have proposed different structures for organizations to adopt for project management, all of which have a generally consistent theme. These are illustrated in Table 3.2.

Table 3.2. Project processes.

Rogers and Slinn (1993)	Slack *et al.* (2007)	Kruger *et al.* (2005)

1. Planning
  a Goals
  b Time and cost estimates
  c Team building
2. Scheduling
  a Resourcing
  b Sequencing activities
3. Controlling
  a Monitoring
  b Revising plans and targets
4. Implementation and operation
	1. Understanding the project environment – internal and external factors
	2. Defining the project – setting objectives, scope and strategy
	3. Project planning – deciding how the project will be executed
	4. Technical execution
	5. Project control
	This model suggests that issues identified by control can be managed through changes to the project definition or corrective action during project planning
		1. Choose the project
		2. Create a capacity plan (internal tasks, outsourced tasks, short term contracts, sub-contracts)
		3. Select a project manager
		4. Select a project team
		5. Plan and organize the project
		6. Manage the workflow and develop the project
		7. Terminate the project

PROJECT PEOPLE

Project managers are those with the skills, experience and sometimes relevant qualifications employed to manage projects, or already working within an organization but with the capacity and ability to manage a project. Their skill set should include:

- an attention to detail;
- an ability to deal with contractors effectively, and assertively;
- an ability to make decisions;
- a knowledge and experience of the responsibilities of all contractors so they understand different people's tasks and can communicate better about these;
- an ability to communicate with different groups and individuals;
- an ability to solve problems logically and quickly;
- an ability to work independently and solve problems;
- an ability to manage time and handle stress and conflict.

A number of other specialists will be involved in projects in the tourism and hospitality sectors including (adapted from Swarbrooke, 2002):

- architects, designers, surveyors;
- builders and tradesmen;
- companies supplying materials;
- decorators and shop fitters;
- landscape gardeners;
- marketers;
- planning and building control officers, conservation advisors and others from the public sector;
- utilities companies including gas and water etc.;
- archivists and education experts;
- interpreters and curators;
- interior designers;
- furniture makers;
- sign makers;
- IT specialists.

PROJECT CONSTRAINTS

There may be a number of factors that constrain a project, and that need to be planned for, but that can be difficult to allocate a time period to. While a project plan (see Managing the Project, pp 49) may be developed in principle and a target given for completion, the factors discussed here all have a direct impact on the timescale, resources and budget for the project, because they determine the project start date and may have a further impact on the project at a later stage.

Planning permission

For a straightforward development, a local authority will suggest a timescale for the planning application, but tourism and hospitality projects are always going to be non-standard because they will have a much greater impact on their surrounding area and are not the usual business of planning officers. While consultation with local communities, working closely with planners, offering additional investment in the local area, carrying out detailed traffic and environmental assessments are all worthwhile ways to pre-empt the issues that may be raised, it is likely that there will still be significant interest in the details of the project and consultation periods will often be extended to allow time for additional independent reports to be carried out. Even after planning permission is granted there will be regular checks on the development by planning and/or building control officers to check the development complies with what was agreed.

Protecting heritage

Many tourism attractions, public parks and hotels are often located in or around historic buildings or parkland, which may be protected by law. In the UK buildings are listed according to their status and there will be rules and regulations not just about how they can be developed, but also around the materials that can be used, the source of materials (such as local stone) and the style of any development, which may substantially increase costs or force the development to be reduced in scale. Similarly, historic landscapes and gardens must be protected, and any potential archaeology under the ground may also need to be investigated. Often, especially in popular historic cities, development of new buildings is quickly halted as the foundations are dug out and historic artefacts revealed, and the subsequent archaeological dig may take many months to complete.

Funding and investment

There are a number of models for funding projects, which may include direct investment by the organization, a bank loan, private investment or sponsorship. While direct investment is simple to manage, for any project that requires external finance time needs to be made available to identify and secure the necessary funding and a process of due diligence may need to be carried out for the investor to check the reliability of the business they are investing in.

Example: Towering costs

The Portsmouth Millennium Tower was to be a flagship attraction to celebrate the Millennium. Planning for the 170-metre high tower with three viewing areas began in 1995, but planning issues, a lack of sufficient funding and issues with the structure of the building led to repeated delays. Construction did not commence until 2001 and the structure was only completed in 2005. Despite the fact the project was not funded from the public purse, the final £35.6 million project cost the taxpayer £11.1 million and was renamed the Spinnaker Tower.

Stakeholders

All projects will have groups of stakeholders, which may include employees, shareholders, investors, local communities, local authorities, business communities and others. The level of power and influence of these different stakeholders can be understood through the stakeholder analysis model shown in Fig. 3.3. Most stakeholders will be able to respond to major developments through the planning process, but in all cases, detailed consultation is often the best strategy to ensure all those concerned about and interested in the project have an opportunity to comment on the plans, to influence them if appropriate and to better understand them, which may in itself alleviate some of their major concerns.

The stakeholders of the most concern, those that are high priority, are those that fall in to the 'manage closely' category. These high-priority stakeholders can be understood and managed with this set of questions (adapted from Slack *et al.*, 2007):

1. What is the stakeholder's positive or negative financial and/or emotional interest in the project?
2. What is the main motivation for the stakeholder?
3. What information does the stakeholder require?
4. What is the most effective and productive way to communicate with the stakeholder?
5. What is the stakeholder's current opinion of the project?
6. Who influences the stakeholder's opinion – and are they consequently also a high-priority stakeholder?
7. If they are unlikely to be positive about the project, how can the stakeholder be persuaded to support it?
8. If they can't be won around, how will the stakeholder's continued opposition be managed?

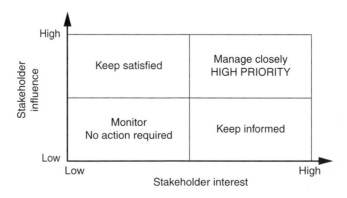

Fig. 3.3. The stakeholder analysis model applied to project management.

MANAGING THE PROJECT

Once all agreements are in place, permissions granted and funding agreed, then the project can begin. It was mentioned earlier in the chapter that project management is about a multitude of skills, of different functions and tasks to manage, with a goal of bringing a project in on time and on budget. A project manager is at the centre of this process, and has to ensure that everyone else is achieving their deadlines.

Before work begins it is important for the project manager to check and confirm that:

- everyone is clear about their duties and responsibilities;
- all insurances and risk assessments are in place;
- all permissions are in place and licences have been obtained;
- all funding is in place.

To support the project manager in achieving this, there are a number of tools available to them, which help to bring together the overall management and control of a project, giving consideration to timescales, logistics, different contractors, budgets, performance and productivity and communication with key stakeholders.

It is also worth noting that in addition to these tools, project managers can also become qualified in the PRINCE II Methodology, which is a useful additional qualification, but is certainly not essential to be recognized as an effective project manager – indeed the effectiveness of a project manager is best measured on their previous performance and their ability to meet deadlines and budgets.

Three specific project management tools are discussed and illustrated within this chapter:

- Gantt charts;
- critical path method (CPM);
- programme evaluation and review technique (PERT);
- work responsibility matrix.

> **Example:** Spending every last penny!
>
> The European Regional Development Fund provided half of the match-funded money for the Peak District Sustainable Tourism Forum project (2004–2006). The project's purpose was to provide business support to tourism and hospitality businesses in the Peak District National Park as a response to the impacts of foot and mouth disease on this rural area, which also has pockets of urban deprivation. The project supported farm diversification, provided conferences and events and provided tourism business advice, with a net result of a 33% increase in profitability and employment across the 100 businesses that benefitted from the project. The nature of the funding meant that the full project monies had to be invested through the project, a process that was reviewed every 3 months to ensure the project was on track and to forecast expenditure to the closure of the project, which hit its final target exactly.

The Gantt chart

The Gantt chart was developed by Charles Gantt in 1917, and in its simplest format is a bar chart that plots the tasks to be done against a timescale, showing the sequence of tasks, the interdependence of tasks and the different deadlines that exist within a project. However, to bring in the necessary level of detail it is useful to break down these tasks into their various component parts, unpacking the project into single work elements that allow for full accountability. Gantt charts can be created 'by hand', but specialist software packages that carry out this function are much more useful and can manage a multiplicity of data, and can be updated with resources allocations, remaining budgets and other detail to help plot the progress of the project. It is also easy to change particular tasks and to find out how small changes may impact on the overall project timescale. The Gantt chart also tends to be used to show milestones for different aspects of the project.

The development of a Gantt chart requires project managers to ask a number of questions in order to compile the chart. These include:

- What is needed?
- When it is needed?
- What needs to be done in what order?
- What tasks can only be started when another task is complete?
- Which tasks can be carried out concurrently?
- When are the key project milestones?
- What budget is allocated to which tasks?
- What are the priority tasks?
- When does the entire project need to be completed?

Figure 3.4 shows a Gantt chart for a project converting disused farm buildings into a self-catering cottage.

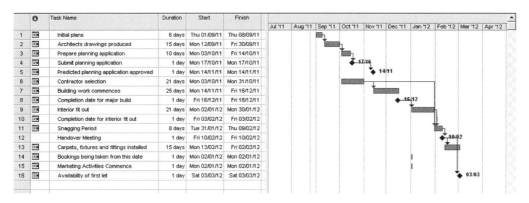

	●	Task Name	Duration	Start	Finish
1		Initial plans	6 days	Thu 01/09/11	Thu 08/09/11
2		Architects drawings produced	15 days	Mon 12/09/11	Fri 30/09/11
3		Prepare planning application	10 days	Mon 03/10/11	Fri 14/10/11
4		Submit planning application	1 day	Mon 17/10/11	Mon 17/10/11
5		Predicted planning application approved	1 day	Mon 14/11/11	Mon 14/11/11
6		Contractor selection	21 days	Mon 03/10/11	Mon 31/10/11
7		Building work commences	25 days	Mon 14/11/11	Fri 16/12/11
8		Completion date for major build	1 day	Fri 16/12/11	Fri 16/12/11
9		Interior fit out	21 days	Mon 02/01/12	Mon 30/01/12
10		Completion date for interior fit out	1 day	Fri 03/02/12	Fri 03/02/12
11		Snagging Period	8 days	Tue 31/01/12	Thu 09/02/12
12		Handover Meeting	1 day	Fri 10/02/12	Fri 10/02/12
13		Carpets, fixtures and fittings installed	15 days	Mon 13/02/12	Fri 02/03/12
14		Bookings being taken from this date	1 day	Mon 02/01/12	Mon 02/01/12
15		Marketing Activities Commence	1 day	Mon 02/01/12	Mon 02/01/12
16		Availability of first let	1 day	Sat 03/03/12	Sat 03/03/12

Fig. 3.4. Example of a Gantt chart.

Network tools

The critical path method (CPM)

The CPM approach helps as an initial planning tool, because it allows project managers to work out the total time for the project based on the key interrelated factors, by scheduling events along a timeline of critical tasks, described by Burke (2006) as the 'time cost trade off'. CPM helps to emphasize the fact that if specific tasks are not completed on time, they will have a detrimental impact on other tasks, thus the critical path is the time line that identifies how long the project should take (Tum *et al.*, 2006).

The problem with this approach is that it is often a best guess and cannot predict the real timescales involved in some elements of the project, such as applying for planning permission. None the less, it can help to identify an approximate point when the project will be completed, and allows organizations to tell their customers, for example, that the new hotel will be open in 2 years time, without being too specific.

In order to assess the critical path, there must be a clear understanding of the types of actions that can be undertaken in 'series', one after each other, and the actions that can be undertaken in 'parallel', alongside each other (Burke, 2006).

Programme evaluation and review technique (PERT)

PERT is very similar in appearance to a CPM, but evolved through an entirely different route and allows for some more complex modelling; including the ability to devise the longest, shortest and most likely time for project completion (see project float, later in this chapter). The guiding principles, which are underpinned by a philosophy of 'logic' for PERT (Kruger *et al.*, 2005) state that:

- activities can flow up and down and from left to right, but never from right to left;
- arrows should never cross each other because this complicates the logic;
- dummy tasks are inserted to maintain the logic;

- there should be a start and finish on every diagram;
- there can be more than one critical path.

Work responsibility matrix

The work responsibility matrix sets out the major activities in the project and identifies the individual or team responsible for that task. This is an important project communication tool because everyone involved is able to see clearly who to contact for each activity that may impact their area of work.

Computer-assisted project management

Enterprise project management has become increasingly popular as a way of managing projects because the details and calculations used for sophisticated critical path analysis can be produced by the computer, as can contingencies, amended plans and resource allocations and requirements. However, in most tourism and hospitality organizations

Table 3.3. Example of a work responsibility matrix.

Project: Development of new central reservation system with online booking for a UK hotel

Tasks/teams	External database developer	Internal web development team	External consultant	Internal marketing team	Internal finance team
Development CRM of database	✓				
Development of website		✓			
Integration of online booking software and EnglandNet compatibility	✓		✓		✓
Launch of new website				✓	
Content management of website		✓		✓	

this is not really necessary – most businesses tend to rely on IT for the production of Gantt charts, but the level of project planning that involves complex calculations and forecasts is often not necessary for the scale of many projects in the sector.

Activity

Think of a project to improve a hotel that you are familiar with.

1. Develop objectives for the project.

2. Outline the tasks that would be required.

3. Using a method of your choice (Gantt, CPM or PERT), plan out the implementation and management of the project.

PROJECT MATERIALS

Although there is little to be said about materials, which will vary from project to project, it is worth noting some of the diversity of materials and equipment that may be involved in a project, especially because these items need to be brought to the site at different times, and must be stored safely and under appropriate conditions. Such materials may include:

- building materials;
- landscaping materials;
- pipes and cables;
- fixtures and fittings;
- indoor and outdoor furniture;
- signage;
- core facility features;
- technical equipment;
- tills, computers, information displays.

MANAGING QUALITY

Quality is important throughout a project, because cutting corners at any stage could impact on the quality of the experience at a later date, could create future hazards and could cost more in the longer term because replacement/repairs may be needed more often. One key quality issue in the tourism and hospitality sector is the decision to open or close. If a business stays open during a project, then it continues to generate (much needed) revenue, but the project must not have a negative impact on the experience – so a hotel undergoing major building works may be able to stay open if work times are constrained and only areas of the hotel some distance from the noise are available.

> **Example:** Keeping the noise down!
>
> When a large three-storey hotel at Heathrow Airport required a new roof, having had repairs and maintenance carried out to the flat surface over a number of years, there were only limited times during the day when the work could be carried out, especially because the restaurant was below a large part of the roof where work was needed. Noise had to be kept to a minimum, as did hazardous fumes from any adhesive that was used. As a result, a special roofing membrane was sourced that required no mechanical or adhesive attachment.

MANAGING ENVIRONMENTAL IMPACTS

Managing environmental issues is an important aspect of project management where large-scale development is involved. This is not to say that smaller scale projects do not have to consider environmental issues, but because smaller projects are managed internally, the existing ethos around sustainability and corporate social responsibility is embedded in the project activity. While at a planning stage most large projects will have carried out some form of environmental impact assessment, many organizations seek to address their triple bottom line, looking at the financial, environmental and social impacts of projects.

> **Example:** Being considerate
>
> The Considerate Constructors Scheme is a voluntary membership scheme for construction businesses, set up in 1997 as a not-for-profit organization aimed at improving the image of construction around environmental issues, the workforce and the general public, making members of this scheme good project partners to select.

MANAGING BUILDING WORKS

Managing building works is a specialist aspect of project management, and one where many operators may not have the necessary skills and 'language' to manage the process effectively. Often an external project manager will be appointed to oversee the development. They may be employed on a freelance basis or may work for either the architects or, most commonly, the principal contractor.

There are essentially two ways to purchase construction work – either as a lump sum agreed in advance, or on a basis of how the final cost will be agreed. The former is always the best option and a contractor should be willing to investigate the project fully to provide such a cost up front. It is important, however, to note that even this can increase or decrease, and it is also common practice for businesses to add penalty clauses to the contract if the work is not completed on schedule.

Contracts tend to be either design and build (all-in-one contract) or conventional contracts (where the construction company builds from designs that have already been prepared). This is very common in the tourism and hospitality sectors because businesses seek to develop environmental buildings incorporating unusual and noteworthy architecture to raise awareness of the business.

To avoid issues, especially for inexperienced organizations, the following principles are important:

- only use experienced and qualified architects and surveyors;
- give designers a clear brief and stick to it;
- let professionals do their job, but do check on their progress;
- ensure all bills are paid on time;
- ensure that the designers and contractors are not put under pressure, thus avoiding them cutting corners to save time and/or money.

These projects are often put out to tender (as are many other types of project) to find the supplier who can offer the best value for money, combined with expertise and understanding of the project.

MANAGING THE TENDER PROCESS

Putting a project out for tender describes a process where different businesses can bid for work. This is common in the public sector, where it is important that there is transparency in decision making, but it is also useful for projects where the contracting organization lacks knowledge. The successful organization is generally chosen based on cost and/or value for money, together with their organizational history, relevant experience, reputation and financial situation. In some instances tenderers may be asked to submit a pre-qualification questionnaire (PQQ) before bidding in order to assess their financial standing and business ethics. This may include their environmental policy, equal opportunities policy and health and safety policy.

FACTORS AFFECTING PROJECT MANAGEMENT

A number of factors can affect a project, and different factors bring with them different levels of severity. These include:

Bad weather	Severe impact on a building project, but may only result in staff absence for other scenarios.
Regulations and legislation	If a project fails to comply with agreed planning rules, or does not have the full set of licences, it may need to be removed or demolished. At best, there will be an extended period of discussion and negotiation.
Health and safety	Assuming that risk assessments are complete and complied with, then only if there is an accident would there be a delay, although this could be substantial if a serious incident has occurred.

Failure of suppliers to deliver	If a replacement supplier can be found, the problem may be mitigated quickly, but special items may take longer to source and manufacture.
Illness and absence	Staff absenteeism can affect the progress of the project.
Disagreements about costs	Issues with costs and payments should be managed with effective contract management at the inception of the project, but if this does not happen serious delays, including a cessation of work, can occur.
Changes to the design	Changes to the design of a building, room or even visitor interpretation can have an impact on so many other interrelated tasks that the project becomes significantly delayed.

A well-managed project should be able to minimize these risks with careful planning and agreements at the start of the project. However, if there are problems, then a contingency may be required.

CONTINGENCY PLANNING

Contingencies are essential, and usually they focus on time and cost because these are the areas most likely to cause problems. Project managers must be able to authorize increases in staffing levels or spending if necessary. Weekly site meetings should be used to manage progress and identify areas where there may be a risk of slippage, that is, the project falling behind the specified timescale.

Project float

Float describes the process of disaggregating tasks through PERT or CPM and identifying the most likely time, and allowing a contingency closer to the maximum time. Assuming that key dates, such as launch parties, are planned for the maximum time, then this spare time becomes the contingency. An experienced project manager may even try to factor in the risk of bad weather and other problems and attempt to build in an estimate of, for example, two weeks of snow, while also considering when a new facility may be weather proof so work could continue inside.

Crashing the network

If a project starts to fall behind time, additional resources can be used to help progress it by introducing overtime working, bringing in additional manpower or sub-contracting some tasks. This reduces timescales if they are behind schedule, or if the project needs to be achieved more quickly, and is known as 'crashing the network', referring to the idea of trying to make the CPM or PERT plan fit a tighter timescale.

> **Activity**
>
> **1.** What are the biggest areas of concern when completing a hotel refurbishment project and how can these be mitigated?
>
> **2.** Debate the network crashing process – is it more effective to employ more people, pay overtime or sub-contract some activities?

MANAGING FOR PROJECT SUCCESS

Slack *et al.* (2007) suggest a set of principles that lead to project success:

- clearly defined goals;
- competent project manager;
- top-management support;
- competent project team members;
- sufficient resource allocation;
- adequate communication channels;
- control mechanisms;
- feedback capabilities;
- responsiveness to clients;
- troubleshooting mechanisms;
- project staff continuity.

COMPLETING THE PROJECT

The completion and handover of a project is very important, and the bigger the project, the greater the importance. Any external companies should be keen to complete the project to a high standard in the hope of gaining future work, and a final meeting is usually held to discuss any outstanding issues.

Before completion of the project, a snagging meeting may be held to inspect the project and check for any outstanding issues and problems to be resolved. These can then be followed up in the final meeting. After this, all outstanding invoices should be paid, all equipment removed and then an internal debriefing meeting held to assess the project.

SUMMARY

This chapter has reviewed project management from a tourism and hospitality perspective and makes clear the importance of effective project management to ensure that the core business of welcoming customers remains at the heart of the business. Clearly it is essential that project management is carried out by suitably experienced staff, and these may exist within the business.

Of most importance, however, is the recognition that effective project management should allow an organization to successfully manage a unique activity to enhance the organization's customer offer.

REVIEW QUESTIONS

1. Define project management and explain how to manage tourism and hospitality projects.
2. Provide an evaluation of the different project management tools.
3. Assess the challenges of managing a building project for a new ride at a theme park.
4. Evaluate the methods that can be used to bring a project back on track when it is overrunning.
5. Carry out a stakeholder analysis for a project of your choice. How would you manage the different stakeholder groups?
6. Create a job description for a project manager for a new hotel development.
7. Compare and contrast the different processes proposed in this chapter for project management.
8. Evaluate the factors that lead to success or failure for project management.
9. Critically evaluate the environmental aspects of a tourism project you are familiar with.
10. Propose a method to manage quality for hotel refurbishment projects.

Case Study

Major restoration of St Pancras train station

When the Channel Tunnel opened in 1989, plans were already underway to provide a high-speed link to London – The Channel Tunnel Rail Link, or CTRL. Victorian St Pancras station was chosen as the terminus, and would on completion replace London Waterloo as the home of Eurostar Services. However, after years of decline and budget maintenance, this once grand flagship station was tired, dirty and dingy. It was far from the salubrious transport terminus required by the Government. To achieve this major restoration project on time and on budget would be a major challenge!

The historic, listed train shed (the large canopy under which were seven platforms), known as the Barlow shed after its original creator, required sympathetic restoration and redevelopment, as did the vast and empty Midland Grand Hotel that faced the main road outside the station and adjoined the train shed behind. The project also required a new station extension to accommodate the long Eurostar trains and engineering work on

(Continued)

Case Study. Continued.

the railway lines and routes outside the station. English Heritage, the public body for the preservation of the historic environment in England, was heavily involved in the design and execution of the plan to create a major transport terminus, which began with the construction of the eastern side of the station extension.

On completion, the existing seven platforms in the old Barlow shed relocated to these platforms to facilitate the rest of the developments around the old platforms inside the shed. By managing the development this way, Midland Mainline services, which provided links with the north of England and Scotland, continued to operate, although the removal of the electric line to the station did mean that local commuter trains were diverted to nearby King's Cross Thameslink station. Logistics such as this required special permission and a degree of planning around timetabling and the services that could be offered.

Once the station no longer received train services it was closed for renovation, but this was no ordinary renovation. As well as a complete reworking of the platform layouts and the sectioning off of a security controlled area for Eurostar travellers, half of the original platform level was removed to give access to the station undercroft, which had historically been used for storing beer being transported to London from the Midlands. This area became a shopping mall, with toilets, Eurostar booking halls and lounges (below the Eurostar platforms), a mainline booking hall and access to the Thameslink platforms (now First capital Connect) and Southeastern Services, accessed from the undercroft and leaving from the far side of the Barlow shed. At the rear of the station, below the hotel, access to London Underground stations was improved and opened up, while the old station roof was also restored and a new subway created to link the station to the adjacent King's Cross Station as part of its £500 million redevelopment, which also included a new concourse and the removal of a 1970s extension to enhance the East Coast Mainline terminus. London Euston station, a short distance in the opposite direction, was also redeveloped to reinstate something of its original character, the 1960s station appearing to be tired and a less than grand terminus for Britain's high-speed west Coast Mainline.

With the further development of the western side of the platform extension, the underground space for the future Thameslink platforms was created, resulting in the closure of the old underground walkways for Thameslink services, meaning Thameslink trains from the north shared the platform with Midland Mainline, while those from the south used the adjacent King's Cross Station. Once this section of the works was complete, trains were able to run through this new space, but platforms and fittings were not part of the St Pancras project, funded instead by a separate programme managed by Thameslink. This would have prevented the new Thameslink station from opening at the same time as St Pancras, despite calls for the Government to provide funding so that St Pancras International could celebrate a full opening, rather than some areas opening later.

(Continued)

Case Study. Continued.

Eventually, in 2006, the Government did provide £50 million to facilitate the station fit out, together with an additional £15 million for signalling and lineside works.

By 2005 planning permission had been granted for the redevelopment of the former Midland Grand Hotel, which was also a listed building, and was, with some sympathetic development and the inclusion of the old booking hall and station entrance, to become a new hotel and apartment block. It was scheduled to open in 2011, exactly 138 years after it originally opened.

In 2006, CTRL was renamed High Speed 1, and with the full platform extension complete, Midland Mainline services (now East Midlands Trains) moved to their new home on the western side of the platform extension, beyond the retail areas, which could be accessed by passengers via escalators or a glass lift. Passengers arriving at the station could view the Eurostar platforms through glass screens, creating a light and open space, while at platform level Europe's longest champagne bar was installed, the old newsagents and platform shops were converted to bars and cafes, and public art was installed in the concourse areas.

On 6 November 2007 St Pancras International enjoyed its official opening, and the key element of the restoration was revealed – the reinstated glass ceiling above the platforms that had for many years been hidden behind sheets of metal and cheap repairs, supported by a blue metal framework that had suffered staining from generations of steam and diesel engines that had terminated at the station.

Completed on time, the project had cost £800 million, significantly more than the projected £310 million, and was the result of 2.7 million man hours, without a single reportable accident. The winner of three Considerate Constructors Awards, three RoSPA Gold Awards (for safety) and BCIA Major Project of the year 2008, the project may have been over budget, but it has also been the catalyst for the regeneration of the surrounding King's Cross communities and has given Britain a transport terminus to be proud of. On 5 May 2011 the London Renaissance St Pancras Hotel was opened to customers.

Questions

1. What have been the keys to success in completing St Pancras Station?

2. This project was massively over budget by the time it reached completion. Critically evaluate the factors that may have led to this overspend.

3. Considering the investment injected into St Pancras, how would you measure the success of this project in the longer term?

4. The new St Pancras Renaissance London Hotel was the final element of this project to be completed. Critically evaluate the importance of the overall project to the tourism and hospitality sectors in the area surrounding the station.

5. What can we learn from St Pancras that could inform the plans for London King's Cross and London Euston stations?

GLOSSARY OF TERMS USED IN THIS CHAPTER

Crashing the network	Reducing project time by employing additional manpower, offering overtime or sub-contracting activities.
Critical path method/ analysis	The method by which the critical time for a project can be established, based on the key tasks for a project.
Enterprise project management	A computer-assisted method of project management.
Feasibility study	A report that assesses a range of operational and environmental factors to establish the viability of a project.
Gantt chart	A graphical illustration of the processes, resources, timescales and budgets for a project.
PERT or performance evaluation and reporting technique	A method used to assess the shortest, longest and most likely time periods for a project.
Project float	The process of embedding time into a project plan as a contingency.
Project management	The coordination of a project, managing processes, resources and budgets to complete the project by the required deadline.
Stakeholders	All the individuals, groups and organizations with an interest in a project.
Tender	A method for organizations to offer work for which businesses can submit a bid or a tender for a project.

REFERENCES AND ADDITIONAL READING

Burke, R. (2006) *Project Management: Planning and Control Techniques.* Wiley, Chichester, UK.

Kruger, R., De Wit, P. and Ramdass, K. (2005) *Operations Management.* Oxford University Press, Oxford.

Nicholas, J.M. (1990) *Managing Business and Engineering Projects: Concepts and Implementation.* Prentice-Hall, Harlow, UK.

Robinson, P. (2010) *Operations Management in the Travel Industry.* CAB International, Wallingford, UK.

Robinson, P., Wale, D. and Dickson, G. (2010) *Events Management.* CAB International, Wallingford, UK.

Slack, N., Chambers, S. and Johnston, R. (2007) *Operations Management*, 5th edn. Financial Times/Prentice-Hall, Harlow, UK.

Swarbrooke, J. (2002) *The Development and Management of Visitor Attractions.* Butterworth-Heinemann, Oxford.

Tum, J., Norton, P. and Wright, J. (2006) *Management of Event Operations.* Butterworth-Heinemann, Oxford.

chapter 4

Feasibility Studies for THE Facilities

Ahmed Hassanien
Edinburgh Napier University

Crispin Dale
University of Wolverhampton

Mohamed F. Hawela
Greenwich School of Management

LEARNING OBJECTIVES

Having completed this chapter, readers should be able to:

- explore the concept and purpose of feasibility studies in tourism, hospitality and events (THE) facilities;
- analyse the key components of a feasibility study;
- discuss the limitations of a feasibility study.

INTRODUCTION

Conducting a feasibility study is crucial for THE facilities if they are to maximize their human, physical and financial resources. A feasibility study will enable the THE facility to assess the viability of any proposed new development. This may include a completely new development such as a restaurant or event venue or the renovation of an existing facility and the addition of new services. The feasibility study enables managers and operators to understand the financial implications alongside its potential market demand. Failing to conduct a feasibility study, or not doing it properly, can result in loss of revenue, increased costs and wasted time. The following chapter will explore the concept, purpose and importance of a feasibility study, while also acknowledging its key elements and limitations.

PURPOSE

Feasibility studies can be defined as the exploration into the costs and benefits of a new facility development or renovation. This assessment will offer a full breakdown of the resources that are required for the development or renovation to be carried out. It is the first stage carried out before the planning process (Hassanien *et al.*, 2010) and is an important part of the facility manager's decision-making process (Swarbrooke, 2002). Because the feasibility study requires some investment of resources, this may lead to managerial decision making that is skewed towards progressing with the project. It is therefore important for facility managers to be fully aware of the objectives of the study in order to provide a critical assessment of the development project.

The management and ownership of THE facilities means that feasibility studies can be a challenging exercise. First and foremost, the key drivers for the feasibility study have to be recognized. Second, THE facilities have to acknowledge the different priorities of the stakeholders they are involved with (Swarbrooke, 2002; Westerbeek *et al.*, 2006; Leask, 2010). The feasibility study enables priority areas to be identified and proposals made on how these can be delivered effectively (O'Fallon and Rutherford, 2011). However, it can also determine whether the development should go ahead at all (Cho, 2010) and enables the THE facility manager to make an assessment of the risk of carrying out the project (Jiang and Fu, 2011). Indeed, this is a crucial part of the process, because existing or potential investors have to be assured of the development project's viability (Nykiel, 2007). It should be noted that the feasibility study is a necessary part of the underpinning for the business plan, but it is not a replacement.

COMPONENTS

The feasibility study will enable the facility manager to assess the extent to which the component parts of the development project will work collectively together and fulfil the economic aims (Westerbeek *et al.*, 2006). As mentioned earlier, the process will require the allocation of resources and the time to collate the information to ensure that the study is carried out effectively. This will involve a number of different components (see Fig. 4.1). Each of these components are inter-related and outlined in the following.

Fig. 4.1. Feasibility study components.

Concept

The feasibility study should outline the concept that is being created and/or developed. The concept provides the overall philosophy and raison d'être for the facility and any related developments. The concept may be broadly descriptive, but should embrace the other study components. Fundamentally, this part of the feasibility study will project the image of the concept (Ransley and Ingram, 2004) and is key to providing a justification of the importance of the proposed development.

Whether this is a new development or an addition to an existing facility, the operator needs to be clear on the extent to which this will add value to the business. This may include improved efficiency, faster delivery of customer services, improved operational functioning and so on. In this respect, the concept should provide sufficient 'strategic fit' (Johnson *et al.*, 2011) with the other activities in the facility and with the wider business. In addressing these issues, an evaluation of the business environment is necessary. This will include the analysis of the macro environment, including political, economic, social and technological factors that are prevailing externally to the facility. Factors such as the economic circumstances have strongly influenced the buying behaviour of customers in Western economies in recent years. Markets have been gravitating towards options that offer value for money. Furthermore, demographic changes in society are generating an ageing society in many nation states, affecting the behaviour and choice of products by consumers. Such factors may influence the facility proposition being offered.

The analysis of the micro-environment will acknowledge competitor offerings and market demand for the facility development. This will also be considered in more detail in the 'market' criterion of the feasibility study. However, part of this process should involve identification of the typology profile of the THE facility. In the context of event venues, Hassanien and Dale (2011) propose a classification typology criterion. This is based on strategic, market, physical, service and activity factors. This will enable the facility operator to consider who they are most closely competing against and on what bases. An effective statement on how the facility is positioned, relative to competitors, can then prevail.

It is also important to acknowledge how the facility will be operated. Obviously, this will be determined to a degree by whether the facility operates in the public, private or voluntary sectors. A publically owned THE facility is likely to have constraints placed on its operation and development. These will be driven by financial issues, in addition to community-based policies, that may drive the development of the facility (Hassanien and Dale, 2012). In the context of the private sector, the facility may be operated independently, as a franchise or management contract, or as part of a multinational business. This will influence the overall goal of the facility concept and its development.

Example – Marriot Courtyard and Concept Development

Marriot Courtyard is part of the Marriott International hotel group. Created in 1983, the original concept was based on focusing on the transient business market, and having fewer than 150 rooms, a residential image, a limited menu restaurant and limited meeting spaces. Though the Marriot brand would be used for recognition, it would not take away markets from the brand portfolio of the wider Marriot offering.

Source: Wind (1989)

Market

Market analysis is another crucial part of the feasibility study. As mentioned in the 'concept' stage of the feasibility study, recognition of external factors will be an important part of this process. This will include analysis of the micro-environment and recognition of the facility's competitors. Understanding industry forces influencing the micro-environment (Porter, 1980) will indicate the viability of the proposed facility development. For instance, to what extent are there barriers to entry for the facility entering the market? The facility will need to be able to distribute its goods and services and access appropriate channels of distribution. It may also need to establish whether it can gain economies of scale in the market. This will be challenging for a facility operator that is acting independently in the market. The facility operator will also need to assess the extent to which there may be a threat of substitutes being able to enter the market. The facility's ability to be able to clearly differentiate itself will be a key basis for ensuring its viability. Indeed, if the facility proposition is easy to imitate or copy by others, then this may undermine its long-term viability unless it is able to develop or acquire the resources that will establish it firmly in the marketplace. This will be influenced by the power of suppliers in the market and the extent to which the facility operator is able to obtain resources to start up and function. The power of buyers will also need to be established. Markets may be attached to other facility brands, on the basis of loyalty, or will encounter switching costs by using your facility. This may be contractual or psychological if the buyer is tied into using another THE facility.

An appraisal of the micro-environment will enable the operator to establish whether the facility can access the markets that it would hope to target. It will also help the facility to understand how it should position itself relative to competitors offering similar goods and services. This will form a key part of the business plan if the feasibility of the facility is deemed acceptable.

Appealing to the needs and wants of all customers is likely to be challenging (Bowie and Buttle, 2004). The THE facility therefore has to understand who it is targeting and whether this market is feasible. Segmenting the market using demographic, geographic, psychographic and behavioural variables will help the THE facility to develop a rationale for targeting a particular market. The facility operator needs to be clear on the viability of the target market. Kotler and Keller (2011) propose five criteria for assessing the viability of a market: homogeneous; substantial, measurable, differentiable and accessible. The THE facility operator can use these criteria to define its target market. In terms of homogenous criteria, the market needs to be clearly identifiable so that an effective marketing strategy can be proposed when targeting them.

The market needs to be substantial. If the market is not large enough and is not able to produce a significant return on investment, then the facility and/or development is likely to be an unviable proposition. Conversely, the facility may be targeting a high-value niche market that is able to generate sufficient revenues to ensure its viability. The market also needs to be measurable, so that any marketing strategy is able to identify the behaviours and characteristics of whoever it is targeting. The market also needs to be differentiable and distinguished effectively from other market segments. Finally, the market should be accessible so that it can be reached by the facility operator. In this respect, the facility needs to be clear on the geographical boundaries in which it is operating. That is, is the facility and/or development targeting local, regional, national or international markets? The location of the facility and the nature and management of the operation will be a key determining factor in this instance.

This analysis of the market will need to be driven through appropriate research, which may comprise surveys, interviews, focus groups and so on. This information can then be used as a means of justification in the feasibility study. It can also be used to clarify and refine the facility proposition. Understanding the requirements of the target market will assist the operator in determining what the size and design features of the facility should be.

Understanding the markets that are being targeted will enable the facility operator to consider the extent to which marketing can be used to attract them to the facility. For example, the facility operator will need to establish the viability of using different off and online promotional methods for attracting its proposed target market. The behaviour of the selected market will determine whether the facility has the resources to be able to promote effectively to them.

Legal

The facility operator will need to acknowledge the legal implications of the facilities development. This is in terms of the national and regional legal frameworks that will be in place. This will include conforming to health and safety, employment legislation and so on. Obviously, the country where the facility is located will determine the legislation that should be conformed to. Sufficient legal advice should therefore be taken as part of the feasibility study process.

The focus and nature of the THE facility will influence the legality of its operation. For instance, if the facility is selling alcohol, or gambling is taking place on the premises, then the operator will need to conform to licensing and gaming legislation. Indeed, alcohol and gaming activity may, in the case of a public house or casino, be the core product of the facility and the reason for clientele visiting the premises. The target market of the facility also determines the legality of its operation. For example, if the facility is primarily targeting minors, then sufficient measures should be put in place to secure the safety of children on the premises (e.g. number of adults to children, safety barriers). This will influence the design of the facility and any related features.

The ownership of the facility, in terms of whether it is under sole ownership, a partnership or a private company, will also determine the legal ramifications concerning its viability. In terms of the physical facility itself, the operator will need to address whether it is being purchased on a freehold or leasehold basis. If it is on a leasehold basis, the time duration should be firmly established. There may also be legal issues concerning the nationality of ownership of the facility that can be imposed in some countries.

There may also be restrictions and covenants that are attached to any future development with the facility. These should be checked closely prior to purchase. In changing market conditions it is not unusual for facilities to have to embark on a process of renovation (Hassanien *et al.*, 2010). This may generate a need for minor or major alteration to the physical premises, such as an extension or even a change of use. Indeed, planning permission will need to be sought if there is a change in use to the existing facility, or a preservation order has been placed on the premises. Any legal barriers that may prevent future development from being able to happen should be closely scrutinized during the feasibility stage.

If the facility is being developed from new or is being considered for further development, appropriate building regulations will need to be conformed to. Any work carried out, such as electrical, gas and plumbing, will also have to be completed by qualified personnel who have appropriate certification. Indeed, if external contractors are being used for the completion of the work, then appropriate documentation should be in place to protect all parties. This is particularly the case for the payment of the work being carried out. Indeed, contractual clauses may be considered for delayed completion of the work, which may result in fines. The measures for judging the performance need to be clearly determined as part of the legal side of the feasibility study.

Technical

Technical aspects of the feasibility study will relate to issues concerning location, design and fixtures and fittings. As previously mentioned in the legal stage, this information is important for any planning application that may need to be submitted. The technical information will also reveal any operational issues that may emerge in the design of the facility. This may concern physical capacity, workflows and so on.

Where the facility is located or is to be located will influence the viability of the proposed development. A new facility will need to be located where its target market(s) are able to access it. Therefore, the availability of sufficient transportation modes (e.g. plane, train, boat, car) will need to be assessed to ensure these markets are able to access the facility.

The market analysis stage of the feasibility study will ascertain the viability of any proposed location. The location of an existing facility will also determine whether any alteration can occur. For example, an extension to a facility will require additional space to be located. If this increases the capacity of the facility then extra space may also be required in the form of car parking and so on. If these factors are unable to be addressed the facility may have to be relocated.

The design of the facility or development will also be an influential factor determining its viability. The needs and wants of the target market will be key to the design and related features that need to be incorporated into the facility. It is important for the facility operator to consider the uniqueness of the physical design and related features so as to differentiate from competitor offerings and appeal to its target markets. Using the measures of net present cost, renewable factor and payback time, Dalton *et al.* (2008) provide a feasibility study for a renewable energy supply in a large hotel. They contend that few case studies have focused on feasibility analysis in this area. When compared with domestic contexts, they further note the high-energy consumption rate that tourist destinations have. This can be compounded by 'high-end' facilities where consumer-driven expectations include air conditioning and 24-hour functioning.

With the fixtures and fittings in the facility, the operator will need to consider what materials will be required and how are they to be sourced. If suppliers are limited or the materials required are at a premium, then this will inhibit the development of a facility. Furthermore, if specialist features, décor or equipment are required in the facility, then this will also influence its viability. The facility operator will also need to consider the role of technology in the facility. Technology will be used for facilitating customer bookings and client management on the premises. The facility operator may need to develop this in-house or decide whether to outsource this to a third party.

Managerial

The management structure is an important consideration when it comes to understanding the feasibility of the facility. The first consideration is the method in which the facility is to be operated. This will be in terms of whether the facility is to be operated independently, is part of a chain or is being run as a franchise or under a management contract. If the latter, then the facility will need to conform to brand standards and methods of operation, as determined by the franchisor.

If the facility is looking to expand, then this may require a reconfiguration of its existing management structure. The facility will need to ascertain whether it has the existing human resources or needs to attract new personnel to the business. The structure of management for the successful operation of the facility will also need to be considered. In a large multinational company where a number of facilities are being operated, a hierarchy with strategic business divisions may be conducive. However, a flat or matrix structure may be more effective for a facility that is smaller in size.

In the context of the management of the facility, the operator will also need to decide whether staff should be provided in-house or outsourced. This will be based on a number of factors such as cost-based and service-driven factors that have been outlined as part of the outsourcing chapter. However, if specialist expertise is required for the functioning of the facility, this will have a bearing on the feasibility of the facility.

Example: Travelodge and 'Men in Black'

The budget hotel operator Travelodge has over 500 premises located in the UK, Ireland and Spain. The chain has created a 'Men in Black' maintenance division that specializes in the upkeep of the estate. This includes plumbing, decorating, maintenance of broken equipment and so on. The management of this team in-house helps Travelodge to act on maintenance queries swiftly when they arise.

Source: http://www.travelodge.co.uk

Example: Little Chef and outsourcing

After carrying out a strategic review of its business, Little Chef decided in May 2012 to outsource parts of the business, including IT, which operated from its headquarters in Sheffield, UK.

Source: http://www.bbc.co.uk

Questions

1. Review the two examples above. What are the management implications for the facilities involved?

2. What will be the advantages and disadvantages of the management approaches discussed?

Financial

The production of a feasibility study enables areas of concern to be raised, thus minimizing the financial risk of any investment incurred (Jagels and Ralston, 2007). Fundamentally, an assessment of how much the facility development will cost should be determined. This will include an acknowledgement of the start-up and running costs. The study will also assess the long-term financial viability of the facility development being proposed (Westerbeek *et al.*, 2006). This is necessary if the facility operator is seeking investment. Indeed, a key part of the feasibility study will be identification of potential funding sources. This may include banks, private investors, shareholdings, sponsors, public grants and so on.

It is necessary for the facility operator to be clear about the indicators that will be used to measure performance. This may include a combination of profitability ratio measures and the amount of turnover that could be generated over a given period. It may also include a projected payback period and breakeven point for the facility development. Additional streams of revenue from the development may also be noted.

Example: RevPAR

In a hotel facility, RevPAR (Revenue Per Available Room) is a measure that is used to calculate its financial performance. It is calculated on the basis of multiplying the average daily room rate by the occupancy rate or by dividing the total room revenue in a given period by the number of available rooms in that period. The RevPAR can act as a key indicator of the feasibility of a facility, though it is acknowledged that this can only be measured accurately once the facility is in operation.

Table 4.1 outlines the key elements and questions that should be posed when compiling a feasibility study.

LIMITATIONS

The facility operator needs to be aware of the limitations that can be associated with feasibility studies. These include the following.

Uniqueness of THE facilities

THE facilities are different in their composition, ownership, size, operation and management (Page and Connell, 2006; Hassanien and Dale, 2011). When compiling a feasibility study, comparing one THE facility with another is likely to impair the validity and reliability of the feasibility study. Indeed, facility managers and operators should be cautious when making a judgement on the viability of a potential facility in this respect.

Table 4.1. The feasibility study: key elements and questions for THE facilities.

Component	Key elements and questions
Concept	Overview • What is the nature of the THE facility concept? • What is the typology profile of the THE facility? • Will it 'add value' to the facility and/or wider business? • Will it provide 'strategic fit'? Sector and composition • What sector will the facility development operate in (e.g. public, private, voluntary)? • How will the facility/facility development be operated (e.g. franchise, management contract, as part of a multinational)? Competition and markets • Who are the competitors and potential markets?
Market	External factors • How will macro- and micro-environments influence the development of the facility? • What are the barriers to entry for the facility? • Is there a threat of substitute facilities emerging? • What is the power of buyers and suppliers in the marketplace? • How is the facility positioned relative to competitor offerings? Target markets • Where will the facility be located? • Have the appropriate criteria been used to establish the viability of the market (e.g. homogeneous; substantial; measurable; differentiable; accessible)? • What is the target for the facility and/or development (local, regional, national or international markets)? • Is this a niche market? Promotion • What methods of promotion will be used to market the facility (e.g. off and online)?
Finance	Costs and cash flow • How much will the facility development cost? • What is the projected payback and breakeven point for the facility development? • What will be the turnover of the facility over a three-year period?

(Continued)

Table 4.1. Continued.

Component	Key elements and questions
	Profitability • What will be the projected profits? • What potential revenue streams will the facility and/or development generate?
	Funding sources • What funding sources will be required to support the development (e.g. banks, private investors, sponsorship, social enterprise)?
Technical	Location • Where will the facility be located? • If this is a development to an existing facility, how will it affect the existing location? • Is the current location appropriate? • Will the facility need to be relocated? • Are there sufficient methods of transportation to and from the facility?
	Design • How will the facility or development be designed? • What design features will be incorporated? • To what extent will the design and features be unique?
	Fixtures and fittings • What materials will be required for the development of the facility? How accessible are these and will there be appropriate suppliers? • What equipment will be required for the facility to be operated effectively? • What technology will be required? Will this technology need to be developed in-house or outsourced?
Managerial	Structure • How will the facility be managed and operated (e.g. franchise, independent, multinational)? • How will the management of the facility be structured (e.g. flat or tall hierarchy, matrix)?
	Staff and services • Will the management, employees and services of the facility be provided in-house or outsourced?

(Continued)

Table 4.1. Continued.

Component	Key elements and questions
Legal	Ownership • Will the facility be under sole ownership, a partnership or a private company? • Will the facility be freehold or leasehold?
	Health, safety and employment • Will the design, construction and operation of the facility conform to appropriate health and safety and employment laws?
	Licensing • Will the facility be providing alcohol and need to become a licensed premises? • Will gambling legislation need to be conformed to if this activity is being provided on the premises?

Dynamic and uncertain external environment

The dynamic nature of the external environment can make the compilation of the feasibility study difficult. THE industries are often in a state of change and flux and are affected by a range of political, economic, social, technological, environmental and legal factors. Therefore a feasibility study can only capture a 'moment in time' that is likely to have changed by the formal business planning stage. The timescale for developing the facility from the point of feasibility study to actual operation will depend on a number of factors, but could take anything up to 3 years (Rushmore, 2011). The facility manager should be constantly attuned to changing environmental, competitive and market conditions that will affect the compilation of the feasibility study.

Cost

The compilation of the feasibility study can be a costly and time-consuming exercise (Lawson, 2000). The nature of the study is such that its individual parts have to be performed sequentially, as listed in this chapter, yet also feed into one another. This can make the activity quite protracted and costly when resources have been used to develop the study. This may include preliminary market research, such as questionnaire and interview surveys, requiring expertise and investment in money and time.

Accurateness

The feasibility study may begin with a desire to ensure that the facility project is appropriate to develop. This can be influenced by the operator's blind judgement, which then precludes alternative views. It is important to recognize that the feasibility study is an initial exercise to test the viability of the offer. The cost in taking it further will be more significant if the study has been biased by inaccurate or subjective information that lacks sufficient justification.

Decisional factors

It is important to acknowledge that the feasibility study is the basis on which further decision making can be made on the way forward. It should not be seen as a total justification for proceeding further with the development of the THE facility. In contrast, it should be used as a tool to guide the facility operator on a plan of action concerning investment decisions and possible stakeholder reactions.

SUMMARY

The chapter has discussed the purpose, process and limitations of a feasibility study. The facility manager and operator should use the feasibility study for their decision making on whether to proceed with any development. This can only be accomplished successfully if the respective stages of the feasibility study are addressed comprehensively. Though it can be a time-consuming and costly exercise, if conducted appropriately it will act as an excellent foundation for the future success of the THE facility.

REVIEW QUESTIONS

1. Consider a THE facility that you may develop for the future.
2. Conduct a feasibility study for that facility. Use Table 4.2 to assist you in compiling the study.
3. Make a decision on the feasibility of the facility for future development.

Case Study

Sports and recreational feasibility study, City of Cambridge, Ontario, Canada

The City of Cambridge, Ontario, Canada, has a range of leisure and recreation facilities that are operated by both the public and private sectors. Because existing facilities were a number of years old and in need of renewal and renovation, the City of Cambridge conducted a feasibility study. This was initially done to assess the viability of introducing a major sports and entertainment centre or alternatively to develop a new multi-purpose recreational facility.

The city has a particular focus on Ice Pad facilities, with the provision of a single municipal ice pad for every 15,000 residents. Currently, via a partnership arrangement, the City of Cambridge provides 28 hours of ice time per week at the Cambridge Ice Park. Though demand is relatively high, especially during peak periods, the Ice Pads are not fully maximized during low periods such as early weekday and weekend mornings.

(Continued)

Case Study. Continued.

The population is forecast to expand by 63,000 from 2010 to 2030, with a significant growth in the 0–19 age category, meaning that up to five additional ice pads would be needed.

Current market
Existing facilities within a 100-km radius of the City of Cambridge include the following:
- The Aud, Kitchener: Fixed seating for 7100 spectators.
- The John Labatt Centre, London: Fixed seating for 9090 spectators.
- The Sleeman Centre, Guelph: Fixed seating for 4500 spectators.
- Copps Coliseum, Hamilton: Fixed seating for 17,383 spectators.
- The Powerade Centre, Brampton: Fixed seating for 4980 spectators.

Figures show a decline in attendance and spending at these facilities. Furthermore, major sport franchises require a minimum of 80–120 km separation. Locational factors, therefore, suggest that a new sporting team would need to be created in the City of Cambridge.

Costs and revenues
A number of facilities within a 100 km or an hour's drive have been developed in Canada in recent years. The cost of these facilities ranges from CAN$8000 to CAN$14,000 per seat. The development of these municipally owned facilities was driven by a combination of government and private assistance.

The cost of constructing a new 6000-seat facility would be in the region of CAN$56 million, which excludes land costs. Money to develop the facility would have to be raised through a combination of existing city capital, grants, partnerships and loans. This would also depend on these sources being available.

The facility could potentially generate CAN$2.4 million in revenues. However, generating revenues from ticket sales, advertising, rental and so on to cover the operating costs and loans against the facility has been challenging for existing multi-purpose venues. In addition, operating costs could potentially total CAN$2.6 million.

The City of Cambridge has based its estimates on three different funding scenarios, as outlined in Table 4.2.

Table 4.2. Capital and financing scenarios for the multi-purpose facility.

Scenario	% capital costs to be paid by the City	% to be financed	CAN$ to be financed
A	100	70	39.5 million
B	89	60	33.5 million
C	50	21	11.5 million

(Continued)

Case Study. Continued.

The development of the facility would depend on changing macro environmental conditions facilitating additional demand for events and advertising at the venue; and whether the City of Cambridge is able to accept operating on an annual deficit and prepared to subsidize the facility based on the potential economic effects from its construction (e.g. employment, taxes).

Alternatives

A 2000- or 750-seat venue focusing on the local community would be an alternative to building the proposed facility. These facilities would house ice pads, gymnasia, swimming and meeting rooms and cost CAN$29 million and CAN$24.6 million respectively. However, it is noted that few community-based multi-purpose facilities have more than 1000 seats. The funding model would be based on the scenarios outlined in Table 4.3.

Recommendations

The lack of a key tenant for the facility would suggest minimal financial viability for the development of a multi-purpose sports and entertainment facility. Furthermore, there is low market demand for a 6000-seat centre in the City of Cambridge. It is therefore proposed that a 750-seat facility is a viable alternative option. This is based on the facility targeting community groups, having reduced costs and having the potential for staging smaller events that would benefit the local area.

Table 4.3. Capital and financing scenarios for smaller multi-purpose venues.

Facility	Scenario A	Scenario B	Net cost over a 25 year period (CAN$)
2000 seat	100% financed by the City	75% financed by the City	19.6–27 million
750 seat	100% financed by the City	70% financed by the City	15.7–21.9 million

Source: Adapted from City of Cambridge Multi-Purpose Sports and Entertainment Feasibility Study, http://www.cambridge.ca

Questions

1. To what extent has the feasibility study addressed the different components? Use Table 4.3 to assist you in answering this question.

2. Consider the strengths and weaknesses of the alternative options and evaluate the proposed recommendation from the study. To what extent do you believe this is the most suitable option for the City of Cambridge? Provide a rationale for your answer.

GLOSSARY OF TERMS USED IN THIS CHAPTER

Concept feasibility   The feasibility study should outline the concept that is being created and/or developed. The concept provides the overall philosophy and raison d'être for the facility and any related developments.

Feasibility studies   Feasibility studies can be defined as the exploration of the costs and benefits of a new facility development or renovation. This assessment will offer a full breakdown of the resources that are required for the development or renovation to be carried out. It is the first stage that is carried out before the planning process and is an important part of the facility manager's decision-making process.

Financial feasibility   An assessment of how much the facility development and operation cost, the long-term financial viability of the facility development being proposed and identification of potential funding sources.

Legal feasibility   The facility operator will need to acknowledge the legal implications of the facility's development. This is in terms of the national and regional legal frameworks that will be in place. This includes conforming to health and safety, employment legislation and so on.

Managerial feasibility   The management structure is an important consideration when it comes to understanding the feasibility of the facility.

Market feasibility   The analysis of the micro-environment and recognition of the facilities competitors.

Technical feasibility   Technical aspects of the feasibility study relate to issues concerning location, design and fixtures and fittings.

REFERENCES AND ADDITIONAL READING

Baud-Bovy, M. and Lawson, F. (1977) *Tourism and Recreation Development*. Architectural Press, London.

Beals, P.A. (1989) A critical evaluation of lodging-industry feasibility reports. Doctoral dissertation, Cornell University, Ithaca, New York.

Bowie, D. and Buttle, F. (2004) *Hospitality Marketing: An Introduction*. Butterworth-Heinemann, Oxford.

Cho, S.-M. (2010) Hotel feasibility in the recessionary economy of 2010: a case study in Reno, Nevada. MBA and MSc dissertation, University of Nevada, Reno, Nevada.

Dalton, G.J., Lockington, D.A. and Baldock, T.E. (2008) Feasibility analysis of stand-alone renewable energy supply options for a large hotel. *Renewable Energy* 33, 1475–1490.

Hassanien, A. and Dale, C. (2011) Toward a typology of event venues. *International Journal of Event and Festival Management* 2(2), 106–116.

Hassanien, A. and Dale, C. (2012a) Drivers and barriers of new product development and innovation in events venues: a multiple case study. *Journal of Facilities Management* 10(1), 75–92.

Hassanien, A. and Dale, C. (2012b) Product innovation in events venues: directions, process and evaluation. *Journal of Facilities Management* 10(4), 266–286.

Hassanien, A., Dale, C. and Clarke, A. (2010) *Hospitality Business Development*. Elsevier, Oxford.

Jagels, M.G. and Ralston, C.E. (2007) *Hospitality Management Accounting*. Wiley, Hoboken, New Jersey.

Jiang, X. and Fu, L. (2011) Feasibility study – youth rental community in Beijing. MSc thesis Master's Design and Construction Project Management, Chalmers University of Technology, Gothenburg, Sweden.

Johnson, G., Scholes, K. and Whittington, R. (2011) *Exploring Corporate Strategy*, 9th edn. Pearson, Harlow, UK.

Kotler, P. and Keller, K.L. (2011) *Marketing Management*, 14th edn. Prentice-Hall. Upper Saddle River, New Jersey.

Lawson, F. (2000) *Congress, Convention and Exhibition Facilities*. Architectural Press, Oxford.

Leask, A. (2010) Progress in visitor attraction research: towards more effective management. *Tourism Management* 31(2), 155–166.

Luckmann, J. (1967) An approach to the management of design. *OR* 18(4), 345–358.

McDonald, M.T. (2004) *Lodging Hospitality* September, 48–50.

Nykiel, R. (2007) *Handbook of Marketing Research Methodologies for Hospitality and Tourism*. Haworth Hospitality and Tourism Press, New York.

O'Fallon, M.J. and Rutherford, D.G. (2011) *Hotel Management and Operations*, 5th edn. Wiley, New York.

Oxford Dictionaries (2012) Feasible. Available at: http://oxforddictionaries.com/definition/feasible?q=feasible (accessed 16 February 2012).

Page, S.J. and Connell, J. (2011) *Tourism: A Modern Synthesis*, 3rd edn. Cengage Learning EMEA, London.

Porter, M.E. (1980) *Competitive Strategy*. Free Press, New York.

Ransley, J. and Ingram, H. (2004) *Developing Hospitality Properties and Facilities*, 2nd edn. Butterworth-Heinemann, Oxford.

Rushmore, S. (2011) The truth behind hotel feasibility studies. *Lodging Hospitality* 01480766.

Swarbrooke, J. (2002) *The Development and Management of Visitor Attractions*, 2nd edn. Butterworth-Heinemann, Oxford.

Westerbeek, H., Smith, A., Turner, P., Emery, P., Green, C. and van Leeuwen, L. (2006) *Managing Sport Facilities and Major Events*. Routledge, London.

Wind, J. (1989) Courtyard by Marriott: designing a hotel facility with consumer-based marketing models. *Interfaces* 19(1), 25–47.

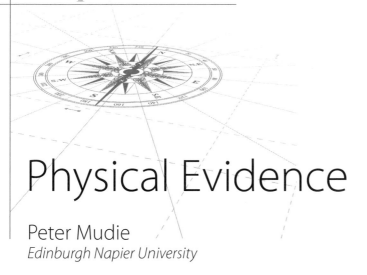

chapter 5

Physical Evidence

Peter Mudie
Edinburgh Napier University

LEARNING OBJECTIVES

Having completed this chapter, readers should be able to:

- understand the concept and dimensions of physical evidence;
- explore services by function and nature for physical evidence;
- investigate how physical evidence might work in terms of its role and impact in the service setting.

INTRODUCTION

As Levitt (1981) observed, common sense tells us and research confirms that people use appearances and external expressions to make judgements about realities. By managing the evidence a service provider can send out signals to anyone interested in using that service. While it may not always be an accurate indicator of the actual service reality, it nevertheless should remain a guide in service selection. Despite its claimed importance, however, there's been a surprising lack of empirical research or theoretically based frameworks addressing the role of physical surroundings in consumption settings. Unlike many other aspects of service, this is arguably due in part to the inherent challenges the servicescape poses in determining how and why (even if) the various dimensions shape and influence the responses of those engaged in service settings. Accordingly, this chapter will explore and evaluate the concept, importance, nature and dimensions of physical evidence in tourism, hospitality and events (THE) facilities.

WHAT IS PHYSICAL EVIDENCE?

There is no definitive list of elements or dimensions of physical evidence. Such a list will vary by service and situation. Table 5.1 is an indication of what it involves.

Both individually and collectively, the above elements or dimensions will say something about a service. The challenge for the designer is one of creating a physical environment that will meet the expectations of potential customers and enable the service to operate efficiently.

INTANGIBILITY: THE RATIONALE FOR PHYSICAL EVIDENCE

One of the most basic and often quoted differences between goods and services is intangibility. It is one of the five key distinguishing characteristics of services, the others being inseparability, perishability, variability and lack of ownership. Unlike tangible goods, services cannot generally be seen, tasted, felt, heard or smelled before being consumed. Even during and after service delivery, customers are often unable to perceive the service. In the case of car repair, customers frequently cannot see what is being done and unable to evaluate what has been done. To mitigate or limit the effects of tangibility, services came round to the view that physical evidence could act as a facilitator by helping consumers judge the likely quality and attractiveness of a particular service.

Difficulties in assessing the quality of a service in advance of using it meant that physical evidence (or servicescape[i], as it has come to be known; Bitner, 1992) has become a key aspect for addressing the problem of intangibility. Leading authors in the field of services have noted its critical role and importance in the management of customers (their expectations and degree of pleasure/satisfaction) and employees (their productivity, motivation and satisfaction).

The background for this developing interest in servicescapes emanates from the field of environmental psychology, a field so vast not only in terms of interest (from psychology, sociology, architecture, design, geography, economics) but application (from large-scale urban and

Table 5.1. Elements or dimensions of physical evidence.

Exterior of a building or facility	Uniforms
Signage	Business cards
Parking	Furnishings
Surrounding grounds	Brochures
Equipment	Websites
Technology	Ambient conditions, e.g. scent, temperature

[i] Scape – denoting a specified type of scene; originating on the pattern of (land)scape.

natural environments to institutional environments such as hospitals, prisons and schools). While service authors and researchers seek to understand relationships between environmental cues and responses, it is worth bearing in mind from environmental psychology the myriad of stimuli that confronts us in any environment (Donovan and Rossiter, 1982). With that in mind a taxonomy of environment cues/stimuli has developed for the services literature (see later in this chapter). What these environmental cues/stimuli in the form of physical evidence were intended to create was an 'atmosphere' or 'ambience'; in effect the pervading tone or mode of a place or situation[ii]. A hotel may win an award for its friendly, welcoming atmosphere. For the student of physical evidence the challenge would then be one of understanding how it might have contributed to the creation of such an atmosphere. One of the earliest contributions (in the marketing literature) to comprehending atmosphere came in an insightful article entitled 'Atmospherics as a marketing tool' (Kotler, 1973–74). In the article Kotler reminded businessmen of the importance of aesthetics in consumption and as a 'silent language' in communication. Just as today we embrace body language, physical evidence or servicescape is seen as a spatial language. Hence, atmospherics came to be described as 'the conscious designing of space to create certain effects in buyers' (Kotler, 1973–74, p. 50; as well as the impact on employees in service situations).

From Kotler's contribution it is now generally recognized that physical evidence and the accompanying atmosphere shape customer experiences and behaviour as:

- an attention-creating medium – using external appearance to distinguish itself from competitors and serve as an attractive proposition for potential customers;
- a message-creating medium – using exterior and particularly interior design to convey the service provider's intentions in terms of quality and customer experience;
- an effect-creating medium – using colours, sound, aromas and spatial design to engineer appropriate feelings and responses that management desire for customers.

THE SIGNIFICANCE OF SERVICE TYPOLOGY IN THE CREATION OF ATMOSPHERE

Understanding should increase as we seek to categorize in terms of criteria or dimensions what appears at times to be a bewildering array of service context or situations. Typologies (Bitner, 1992) or classifications of services (Lovelock and Wirtz, 2007) have developed in the process. For physical evidence, the significance of classification lies in the role it can and should play along with insights that may follow. In terms of atmosphere (a primary function of physical evidence), a number of criteria are worthy of consideration:

- Nature of customer contact from limited or passive (e.g. dry cleaning) to extensive and intense (e.g. health spa).
- Time spent in service from brief (e.g. car repair) to lengthy (e.g. hotels).

[ii] *The New Oxford Dictionary of English.*

- Degree of segmentation from homogeneous (e.g. libraries) to heterogeneous (e.g. restaurants).
- Type of service from standardized (e.g. hospitals) to customized (e.g. private health insurance).

Important differences exist among services. This can be simply illustrated by considering customer involvement (comprising contact time and nature of contact) in the following four services:

- using a courier service to transmit a package;
- spending a weekend at a health spa;
- contacting a plumber to repair or replace a leaking pipe;
- travelling first class on a long-haul flight.

What should be evident from the above examples is that services do differ in respect of customer involvement.

Several authors have sought to establish critical dimensions of services as in equipment-vs people-based (Thomas, 1978), client contact and customization (Maister and Lovelock, 1982), customer contact, routinization and objects of the service process (Wemmerlöv, 1989). Most notably Lovelock and Wirtz (2007) developed a more general classificatory framework by categorizing services into four broad groups based on tangible actions to either people's bodies or to their physical possessions and intangible actions to people's minds or their intangible assets. The purpose of these developments was to facilitate the design and management of services. Most of the typologies focused on issues that would be of significance for marketing, operational or process management and human resource management. While lessons or insights for physical evidence could be inferred from the above approaches, attempts to classify more specifically for physical evidence have been limited.

One noteworthy contribution was developed by Bitner, who categorized services on two dimensions that would, according to her, capture important differences in the management of the servicescape. The vertical dimension related to who is performing actions within the servicescape – the customer, or the employee or both. This would range from the 'self-service' organization in which few if any employees are present and the level of customer activity is high to the other, remote service where involvement by the customer/employee is limited, e.g. automated voice messaging services. Between these two extremes are 'inter-personal' services, where customers and employees are present and performing actions, e.g. hotels, restaurants, hospitals, banks. The horizontal dimension captures the physical complexity of the servicescape, ranging from elaborate, e.g. websites (self-service customer only) to lean, e.g. telephone mail order desk (remote service employee only). In the middle would be dry cleaning services and hair salons, for example (interpersonal involvement, between customers and employees). While extremes of self service and remote service could have physical evidence significance in terms of user friendliness for the customer and reliability for the employee, it is interpersonal services where most of the interest has been focused. Here, it is not only the time spent in the service facility that deserves attention but also the nature and quality of the social interaction within the service.

Whereas Bitner focused on the participants within the servicescape and the complexity of the servicescape, Fig. 5.1 offers an alternative classification in the quest for understanding the contribution and impact of physical evidence in service settings.

It is proposed here that the dimensions should be standardization vs customization and utilitarian vs hedonic. They are defined as follows.

Dimension 1: The construction of the service design

Standardization occurs when a service appears the same every time and in every place. It is in effect the industrialization of a service where, to coin a phrase, 'one size fits all'. It is a means of decreasing costs, increasing productivity and where appropriate lowering prices, e.g. Premier Inn.

Customization occurs when a service is modified to suit a particular individual or group. To coin another phrase it is 'tailor made', a deviation from or alteration of the standard service. The service offer will invariably be quite different from the version on offer and often come at a significantly higher price. Consequently it can be perceived as the preserve of the wealthy.

Dimension 2: The function of the service design

Hedonic services provide more experiential consumption, fun, pleasure and excitement.

Utilitarian services are more cognitive-driven, instrumental and focused on accomplishing a practical task.

It has to be acknowledged that with many 2 × 2 matrices (as in Fig. 5.1) the distinctions between the cells may not always be clear cut, not only in terms of the labels but also with

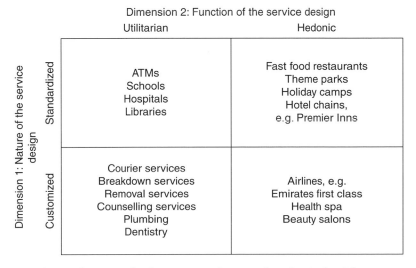

Fig. 5.1. A typology of services by function and nature for physical evidence.

respect to correctly locating the examples. For Fig. 5.1 the boundary between standardization and customization can be porous if we consider mass (standardized) customization where some individualized service elements are offered to a large number of customers. In this context, Normann (1991) has referred to peripheral services such as choice of wines in aeroplanes or special extra service in a hotel, e.g. gathering opera tickets for a client. However, this appears to lie within the domain of personal service rather than have any significance for physical evidence. For customized utilitarian services physical evidence can be viewed as both an input (e.g. removal services) and in a more unorthodox way input and output (e.g. plumbing services). The customized work can be viewed as the output (individualized work done) as well as an input in terms of evidence for a potential customer. In the case of standardized utilitarian services we have come to expect, because of the nature of these services, a relative standardized design where physical evidence can be construed as background and/or peripheral/supportive of the agreed uniform activities that occur in such facilities.

Standardized hedonic services are even more standardized than standardized utilitarian services in that regardless of location the design of physical evidence is identical, e.g. Premier Inns in the UK where the decor, beds, uniforms, signage is identical in every facility. As hotel chain of the year for 2011, Premier Inns has demonstrated through its advertising how physical evidence can contribute to an enjoyable, comfortable experience for customers. Its signage is an excellent intimation of its proposition, a good night's sleep. Other service facilities in the standardized hedonic cell give equal prominence to the role of physical evidence in delivering 'a good time for customers'. For the customized hedonic cell, physical evidence can be said to almost constitute the service itself. For a health spa customized unique experience designed for relaxation and rejuvenation can be delivered through the medium of physical evidence. Through the creation of individual spa rituals and treatments balance can be restored, the body purified and the senses stimulated. It is an atmosphere of sheer indulgence and escapism. Equally flying first class on the Emirates airline offers customers a private suite/shower, adjustable seat and flat bed, vanity table, wardrobe and mirror along with adjustable ambient lighting in what can only be described as a sumptuous, luxurious environment.

It is evident from the above discussion that the significance of physical evidence in the design, delivery and response to a service can range from disinterest, distraction and background to involvement, prominence and delight. Furthermore it should be regarded not only in terms of the service setting but also as a part of the service output.

MODELS AND FRAMEWORKS

Over a number of years several conceptual frameworks have been developed, aimed at increasing our understanding of how physical evidence might work in terms of its role and impact in the service setting. Unfortunately, and the reasons for this seem less than clear, there has been a surprising lack of research and empirical findings that would confirm its significance for service environments. Notwithstanding the lack of research, however, the advances made through the literature do offer intriguing and logical insights into how we might understand the effects of physical evidence.

The Mehrabian–Russell Model

To help explain the effects of the service environment on consumer behaviour, environmental psychologists applied a stimulus/organism/response (SOR) model. Mehrabian and Russell (1974) deployed such a model to study the effects of retail store atmosphere on shopping behaviour. Figure 5.2 summarizes the model.

It focuses on the intervening variables and response areas, but neglects the stimulus element. This, according to Donovan and Rossiter (1982), is 'not unexpected in an area such as environmental psychology simply because of the myriad of stimuli that confronts us in any environment'.

The model assumes that all responses to an environment can be considered as approach or avoidance behaviours, which are regarded as having four aspects:

1. pleasant and arousing would be termed exciting;
2. pleasant and not arousing would be termed relaxing;
3. unpleasant and arousing would be termed stressing;
4. unpleasant and not arousing would be termed gloomy.

Such behaviours, it is argued, are a consequence of emotional states people experience within any environment. These emotional states, according to the model, can be portrayed as a combination of two major dimensions – pleasure and arousal and to some extent, a third, dominance. The responses are known by the acronym PAD.

Pleasure refers to the degree to which a person feels good, joyful, happy or satisfied in a situation.

Arousal refers to the degree to which a person feels excited, stimulated, alert or active in a situation. As a measure of environmental stimulation Mehrabian and Russell draw on what is termed the information rate or 'load' of an environment. This is assumed to be directly related to the degree of arousal induced by an environment. Therefore a high loaded environment (i.e. novel, surprising, crowded) will make a person feel stimulated, excited and alert, whereas a low load environment will induce feelings of calm, relaxation and sleepiness.

Dominance refers to the extent to which a person feels in control of, or free to act in, a situation.

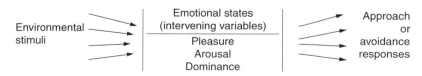

Fig. 5.2. The Mehrabian–Russell model.

Taking all three intervening variables and in terms of the quality of the customer experience,

- a pampered customer would report pleasure, low arousal and submissiveness;
- an excited customer would report pleasure, high arousal and dominance;
- an upset customer would report displeasure, high arousal and submissiveness.

While the focus for the model was retail settings, the authors do provide significant empirical support for the impact of their three variables on shopping behaviour.

The model specifies a conditional interaction between pleasure and arousal in determining approach/avoidance. This means that:

- in a neutral (i.e. neither pleasing nor displeasing) environment, moderate arousal enhances approach behaviour, but very low or very high arousal leads to avoidance behaviours;
- in a pleasant environment, the higher the arousal, the greater the approach behaviour;
- in an unpleasant environment, the higher the arousal, the greater the avoidance behaviour.

The Russell and Pratt Model

Russell and Pratt (1980) proposed a modification of the Mehrabian–Russell model. They deleted the dominance dimension because evidence for its application over a range of situations appeared weak. In addition, dominance was interpreted more as a cognitive rather than affective (emotional) response. Pleasure and arousal were believed to be sufficient for representing people's emotional or affective responses across a range of environments. In the preamble to the model, Russell and Pratt suggest that 'most of us would acknowledge pervasive if subtle influence of affective responses on person–environment interactions'. They recognize, again like most of us, that hundreds of words can be used to described what they term 'the affective quality of places'.

The model itself encapsulates pleasure and arousal in a 2-dimensional space (Fig. 5.3).

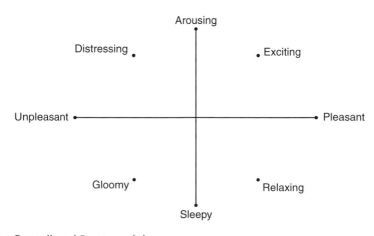

Fig. 5.3. The Russell and Pratt model.

Each quadrant is represented by an overriding affective quality attributed to environments as follows: exciting – pleasant and arousing; relaxing – pleasant and unarousing; gloomy – unpleasant and unarousing; distressing – unpleasant and arousing.

The attractiveness of the model is that it enables service environments to be classified in terms of how consumers are expected to feel, e.g. the hospitality industry will seek to embrace the exciting and relaxing quadrants as the physical environment becomes more integral to the service offer. Equally, through neglect by the provider, hospitality environments may be perceived as gloomy or distressing.

The Bitner Servicescape Model

Building on previous models, Bitner (1992) sought to provide a framework (Fig. 5.4) that would express in more detail the influence of the servicescape on behaviours of customers and employees.

According to Bitner, attention centres first on the behaviours that may be influenced by the servicescape, then on the internal responses and the controllable dimensions that constitute the servicescape. With reference to the approach and avoidance behaviours cited by Mehrabian and Russell, Bitner draws attention to how poorly designed/operated features (e.g. inadequate signage, inaudible acoustics and poor ventilation) can negatively impact on the customer's experience. Similarly inadequate physical surroundings are said to affect employee feelings and performance. Social interaction and behaviour will also be a product of the physical setting. In other words, it should provide guidance as to how people are expected to behave with and towards each other. Just think of how the design of a 5-star hotel communicates expectations for how one should conduct oneself, whether as customer or employee.

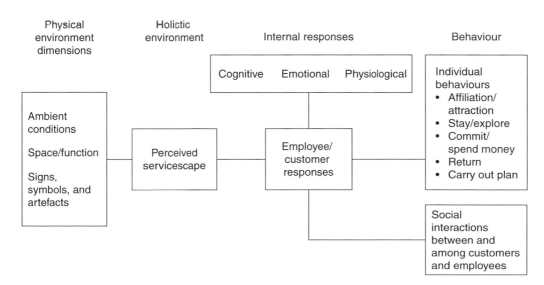

Fig. 5.4. The Bitner servicescape model.

The actual behaviours cited by the model are the product of internal responses from customers and employees. These responses are categorized as:

- Cognitive responses, which refers to the beliefs people hold about a service provider's place of business and where appropriate the users of that facility. Judgements on value for money, exclusivity, competence, trust and others will inevitably be made. For the service-scape questions can and should be raised over how far and in what respects it offers a credible communicator and sign of trust, competence etc.
- Emotional responses, which have been captured according to previous models mentioned by the dimensions pleasure/displeasure and degree of arousal, i.e. amount of stimulation or excitement. Customers can emit a whole range of emotions (anger, excitement, frustration, calm, enthusiasm, joy, panic, humiliation and so on) in response to a servicescape, including peripheral elements as well such as websites and self-service.
- Physiological responses, which addresses the impact of the working environment on the human body. Ergonomics is one of a range of specialist areas studying working conditions. Overall physiological conditions can cause discomfort or deliver satisfaction for employees and customers. Such areas include level of noise, air quality, glare of light and the degree or intensity of heat.

While all three (cognitive, emotional and physiological) have the potential to impact on customers and employees, customers have more scope to avoid and also to react within service environments. What does not appear to have been greatly acknowledged or researched (in the service management literature) is the response of service employees working in these environments (Parish *et al.*, 2008). The models developed so far seem to be more at the disposal of customer feelings and responses. Most notably employee emotional responses have been omitted.

Bitner's model appears to give equal weighting and prominence to customer and employee. It is however widely recognized and reported in the services literature and elsewhere that front office employees must project an emotional neutrality and professionalism regardless of the ambient conditions at the service facility. Employees in non-professional services are subject to what is known as emotional labour (Hochschild, 1983) where feelings must be hidden/faked. Equally, professional services employees are subject to a code of standards regardless of their surrounding environment. It almost begs the question, what's the point of researching emotions when they are self evidently in check over long periods time? On physiological responses employees spend a great deal more time in the service environment than customers. On cognitive responses the small matter of employment prospects and continued employment could eclipse any misgivings in respect of the servicescape, unlike potential customers. Their judgement may be central to whether they approach or avoid. Adverse conditions for service employees have to be endured, e.g. consider the case of the uniform, an element of the servicescape (Mudie and Pirrie, 2006). Customers can steer clear of perceived adverse conditions.

Bitner goes on to suggest that customer and employee responses may be moderated by individual personality traits, the purpose for being in an environment, mood states and expectations. These factors may be of interest for furthering our understanding but must be set against the reality of a service provider being largely unable to quickly and easily modify the servicescape to accommodate them.

Before discussing the significance and impact of individual stimulus factors on behaviour, Bitner correctly includes the influence of the 'perceived servicescape'. Schiffman and Kanuk summarize it well by noting that 'people do not experience the numerous stimuli they select from the environment as separate and discrete sensations; rather, they tend to organize them into groups and perceive them as unified wholes. Thus, the perceived characteristics of even the simplest stimulus are viewed as a function of the whole to which the stimulus appears to belong. This method of perceptual organization simplifies life considerably for the individual' (2010, p. 182). This approach is often referred to as Gestalt psychology (Gestalt, in German, means pattern or configuration). In common parlance, it could be captured by the question 'What's your overall impression?' This overall image should not be underestimated in the search for understanding responses to a servicescape. The attractive Gestalt approach contrasts with the inherent challenges and difficulties of determining the influence of individual stimuli such as music, colour and lighting.

Bitner brackets stimuli into three categories under the heading environmental dimensions. Ambient conditions would probably be high on the agenda of many if asked to list aspects of the service environment. The conditions refer to those characteristics of the environment that relate to your five senses.

- Visual stimuli (brightness/darkness; colours; shapes).
- Aural stimuli (the volume, pitch and character of sounds).
- Olfactory stimuli (fresh or foul scents and smells).
- Oral stimuli (bitter, sweet tastes, and hot/cold ingredients).
- Tactile stimuli (the texture in food products, the softness in furnishings and the level of comfort with the temperature).

Thinking back to the concept of arousal, extreme stimulation can cause varying degrees of physical discomfort, ranging from the mildly aggravating to the medically threatening.

Although many studies have been undertaken of how ambient conditions influence employee performance and job satisfaction, research on the influence of ambient conditions on customers has been limited. Of the five senses, music (aural stimuli) appears to be the most commonly researched ambient variable because according to Yalch and Spangenberg (2000) 'it is relatively inexpensive, easily changed and has predictable appeals to consumers based on their age, gender and lifestyles'. Many of these studies have been on supermarkets, e.g. how music affects pace of shopping, length of stay and amount of money spent. On restaurants one study found that diners who listened to loud, fast music ate more food and those who listened to Mozart or Brahms ate less and more slowly. The researchers concluded that diners who choose soothing music at meal times can increase weight loss by at least 5 pounds a month (Edmondson, 1989). Milliman (1982) discovered that music tempo influences customer time at tables and bars.

Alongside music, colour is seen as a major cue in a servicescape. There are no definitive 'rules' for the use of colour or how it might work. For the service setting the symbolic nature of colour is important in terms of meanings conveyed and corresponding relevance for the nature of the service activity being undertaken.

A number of valuable insights into colour psychology have been drawn and a summary of these are listed below (for further reading see Cumming and Porter, 1990; Lewison, 1991):

- Red – the colour of fire and passion, suggesting activity, energy, joy. Associated with love, romance, warmth and excitement.
- Orange – improves social behaviour, delivering warmth, openness and friendliness.
- Yellow – stimulates concentration but used too strongly can induce stress.
- Blue – symbolizes authority and implies truth, prudence and wisdom. A 'cool colour', it is said to convey calmness.
- Green – symbolizes the natural world and is widely believed to be a calming colour. It suggests restfulness, freshness and softness.
- Purple or Violet – indicates sensitivity, taste, class and wealth.

Each colour can of course differ in terms of brightness, intensity and purity. A deep, pure red for example may indicate class and exclusivity, whereas a bright, lighter red conveys fun and inclusivity.

The atmosphere of a service environment can also be affected by smell. Scented air is becoming an attractive proposition for stirring emotions, creating a calming feeling or relaxed mood. Just how a service is meant to smell is an interesting and challenging issue for the scent marketers. Lighting is another ambient condition with a role to play. It has been suggested that 'consumers talk more softly when the lights are low, the service environment is perceived more formal, and the pace of the encounter slows. In contrast, brightly lit service environments are louder, communication exchanges among customers and between customers and employees are more frequent, and the overall environment is perceived as being more informal, exciting and cheerful' (Hoffmann *et al.*, 2009, p. 284).

In addition to the ambient conditions, the designer and in some cases an architect will have to address how an empty, or to be refurbished, space is to be configured or laid out. Overall they will have in mind the task of finding a harmonious balance between:

- image;
- style;
- comfort;
- operating efficiency.

More specifically they will need to consider:

- user friendliness;
- aesthetic appeal;
- special needs provision;
- capacity level;
- flow/work method;
- profit and income generation;
- health and safety/security;
- environmental friendliness;
- ease of maintenance;
- size and shape as well as arrangement of machinery, equipment and furnishings;
- the visual appearance and placement of signs.

As previously noted, the main objective is one of harmony. This is not always the case, because efforts to contain costs may come at the expense of customer satisfaction.

RESEARCH AND THE SERVICE SETTING

It does seem somewhat paradoxical that writers in this area of service have referred to the importance of stimulus factors as a determinant in particular of consumer behaviour while saying little on how we are to understand customer responses to these factors. Neglect of the physical environment and the search for detailed understanding of responses to stimuli may be attributed to one of the basic principles of Gestalt psychology, namely figure and ground. Consider the stimulus of music (Schiffman and Kanuk, 2010). People can either bathe in music or listen to music. In the first case, music is simply background to other activities; in the second it is the figure. Figure is more clearly perceived because it appears to be dominant; in contrast, ground appears to be subordinate and, therefore, less important. Coupled with that is another basic principle of Gestalt psychology called grouping. This was referred to earlier in the chapter as 'What is your overall impression?' Closure suggests that people tend to group stimuli so that they form a unified picture or overall impression.

With that in mind questions should be asked as to how important or relevant is the design of the service setting, particularly weighted against other aspects such as response to complaints, speed of service, value for money, the company culture. For some of these the physical environment will contribute but it does raise the question of how integral the physical environment is to the delivery of a service. Is it simply perceived as a background composition of colour, music, aroma, lighting etc.? Answers to that will inevitably depend on the type of service (see Fig. 5.1).

Furthermore, how do consumers interpret the servicescape and what impact do they believe it has on them? A fruitful avenue to explore is the language expressed by consumers in comparison with that of the designers. Just as consumers are said to not fully comprehend the copy, imagery and theme of an advertisement, particularly in regard to the link with the product, the creativity of designers could be beyond the consumer. How far, for example, do people appreciate the exposure to blue has a calming influence, lowering blood pressure, pulse rate and brain waves? Surely in any research the intention of the designer should be made clear as to how the design is meant to impact on users. Comparisons can then be drawn with users' perceptions. Where a gap appears, to the extent of consumers contradicting the design rationale, can it be attributed to language, knowledge of understanding?

As for how one might research attitudes towards and perceptions of service, a number of methods and tools have been, and continue to be used, e.g. surveys, mystery shopping, focus groups, observation. However, given that design in the form of the service setting is a visual medium, the above-mentioned approaches have limitations. In an interesting article on hotel design research, Pullman and Robson (2007) argued for a camera- or image-based research methodology. According to them 'images are important in communicating impressions of the physical world and, so we believe a photography-based method might be beneficial when evaluating experience design issues. Used in conjunction with language-based methods, photographic images offer a valuable tool for assessing the guest experience in hospitality environments'. They admit surprise at how little this research method appears to have been used in hotels, resorts or restaurants. A key to understanding why may be found later in the article where they address some practical problems surrounding the application of such an approach. Notwithstanding the difficulties however, an image-based methodology should remain an attractive proposition for researchers alongside developments in computer-simulated, virtual tours.

SUMMARY

Whether we refer to the focus of this chapter as physical evidence, service setting or service-scape is incidental. What matters is its importance or relevance for the conduct of service activity. Given that much service activity occurs in a facility of one kind or another, it seems paradoxical that so little attention has been directed toward it. On the other hand, service quality, service encounter, service productivity, managing people and demand have been the subject of significant research and comment. Physical evidence is a factor in these issues but it appears insignificant.

Where the service issues cited above continue to be controversial and draw on other disciplines, physical evidence seems to be built around deterministic, stimulus-response models and largely devoid of input from other disciplines. As a result, the service literature on physical evidence appears limited. Furthermore, the focus of research has largely been on retail outlets and the influence of ambient conditions on sales revenue. The research, limited as it is, focuses on the consumer rather than the employee.

Retail outlets over the years have been portrayed as psychological laboratories where experiments can be conducted by varying stimulus factors. This is manipulative and not factored into or considered by the models. Employees are equally manipulated but research and experiments are undertaken for the benefit of increased productivity. But what of employee satisfaction? Overall the impact of facility conditions on employees is largely ignored by service management writers, even though there is a vast amount of literature on this topic.

While physical evidence is a valuable addition to the service domain, it should be developed by drawing on subjects such as sociology, anthropology and environmental psychology. At the very minimum there should be incorporation of design principles and designer experiences. Controversy has stalked many areas of services but physical evidence appears to have escaped the spotlight. The effectiveness of the servicescape can only be enriched through embracing a wider perspective.

REVIEW QUESTIONS

1. Define the concept of physical evidence and examine its significance within the context of the THE facilities.

2. Explore services by function and nature for physical evidence.

3. How might physical evidence work in terms of its role and impact in the service setting?

Case Study

The development of Marriott Courtyard

Introduction

This case study centres on the design of Marriott Courtyard hotel. With the assistance of a conjoint analysis, specific guidelines were provided for selecting target market segments, positioning the hotel within the market and most importantly, for the servicescape, designing an improved facility in terms of physical layout and services.

While design has largely been within the domain of designers, architects and R&D engineers, this study sought to demonstrate how marketing science through the use of conjoint analysis can be of help.

Outside consultants were hired to conduct a large-scale consumer study among business and non-business travellers aimed at establishing an 'optimal' hotel design.

Design facets

The focus of the research would be features of a hotel and for this study they were summarized under seven sets (called 'facets') of attributes. These are shown in Table 5.2.

(Continued)

Case Study. Continued.

Table 5.2. The seven design facets. (Note: Within the seven facets, there were 50 factors or attributes and 167 levels describing hotel features and services.)

Design facets	Attributes
External factors	Building shape, landscape design, pool type and location, hotel size.
Rooms	Room size and decor, type of heating and cooling, location and type of bathroom, amenities.
Food-related services	Type and location of restaurant, room service, vending services and stores, in-room kitchen facilities.
Lounge facilities	Location, atmosphere and type of people (clientele).
Services	Reservation, registration and check-out, limo to airport, bellman, message centre, secretarial services, car rental and maintenance.
Facilities for leisure-time activities	Sauna, exercise room, racquetball courts, tennis courts, games room, children's playroom.
Security factors	Security guards, smoke detectors, surveillance.

The central aim was one of determining, out of all the various hotel features and services, which combination should be offered that would meet management's profit and growth objectives, offer consumers good value for money and establish a market positioning that offered management a substantial competitive advantage.

The study

The study itself is clearly comprehensive and detailed. It considered 50 attributes, each ranging from two to eight levels. If we take the 'rooms' facet as an example, the research format would appear as in Table 5.3.

At each level in the rows respondents were asked to indicate:

- the block that comes closest to describing your current hotel;
- the block(s) that you find to be completely unacceptable;
- the blocks that represent what you want and are willing to pay for.

The hotel's cost accounting department developed prices and respondents were asked to indicate whether the price combination was:

- completely unacceptable;
- most preferred;
- acceptable.

(Continued)

Case Study. Continued.

Table 5.3. Research format.

Features[a]/ attributes	Levels				
Entertainment	TV	TV with movies that are 9 months ahead of HBO	TV with 30-channel cable	TV with HBO movie channel, sports news channel	TV with free in-room movies
Bathroom features	None	Shower massage	Whirlpool (Jacuzzi)		Steam bath

[a] These two features have been selected from a total of eight features.

Once the respondents had evaluated all seven facets, they were asked to add the total incremental costs of the features and services they selected. If the total of the charges plus the base room price were higher than they were willing to pay on a regular business (or pleasure) trip, they were asked to go back and select the enhancements they were willing to forego in order to arrive at an acceptable room price. Ultimately each respondent was shown five cards, each one containing a full profile description of a 'complete' hotel offering and had to state for each profile whether they would 'stay there almost all the time' through to 'would not stay there'.

To help position the hotel's image, respondents were presented with a number of hotel descriptions and asked to evaluate each in terms of several desired characteristics. The descriptions included such characteristics as:

- a place kids really like;
- gives a complete break from the usual routine;
- gives safe and secure feeling;
- has stimulating/exciting atmosphere;
- good for people who do not want to be hassled;
- a good place for people on a budget;
- provides a comfortable room for when you are alone;
- has charm, warmth;
- a busy, efficient, modern hotel;
- a good, no-frills, basic hotel;
- an informal, quiet, relaxing hotel with charm and personality;
- a casual feeling in a hotel with understated elegance;
- an exciting, action-oriented hotel with spectacular, modern architecture.

(Continued)

Case Study. Continued.

Results

The study clearly suggested that some business and leisure travellers were dissatisfied with current hotel offerings. The problem seemed to be that some hotels cost too much and offer features not valued by the traveller, while others that cost less offer too few of the desirable features.

Additionally, both types of hotels appeared to lack the personalization of features that travellers seek. From this a positioning of 'a special little hotel at a very comfortable price' was chosen. This was reinforced by the leisure and non-business travellers' selection of the following description as the most preferred hotel – 'an informal, quiet, relaxing hotel or motel with charm and personality'.

Implementation

The resulting hotel followed almost to the letter the recommendation of the study. All of the features and services offered were among the highest valued by the customers. Development team members from several corporate departments provided expertise in the direct translation of the research results into final product design.

Impact

The study had a major impact on the profitability and growth of the hotel group, resulting in a new product line or sub-brand (i.e. Marriott Courtyard) with a clear appeal to a distinct target market segment.

Questions

1. How significant are the facets used in this case study for portraying the servicescape in hotel design?

2. How suitable is conjoint analysis for hotel design? What other methods/tools could be used and what are their strengths and weaknesses?

3. Should hotel design be left to the designers? Explain.

4. In light of the models/frameworks developed to assist our understanding of how physical evidence might work, what approach would you suggest for determining whether they do or do not work?

GLOSSARY OF TERMS USED IN THIS CHAPTER

Cognitive responses They refer to the beliefs people hold about a service provider's place of business and where appropriate the users of that facility. Judgements on value for money, exclusivity, competence, trust and others will inevitably be made.

Customization	Customization occurs when a service is modified to suit a particular individual or group.
Hedonic services	Hedonic services provide more experiential consumption, fun, pleasure and excitement.
Intangibility	Unlike tangible goods, services cannot generally be seen, tasted, felt, heard or smelled before being consumed. Even during and after service delivery, customers are often unable to perceive the service.
Physical evidence	It refers to the different elements or dimensions of the physical environment that help service organizations to meet the expectations of potential customers and enable the service to operate efficiently.
Physiological responses	They address the impact of the working environment on the human body.
Standardization	Standardization occurs when a service appears the same every time and in every place.
Utilitarian services	Utilitarian services are more cognitive-driven, instrumental and focused on accomplishing a practical task.

REFERENCES AND ADDITIONAL READING

Bitner, M.J. (1992) Servicescapes: the impact of physical surroundings on customers and employees. *Journal of Marketing* 56, 57–71.

Cumming, R. and Porter, T. (1990) *The Colour Eye*. BBC Books, London.

Donovan, R.J. and Rossiter, J.R. (1982) Store atmosphere: an environmental psychology approach. *Journal of Retailing* 58, 34–57.

Edmondson, B. (1989) Pass the meat loaf. *American Demographics* 19 January.

Hochschild, A. (1983) *The Managed Heart: Commercialization of Human Feeling*. University of California Press, Berkeley, California.

Hoffmann, K.D., Bateson, J.E.G., Wood, E.H. and Kenyon, A.J. (2009) *Services Marketing: Concepts, Strategies and Cases*. Cengage Learning, London.

Kotler, P. (1973–74) Atmospherics as a marketing tool. *Journal of Retailing* 49, 48–64.

Levitt, T. (1981) Marketing intangible products and product intangibles. *Harvard Business Review* May–June, 94–102.

Lewison, D. (1991) *Retailing*. Macmillan, Basingstoke, UK.

Lovelock, C. and Wirtz, J. (2007) *Services Marketing: People, Technology, Strategy*. Prentice-Hall, Englewood Cliffs, New Jersey.

Maister, D.H. and Lovelock, C.H. (1982) Managing facilitator services. *Sloan Management Review* Summer, 19–31.

Mehrabian, A. and Russell, J.A. (1974) *An Approach to Environmental Psychology*. MIT Press, Cambridge, Massachusetts.

Milliman, R.E. (1982) Using background music to affect the behavior of supermarket shoppers. *Journal of Marketing* 46, 86–91.

Mudie, P.M. and Pirrie, A. (2006) *Services Marketing Management*. Butterworth-Heinemann, Oxford.

Normann, R. (1984) *Service Management*. Wiley, Chichester, UK.

Parish, J.T., Berry, L.L. and Lamb, S.Y. (2008) The effect of the servicescape on service workers. *Journal of Service Research* 10, 220–238.

Pullman, M.E. and Robson, S.K.A. (2007) Visual methods: using photographs to capture customers' experience with design. *Cornell Hotel and Restaurant Administration Quarterly* 48, 121–144.

Russell, J.A. and Pratt, G. (1980) A description of the affective quality attributed to environments. *Journal of Personality and Social Psychology* 38, 311–322.

Schiffman, L.G. and Kanuk, L.L. (2010) *Consumer Behaviour*. Pearson, Harlow, UK.

Thomas, D.R.E. (1978) Strategy is different in service businesses. *Harvard Business Review* July–August, 158–165.

Wemmerlöv, U. (1989) A taxonomy for service processes and its implications for system design. *International Journal of Service Industries Management* 1, 20–40.

Yalch, R.F. and Spangenberg, E.R. (2000) The effects of music in a retail setting on real and perceived shopping times. *Journal of Business Research* 49, 139–147.

chapter 6

Information Technology and THE Facilities

Neil Robinson
Salford University

Crispin Dale
University of Wolverhampton

LEARNING OBJECTIVES

Having completed this chapter, readers should be able to:

- discuss the historical context of information technology (IT) in tourism, hospitality and events (THE) facilities;
- explore different types of technologies in THE facilities;
- consider the role of IT in THE facilities.

INTRODUCTION

A range of technologies are used by THE facilities to facilitate their efficient management. This includes technologies that enable customers to interact with the facility more effectively through to technologies that are used in the actual design of the facility itself. While the evolution of IT has mushroomed over recent years, it can be argued that such developments have originated from the technological arms race of yesteryear and the space race of the 1960s. Indeed, while much of the technological developments of today have themselves been developed since the 1960s, the initial technological developments are deeply rooted in a darker past. The internet, mobile phone, personal computer and even satellite navigation are manifestations of tools originally developed to assist governments during a period of sustained war or conflict. While such Armageddon-like scenarios were fortunately not played out on the global stage, their inheritance and subsequent evolution have had many positive spin-offs within the world of consumerism. Debating the evolution of IT is in itself a little like weather forecasting. We have some information that can identify particular patterns of development, but such developments can themselves be impacted upon by unforeseen external pressure such as recession, availability of resources, global conflict, consumption, trends and ultimately buyer awareness/trust.

The IT landscape that lies ahead of us has been shaped by the past. A larger less unpredictable future will see mass user interface and consumption being directly affected by the end user. Gone are the days of IT developments that took little interest in industry needs and with it limited understanding of consumer preferences. This autocratic, totalitarian manner has given way to mass user configuration, a method where users are at the forefront of development and in some cases are actively encouraged to engage in the design process. Such examples include the 'app' (application), user-enhanced systems in which the power of the large multinational is somewhat diminished and where user-driven interface and software development is actively encouraged. Debating this further, we can naturally see a time when IT development might itself become totally user-driven, where technology is developed quickly and effectively to aid everyday service activities and transactions. This is being employed by many of the large multinational THE chains in an attempt to further market and develop consumer loyalty. The future will see organizations attempting to attract and retain business by employing smart IT devices, designed to predict consumption and purchase patterns based around data already collected from the user and the external market conditions. While society has yet to fully realize the potential of IT developments, those industries based in the service sector have themselves been at the forefront of this evolution; the next section of this chapter will debate such issues further.

DEFINITION AND HISTORICAL CONTEXT

While many have attempted to define IT, and indeed some have been successful, the authors define IT as 'a generic term that encapsulates the management processes of information retrieval, storage and use, and the subsequent dissemination of this data by electronic means'. By this the authors intentionally steer away from specific reference to man and machine and purposefully chose a more information-based paradigm that recognizes the importance of information and its manipulation; in an attempt to better predict, aid and facilitate management thinking. If we are to look at the developments associated with IT over the last 20–30 years one would be hard pressed to recognize any of the bulky, often unreliable IT systems of the past, in relation to those of today. This post-modern, brave world is now more focused on user needs and ease of use, ensuring that information management is more user-driven, as opposed to the traditional technological-driven system of previous years. If we are to compare the evolution of the motor-car, we can observe that its linear-like development is now more focused on user needs, reliability and comfort. Likewise, the IT evolution is now attempting to match user needs with systems development; the smart phone with its many manifestations is a good example of this, as are the user-driven development of communication tools manifesting in the market (these include, but are not exclusive to Twitter, Facebook and Bebo to name but a few).

IT has itself seen a number of generational changes over recent years. Gone are the 'information for information sake' days when IT was employed in suit-wearing, male-dominated boardroom environments, where decisions were made based around an information in and information out scenario. This often resulted in output that meant little to its user and even less to the end user, i.e. the consumer. While many have been dismissive of IT as a management tool, we must remember that such time periods were greatly driven by technological developments, rather than a study of user needs. Indeed one of the great developments to emerge from the 1980s and 1990s was the importance of the consumer and with this IT became more bespoke, less one-size-fits-all and ultimately responding to user needs. We can also add at this point that suppliers and manufacturers have also become more user- and customer-driven and those that have not done so have merely disappeared or have had to modify their business plans. One such example relates to IBM and its huge dominance in the mid 1970s and early 1980s, losing its markets years later to smaller organizations that saw the future as being consumer-driven PCs in the home and not exclusively just for industry.

IT and the evolution of society are themselves inextricably linked. Take for example the evolution of social media and its relationship with youth culture and music that has itself spawned a sub-culture in terms of customer interface and loyalty. Those users who align themselves to the Apple Mac brands and refute all other IT systems would be good examples of brand loyalty. Indeed, the 1960s were typified by a musical revolution and with it many cultural spin offs often manifesting in dress style, musical genre consumption, tribal loyalty associated with music (i.e. the Mods vs Rockers) and ultimately the demise and possible disrespect of authority. While the IT-savvy generation of the mid to late 1990s and the period post 2000 has not so much turned on, tuned in and dropped out, more the case of uploaded, controlled and actively engaged, and as a result become key developers in the IT revolution. Such is the depth of loyalty shown by these tribally loyal consumers that everyday icons of commerce are themselves becoming 'technoised' (a term developed by the authors to describe the process of technology impacting on consumer choice and methods of consumption). For example, the employment of bar coding and information applications that can be employed by differing user interfaces such as Apple OS, Android or a multitude of other formats. Such methods of information retrieval and storage have parallels with the VHS and Betamax format for VCR viewing in the late 1970s and also presently taking place between Blue ray and Toshiba DVD play formats. A key factor in information distribution and retrieval for everyday consumers in the future will be the power of those industry giants that back the most popular and common, easily used formats to product place information to aid profitability.

In the context of facilities, technologies are having a significant impact and the following will discuss how these are being used to facilitate the management and operation of THE premises.

TYPOLOGY OF IT IN THE FACILITIES

Technologies can be classified from a number of perspectives. The following discussion classifies technologies using a typology based on consumer-, employer-, employee- and supplier-driven needs.

Consumer-driven

Consumer-driven technologies are those that are by definition demand-driven by the workforce and user population. A main difference here between consumer- and employer-driven is the fact that the end user has been fundamental in its creation and design. This area is very much the arena for the inventor or technopreneur (a term designed by the authors to categorize inventors who dabble with all things IT-related, including design, procurement and promotion), who recognizes problems as potential opportunities for the creation and sales of solutions. While the role of the consumer is key, it is not always the case that the consumer designs and patents the product; in some cases their role may be merely consultative, in so much that a third party asks the user/consumer to list attributes, likes and dislikes, and a product is designed accordingly. In THE facilities, 'App'-based technologies have facilitated some interesting developments. A number of providers have produced apps for the management of their events, as the examples below illustrate.

Example: App technologies in THE facilities

Ticketscript and Kawet developed a plug and play mobile event app. The App enables event organizers to produce their own event app for event participants to download and use. The app enables users to promote the event, manage ticket purchasing and view event information.

Propeller Mobile developed a customizable app that can be used by event organizers to produce a show guide, facilitate push notifications on event information and collect information on which parts of an event are popular. These data can then be used to direct visitors to parts of the event based on their own interests.

IBTM Event Portfolio Shows produced an app that enables attendees to access event information and social media, view exhibitor appointment diaries and participate in live voting and surveys.

Source: http://www.eventindustrynews.co.uk, http://www.eventmagazine.co.uk

---

Questions

1. Consider an app that could be used by a THE facility. Outline the rationale for why it should be produced.

2. What would be the benefits and challenges of using this app for the facility?

Employer-driven

Employer-driven technologies are those that are by definition driven by the designer, manufacturer and industry, with a sole purpose of facilitating an organizational issue. In many cases such designs do later have commercial application and might be developed and modified to accommodate the needs of individuals. A good example might be the evolution of the home computer. Who would have foreseen the evolution of large industry-driven mainframe computers of the 1960s to the slimmed-down home PC some two decades later? Indeed many large computer companies of the 1960s missed this at their peril and possibly lacked foresight to see the explosion in demand in the home PC market, choosing to concentrate on industry needs and at the same time not exploring new demand markets in the home PC sector.

Employee-driven

Employee-driven technologies are those that are developed by the employee, an individual working with an organization who possibly sees an alternative way of doing something and acts accordingly. The design itself could relate to a piece of software or even a component of technology that is designed or modified to facilitate a process. A recent manifestation in this kind of format would be the app (application), designed in many cottage industries and sold to facilitate a transaction or ease a laborious process, or to even facilitate human interaction and fun (see angry birds app).

Supplier-driven

Supplier-driven technologies are in part value chain-driven and are often created by a process of reverse engineering. This is to say that many suppliers improve their distribution process by identifying opportunities in the value chain and in turn re-engineer certain stages in the distribution process to speed up the distribution process. For example, the utilization of PayPal by certain on-line retail outlets has reduced fraud, ensuring that buyers are more trusting of on-line suppliers; by identifying on-line fraud as a major inhibitor to on-line trade, a more trusting ethos is created, enhanced by safety and refund guarantees.

Questions

1. Choose a THE facility with which you are familiar.

2. Classify those technologies that are consumer-, employer-, employee- or supplier-driven.

3. Make suggestions on how the facility could utilize technology further to maximize its efficiency and effectiveness.

THE FACILITIES AND IT

Technologies are used in THE facilities in a number of different ways. Some technologies are used generically across the sectors, whereas others are unique to the respective sectors.

The tourism industry has been an active participant in the evolution and employment of technology to successfully facilitate global activities. Indeed, while one could argue that the industry has successfully evolved without technology (Thomas Cook did not have a laptop, at least during his lifetime), one would surely recognize the importance of technology in today's tourism industry. Demand, the need for heightened security and increasing customer expectation means that users require information in increasing amounts and the role of technology has aided this process. This includes baggage handling and security scanner technologies at airports to ensure the safety of passengers. Airport touch screen check-in technologies are used to increase the efficiency of passengers through the airport facility.

The hospitality sector has embraced IT evolution and this has enabled a more professional and accurate level of service to be delivered. A certain level of expectation has arisen among consumers because of the increasing use of IT and this relates to the ease of booking, viewing a product before purchase (facilitated by a web page), secure ease of payment methods, quick billing and pre-purchase information apps. Such mechanisms are now no longer the preserve of the large multinational hospitality conglomerates, but also of the smallest hospitality enterprises, ensuring that geographical distance, time difference, language issues and limited promotional budgets are no longer barriers to trade and can be facilitated by the hospitality owner-proprietor relatively cheaply and aided by technology.

In a hospitality context, technology can be used in THE facilities to encourage sustainability and reduce costs. This can be in the form of energy consumption and the use of systems to generate power such as solar panelling, or energy management systems that control the use of power in the facility such as key card control and low emission lighting.

Example: Technology and eco-friendly hotels

The University of Nottingham in England, UK, developed an up-market eco-friendly hotel with 200 executive-style rooms. The £20 million facility is located on the main University Campus and opposite the East Midlands Conference Centre (EMCC). This combined facility is able to house visitors to both the EMCC and the University. The construction of the hotel is based on technology that ensures that carbon emissions are kept to a minimum. This includes solar photovoltaic panels, ground-source heat technology and a lower energy-assisted cooling ventilation system.

Premier Inn is another hotel provider maximizing the use of technology for the purposes of sustainability and cost reduction. For example, the Premier Inn in Cornwall, UK is under a

(Continued)

Example. Continued.

constant state of technological renewal to ensure the latest in eco-friendly developments. This includes solar panelling, offset charging points for electric cars and low-energy lighting and high-efficiency equipment such as heating and refrigeration in the kitchens.

Source: http://www.colorcoat-online.com

In events, technology has been used for the purposes of facilitating pre, during and post inter-action. Before the event app-based technologies, as highlighted in the example earlier, have been used to enable mobile bookings to occur. During the event technologies are used to coordinate attendees in and around the event. Following the event, technologies are used to maintain a connection with the customer for feedback and future bookings.

For example, wristband technology has had a significant impact on the way events manage transactions with customers. They have user information embedded in a chip that is contained within the wristband. There are a number of advantages to using event and festival wristbands. From a user perspective, the wristbands can be used for the payment of items on site. Kiosks are made available at the event so that visitors can 'top-up' their wristbands. Cash is therefore kept to a minimum, enabling greater security for visitors. From an event provider's perspective, the wristbands can be used for entry to the event, ensuring better queue management and a greater deterrent for counterfeit ticketing. With Radio Frequency Identification (RFID) they can also be used for monitoring visitor numbers and enabling crowd control. However, the challenges of using wristband technologies include data protection and the cost effectiveness of their use.

Example: Wristband technology at the Isle of Wight Festival

Though used in the United States at festivals such as Coachella, digital wristband technology was used for the first time in the UK in 2011, at the Isle of Wight Festival. The festival operators, Solo Promoters, worked with a number of technology and credit card partners in delivering the service. This included ID&C, Intelligent Event Solutions and MasterCard. The wristbands were used for entry to the festival as well as being used for the payment of food, drink and merchandise. Festival operators commented that in the past, a limitation of wireless payment technologies had been the open field environment. Limited signal radiuses had, therefore, impacted on the efficiency of transactions between vendors and visitors. It was commented that a typical online authorization time of 3–4 seconds had been achieved, which had been far better than at previous events. Research by MasterCard at the event found that 100% of users would use the wristbands at other events.

Source: http://www.eventindustrynews.co.uk

SUMMARY

The chapter has discussed different technologies as they relate to THE facilities. In addition to discussing the historical context of technologies, the chapter has presented a typology for understanding their application in THE facilities. The chapter has then gone on to discuss specific technologies in THE facilities. The pace of technological developments is likely to bring new innovations to the management and operation of THE facilities. The developments will be driven by political and economic factors to meet evolving consumer demands.

REVIEW QUESTIONS

1. Historically, evaluate the impact of technologies on THE facilities over the last 50 years.
2. Identify and discuss technologies that can be associated with each of the IT and facility typologies.
3. Speculate and develop examples for what the future might be for technology in THE facilities.

Case Study

Nosnibor & Elad Hospitality and Travel Services

Overview

Nosnibor & Elad Hospitality and Travel Services (NEHTS) specializes in predicting customer demand and purchase patterns for businesses associated within the hospitality and tourism sectors. The business has been established for 10 years and has experienced much success in predicting future trends and demand for travel-related products, including hospitality services. In previous years it advised its clients on some of the pitfalls associated with developing business ideas within the hospitality and tourism sector. As part of its business portfolio, it has acted as consultant for a number of multinational blue-chip companies, tasked with identifying consumption patterns and user preferences associated with hospitality and tourism.

Technologies profiled

It is important for any organization to have a clear picture as to their customer types and purchase patterns; identifying future trends is one of NEHTS specialisms. Previous work has included:

- EPOS assessment needs

This includes point of sale systems facilitating stock control and revenue management of goods. In addition to facilitating payment, EPOS provides clients with specific information

(Continued)

Case Study. Continued.

on sale items that are in demand. Clients have then been able to provide goods that will maximize sales and provide better customer satisfaction.

- Aviation ticketing systems

Ticketing systems have been developed to maximize ticket sales through effective inventory management. The systems also enable effective ticket recording, enabling efficiency in customer reservation management when booking. The software has been developed to link directly with related Global Distribution System (GDS) networks.

- Bespoke hospitality software

NEHTS has advised on the development of personalized hospitality software tailored to the needs of the outlet. This has included software ranging from stock control to mobile app technologies facilitating greater customer interaction and relationship management.

- Event ticketing and electronic wristbands

Event ticketing systems have enabled clients to maximize visitor volume and manage customer flows at the event venue. Embedded RIFD technology has enabled customers to be directed more efficiently in and around the event venue.

- Smart electronic security baggage systems

Scanners incorporating x-ray technology for enhanced security in airports and hotels ensures greater customer security. NEHTS has also advised on the use of embedded RFID baggage technologies. Baggage can be monitored and tracked for both security and customer satisfaction in case of loss.

- Intelligent software

NEHTS has suggested the use of software for predicting yield management trends for the lodging sector. Based on previous occupancy data and consumer demand, the software calculates peak and low periods throughout the annual cycle. This enables an assessment to be made of future trends and facilitates pricing strategies to maximize customer sales.

- In-house customer-directed web sites and social media

Website creation and social media are paramount for travel and hospitality firms. NEHTS has made recommendations to clients on design features to best maximize customer interaction and booking. Social media technologies incorporating Facebook, Twitter and YouTube have also been suggested to encourage customer purchase and repeat sales.

Future opportunities

NEHTS has been approached by a large multinational Middle Eastern conglomerate (Dubai technologies) looking to develop its profile and move into the European travel and hospitality sector. Dubai technologies is looking for investment opportunities within the European hospitality and tourism sector. By identifying investment opportunities via its consultant NEHTS, it hopes to gain a foothold in the market.

Questions

1. How will the future development of technology facilitate travel choice for customers within the next 5–10 years?

2. Using secondary data from reliable sources, how can cost savings be made from employing IT systems within the hospitality and tourism sector?

3. The above points should be covered in a 15-minute presentation that will be delivered to your clients next week in London. It is important to note that any recommendations made should be justified with evidence.

GLOSSARY OF TERMS USED IN THIS CHAPTER

Consumer-driven technologies	Demand driven by the workforce and user population.
Employee-driven technologies	Developed by an individual working within an organization who possibly sees an alternative way of doing something and acts accordingly.
Employer-driven technologies	Driven by the designer, manufacturer and industry, with a sole purpose of facilitating an organizational issue.
Information technology	The management processes of information retrieval, storage and use, and the subsequent dissemination of these data by electronic means.
Supplier-driven technologies	Value chain-driven and often created by a process of reverse engineering.
Technopreneur	Inventors who experiment with all things IT-related, including design, procurement and promotion.

REFERENCES AND ADDITIONAL READING

Aldebert, B., Dang, R. and Longhi, C. (2011) Innovation in the tourism industry: the case of Tourism@. *Tourism Management* 32, 1204–1213.

Allen, J. (2002) *The Business of Event Planning: Behind-the-scenes Secrets of Successful Special Events.* Wiley, Mississauga, Canada.

Allen, J., Harris, R. and Huyskens, M. (2000) *Event Management: An Australian Bibliography.* University of Technology, Sydney, Australia.

Allen, J., O'Toole, W., McDonnell, I. and Harris, R. (2002) *Festival and Special Event Management,* 2nd edn. Wiley, Brisbane, Australia.

Buhalis, D. and Law, R. (2008) Progress in information technology and tourism management: 20 years on and 10 years after the Internet – the state of eTourism research. *Tourism Management* 29(4), 609–623.

Chanter, B. and Swallow, P. (2007) *Building Maintenance Management,* 2nd edn. Blackwell, Oxford.

Clarke, A. and Chen, W. (2007) *International Hospitality Management.* Butterworth-Heinemann, Oxford.

DomainTools (2010) Domain counts & internet statistics. Available at: http://www.domaintools.com/internet-statistics (accessed 10 November 2010).

Goldblatt, J.J. (2002) *Special Events – Global Event Management in the 21st Century*, 3rd edn. Wiley, New York.

Ip, C., Leung, R. and Law, R. (2011) Progress and development of information and communication technologies in hospitality. *International Journal of Contemporary Hospitality Management* 23(4), 533–551.

Litvin, S., Goldsmith, R. and Pan, B. (2008) Electronic word-of-mouth in hospitality and tourism management. *Tourism Management* 29(3), 458–468.

Montgomery, R.J. and Strick, S.K. (1994) *Meetings, Conventions, and Expositions: An Introduction to the Industry*. Van Nostrand Reinhold, New York.

Muller, C. (2010) Hospitality technology: a review and reflection. *Worldwide Hospitality and Tourism Themes* 2(1), 9–19.

Yeoman, I., Robertson, M., Ali-Knight, J., Drummond, S. and McMahon-Beattie, U. (eds) (2003) *Festival and Events Management: An International Arts and Culture Perspective*. Butterworth-Heinemann, Oxford.

chapter 7

Outsourcing and THE Facilities

Ahmed Hassanien
Edinburgh Napier University

Crispin Dale
University of Wolverhampton

LEARNING OBJECTIVES

Having completed this chapter, readers should be able to:

- explore the concept and scope of outsourcing in tourism, hospitality and events (THE) facilities;
- understand the importance of outsourcing for THE facilities;
- discuss the advantages and disadvantages of outsourcing;
- analyse the outsourcing decision criteria.

INTRODUCTION

Outsourcing has become a key part of THE facility management. There are a number of motivations for a facility to engage in outsourcing and these will be explored fully within this chapter. Outsourcing has been in existence in non-THE organizations for a long time and as a concept is not new. Manufacturing organizations have often outsourced functions as a means of drawing on the resources of others and for driving down costs. Examples include Nike and Apple who outsource their production overseas but retain a focus on research and development.

Outsourcing in the THE industries has been in existence for a number of years but its role has grown in significance as facilities seek to gain a competitive advantage. Indeed, external pressures have resulted in THE facilities seeing outsourcing not only as a means of cutting costs but also as a basis for adding value to the end product/service. This chapter will explore and evaluate the concept, scope, importance, process and advantages and disadvantages of outsourcing in THE facilities.

THE CONCEPT AND SCOPE OF OUTSOURCING

The concept of outsourcing is difficult to clearly define and numerous definitions exist (Atkin and Brooks, 2000). This is complicated by a lack of clarity on the scope of what it encompasses. Indeed, outsourcing has been in existence for a number of years (Gay and Essinger, 2000) but has been intellectualized in recent times with the acknowledgement that it can contribute to an organization gaining a competitive advantage. This advantage maybe gained through a reduction in costs, improved quality and maximizing resource capabilities (Fill and Visser, 2000).

Furthermore, outsourcing has been driven by the dynamic nature of the competitive environment, changing market demands and rising expectations of services (Greaver, 1999). This is coupled with the growing challenge of reduced internal resources (McIvor, 2005). The term outsourcing is often used interchangeably with others such as sub-contracting, sourcing, partnering and contracting out (Gay and Essinger, 2000).

Table 7.1 outlines a number of definitions that have been associated with outsourcing.

Table 7.1. Definitions of outsourcing.

'Where an organisation passes on the provision of a service or execution of a task previously undertaken in house, to a third to perform on its behalf' (Reilly and Tamkin, 1996, p. 5)
'The generic term to describe the process by which the user employs a separate organisation (the supplier), under a contract to perform a function, which could, alternatively, have been performed by in-house staff' (Barrett and Baldry, 2003, p. 134)
'The act of transferring some of an organisation's recurring internal activities and decision rights to outside providers, as set forth in a contract' (Ghodeswar and Vaidyanathan, 2008, p. 25)

> **Activity**
>
> Review the definitions in Table 7.1 and answer the following questions:
>
> **1.** What key themes emerge from these definitions?
> **2.** What do you understand by the key themes?
> **3.** How much difference is there between outsourcing other related terms such as sub-contracting, sourcing, partnering and contracting out?

Definitions are often determined by the provision of a service, function or task that would have been completed by the facility but is now contracted out to an external third party (Barrett, 1995; Reilly and Tamkin, 1996; Atkin and Brooks, 2005). The key components of outsourcing definitions, therefore, include some aspect of the following.

In-house service, task or function

In the context of THE facilities these services, tasks and functions can be classified on a micro and macro scale. For example, in a hotel, the laundry function can be outsourced to an operator that has the capability for offering this service. In a branded hotel chain, certain functions such as coffee bars may be outsourced to other branded providers. For example, Village Hotels, which is part of the De Vere group, incorporate the Starbucks brand into their outlets.

Various in-house services, tasks or functions may be outsourced to different providers. This can include the financial, human, legal and physical resources associated with the service being undertaken. For example, catering at events may be serviced by one single provider or there could be many suppliers offering alternative delicacies to suit the demands of the market that the event is catering for.

These are often non-core activities and are therefore not the central focus of the facilities' activities. Nevertheless, they are likely to be key to the overall facilities offering and can add significant value to the end service delivery.

Contractual

A binding contract will exist between the facility and third party. Terms and conditions would form part of the contract (Barrett and Baldry, 2003) and it may be long, medium or short term in nature, depending on the service, task or function being undertaken. The contract will also be influenced by the size and scale of the outsourced service, task or function. Management contracting, 'where a company (owner) contracts another firm (operator) to manage and run the business' (Hassanien *et al.*, 2010, p. 191), could be classified as a form of outsourcing.

External to the organization

The provider supplying the service, task or function will be external to the organization (Lankford and Parsa, 1999). These external organizations may be corporate providers of outsourced functions, or small operators supplying a specific service.

Activity

Select a THE facility of your choice and answer the following questions:

1. What in-house service, task or functions could be outsourced and what would your justification be for this?
2. What are the advantages and disadvantages for outsourcing these aspects of the facility?
3. What factors would the facility manager need to consider when outsourcing these services, tasks or functions?

LEVELS AND TYPES OF OUTSOURCING

Outsourcing can be classified into different levels and types. These levels and types each have their own features and drivers, which THE facilities are able to exploit for the operation of their business. Outsourcing can be referred to in terms of 'core' and 'non-core' activities, and it is important to understand what this means. Core activities of the business are those that provide the primary function of the facility as outlined in Chapter 2. This may include the staging of the performance for an event or food and drink for a restaurant. Non-core activities are those that lead to the servicing of the core function of the facility. In the context of THE facilities this may include back office functions such as security, maintenance, cleaning and landscaping and also front office functions such as customer services (Barrett, 1995).

Outsourcing is a key theme of Handy's (1989) 'shamrock organisation'. This is an organization that has a core body of permanent employees that is additionally supported by contracted or 'outsourced' staff who can provide specialist skills and potentially be more cost efficient. The measurement of their performance is based on their level of output and results produced. The third layer of the shamrock is the flexible and casual workforce. Facilities managers have to delineate between those activities that are core to the business and those that would be more productively 'outsourced'.

Brown and Wilson (2005) note the following three levels of outsourcing.

* **Tactical:** Tactical outsourcing is used to resolve a current problem. This may be due to a lack of expertise in a specific area that requires a short- or medium-term solution. In THE facilities, manpower is part of the operation that can be tactically outsourced. The fluctuating demand cycles of THE facilities results in organizations often requiring casual labour, which can be outsourced to an external operator. Furthermore, there may be

the requirement for specific skills that the facility is unable or even unwilling to service on a permanent basis. The relationship is tactical in as far as that it is often short term and task-driven with the aim to complete the job at a lower cost (Kedia and Lahiri, 2007). For example, security at events can be outsourced to a third party. Deploying this function to an external provider enables the facility to draw on the specialist skills and expertise that are required for this function to be carried out while simultaneously reducing the cost burden that this can bring to the overall operation of the business.

- **Strategic:** Strategic outsourcing is more long term in nature with the aim to generate value to the final service proposition for the facility. The onus here is not purely on cost reduction but on value creation for the facility and the outsourced operator. The outsourced functions may be few in number, enabling the facility to develop a resource-based advantage over time (Kedia and Lahiri, 2007). Kedia and Lahiri (2007) provide the example of Qatar Airways, which outsourced its revenue accounting and recovery processes to the India-based Kale Consultants. This enabled Qatar Airways to focus on the core activity of the business.

- **Transformational:** Transformational outsourcing is as it implies. To transform the business so it is able to compete in a volatile and dynamic external environment. It seeks to be rapid and sustainable in nature with the aim of improving overall business performance (Linder, 2004). This may include the rapid scaling of the business, removing business growth constraints and cultural change and renewal of the business (Linder, 2004). This involves the facility outsourcing aspects of its business that can lead to a transformation effect. According to Kedia and Lahiri (2007), this is further driven by the need for greater risk sharing, flexibility and business transformation.

Example: Six Nations Rugby and Twickenham

The staging of England's six nations rugby games at Twickenham Stadium results in a large-scale hospitality operation taking place for fans visiting the site. This includes the playgrounds and fields of local schools and the car park of a self-storage unit which becomes the 'Orchard Enclosure'. The temporary structures and infrastructure that are used at the site have been supplied for the last 25 years by GL events Owen Brown. The structures are made into private dining suites, with their own entrance doors, and supporting kitchens, bars and offices.

Source: http://www.eventindustrynews.co.uk

Questions

Read the example above and answer the following questions:

1. How would you classify the level and type of outsourcing that is illustrated in the example?
2. What have been the drivers for this outsourcing provision?
3. What factors should Twickenham Stadium consider when undertaking outsourcing?

WHY OUTSOURCING?

Outsourcing has the potential to be a key strategic tool for organizations in gaining a competitive advantage (Barrett and Baldry, 2003). Indeed, there will be a number of motives for an organization wishing to pursue a strategy of outsourcing and these can be classified as follows.

Financial

Essentially the organization may be seeking to use outsourcing to reduce its costs. O'Brien and Shaw (2002) recognize the use of independent meeting planners as outsourced provision in convention centres as facilities seek to become leaner operationally. Though outsourcing has the potential to reduce costs, facility managers still have to ensure that the service, task or function is integrated successfully into the wider operation of the business. This in itself will incur a cost and THE facilities should approach outsourcing with this in mind. The outsource provider may also have a lower cost structure. If they are operating in a specialist area of the business, then they may have been able to capitalize on the experience curve of driving down costs. These benefits will far outweigh the facility operating the task or function from the beginning. This then enables cash-flow advantages to occur, freeing up cash in the facility, which would otherwise go to operating the task or function.

Physical

Outsourcing enables the facility to utilize its space more effectively. First it releases space that can be used for another activity and second it enables occupied space to be maximized by the outsource provider delivering the service. If the outsource provider is being asked to operate on the physical premises, then they may be better equipped to know how to make the best use of space in the facility.

Human

The facility is able to gain expertise that it otherwise would have to develop itself and that would be resource intensive and draw the business away from its core activities, as well as incur cost disadvantages. Outsourcing ameliorates skills shortages that may be apparent in the facility. If the facility is unable to undertake a task or function due to a lack of expertise or knowledge then outsourcing can provide the solution. This is particularly the case with highly specialized tasks and functions such as information technology. Outsourcing can also generate managerial efficiencies, with human resources being directed towards activities in the facility where they can be better utilized.

Operational

Outsourcing aspects of the facility can generate both cost and operational efficiencies. If the facility has limited resources to operate particular tasks or functions, then external providers can provide the expertise and knowledge to do this more effectively. This can also enable the facility to be less distracted by having to undertake this task or function. For example, in nightclubs or at festivals, it is not unusual for external firms to provide the security. The service delivery and performance can then be enhanced by personnel who have the specialist expertise to perform the task. Outsourcing can also generate better operational flexibility for the facility. Aspects of the facility, such as technology provision, may be outsourced to external providers in order to be able to switch to alternatives as the technology evolves. This offers the facility greater flexibility and autonomy while also offsetting costs (Wise, 2007, pp. 60–61). Clark (2005) discusses how convention centres can use outsourcing in the functional practices of their facility. Carlsen (2005) identifies how the Perth Convention and Exhibition Centre in Australia uses outsourcing to perform the functional areas of catering, cleaning, marketing, security and car parking.

Example: Dragon Security, Ontario, Canada

Based in Ontario, Canada, Dragon Security is a specialist security firm providing services to bars, nightclubs and events. Staff are equipped to deal with ID and person searching, conflict management etc. Staff are licensed security guards and 'Smartserve' certified. The firm has been responsible for the YouthFest, WingFest and Niagara Wine Festival events in Canada, as well as for ensuring security at the home games of the Toronto Nationals Lacrosse team.

Source: http://www.dragonsecurity.ca

Strategic

Refocusing resources can be a key advantage for the facility. Indeed, outsourcing can provide the opportunity for the facility to refocus its resources on the key components of its core activities (McCarthy, 1996). For example, in a hotel the outsourcing of the laundry to an external provider enables the facility to use the resources that it would have allocated to this function to its core business such as accommodation and food and beverages. It enables facility managers to utilize their expertise in areas where they may be most productive and can gain an advantage (Gilley and Rasheed, 2000). Strategically, it can also improve the facility's focus on its core competences. This may be in terms of innovation, renovation, quality and so on, though the facility would need to consider how those outsourced tasks and functions can develop the core competencies of the business. Outsourcing can potentially improve the quality of the offering from external providers. A marketplace for outsourced provision is generated and competitors will seek to ensure that their offering provides the best quality to the facility. This can add value to the facility by enhancing its image and reputation through its association with an established outsource provider.

Outsourcing can provide the facility with enhanced opportunities for accessing and entering new markets. Franchising and management contracting are relevant examples where organizations have used external providers to grow and develop their businesses in new markets. Strategically, outsourcing enables the facility to spread and offset risk that it would have incurred by investing in the task or function. This risk is then transferred to the outsource provider, though an assessment of risk would still need to be undertaken by the facility when considering to outsource a task or function.

LIMITATIONS OF OUTSOURCING

Though the advantages of outsourcing are clearly apparent, the limitations should also be acknowledged (Barrett and Baldry, 2003; Atkin and Brooks, 2009). These are outlined as follows.

Financial implications

Though the financial advantages have been previously highlighted as the main driver for outsourcing, the partnership should be more than just about reducing costs to a minimum. Indeed, the outsourcing arrangement could be financially detrimental to the facility if it is tied into a long-term contract that is difficult to break free from, and switching costs will subsequently be incurred. The management of the outsourced provision may not meet the requirements originally intended and could potentially become a time-consuming exercise.

Organizational implications

The facility potentially loses control of the task or function to the outsource provider. Therefore, the facility needs to ensure that it has outsourcing selection criteria in place so that the risks of the loss of control are established. The facility will need to coordinate its day-to-day activities with the outsource provider so that they can be integrated effectively into the business.

Differences in work ethic between the facility and outsource provider can result in a tense relationship and potential conflict. If the outsource provider is unable to perform to the standard that is required by the facility, this can lead to poor service quality and overall performance in the business. Conflict can also result if the implementation of the outsourced provision has not been properly managed. The example below illustrates this point.

Example: Hyatt Regency, Boston, USA

In August 2009, the Hyatt Regency in Boston, USA decided to restructure its housekeeping provision to an outsource provider, Georgia-based Hospitality Staffing Solutions. Over 100 employees were affected by the move to outsourced provision and lost their jobs. The Hyatt hotel was seeking to drive down costs in a volatile economic period. However, the job losses resulted in instant action by the employees who picketed in protest at the action.

Source: http://www.boston.com/business

Strategic implications

Outsourcing key components of organization may lead to a lack of innovation and development of core competencies (Gilley and Rasheed, 2000). Operating the task or function can enable the facility to develop it as a strategic resource or core competence over time. The facility may reduce its capacity to develop knowledge resources that can influence other aspects of the business.

A lack of synergy may also occur. This may be because of cultural conflicts or incompatible systems and operating procedures between the facility and outsource provider. Furthermore, the outsource provider could potentially become overstretched with the number of activities and organizations undertaken, and therefore be unable to fulfil the obligations required.

Ticketing can be an area that an event facility may consider outsourcing. However, it will need to decide to what extent this is a core or non-core aspect of the business. Table 7.2 illustrates the advantages and disadvantages when evaluating this (Yeoman *et al.*, 2003).

OUTSOURCING DECISION CRITERIA

To maximize the benefits and offset the risks associated with outsourcing a number of criteria can be considered. These criteria can be associated with whether the facility is considering outsourcing as a new innovation to the business, or is managing an existing partnership with an outsource provider. However, when undertaking this decision an important maxim to consider is to 'never outsource what you don't understand' (Johnson, 1997, p. 23). This is important so that facility managers are able to understand the task or function that is being outsourced.

Table 7.2. An evaluation of outsourcing ticketing for an event facility.

Advantages	Disadvantages
Mitigates lack of in-house expertise	Reduced ticket yield for the event facility
Reduced up-front costs on equipment and box office space	Additional booking fee transferred to customers increasing ticket cost
Reduced staffing costs	Reduced control over customer service
Reduced IT costs and enhanced IT service delivery by outsource provider	Reduced knowledge of event facility by ticket provider
Maximizes capacity by providing a back up to any in-house box office service	Inability of ticket provider to manage queries connected to the event facility, such as complaints, priority bookings
Provides multiple channels of distribution	Customer data are under the ownership of the ticket provider

They will then be better equipped to understand the terms, conditions and delivery of the task or function being outsourced. The decision criteria are outlined in the following.

Type of decision

It is contended that outsourcing can take a rational or ad hoc approach (Reilly and Tamkin, 1996). A rational approach takes a long-term view of outsourcing and considers the costs and benefits to its implementation in the facility. In contrast an ad hoc approach is more reactive and short term in nature. Priorities may be driving down costs in the short term in reaction to a volatile external environment (Hunter *et al.*, 1993). The decision should also acknowledge both 'hard' and 'soft' criteria. Hard criteria such as cost cutting and soft criteria associated with service quality and customer satisfaction need to be counter balanced and not one take priority over the other (Atkin and Brooks, 2005). The facility will also need to appraise the core and non-core activities that have outsourcing potential. Strategically, those activities that differentiate or add value to the facility may not be considered viable for outsourcing (Fill and Visser, 2000; Atkin and Brooks, 2005).

The value chain (Porter, 1985) can be adopted by THE facility managers as a basis for considering the viability of an outsourcing option. According to Porter the value chain can be seen as a combination of primary and support activities. Primary activities include inbound logistics, operations, outbound logistics, marketing and sales and services. The primary activities are facilitated by a number of support activities, which include procurement, human resources, infrastructure and technological development (see Fig. 7.1). In the context of a THE facility, activities may include the supply of goods, the internal operations such as housekeeping, maintenance, security and the delivery of the service to the end user/customer. Support activities may include recruitment, selection and training, functions concerned with the design and general upkeep of the facility, technology systems and general management such as legal and financial aspects.

Determining the primary and support activities of the THE facility enables it to assess their relative importance to the business and stakeholders; establish the cost of each activity in the production of the service to the customer; and assist in understanding the connections between the different internal and external activities in delivering value to the end user. The THE manager may consider outsourcing as a basis for gaining a competitive advantage. That is by being the lowest cost provider in the sector or as means for differentiation (Porter, 1985). In doing so the THE manager will need to perform a value chain analysis of the business to identify which activities could potentially be viable for outsourcing as a means of further generating value.

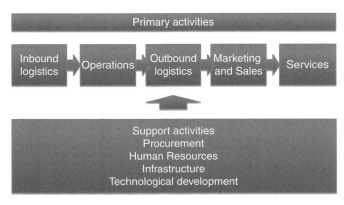

Fig. 7.1. The value chain.

On the other hand, the facility manager may not want to outsource a vital activity of the business, which acts as a strategic capability or competence and enables it to gain a competitive advantage in its own right. When assessing the viability to outsource, it is therefore crucial to establish the significance of an activity to the facility. A critical activity in which the organization possesses a distinctive capability will have to receive a considerable level of strategic attention in order to maintain such a position (McIvor, 2005).

The outsourcing decision matrix (Fig. 7.2) is another tool that can be used by facility managers to help decide whether to outsource an activity or function. If the activity or function is core to the facility but does not contribute significantly to operational performance then a strategic partnership or alliance should be considered. If the activity or function is high on strategic importance and contributes significantly to the operational performance of the facility, then this should be maintained. The activity or function may act as a core competence and will therefore have strategic value to the facility. If the activity or function has low strategic importance and does not contribute to

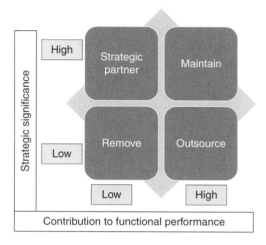

Fig. 7.2. Outsourcing decision matrix.

operational performance, then it should be removed. If the activity or function is low on strategic importance but high on operational performance, then this has potential for outsourcing.

Questions

1. Choose a THE facility and conduct a value chain analysis.

2. Using the outsourcing decision matrix, identify and justify those activities that are central to the facility and should not be considered for outsourcing.

3. Which activities of the facility could be outsourced to generate further value and gain a competitive advantage?

Responsibility for outsourcing

Though outsourcing decisions are argued to be subjective or objective (Atkin and Brooks, 2005), the THE facility will need to consider who is responsible for undertaking the decision and how this will be implemented and coordinated. This will depend on the size, structure and ownership of the facility. The decision in a small THE facility is likely to be undertaken by the owner/manager. In small hospitality facilities research suggests that outsourcing decisions are often driven by the owner-managers (Jones, 2002). In a larger corporate business the decision may be carried out by the directors or operations managers of the firm. Indeed, as outsourcing can enable a facility to gain a competitive advantage, it is argued that it should be central to those responsible for the strategic decision making of the firm (Johnson, 1997).

Standard of service

The impact on service delivery is key to any outsourcing decision. The overall satisfaction of the customer is paramount in determining whether outsourcing is a viable option. Outsourcing should act as an empowering enabler of adding value throughout the facility. The danger lies when outsourcing draws negatively on the resources of the facility and fails to add value to the end user.

Risk and control

The facility will need to consider the risks that may be associated with outsourcing and assess the costs and benefits of any decision that is made. Though it is argued that outsourcing provides a low degree of risk, the potential loss of control of an aspect of the facilities operations should be properly evaluated. Indeed, the facility may actually have the resources and capabilities to resolve or perform the activity/function that is being considered for outsourcing. The direct and indirect costs of outsourcing provision on a like-for-like basis in the facility should be recognized (Atkin and Brooks, 2005). Once the facility is committed to an outsourcing arrangement, who takes overall responsibility for implementing and managing this should be properly established. Effective channels of communication should also be clearly apparent between the facility and outsource provider.

Trust

Trust should be a key concern when developing a partnership with an outsource provider. The outsource provider has the potential to gain expertise from the THE facility it is working with and utilize this in a different context and to its advantage. Clear terms of agreement should be presented as part of the contractual obligations between the facility and the outsource provider.

Performance measures

The performance and evaluation of the outsourcing agreement should be properly evaluated at regular intervals to ensure it is adding value to the facility (Atkin and Brooks, 2005). Key performance indicators should be clearly outlined in the contractual agreement, with remedial measures necessary for inadequate performance by the outsource provider. The facility and outsource provider should be able to clearly outline any exit strategy from the arrangement. This may be during or after the completion of the contractual terms. The facility will need to factor in the switching costs (Porter, 1998) of going to another outsource provider or deciding to develop the activity or function in-house.

THE OUTSOURCING PROCESS

Though outsourcing is widely discussed in the literature, the process for outsourcing is not as well documented (Perunović and Pedersen, 2007). Atkin and Brooks (2005) suggest that the process of outsourcing is comprised of three main stages: strategy, tender documents and tendering process. Each of these stages will be discussed in the following.

Strategy

Strategy includes the definition of services, current arrangements, the position of stakeholders and legislation affecting employment and procurement. When defining services the THE facility needs to ensure that the scope of what is to be undertaken is outlined. For example, in event security, does this include queue management and ticketing as part of the contract? The facility should clearly outline what current arrangements are in practice. This includes information relating to the in-house (number of employees and employment details) and outsourced (expiration date of contract, contract value and scope) services provided. Stakeholders will need to be identified. Those key stakeholder players who have the most power and influence (Mendelow, 1991) will determine the overall strategy of the facility for outsourcing. For example, a THE facility operated by a corporate chain may find major financial investors and banks as the key players. In this respect, the need for a return on investment may drive the facility to seek ways in which it can become more efficient and cost driven. Employment and procurement legislation will be critical when preparing for outsourcing. Legislation will relate to existing employees of the THE facility as well as to those employees of the outsource provider. Legislation relating to procurement will also influence the tendering process. This includes ensuring that the contract is non-discriminatory, objective and transparent.

Tender documents

This stage of the outsourcing process relates to the contract service specifications, agreement and conditions. The service specification will document the expected standard of service required by the facility from the outsource provider. This may include facility requirements, policy and heath and safety principles. The service level agreement expands on the service specification and documents the quality standard and expectations of performance. The service level agreement should be dynamic and flexible when the outsourcing arrangement is underway. This is so that both the facility and the outsource provider can learn from accepted practice over time. The conditions of contract should adhere to a standard format. The purpose is to formalize the process and ensure the legal process is adhered to. Performance indicators and penalty clauses may be outlined. However, the conditions should not be so rigid as to prevent any changes occurring in the future.

Tendering process

The tendering stage will involve the briefing and assessment, the contract award, the pre-contract meeting and mobilization and review. The prequalification stage of the tendering process will, under normal circumstances, be open and transparent. Interested parties will have to demonstrate their ability to fulfil the terms of the contract. This includes evidence of the service of previous and existing contracts, and the resources of the provider to be able to undertake the contract.

This may also include a briefing to prospective outsource providers detailing the core business of the facility and an overview of the expectations of the contract. As discussed previously, the aim of the contract may not be entirely cost-driven and this should be articulated to prospective outsourcers. The tendering period should ensure that sufficient time is given for any prospective clients to submit a contract bid. This could be anything from one to four weeks, depending on the nature and size of what is being outsourced. Although, for private providers, there is no set standard timeframe, common sense should prevail so as not to impede the process. The assessment of bids should conform to a set list of criteria to ensure consistency of evaluation. This will include an assessment of the competences and capabilities of the outsource provider, in addition to an assessment of risk relating to financial, legal and staffing factors. When balancing an assessment of cost with quality, benchmark standards may be used as a key indicator of previous performance by the outsource provider. This may include their financial performance, position in the market, reputation and so on. Once a decision has been made, the THE facility will award the contract. This will involve a pre-contract meeting where the start terms, insurance details and administration should be considered. This stage will also involve the outsource provider being given sufficient time to mobilize its resources. It may also include the exiting of an existing provider and/or in-house staff. This should be given due care and attention to ensure the transition is as smooth and efficient as possible. Once implemented the arrangement should be kept under review as per the terms of the contract. The number and timing of the reviews should be agreed between the facility and outsource provider. The early stages of implementation may require closer attention so any initial problems can be ameliorated.

SUMMARY

Outsourcing can generate many benefits for THE facilities. The chapter has outlined the ability of outsourcing to reduce costs, enhance service delivery and generate a more efficient operating environment. However, outsourcing also has the potential to erode the central focus of a facility and render it incapable of developing resources and core competences that can ensure its long-term survival. Whether the facility decides to outsource its non-core activities is a decision that should be taken using the criteria that have been outlined in this chapter. THE managers will then be in a better position to acknowledge the costs and benefits of outsourcing and whether it is a viable option for their facility.

REVIEW QUESTIONS

Select a THE facility and consider an activity or function that could be outsourced. Using the outsourcing decision criteria, consider the following questions:

1. To what extent would this be a rational or ad-hoc approach to outsourcing?
2. Who should be involved in, and responsible for, the outsourcing decision?

3. What 'hard' and 'soft' criteria should be considered as part of the decision?

4. What will be the impact on the service delivery to the facility? How will outsourcing add value to the facility?

5. What will be the implied risks of outsourcing? Perform a cost-benefit analysis.

6. What performance measure will be set in place to ensure the effectiveness of the outsourced provision?

7. What would be the exit strategy if the facility wished to leave the outsourcing arrangement or the contract had ended?

Case Study

Outsourcing in airline and airport facilities

The demand for air travel has grown significantly over the last 30 years. The increased propensity for travelling for leisure or business purposes has necessitated the growth of the aviation sector and its related facilities. Alongside this increased demand has been the proliferation of airline companies targeting passengers with different budgets, needs and expectations. The number of airports has also grown, with major and hub airports facilitating air travel. The traveller's time spent at an airport is an opportunity to generate further revenue for airport operators and airports have become a travelling experience in their own right, offering facilities that cater for varying consumer tastes and preferences. This includes retail, amusement, eating and dining facilities.

For airline companies and airport operators, supplying the day-to-day needs of customers is resource intensive and not necessarily best serviced by the companies themselves. The focus for airlines and airports is to ensure that passengers are able to get to their destination as efficiently, comfortably and safely as possible. However, offering a multitude of facilities and services to travellers can be challenging and potentially distract airline and airport operators from their core product. Outsourcing has therefore become increasingly prevalent in the air travel sector.

Airlines use outsourcing in a number of ways and a number of providers have emerged offering related services in catering, maintenance and cleaning. For example, the Gate Group based at Zurich Airport in Switzerland includes a number of subsidiary brands including Gate Gourmet. Gate Gourmet provides the on-board catering for national carriers including British Airways and United Airlines and budget carriers such as easyJet. Indeed, catering on airlines is often outsourced to an external operator with companies such as Servair and LSG Sky Chefs providing in-flight catering. Services related to aircraft ground handling, which involve maintenance, repair and overhaul (MROs), and the cleaning of aircraft are other areas that can be outsourced. Examples include MRO companies such as Aeroman and Donbassareo, and cleaning companies such as Gate Aviation and OCS.

(Continued)

Case Study. Continued.

Outsourcing such services is not without its challenges. For instance, in August 2005, and due to what was described as 'outdated working practices', Gate Gourmet made 350 employees based at Heathrow Airport redundant. Gate Gourmet's revenue streams had been impacted on by rising fuel costs from the airline carriers. However, the redundancies culminated in strike action not only within the company itself but also among the ground staff working for British Airways. Operationally, this generated 24 hours of chaos for British Airways who had to supply passengers with hotel accommodation and food and drink at their own expense (Dale, 2009). Maintenance contracts can also provide challenges for airlines. For example, Taeco, based in the South Chinese city of Xiamen, provides the maintenance for long-haul aircraft for airlines such as Air France, British Airways, American Airlines, Emirates and Lufthansa. In December 2011, Air France temporarily stopped its cooperation with Taeco after 30 bolts were found to be missing from the aircraft security panel of an A340.

Customers need to be transited through the airport with ease, ensuring their safety, security and comfort. Airports are run by operators such as the Spanish-owned BAA, which presides over six airports in the UK including Heathrow airport. Airports have a number of functions that can be outsourced. These can include everything from entry to the airport right through to processes involved with disembarking. The rationale for outsourcing is to draw on knowledge and resources and to capitalize on the economies of scale that the provider may have to operate the facility (Graham, 2008). For example, car parking at airports can be handled by operators who have expertise in the infrastructure and functioning of the facility. For example, National Car Parks (NCP) manages the car parking facilities at Heathrow airport, though it is acknowledged that airport car parking may be kept in-house due to the minimal degree of expertise that is required for their operation. For those wishing to stay overnight before or after flying, accommodation at the airport will be provided by external hotel operators such as Holiday Inn or Ibis.

Once the customer is in the airport a number of facilities will be provided including retail, dining and lounge services. External operators will supply many of these services. For example, shopping and dining facilities may be provided by well-known branded outlets that are familiar to the customer, for example fast food operators such as McDonalds or Burger King and coffee outlets such as Costa or Starbucks. These facilities may be offered as a retail package to a 'master concessionaire' who will seek contracts for the airport (Graham, 2008). Lounge facilities can also be operated by external providers. For example, in 2009, Performa, a subsidiary of Gate Group, was awarded the contract to operate the global airline alliance SkyTeam lounge at Heathrow airport. This includes the design of the facility, the menu offerings and the day-to-day operation of the facility. In terms of information technology (IT)-related services at airports, these can be outsourced to external providers who have the expertise in this area. For example, in April 2011, BAA forged an outsourcing agreement with Capegemini UK plc to supply the IT logistics for

(Continued)

Case Study. Continued.

their UK-operated airports. This included IT services ranging from those related to the landing of planes to security queues and handling.

The introduction of outsourced facilities to the airport may provide it with an opportunity to reinvigorate the holistic airport experience. However, a number of criteria should be considered by airport operators when outsourcing. First, the needs of the target markets that use the airport. This includes the percentage share that the airport comprises of business, long-haul, short-haul, domestic, family, holidaying and expatriate passengers. The behaviour of these different markets should influence the composition of the airport's facilities and their location. This may include factors such as the length of time that the passenger spends at the airport and the type of facilities that should be provided in the airside or landside part of the airport. Second, the type of experience that the airport is wishing to convey to its markets based on the make up of its facilities. This may include designer boutiques or high cuisine restaurants for airports whose markets are primarily premium or business-class driven. The composition of facilities can provide the airport with an opportunity to differentiate itself from other airports and airport operators. Third, the contract terms should be clearly outlined, including the percentage return that the facility will pay to the airport operator. This is likely to be based on the number of sales generated at the facility. Fourth, the length of the contract, which needs to be sufficient to enable the operator to generate a return on investment. Fifth, the responsibility for the design and renovation of the facility. This will normally be the responsibility of the facility provider, who will require the physical entity to reflect brand standards. Sixth, the legal and planning issues required for the facility at the airport.

The challenge for airport operators outsourcing their functions and facilities is the increase and range of stakeholder interests that will have to be balanced. Conflicts of interest may emerge between the airlines and airport operators and the desire to maximize revenues (Graham, 2008). It should be noted that a concession tender code exists for airport operators engaging in the tender process, which has been devised by the Airports Council International (ACI Europe).

Questions

1. Choose an airport or airline. Identify which services are outsourced. Perform a value chain analysis and explore to what extent these outsourced services add value to the airline or airport offering.

2. What markets are primarily attracted to the airline or airport? To what extent does this influence the services and facilities that are outsourced?

3. Using examples illustrated in the case study, identify which stakeholders have the most power and influence in outsourcing decisions.

GLOSSARY OF TERMS USED IN THIS CHAPTER

Outsourcing
The generic term to describe the process by which the user employs a separate organization (the supplier), under a contract to perform a function, which could, alternatively, have been performed by in-house staff.

Service level agreement
An outsourcing tender document that expands on the service specification and documents the quality standard and expectations of performance.

Service specification
An outsourcing tender document that comprises the expected standard of service required by the facility from the outsource provider. This may include facility requirements, policy and heath and safety principles.

Strategic outsourcing
Strategic outsourcing is more long term in nature with the aim to generate value to the final service proposition for the facility. The onus here is not purely on cost reduction but on value creation for the facility and the outsourced operator.

Tactical outsourcing
Tactical outsourcing is used to resolve a current problem. This may be due to a lack of expertise in a specific area that requires a short or medium-term solution. In THE facilities, manpower is part of the operation that can be tactically outsourced.

Tendering
The tendering stage of the outsourcing process involves briefing and assessment, the contract award, the pre-contract meeting and mobilization and review.

Transformational outsourcing
Transformational outsourcing is as it implies. To transform the business so it is able to compete in a volatile and dynamic external environment.

Value chain
A combination of primary and support activities. Primary activities include inbound logistics, operations, outbound logistics, marketing and sales and services. The primary activities are facilitated by a number of support activities, which include procurement, human resources, infrastructure and technological development.

REFERENCES AND ADDITIONAL READING

Allen, J., O'Toole, W., Harris, R. and McDonnell, I. (2008) *Festival and Special Event Management*, 4th edn. Wiley, Milton, Australia.

Atkin, B. and Brooks, A. (2000) *Total Facilities Management*, 1st edn. Blackwell Science, Oxford.

Atkin, B. and Brooks, A. (2005) *Total Facilities Management*, 2nd edn. Blackwell Science, Oxford.

Atkin, B. and Brooks, A. (2009) *Total Facilities Management*, 3rd edn. Blackwell Science, Oxford.

Barrett, P. (1995) *Facilities Management – Towards Best Practice*. Blackwell Science, London.

Barrett, P.S. and Baldry, D. (2003) *Facilities Management – Towards Best Practice*, 2nd edn. Blackwell Science, Oxford.

Bowdin, G., Allen, J., O'Toole, W., Harris, R. and McDonnell, I. (2006) *Events Management*, 2nd edn. Elsevier, Oxford.

British Institute of Facilities Management (BIFM) Available at: http://www.bifm.org.uk/bifm/home

Brown, D. and Wilson, S. (2005) *The Black Book of Outsourcing – How to Manage the Changes, Challenges, and Opportunities*. Wiley, Hoboken, New Jersey, pp. 19–43.

Carlsen, J. (2005) Issues in dedicated convention center development with a case study of the Perth Convention and Exhibition Center, Western Australia. *Journal of Convention & Event Tourism* 6, 45–61.

Chanter, B. and Swallow, P. (2007) *Building Maintenance Management*, 2nd edn. Wiley, Oxford.

Clark, J.D. (2005) Considering a convention center. *Journal of Convention & Event Tourism* 6, 5–21.

Dale, C. (2009) Business planning and strategy. In: Robinson, P. (ed.) *Managing Operations in the Travel Industry*. CAB International, Wallingford, UK.

Fill, C. and Visser, E. (2000) The outsourcing dilemma: a composite approach to the make or buy. *Management Decision* 38, 43–50.

Fyall, A., Leask, A., Garrod, B. and Wanhill, S. (2008) *Managing Visitor Attractions – New Directions*, 2nd edn. Elsevier, Oxford.

Gay, C.L. and Essinger, J. (2000) *Inside Outsourcing: An Insider's Guide to Managing Strategic Outsourcing*. Nicholas Brealey, London.

Ghodeswar, B. and Vaidyanathan, J. (2008) Business process outsourcing: an approach to gain access to world-class capabilities. *Business Process Management Journal* 14, 23–38.

Gilley, K.M. and Rasheed, A. (2000) Making more by doing less: analysis of outsourcing and its effects on firm performance. *Journal of Management* 26, 763–790.

Graham, A. (2008) *Managing Airports: An International Perspective*. Butterworth-Heinemann, Oxford.

Greaver, M.F. (1999) *Strategic Outsourcing: A Structured Approach to Outsourcing Decisions and Initiatives*. AMACOM, New York.

Handy, C. (1989) *The Age of Unreason*. Harvard Business School Press, Cambridge, Massachusetts.

Hassanien, A., Dale, C. and Clarke, A. (2010) *Hospitality Business Development*. Elsevier, Oxford.

http://yznaem.info/air-france-had-a-quarrel-with-the-chinese-because-of-the-30-missing-bolts

Hunter, L., McGregor, A., MacInnes, J. and Sproull, A. (1993) The 'flexible firm': strategy and segmentation. *British Journal of Industrial Relations* 31(3), 383–407.

Johnson, M. (1997) *Outsourcing – in brief*. Butterworth-Heinemann, Oxford.

Jones, C. (2002) Facilities management in medium-sized UK hotels. *International Journal of Contemporary Hospitality Management* 14, 72–80.

Jones, C. and Jowett, V. (1998) *Managing Facilities*. Butterworth-Heinemann, Oxford.

Jones, O. (2000) Facility management: future opportunities, scope and impact. *Facilities* 18, 133–137.

Kamarazaly, M.A. (2008) Outsourcing versus in-house facilities management: framework for value adding selection. MPhil. thesis, Massey University at Wellington, New Zealand.

Kedia, B.L. and Lahiri, S. (2007) International outsourcing of services: a partnership model. *Journal of International Management* 13, 22–37.

Lamminmaki, D. (2007) Outsourcing in Australian hotels: a transaction cost economics perspective. *Journal of Hospitality & Tourism Research* 31, 73–110.

Lankford, W.M. and Parsa, F. (1999) Outsourcing: a primer. *Management Decision* 37, 310–316.

Linder, J.C. (2004) Outsourcing as a strategy to drive transformation. *Strategy and Leadership* 32, 26–31.

Mallen, C. and Adams, L. (2008) *Sport, Recreation and Tourism Event Management: Theoretical and Practical Dimensions*. Butterworth-Heinemann, Oxford.

Matthews, D. (2008) *Special Event Production: The Process*. Elsevier, Oxford.

McCarthy, E. (1996) To outsource or not to outsource: what's right for you. *Pension Management* 32, 12–17.

McIvor, R. (2005) *The Outsourcing Process*. Cambridge University Press, Cambridge, UK.

Mendelow, A. (1991) Stakeholder mapping. *Proceedings of the 2nd International Conference on Information Systems*. Cambridge, Massachusetts.

O'Brien, E. and Shaw, M. (2002) Independent meeting planners. *Journal of Convention & Exhibition Management* 3, 37–68.

Perunović, Z. and Pedersen, J.L. (2007) Outsourcing process and theories. In: Gupta, S. and Coelho, J. (eds) *Proceedings of the 18th Annual Conference of the Production and Operations Management Society*.

Porter, M.E. (1985) *Competitive Advantage*. The Free Press. New York.

Porter, M. (1998) *Competitive Advantage*. Macmillan, New York.

Ransley, J. and Ingram, H. (eds) (2004) *Developing Hospitality Properties and Facilities*, 2nd edn. Butterworth-Heinemann, Oxford.

Reilly, P. and Tamkin, P. (1996) Outsourcing: a flexible option for the future? *Institute of Employment Studies Report* 320.

Swarbrooke, J. (2001) *The Development and Management of Visitor Attractions*, 2nd edn. Butterworth-Heinemann, Oxford.

Wise, D. (2007) *Agility Spotlight and Leadership in Project Management*. Project Management Institute, Huddersfield, UK.

Yeoman, I., Robertson, M., Ali-Knight, J., Drummond, S. and McMahon-Beattie, U. (eds) (2003) *Festival and Events Management: An International Arts and Culture Perspective*. Butterworth-Heinemann, Oxford.

chapter 8

Cost Management

Abel Duarte Alonso, Michelle O'Shea and Vlad Krajsic
University of Western Sydney

LEARNING OBJECTIVES

Having completed this chapter, readers should be able to:

- explain project cost management principles, concepts and terms;
- identify, analyse and discuss cost management in the contemporary tourism, hospitality and events (THE) facilities context;
- critically discuss and apply cost management principles, including opportunity costs, revenue management and other principles relevant to THE operations' bottom line;
- illustrate the ability to apply gained understanding by completing the simulations and case studies provided throughout the chapter.

INTRODUCTION

This chapter focuses on cost management, including managing and maximizing the capacity, space and resources available within THE facilities' context. Additionally, the chapter explores opportunity cost and its implications for budgeting, daily operations and strategic planning. The chapter seeks to provide a clear and implicit link between cost and revenue management, and discusses issues relevant to opportunity costs; for example, when businesses fail to maximize existing physical resources, such as when equipment or structural damage prevents the successful execution of events. Case scenarios presented in the chapter will allow readers to analyse, calculate, discuss and apply findings. The objective of these case studies is to facilitate a deeper understanding, awareness and, importantly, the practical application of cost-related issues to THE operations.

IMPORTANCE OF COST MANAGEMENT IN THE SECTORS

With unpredictable and sporadic growth cycles in the global hospitality and other sectors, the area of tourism, hospitality and events facilities management is of continued contemporary relevance. Increasing tourist visitation numbers to a variety of traditional and non-traditional destinations (Lai and Yik, 2008), unprecedented growth in the events and conferencing sector, and the popularity of meetings and conventions (Tay, 2006) are just several industry trends affecting the demand for accommodation and other physical facilities. The rise and fall of many tourist destinations is in part illustrative of competitive regional and global tourism industries, with direct and indirect consequences for THE enterprises. Strong competition is contributing to renewed efforts among many THE facilities managers to address the needs and wants of customers. The phrase 'the customer is always right' has taken on renewed significance. In an environment strongly influenced by supply and demand factors, customer expectations are rising, including among hotel guests concerning the amenities, usability and overall performance of hotel facilities (Lai and Yik, 2011).

Those rising expectations, together with the vital importance of hotel guests and other consumers for the long-term survival of the business, illustrate the key role of THE facilities managers in ensuring the on-going maintenance and operation of facilities, including elevators, air-conditioning, fire service and lighting (Lai and Yik, 2008). Because addressing guests' expectations may lead to considerable expenses in real estate purchases, or in construction, maintenance and renovation of many THE buildings, today's managers need a variety of skills to seek and maximize any available space. Arguably, in many cases THE facilities managers are hesitant or resistant to make needed investments. In turn, managers lack the creativity and innovation necessary to make under-used or presently non-used spaces profit-generating.

Hassanien and Losekoot (2002), and subsequently Hassanien (2007), observed resistance and hesitation when evaluating managerial decisions related to hotel renovation. Hotel owners appeared to undervalue the renovation process and did not see renovations or modernizing infrastructure as a means of extending hotels' useful life, and therefore adding value to their business. By contrast, Okoroh *et al.* acknowledged: 'Construction and facilities maintenance contributes to the derivation of value by all stakeholders in hotels' (2003, p. 32). Consequently, with appropriate cost management skills, investment in facilities maintenance and in other areas of hotel facilities management can clearly contribute to the life span of the business and also have positive direct and indirect impacts on personnel, guests and other business stakeholders (e.g. suppliers and surrounding community). Indeed, in regard to hotels, Okoroh *et al.* identify the management of physical assets and infrastructure as critical to effective strategy and operations: 'effective management of the physical aspects … is essential for maximum efficiency' (2002, p. 239). Efficiency in this context not only relates to management's ability to utilize available spaces and human resources in a THE facility, but also their skills to manage costs and revenues successfully.

Despite the growing relevance of cost management of facilities maintenance for THE practitioners and researchers, to date only a handful of textbooks written on this topic devote any space to discussing costs in the context of THE businesses. Stipanuk (2002, 2006) is among the few authors who critically reflect on the multiplicity of areas in hospitality operations where unexpected or rising costs of hospitality/events facilities can occur, and subsequently have direct and indirect business implications for the organization. Ransley and Ingram (2004) also referred to costs when they presented scenarios describing the significant capital costs associated with 'start up' hospitality enterprise. In the case of independent restaurants, Ransley and Ingram (2004) calculated that as much as €10,000 per seat was needed to simply commence operations. The bulk of this amount is devoted to construction and furnishing of front- and back-of-house, while the remainder is used as working capital, or to buy supplies and small wares.

Even higher are the costs of chain restaurants and franchise operations (€18,000). Ransley and Ingram (2004) found, however, that the rooms department (hotels) is where most expenses are incurred. For example, while in small hotels a room may cost up to €80,000, a full-service hotel would require almost €150,000. Full renovation costs per room of a 4-star hotel would cost approximately €7000, and that of a restaurant's dining room €2000 per seat (Ransley and Ingram, 2004). Given the additional and continuous utility, labour, maintenance, repair or insurance costs, and the sometimes unpredictable nature of THE business environments, amortizing the resulting significant figures can be very daunting and a long-term proposition for most operators.

Exercise: Amortizing investment

Assume the following scenario: You are required to calculate the approximate time in years to amortize the costs of a new 100-seat restaurant (use Excel or similar spreadsheet). The following information is provided:

Cost per seat: $4000

Revenues:

First year after opening: −$50,000 (first year the business incurs a net loss).

Second year: $15,000 profit.

(Continued)

Exercise. Continued.

Third year: $120,000 profit.

Fourth year: $175,000 profit.

Fifth year: $195,000 profit. Please note that inflation and other aspects are not considered in this exercise; however, consider the potential overall long-term 'loss' in value of your cash investment.

A number of contemporary issues are affecting many organizations and entire sectors, thus reinforcing the notion of unpredictability. In fact, a long and recurring recession, whereby consumers are more hesitant to spend their hard-earned income, the unpredictability of natural phenomena or even the alleged effects of climate change and associated proposed government policies may all play a part in affecting the potential of many THE businesses. High labour, supply, food costs and/or oil prices can have direct and indirect impacts on utility, maintenance, renovation and related costs incurred by THE operations. Utility prices, for instance, can dent an operation's revenue maximization significantly. Almost a decade ago, average expenses in energy costs at restaurants comprised more than 5% of establishments' total sales (Birchfield and Sparrowe, 2003).

More recently, Jones and Zemke (2010) examined several scenarios to assist hospitality managers in making informed decisions when purchasing kitchen equipment. These authors critically considered utility costs, comparing different types of hotels and percentage of utility costs vs total revenues. At one end, all limited-service hotels appear to incur most utility costs (5.3%) compared with total percentage of revenues, while at the other end, convention hotels (3.9%) spend less. Similarly, all limited-service hotels spend more on operations and maintenance (5.8%), while convention hotels (4.7%) once again account for the lowest percentage.

While current knowledge of the effects that age, quality and occupancy rate have on hotels may be limited and therefore require further investigation, in their study of Hong Kong hotels Lai and Yik found evidence that these 'are potential factors affecting the costs for operating and maintaining the facilities' (2008, p. 288). Lai and Yik (2008) explain that 'hard service' components such as maintenance of building services (air-conditioning, fire protection installation), or the builder's works (furniture, building fabric) can have a strong impact on customers' satisfaction, subsequently affecting hotels' income and resources available to perform maintenance. These scenarios illustrate very critical implications for hospitality managers, because, as Okoroh *et al.* explain, regardless of the size of the hotel, 'the manager/owner plays a significant role in most FM tasks' (2003, p. 30).

Exercise: Utility costs

Assuming yearly revenues of $1,250,000 (all limited-service) and $2,200,000 (convention hotels), calculate the total dollar value in utility costs for both businesses (5.3% and 3.9%, respectively). Use the same figures to calculate dollars and cents of maintenance costs for both scenarios (5.8% and 4.7%, respectively).

DEFINING COST MANAGEMENT

The findings and insights from previous studies clearly underline the importance for managers of THE sectors to understand practical principles of cost management. McNair *et al.* refer to cost management in general terms: 'Advanced cost management studies and practices suggest a variety of different tools that help us understand the relationship between value and cost' (2001, p. 33). McNair *et al.* also mention that 'cost management techniques' (2001, p. 34) can assist in increasing product or business profitability, improving quality, cost allocation and product mix decisions. Similarly, El Kelety points out: 'cost management looks to the long-term competitive success of the firm' (2006, p. 1). There is an important link that needs to be made between cost management and the organization's short-term and long-term strategic plan. Failing to identify and continuously address cost management through key performance indicator (KPI) development and yearly assessment will ultimately affect the organization's bottom line and its long-term financial viability.

Example: Riverside Oaks

Riverside Oaks Resort Golf Course is rated among the top resort courses in Australia. The resort is set on nearly 250 hectares of natural bushland 75 minutes' drive north-west of the Sydney central business district. Opened in 1988, Riverside Oaks hosted the Australian PGA Championship from 1988 to 1990 and has also hosted the New South Wales PGA Championship.

As well as a championship-standard golf course, the resort boasts an award winning restaurant, various conference facilities, function rooms and both luxury villa and lodge style accommodation. Having had a number of owners in its 22-year history, Riverside Oaks has a new lease of life with new owners, new management and plans for upgrades of the course, clubhouse and facilities. Nanshan Group, which owns 15 golf courses in China, recently purchased Riverside Oaks and has enlisted golf course management company Troon Golf to manage the operation. Work has recently been completed on the first phase of renovations on the clubhouse with work soon to commence on the public golf course. A driving range and a new practice range have been completed and Nanshan plan to continue developing Riverside Oaks with construction of an additional 18-hole golf course. The 'tired' fleet of golf carts will soon be replaced.

The recently renovated two-storey clubhouse is a popular venue for weddings and corporate functions. In addition to its golf course, Riverside Oaks provides conference venues, with several meeting options from small conference rooms to full banquet rooms with seating for 300 guests.

(Continued)

Example. Continued.

The new owners will also be expanding the onsite accommodation, with plans to build more three- and four-bedroom golf villas and a 300-room hotel in the near future.

Having already invested considerable funds, and proposing to invest more in a facility that is not fully utilized, the owners must look at opportunities to maximize their revenue from the various facilities.

If you were the General Manager, discuss what strategies you could adopt regarding the:

- golf course;
- accommodation;
- conference facilities;
- restaurant.

Remember to consider 'packaging'.

Source: http://www.riversideoaks.com.au

Other studies refer to target costing in conjunction with cost management as a tool to reduce overall cost of a product over its entire life cycle (Nicolini *et al.*, 2000). To date, however, cost management has not been clearly defined in relation to THE facilities management, or even broadly discussed in THE literature. In addition, there appears to be a scarcity of research conducted on cost management-related areas, including cost analysis, benchmarking and maintenance in the hotel industry (Chan, 2008). In this chapter, cost management is emphasized as a vital concept for THE facilities managers to limit or minimize expenses without compromising performance, quality or safety of the operation, while allowing them to maximize revenues. Furthermore, cost management is a tool that assists in 'balancing' the complex process THE managers experience when seeking to add value to the products their businesses provide, and monitor the always-looming costs associated with running a THE businesses effectively and efficiently.

OPPORTUNITY COSTS

The modern THE manager must not only be aware of external events and challenges, such as the increase of utility and food prices, but also learn to manage, maximize or at least balance efficiently the physical resources available to the organization. Equally important is to understand unexpected or unforeseen events, including delays or increased costs during the construction phase, referred to as 'scope creep' (Shane *et al.*, 2009), and resulting opportunity costs. Palmer and Raftery refer to opportunity cost as 'Benefits forgone by particular use of resources' (1999, p. 1552). Other definitions include Tranter *et al.*'s explanation: 'the cost of taking any action is the loss of opportunity of taking any alternative action given the same time and resources' (2009, p. 324).

Opportunity costs: Scenario 1

Ignacio has a small restaurant with capacity for 100 people. He has recently been invited to speak at a forum in city X (about 30 minutes' drive from his restaurant) on a Tuesday evening. Tuesdays are usually quiet, with an average of 45 meals sold at $17 each. Because he is the only one cooking at the restaurant, and with no time to find anyone else to replace him, he has decided to close the restaurant this coming Tuesday. What are Ignacio's opportunity costs in dollars and cents? Beyond simply dollars and cents? What opportunities may lie ahead by Ignacio attending the event?

Unpredictable and unforeseen events such as damaged golf turf from drought or floods, breakdown of a cruise ship or malfunctioning hotel/restaurant equipment can lead to unexpected cancellations of bookings and resulting loss of benefits for the business. Among hotels, fluctuating demand and resultant room vacancies can lead to 'profit instability'; hence the need for management to maintain high revenue levels (Graham and Harris, 1999). Investments in labour, supplies, outside entertainment and other areas often have to be arranged well in advance of the start of the events.

Opportunity costs: Scenario 2

Sharon's small restaurant business has not been performing very well lately. Sales are decreasing and more small restaurants with cheaper options are cropping up in the neighbourhood. Over the last five years, Sharon has offered a menu featuring different international dishes with several courses each that on average cost $30 per person. During this time, she has seen her loyal customers grow from 15 to 150, spread out throughout the week, and to date no other restaurant in the neighbourhood provides such high-end product and service. However, given the current situation, she is considering an overhaul of the menu content; the idea is that customers have an array of meals that on average cost $12. She is also considering doing without tablecloths and linen napkins, and letting two very skilled staff go. What might be some of the opportunity costs associated with Sharon's decision, especially during the first year?

Hence, apart from foregoing revenues, the business may also incur expenditures on already agreed on arrangements or products without any imminent opportunity to recover that investment. THE managers face these sorts of situations on many occasions; when they occur, managers must find ways to alleviate any potential losses. In the case of labour already allocated to work at an event, management must be careful to find a balance between looking at the bottom line (expenditures vs idle labour) and maintaining a working environment that nurtures workers' commitment, productivity and morale. The following simulation illustrates an opportunity cost scenario.

Example: Opportunity costs

The Y Hotel is a season hotel (open April through October) located in the northern hemisphere in a valley in the midst of a pristine natural environment with opportunities for walking, hiking and playing golf. The hotel features 230 rooms, a restaurant that can seat 110 patrons, a bar with capacity for 75, and a ballroom with space to host banquets, weddings and other events that can cater for 300 people. Before its yearly re-opening, the maintenance team spotted a problem in the heating system that will require the replacement of some of its parts. Because this April has been unusually cool, the hotel's managers are opposed to going forward with the re-opening and risking customers' discomfort and their resulting dissatisfaction, which may lead to even more serious problems (e.g. negative word-of-mouth advertising). The cost of the parts to be replaced amounts $75,000, including labour and delivery from a city Z located about an hour away by car.

What is worse, the re-opening of the hotel will have to be postponed from Saturday to Monday. On Saturday, 185 rooms (215 guests) were booked and 125 rooms (175 guests) on Sunday; the average price per room is $120 and includes breakfast. Usually, all guests dine at the restaurant (average revenues per guest: $20); also, on average some 25 locals dine at the restaurant each evening during the season (average revenues per guest: $27). One wedding for some 185 people was booked in the ballroom on Saturday evening; the expected average revenue per guest was $37. On Sunday, the annual rotary club meeting was scheduled; 150 guests were booked and average revenue of $17 per guest was expected, plus $1500 for the ballroom booking. Finally, the bar was expecting to be 'buzzing' in the first two evenings: some 200 clients were expected per evening, both from the hotel and residents of the area combined. Last year's average consumption at the bar was worth $21.

The hotel had already arranged to be assisted by 20 hotel cleaners and three housekeepers to do the work Sunday and Monday for those guests staying Saturday and Sunday. In addition, 15 waiting staff, four restaurant managers, 11 cooking staff, two head chefs, 10 kitchen staff, 10 ballroom staff and six bar staff had been secured to work Saturday and Sunday. Last year, the hotel paid an average of $38.5 per hour, including benefits.

1. Calculate total revenues foregone.
2. Calculate total employee costs, assuming that all employees will be paid for two entire working shifts (8 hours per shift).
3. Calculate total opportunity costs (include repairs of heating system).
4. Discuss the implications of the hotel's decision to shut down, including other aspects of the opportunity costs associated with this case (e.g. food and other supplies, maintenance, utilities, insurance).
5. Can the management make arrangements with personnel during this time of crisis? For example, what could be some of the consequences of awarding mandatory leave to part of the staff until the hotel is fully operating?

BREAK-EVEN POINT ANALYSIS

Investing in the business operation's physical facilities in maintenance, renovation or construction, while often necessary, can be a source of uncertainty for THE managers, particularly concerning the time and energy needed to recuperate or financially benefit from investments. Many THE business managers use break-even and profit-and-loss analysis to generate a picture or have an idea of what it would take for their business to recuperate any investments. Break-even is defined as 'The point at which a firm's revenues exactly equal its expenses' (Hayes and Miller, 2011, p. 55), and it is often illustrated in different financial and accounting textbooks as follows:

Profit = Revenue − Expense.

Different sources (internet, textbooks) also feature equations using numbers and letters to calculate the break-even point:

RX = FC + VX,

where RX represents revenues per item, VX variable costs per item and FC fixed costs.

For example, a fruit seller pays $50 per day for a stand at a market, and an average of 50% of the total sale price of each case of oranges he will sell at the market. If he sells each case for $25, how many cases will he need to break even? Solution:

25x = 50 + 12.5x

We need to move 12.5x to the left to isolate both the x and non-x figures. 12.5x therefore changes sign from positive to negative, thus:

25x − 12.5x = 50

Then, solving for 'x':

12.5x = 50

x = 50/12.5

x = 4

thus, at 4 = 4 a break-even point is a achieved. Therefore, the fruit seller will need to sell four cases of oranges to break even. Only from that point on will he be able to make profits if he manages to continue selling his oranges.

While most cases in real-world THE environments are obviously not this straightforward, when properly calculated break-even analysis can help managers, if only 'symbolically', informing or suggesting aspects (sales, time) that are needed to offset any previous financial investments. According to Graham and Harris, while break even 'is not an end objective in itself, it is a critical intermediate point which must be reached before profits are realised' (1999, p. 201). Overall, in the absence of a more financially favourable situation, break-even is the least managers should be achieving in order to work towards the future well-being of the business. Thus, it is very important for managers to design and execute strategies that would lead to more maximization of revenues and resources. The following provides an opportunity for students to calculate break-even.

Example: Bodegas Monje

Bodegas Monje is one of the most traditional (older) wineries in the Canary Islands, Spain. Open to the public since 1956, but with several generations of family history, after the establishment of designations of origin in the islands' wine regions, this winery has led a pioneering role in wine tourism. Today, the winery not only offers guided tours, a full-service restaurant and wine tastings, but also organizes musical events, meetings, art exhibits as well as other activities that draw some 9000 customers to its facilities at El Sauzal (Tenerife Island) each year.

To draw and maintain consumers' interest in a very competitive wine sector, the owner Felipe Monje and the approximately ten employees of the winery consistently need to offer high-quality products and services. In addition, the management of costs and expenses in this type of business is of paramount importance for its viability. Concerning the aspect of cost management, Mr Felipe comments: 'The manager of any hospitality establishment must know the area of cost management and that of maximization of resources very well. In my case, for a long time I have acquired information technology packages that allow me to track costs and expenses very rapidly.'

In 2010, the winery completed the construction of an underground space to host concerts, art exhibits and even a wine 'safe' for the winery's clients to buy wines and store them in their own (rented) safe for consumption at a later time. The construction of this space took three and a half years and cost approximately €2,500,000. In 2011, an ample terrace outside the winery's restaurant overlooking the vineyard and the Atlantic Ocean was completed at a cost of around €80,000.

Although investments in terms of money, time and work have been significant, Mr Felipe is positive about the future of the winery. Moreover, Mr Felipe not only expects to continue being a leader in the production of excellent wines, or offering quality wine tourism and restaurant products and services, but also in organizing events and activities compatible with the interest of wine- and non-wine- aficionados.

Case study questions:

1. Break-even analysis: Assume that the average consumption per visitor of Bodegas Monje is €22.50, and that of the expenses incurred per customer served (labour, maintenance, utilities, etc) is €6.75. Calculate the approximate number of winery visits needed to offset the expenses incurred in the construction of the underground space. Tip: follow the following formula:

$$22.50x = 6.75x + 2,500,000$$

(Continued)

Example. Continued.

2. Break-even analysis: If 4000 clients visited the winery's terrace per year and spent an average €16.75 per person, while the costs per served client (labour, maintenance, utilities, etc) were €6.75, calculate the approximate time needed to offset the costs of construction of the winery's terrace. Tip: Use the same formula as in (1). Then divide €80,000 by your answer.
3. Propose ideas/strategies for Bodegas Monje to increase its revenues and/or the value of its individual sales.

Source: http://www.bodegasmonje.com/

Despite its practical usefulness, there is an argument that the break-even concept has been ignored or underrated (Graham and Harris, 1999). Similarly, there appears to be a lack of discussion concerning other aspects or elements required in the process of recuperating financial or other forms of investment that are often unaccounted for when computing break-even financial analysis. For example, the price paid in the process of breaking even may include among other aspects the effort made (physical/mental), the extent to which human resources are invested (e.g. working overtime), and resulting costs at personal or social level in the case of heavy work-schedules placed on workers. Given the complexity and potential financial, work and social implications of these additional aspects related to breaking even, the modern THE manager must have a sound knowledge of different alternatives, or be able to allocate resources.

DEVELOPING ALTERNATIVE REVENUE STREAMS

Increasingly, hospitality, leisure and event venues and facilities are required to consider utilization strategies that fall outside their 'core' business. Facility managers are beginning to consider alternative, creative and innovative ways to increase usage, patronage and ultimately their bottom lines. One example can be seen when considering the Sydney Olympic Park facility usage legacy. Although purpose-built for elite sport, many of these venues are developing business strategies that have a hospitality, entertainment and business event focus. Many of these strategies relate to criticisms that the venues are a drain on public funds and that they are 'white elephants'.

Exercise: Utility and maintenance costs

The following table shows the percentages (of total revenues) of power costs (Table 8.1), and those of maintaining the turf of the hotels' golf courses (Table 8.2) for the last 6 years in all five resorts that belong to Palmera Hotel Company. Calculate dollar values for each hotel. Then, graph the results, identify any patterns and discuss the implications of the results for Palmera Hotel Company.

(Continued)

Exercise. Continued.

Table 8.1. Percentages (of total revenues) of power costs.

	Average revenues	2008	2009	2010	2011	2012
Resort 1	$3,750,000	4.5	4.9	5.2	5.7	5.9
Resort 2	$4,900,000	5.8	6.3	7.2	7.1	8.0
Resort 3	$2,800,000	3.7	5.3	5.9	6.1	6.3
Resort 4	$5,700,000	5.4	6.1	6.3	6.4	6.5
Resort 5	$1,950,000	3.2	4.5	6.3	7.1	7.5

Table 8.2. Percentages of maintaining the turf of the hotels' golf courses.

	Average revenues*	2008	2009	2010	2011	2012
Resort 1	$4,750,000	2.3	3.3	4.5	5.5	7.5
Resort 2	$5,950,000	4.0	4.5	6.3	7.4	8.3
Resort 3	$3,400,000	2.7	5.3	4.9	7.1	3.3
Resort 4	$6,800,000	3.4	4.1	5.3	6.4	7.5
Resort 5	$2,350,000	4.2	5.5	6.3	7.2	8.5

* Revenues include those achieved through golf course memberships and fees to play.

Similarly, the Aquatic Centre at Sydney Olympic Park has considered the opportunity to yield additional revenue by considering the community and family market together, hiring out the venue for gala events, corporate functions and business meetings. The venue's unique appeal has seen significant financial returns. The venue has hosted fashion launches; sit-down three-course functions for in excess of 500 guests by night and returns to its aquatic operations by day. Although there are significant financial returns, the approach is not without difficulty. The staff needed to 'bump in and out' event infrastructure is notable, together with the required capital investment. However, the venue has been able to strategically increase venue utilization and their bottom line with minimal effects on the organization's core operations. Cashman (2002) further reflects on the Aquatic Centre's strategy as a good example of a dual-purpose venue in that it housed both the best facilities for elite sport as well as 'sport-for-all'. This last element includes play areas for children, community outdoor-orientated recreation facilities together with a capacity to host non-sporting events and programmes.

Example: Managing events in a wine tourism destination

Wandin Valley Estate is a winery located in Hunter Valley, a popular tourist destination in Australia, approximately three hours' drive from Sydney, a city of four million people. Hunter Valley is home to dozens of wineries, olive groves, music festivals and other activities that attract several million visitors each year. The Hunter Valley and surrounding towns boast a large variety of accommodation opportunities, from high-end to backpacker motels.

Apart from cellar door visits to taste a range of estate wines, Wandin Estate has positioned itself as one of the region's leaders in catering events, especially weddings. That the winery has become a multifunctional business is not surprising. The surrounding landscape, the estate's vines, its undulating hills, its pristine long entrance and the physical facilities (the winery and multiple ceremony locations) provide a romantic, family and very convenient environment for organizing weddings and other events.

Mercedes Mendoza, weddings and events manager, explains that the events season (weddings) coincides with the seasons and is from March to May and September to December. From a cost management perspective, this approximately 6-month opportunity must be maximized. Mercedes states that given the very competitive nature of the local market, with different wineries offering events, Wandin Valley Estate needs to match and exceed customers' expectations. To address those expectations, attention must be paid to detail, especially by providing high-quality service and product (e.g. food) at competitive prices.

One of the key challenges for the events department, according to Mercedes, is securing skilled personnel who are willing to commit long-term. Several issues exacerbate this challenge, such as the lure of more hours and higher wages on offer elsewhere, and the nature of the wedding market itself, whereby event employees may have many working hours in some weeks and fewer working hours in others. In addition, finding alternative business opportunities during the months with less event activity is also an area where the winery could improve.

The winery is involved with the local community in different ways. For example, it provides employment to local residents, and from-time-to time hosts events or offers discounts for local groups to carry out events onsite.

1. If you were Mercedes, what potential alternatives would you suggest for Wandin Valley Estate to maximize returns during the approximately 6 months of less event activity (winter and mid-summer in Australia)?

2. Expand on your choices, discussing the potential revenue streams (e.g. menus, personnel), as well as costs incurred in the process.

Sources: Masanauskas and Deery (2011); Media release (2011); Wandin Valley Estate Winery (2011)

SUMMARY

The concept of cost management for hotel facilities management is critical for the current and future well-being of THE businesses, as is that of revenue management. Hotel managers need to have an understanding of the different aspects entailed in the effective and efficient management of existing resources. For example, cost of utilities, equipment, maintenance or renovation can easily deplete a business financially, potentially weakening its foundation and threatening its future. Equally critical are opportunity costs, or the costs associated with choosing one course of action over another with similar time and similar resources, and foregoing or losing potential or real business opportunities in the process.

THE managers must be aware of the financial and other consequences of choosing available alternatives. Learning basic financial principles, such as the pros and cons of choosing different scenarios and how doing so may affect the business operation's bottom line, or the demands placed on a business to break even after considerable investments, is paramount. This chapter provides some basic scenarios and drills for future hotel managers to gain awareness of the implications of business decisions. However, this chapter is only a beginning in a long journey, whereby future THE facilities managers will unearth opportunities and face numerous challenges. Therefore, students should continue their quest for life-long learning and mastering of practical calculations in order to be prepared for the future challenges of the industry.

REVIEW QUESTIONS

1. Define the concept of cost management and explore its contributions to THE facilities.
2. The modern THE manager must not only be aware of external events and challenges, such as the increase of utility and food prices, but also learn to manage, maximize or at least balance efficiently the physical resources available to the organization. Discuss.

Case Study

Laundry troubles

The Dove is a 60-bedroom boutique hotel that has survived changing times and has been passed on from generation to generation. Marty O, the present owner, has successfully managed the hotel for three decades. However, recently some of the laundry equipment (the cooling system, washing machines and tumblers/driers) is beginning to be affected by constant use, and wear and tear is having an impact. To make matters worse, one of the most loyal and efficient employees who managed to work under difficult conditions, enduring the increasing problems of the laundry's heat and the breakdown of machines, is retiring.

(Continued)

Case Study. Continued.

With only two less-experienced employees to rely on in the laundry department, Marty is confronted with fixing the malfunctioning equipment. He will need to (a) outsource the washing, drying and ironing of the hotel's linen for the next 2 months, and (b) find additional work for the two local employees who also do the hotel's housekeeping as well as their laundry duties. Outsourcing means that the laundry will be picked up and sent to a central laundry some 2 hours' drive from the village where the hotel is located. The hotel has a loyal clientele and occupation in the next three (summer) months is expected to be at its maximum (almost 100%), while the rest of the year occupation is around 70%.

Each weekly batch of outsourced linen costs $1400; the outsourcing company sometimes does not keep its return delivery promises. Marty calculated estimated costs of cleaning the laundry at the hotel at $1100. However, now much of the equipment will need to be replaced at a cost of $27,000 for new machines, and $5800 for the laundry's cooling system. Other useful information: The average price of each room is $100; overall, costs (labour, insurance, utilities, etc.) represent 55% of revenues; the laundry's size is approximately 25 square metres.

Questions

1. How much will outsourcing the laundry cost in total, while repairs take place?
2. Approximately how long will it take Marty to break-even if he decided to do the repairs?
3. What other alternatives may Marty consider, including maximizing labour or space?
4. What may be some of the implications of the different scenarios Marty could potentially choose? Discuss.

GLOSSARY OF TERMS USED IN THIS CHAPTER

Break-even	Reaching a point whereby THE operations only manage to cover incurred expenses, but without any apparent monetary benefits.
Labour maximization	Successfully managing, utilizing and/or obtaining benefits (more income, more guests, more services, improved services, more products, improved products) by fully utilizing the available human resources.
Opportunity costs	Costs associated with taking one course of action over another with similar time and resources available, potentially foregoing opportunities in the process.
Space maximization	Successfully utilizing and/or obtaining benefits (more income, more guests, more services, more products) by taking advantage of available physical resources, especially more available space.

Unaccounted-for elements related to break-even and opportunity cost	Those elements that may not have a defined or clear price/value but that can have a significant impact on THE operations. In business environments, investments or price paid physically or psychologically; also, the social aspects (hiring and firing) in the process of achieving break-even point or when foregoing opportunities.

REFERENCES AND ADDITIONAL READING

Birchfield, J.C. and Sparrowe, R.T. (2003) *Design and Layout of Foodservice Facilities*, 2nd edn. Wiley, Hoboken, New Jersey.

Cashman, R. (2002) University lecture on the impact of the games on host communities. Educational Project of the Centre d'Estudis Olímpics, Universitat Autònoma de Barcelona, Spain.

Chan, K. (2008) An empirical study of maintenance costs for hotels in Hong Kong. *Journal of Retail and Leisure Property* 7, 35–52.

El Kelety, I.A.E.M.A. (2006) Towards a conceptual framework for strategic cost management. The concepts, objectives, and instruments. PhD thesis. Chemnitz University of Technology, Chemnitz, Germany.

Graham, I.C. and Harris, P.J. (1999) Development of a profit planning framework in an international hotel chain: a case study. *International Journal of Contemporary Hospitality Management* 11, 198–204.

Hassanien, A. (2007) An investigation of hotel property renovation: the external parties' views. *Property Management* 25, 209–224.

Hassanien, A. and Losekoot, E. (2002) The application of facilities management expertise to the hotel renovation process. *Facilities* 20, 230–238.

Hayes, D.K. and Miller, A.A. (2011) *Revenue Management for the Hospitality Industry*. Wiley, Hoboken, New Jersey.

Jones, T. and Zemke, D. (2010) *Managing the Built Environment in Hospitality Facilities*. Prentice-Hall, Upper Saddle River, New Jersey.

Lai, J.H.K. and Yik, F.W.H. (2008) Benchmarking operation and maintenance costs of luxury hotels. *Journal of Facilities Management* 6, 279–289.

Lai, J.H.K. and Yik, F.W.H. (2011) A probe into the facilities maintenance data of a hotel. *Building Services Engineering Research and Technology* 32, 1–17.

Masanauskas, J. and Deery, S. (2011) Melbourne's population closes gap on Sydney as new suburb planned. Available at: http://www.heraldsun.com.au/news/more-news/new-inner-west-suburb-on-the-way/story-fn7x8me2-1226031679786

Media release (2011) NSW government supports Hunter Valley wine and food extravaganza. Available at: http://corporate.tourism.nsw.gov.au/Sites/SiteID6/objLib85/110603_Hunter-Valley-Food-Wine.pdf

McNair, C.J., Polutnik, L. and Silvi, R. (2001) Cost management and value creation: the missing link. *European Accounting Review* 10, 33–50.

Nicolini, D., Tomkins, C., Holti, R., Oldman, A. and Smalley, M. (2000) Can target costing and whole life costing be applied in the construction industry? Evidence from two case studies. *British Journal of Management* 11, 303–324.

Okoroh, M.I., Jones, C. and Ilozor, B.D. (2002) FM application in the hospitality sector. *Facilities* 20, 239–250.

Okoroh, M.I., Jones, C. and Ilozor, B.D. (2003) Adding value to constructed facilities: facilities management hospitality case study. *Journal of Performance of Constructed Facilities* 17, 24–33.

Palmer, S. and Raftery, J. (1999) Opportunity cost. *British Medical Journal* 318, 1551–1552.

Ransley, J. and Ingram, H. (2004) *Developing Hospitality Properties and Facilities*, 2nd edn. Elsevier, Burlington, Massachusetts.

Shane, J.S., Molenaar, K.R., Anderson, S.D. and Schexnayder, C.J. (2009) Construction project cost escalation factors. *Journal of Management in Engineering* 25, 221–229.

Stipanuk, D.M. (2002) *Hospitality Facilities Management and Design*, 2nd edn. Educational Institute of the American Hotel and Lodging Association, Lansing, Michigan.

Stipanuk, D.M. (2006) *Hospitality Facilities Management and Design*, 3rd edn. Educational Institute of the American Hotel and Lodging Association, Lansing, Michigan.

Tay, L. (2006) Strategic facilities management of Suntec Singapore International Convention and Exhibition Centre. *Facilities* 24, 120–131.

Tranter, K.A., Stuart-Hill, T. and Parker, J. (2009) *An Introduction to Revenue Management for the Hospitality Industry: Principles and Practices for the Real World*. Prentice-Hall, Upper Saddle River, New Jersey.

Wandin Valley Estate Winery (2011) Available at: http://www.wandinvalley.com.au

chapter 9

Corporate Social Responsibility

Michelle O'Shea, Abel Duarte Alonso and Vlad Krajsic
University of Western Sydney

> Our position as the world's leading entertainment company could not have been reached – and could not have been sustained – solely from business success. It rests equally on our tradition of social responsibility and community involvement. At the core of this enterprise is the determination to make a difference as well as a profit
>
> (Gerald Levin Chairman and CEO, Time Warner, Inc.)

LEARNING OBJECTIVES

Having completed this chapter, readers should be able to:

- conceptualize/define corporate social responsibility (CSR) from the perspectives of a range of stakeholder interests;
- critically reflect on CSR as part of the tourism, hospitality and events (THE) organizations' business and marketing philosophy;
- discuss and critically consider the financial (tangible) and engagement/outreach (intangible) outcomes of organizational CSR initiatives;
- reflect on the nature and value of community engagement initiatives incorporating industry, market, government, joint government–industry and educational initiatives;
- help develop a philosophical view of CSR in the context of THE organizational operations.

INTRODUCTION

In an increasingly competitive business world, many companies are expected to address a number of new and existing challenges. Uncertain economic times, changes in consumer demographics and other external demands are some of the pressures placed on contemporary THE organizations. Amidst these developments, CSR has emerged as a relevant issue in the corporate world, most noticeably in the past two decades. The THE industry has responded to, and been actively involved in, CSR initiatives in various innovative ways (Lee and Heo, 2009). As early as the 1960s, scholars and practitioners were considering the positive outcomes associated with CSR for organizations' reputations as well as employee health and wellbeing outcomes (Salzmann *et al.*, 2005). However, the 'strategic business case' for CSR and strategies to maximize business objectives through CSR have only recently been explored.

Involvement in CSR at the organizational level is in part the result of a growing expectation for organizations to conform to transparent ethical and social principles. This growing expectation serves as a reminder to corporations of their duty to behave in a legal, ethical and socially responsive manner (Carroll, 1979). Additionally, organizations' role as commercial enterprises, together with their social agenda, have raised consumer expectations to the extent that phrases including 'community benefactor' and community 'guardian' produce trust expectations. Expectations also are also growing of a need to build positive alliances and social networks with relevant stakeholders of which, for THE organizations, consumers are a considerable and fundamentally important group.

THE organizations, like many other organizations, can no longer continue to engage in 'business as usual' because consumer and employee expectations have shifted significantly. The heightened expectations placed on many organizations to be socially conscious, in part through their involvement in social causes, philanthropic activities and gift giving, is triggering continued dialogue about CSR within the services sector globally. However, organizations are not evaluated based on words and rhetoric, but instead on their actions. Consequently, 'in recent years there has been a rapid increase in the number of businesses that have become involved in community and social projects' (Makaros and Zehavi, 2008, p. 40). Thus, concepts such as social responsibility, social capital (Putnam, 1995) and sustainability have gained in relevance, becoming key components of many modern organizations' daily operations. This movement underlines the growth from CSR as philanthropy and philosophy to CSR's role as part of an organization's core and reported business activity (Burke and Logsdon, 1996).

CSR DEFINED

Just what does CSR mean anyway? CSR is referred to in a number of ways, including social responsibility (SR), corporate citizenship, corporate social enterprise and, in the case of tourism, corporate sustainability. Definitional debates and the growing plurality of perspectives on CSR are in part the result of differing viewpoints regarding the role that business 'does' or 'should' play in society, leading to the question: for what primary reason does the organization (and hence THE enterprises) exist?

The 'classic view', based on neoclassical economic theory, rests with the organization's capacity to make money. In the neoclassical view, the 'shareholder value maximization model' is applied to the organization and its activities (Grossman and Stiflitz, 1977). By contrast, the 'enlightened stakeholder perspective' is more socially orientated, contending that companies have a social responsibility that extends beyond profit generation (Jensen, 2002). In this approach, the interests of stakeholders are taken into account when making organizational decisions (Jensen, 2001). Margolis and Walsh explain that the challenge that those organizations advocating corporate social initiatives face is finding ways 'to promote social justice in a world in which the shareholder wealth maximization paradigm reigns' (2003, p. 273). One relevant example for the THE industry can be identified when considering Comfort and Hillier's (2006) research exploring the CSR initiatives of pub operators in the United Kingdom.

For the industry, a tension exists between financial gains, social agendas and community expectations. In response, the industry has engaged member organizations attempting to strike a balance between the responsibilities of stakeholders (producers, retailers, government, regulators and consumers). Consequently, the development of a 'responsible marketing strategy' (Comfort and Hillier 2006, p. 334) designed to 'communicate a responsible drinking message to consumers' is an example of the industry's response to socially responsible practice. However, whether this response is genuine, CSR or simply ethically and perhaps legally required action remains a contentious issue, especially for operators in the liquor and gaming industry.

The mentioned THE organizational response also raises debate regarding an appropriate definition for the CSR concept, hence the questions: what is CSR? How do THE organizations conceptualize? This ongoing debate is in part the result of calls that CSR is vague, subjective and intangible, and therefore does not allow for a universally applicable definition (Jones *et al.*, 2006). Organizations and THE enterprises have arrived at a variety of lenses to conceptualize, frame and action CSR strategies. In spite of this disparity and difference of opinions, there is considerable common ground between organizational views.

One assessment of CSR from a corporate perspective proposes the following definition: 'Corporate social responsibility is the commitment of business to contribute to sustainable economic development, working with employees, their families, the local community and society at large to improve their quality of life' (Holme and Watts, 2000, p. 10). Some definitions are based on the recognition that organizations should be equally interested in commercial success and the ability to evoke positive community impacts. This definitional approach reflects organizations' acting as 'good corporate citizens' where 'brands do good' and act beyond and in addition to the interests of the firm (McWilliams and Siegal, 2001). Thus, CSR may also relate to moral and ethical issues concerning corporate behaviour and decision making (Branco and Rodrigues, 2007). This definitional approach attests that organizations and society do not operate in a vacuum; instead, they are interwoven and integral to the communities in which they operate.

Using the definitions provided in conjunction with the Pyramid of Global CSR and Performance (see Carroll, 2004, p. 116), it can be concluded that CSR incorporates four primary responsibilities of social responsibility:

- Economic: fulfilling obligations related to global capitalism while enhancing profitability.
- Legal: following requirements by global stakeholders, in that organizations pursue economic and production activities while obeying the law.
- Ethical: addressing expectations by global stakeholders that organizations behave ethically.
- Philanthropic: voluntary roles assumed by companies, desired by global stakeholders; essentially, companies behaving like 'good citizens'.

These responsibilities are a useful way to begin to reflect on, frame and evaluate the degree to which THE organizations and their facilities engage in CSR. These responsibilities also provide a way in which CSR can be used as a stakeholder and as a contingency model in the organizational setting (Carroll, 2004). The following case study addresses the concept of 'corporate social enterprise' as a model where THE enterprises operate sustainably, effecting positive change in disadvantaged communities. Additionally, the case provides a context in which to apply Carroll's (1979) four primary areas of social responsibilities: economic, legal, ethical and discretionary.

Example: Streets International

According to its mission, Streets International (SI) 'is an innovative social enterprise with a purpose to develop and operate sustainable programmes for disadvantaged youth in South East Asia and throughout the world' (http://www.streetsinternational.org). SI's initiative is designed to match the resource demands of the growing hospitality/tourism sectors with the needs of disadvantaged youth. Further, it provides youth with training to prepare them for careers in culinary arts and hospitality service.

Asked to define CSR and the SI business model, Neal Bermas, chairman of SI responded 'it's a timely question and one we are all trying to figure out' (what is CSR?). SI, like other hospitality and non-hospitality enterprises are engaged in the discourse regarding how to frame, define and execute CSR. Importantly, Neal contends, 'definitional and philosophical debates should acknowledge and create an apparent distinction

(Continued)

Example. Continued.

between "corporate social enterprise" and "corporate social responsibility". This distinction is fundamental to the organization's business strategy and philosophy.'

One rationale for this distinction rests in Neal's concern that 'CSR is all too often a marketing ploy for corporate entities that want to seem as if they have better intentions than just return on equity or return on investment'. Consequently, one view is that what corporations do under the 'umbrella of CSR' should in fact just be a matter of course, an expectation based on the necessity for equity and fairness. So, 'Corporate social enterprise' is conceived of as organizations that have as one of their key criteria/objectives 'a return on social investment, where there is return for not just one individual'. Neal contends that social enterprise can be a not-for-profit or for-profit enterprise, indicating 'corporate social enterprise transparently incorporates both not-for and for-profit entities through their legal structure and business philosophy'.

Thus, SI's business model is described by Neal using the following metaphor, 'the parent company is a not-for-profit, the parent [company] owns the subsidiary entity which is SI Vietnam. In Vietnam we are organized as a for-profit enterprise; we have to pay to the extent that we profit, we have to pay taxes. Importantly, the profit goes back into the parent company, which in turn is re-invested into other similar programmes'.

Further, Neal recognizes the approach is one of many, but that in his view 'this is where our focus should be; this is where new ventures need to be happening'. The philosophy is one where the organization does good not to look good, but rather to do good. The organization's purpose is to 'create a sustainable enterprise that is self-supporting, with the primary business objective being to Improve, enhance and change the lives of deeply impoverished disadvantaged young adults'.

Neal's individual desire to assist disadvantaged Vietnamese youth was in part the result of his tourist travels to South East Asia. As he travelled, he came across 'street kid restaurants': 'we didn't invent that concept; however when I went to them, they were started by big-hearted people so that children from orphanages and disadvantage could learn basic kitchen skills, but I was also troubled in a way'. Troubled by the unknowing limitations that charitable operations placed on disadvantaged youth, Neal questions: 'why do we limit their possibilities to dishwashing and kitchen preparation?' Instead, SI's philosophy rests on the assumption that 'with greater expectation you can achieve a lot more' and that hospitality enterprise can be a vehicle through which dignity and choice can be brought to the lives of impoverished individuals and their families'.

Asked to reflect on the programme's structure, Neal alluded to providing life skills in conjunction with a professional hospitality skills programme. SI's vision is to 'bring dignity, choice and freedom to people who would ordinarily not have it'. The organization achieves its vision by providing housing and food, medical care and clothing, basic

(Continued)

Example. Continued.

elements necessary to work and link through to job skills and training. As SI is involved in the hospitality industry, English language training is central to the programme. Hospitality skills' training is seen as a way to increase the life and employment prospects for trainees. The programme has been successful: 'there was 100% employment within a month, in really the best hotels in our area'. Further, 'from an education/training perspective, when I put on my educator's hat, the underlying philosophy is if you expect a lot then you get a lot. And that a person's past does not predict their future potential. I think that especially applies to South East Asia, where children may have only completed the equivalent of the sixth grade because of their disadvantage, because they are so horribly disadvantaged and not because they don't have the potential'.

Source: http://www.streetsinternational.org

Questions and activities

1. Discuss the challenges associated with defining CSR.
2. What words and phrases would you use to define CSR?
3. Identify and critically discuss the difference between corporate social enterprise and corporate social responsibility. To what extent do you agree with this distinction? Discuss why or why not.
4. Discuss the business and legal model being used by SI. Reflect on the concepts 'for-profit' and 'not-for-profit' and how the two can be transparently applied to hospitality enterprises.
5. What other strategies or models could the organization initiate/trial to build and grow their current life skills and hospitality programme?

WHERE DOES CSR FIT INTO THE THE BUSINESS AGENDA?

In addition to definitional debates, significant discourse has emerged regarding the motivations and outcomes associated with an organization's CSR initiatives. Freeman's (1984) stakeholder framework assists with situating and understanding the mentioned definitional debates, theoretical arguments and pragmatic discussions around organizational CSR agendas to the extent that 'the stakeholder perspective has become something which is inescapable if one wants to discuss and analyse CSR' (Branco and Rodrigues, 2007, p. 5). Freeman's (1984) stakeholder theory posits that organizations have responsibilities for their stakeholders as well as other interest groups. Business's major stakeholders include consumers, employees, owners, the community, government, competitors and the natural environment. Increasingly, THE organizations are looking at ways to better manage their profit and cost-maximization philosophy as well as considering stakeholder expectations.

Thus, THE organizations execute CSR activities as part of their broader business strategy for various tangible and intangible benefits. Some of these benefits include improvements in the organization's corporate image/reputation, enhanced capacity leverage and positive stakeholder relationships, including with government and suppliers. Further, CSR is seen as an important component of the marketing/business development strategy. Being that CSR is increasingly embraced and valued by consumers, organizations consider CSR as a way to win favour and bolster positive consumer sentiment.

The role of CSR in reputation building, public relations and marketing has been contested, with some studies concluding that the CSR activities of many THE organizations are clever public relations and marketing ploys rather than a commitment to health, environment and social sustainability. In discussing CSR in the context of tourism and service enterprises, Henderson questions 'the depth of commitment and veracity of statements of intent and achievement which are often very general and not easily validated' (2007, p. 231). This issue raises the question of whether CSR activities portray that a company is 'doing good' as part of its marketing approach or because ethically and morally it is the right thing to do (Holcomb *et al.*, 2007). One further view is that organizations can initiate socially responsible activities that are ethical and altruistic while strategic and with clear commercial imperatives.

CSR AND THE FACILITIES AND ENTERPRISES

To date there is little academic literature exploring CSR in context of the THE industry. Part of the research conducted in this area emphasizes CSR through environmental management. Research by Holcomb *et al.* (2007) provides information regarding the motivations, nature and implementation of CSR initiatives by THE organizations. The purpose of the research was to investigate the degree to which hotels were engaged in socially responsible activities. The research concluded that overwhelmingly hotels were involved in 'some degree' of socially responsible activity: 80% of the top ten hotels reported activities such as community education programmes, humanitarian efforts, fundraising and environmental protection. Additionally, hotels reported activities related to human resourcing, diversity management and employee development and wellbeing programmes. Further, of the hotels studied, 40% featured CSR in their vision or mission statements. In spite of these reported findings, Holcomb *et al.* (2007) conclude that there was a disparity between the organization's ongoing strategy and what might be considered one-off activities. As a result, the motivation for CSR and the potential business case for CSR in the THE context will be explored in further detail.

FINANCIAL OUTCOMES

In some organizational settings, especially in the current uncertain economic climate, it is increasingly important to determine if CSR investment actually increases firm value and profitability. This necessity is also relevant to the hospitality industry (Kang *et al.*, 2010). Given that the bottom line (fundamental goal) for a commercial enterprise is to maximize its value, it has become an important consideration for companies to invest in CSR activities that achieve positive outcomes for the community but, more importantly, simultaneously maximize the firms' value and profitability. Thus, the motivation for and the process of evaluating CSR activities in THE and general business settings is not simplistic.

There is a potential tension between business and social goals, so how can seemingly competing goals and objectives be achieved? In order to answer this question one has to reconsider both the quantitative numerical financial returns associated with CSR together with the intangible or qualitative outcomes, which are inherently more difficult to measure and report. The application of the 'triple bottom line' is perhaps a more appropriate way to conceptualize, measure and report the potential and actual impacts of contemporary CSR.

Rodriguez and Cruz (2007) considered the CSR activities of hotel sites in Spain, while Jackson and Hua (2009) and Lee and Park (2009) investigated the relationship between organizational CSR initiatives and performance in a hospitality, gaming and lodging enterprise. The cases measured returns from CSR in the form of organizational profitability and performance. For hotels, a positive return was reported for profitability and performance; this was not the case for casinos, with no positive impact on either area of organizational performance. Research by Kang *et al.* (2010) further illustrates the difficulty of quantifying and measuring the outcomes of CSR, and with the inconclusive nature of CSR's actual and stated financial benefits, leading to the question: is it beneficial for the THE organization to invest in CSR? The answer, while not clear-cut, highlights the fact that the financial and revenue impacts for THE enterprises perhaps relate to variables such as which part of the industry they belong to and the sensitivities of the market they serve. Further, it could be argued that the hotel industry is more sensitive to CSR issues because of its relationship with the tourist product and the natural, economic, social and cultural environment (Rodriguez and Cruz, 2007). Henderson also considers the cost of CSR for organizations, inferring that 'while there is an assumption that CSR will lead to economic and non-monetary rewards, its direct effect on financial and other results is disputed' (2007, p. 230). Thus, understanding the presence or absence of financial returns highlights the need for THE organizations to better consider and execute their strategic decisions about CSR.

ENGAGEMENT, ORGANIZATIONAL OUTREACH AND SOCIAL CAPITAL

In addition to financial outcomes (frequently perceived as the primary reason for some commercial CSR agendas), organizations undertake CSR activities for philanthropic/altruistic reasons. CSR is an opportunity for organizations to engage communities providing a context in which they benefit from and contribute to the development of 'social capital'. This aspect is discussed by Clopton and Finch (2011), who emphasize the potential contribution of different organizations ('social anchors') in the creation and maintenance of social networks and community outreach. This point is relevant to THE facilities and event enterprise.

The symbolism of buildings, hotels, resorts and event venues can also act as a symbolic source of community. Regarding this aspect, Goodsell contends that physical infrastructure and architecture remind 'citizens that they belong to a comprehensive, organized polity' (1997, p. 92), and 'that they hold their citizenship in common' (1997, p. 92). Further, Macbeth *et al.* (2004) explored the role that regional tourism plays in social and community development. Their research explored the non-economic community outcomes, and the contribution that tourism-related organizations could make in addition to the usually reported financial/economic returns. Their approach recognized that 'the environments for regional tourism systems include the broader communities in which they operate and that these stakeholders should benefit and be engaged' (2004, p. 508). Further, they forwarded 'partnership' to bring about gains for organizations, government and community stakeholders. Another example considered the potential of tourism development in Cape York, Australia, where Bennett (2005) found that indigenous communities greatly benefit from the industry. Moreover, by managing with a CSR agenda there are significant gains for individuals, community and government. Remote indigenous communities can be strengthened at the same time as providing destinations with distinctive competitive advantages. The following case study will further discuss community outreach and the community as beneficiaries in the context of a hospitality facility in the north western suburbs of Sydney, Australia.

Example: Castle Hill RSL Club

The Castle Hill Club (CHC) can be traced back to 1932, when the 'Hills District Returned Sailors and Soldiers Club' was formed to assist World War I veterans and their families. Today the club is one of the premier hospitality and entertainment venues in the north western suburbs of Sydney, Australia. With a membership of 30,000, the mission of the organization is 'to provide members and the community with a modern and progressive community focussed club group that provides the best hospitality, gaming, sporting, entertainment and fitness/aquatic services and facilities' (http://www.castlehillrsl.com.au). Further, the organization's aim is to ensure that club members their families and friends consider the venue their first choice for entertainment, gaming, food, beverages, functions, sporting and fitness/aquatic needs.

Melanie Morson, marketing manager, reflected on the organization's role: 'clubs were established as a social environment, being a returned service men's club it's about connection, celebration and commemoration of the ANZAC (Australian and New Zealand Army) tradition'. In addition to commemoration of fallen and serving (defence force) personnel, CHC's membership philosophy is a welcoming environment for all. In order to achieve this end she reflects on community outreach and organizational leadership. Melanie reflects, 'the organization is a community club, community is at the heart of our brand'. Beyond brand and market positioning, 'giving back' is centrally important to CHC's business philosophy and daily operations.

(Continued)

Example. Continued.

Consequently, the organization's CSR agenda 'has not happened overnight, it has been an ongoing and lasting commitment and investment'. The organization has a yearly reporting structure and 5-year organizational plan; in both, key performance indicators are included relating directly to aspects of CSR and CHC's activities. Additionally, there is a keen emphasis placed on leadership, innovation and continuous improvement.

One example of this continuous improvement is the organization's school mentoring programme (Max Potential), whose goal is to 'maximize engagement with local communities through connections with the business community and young people'.

Industry leaders are encouraged to pass on their experience/values by working with secondary students to complete projects that benefit the community; the programme has positive outcomes for the individuals involved and the broader local community. The general manager's aspiration is that 'the next generation of organizational managerial and leadership staff will result from this programme and that the organization positively contributes to the creation and maintenance of a vibrant sustainable community'.

CHC's commitment to CSR and sustainability is evident in several other programmes. Melanie referred to CHC's role as a 'facilitator' and 'enabler'. In this way, the organization can be conceived of as a 'community anchor, a point where hospitality facility and community connect'. One example of this community anchoring is a yearly fundraising event called the Rattle 'n' Hum Car Show. The event is targeted at car enthusiasts and their families. All proceeds from the car show are donated to the Tallowood Special Needs School (the school provides educative and learning environments for children with multiple disabilities).

The event concept is a valuable example. First, the event idea was the result of the organization instilling in its employees a sense of service and community. The food and beverage manager approached senior managerial staff, he himself a car enthusiast with a desire to conduct an event with a philanthropic and altruistic purpose. Initiatives such as these illustrate CHC's overarching culture, with its staff being encouraged to become involved in outreach/community service activities. CHC's human resource philosophy is people-, wellbeing- and lifestyle-focused.

The fundraising event benefits the club with increased patronage, food/beverage sales and first-time visitation. Community events are hosted during what the club considers non-peak periods, so there are tangible and intangible outcomes. However, the marketing manager indicated these benefits were not the motivations for the event or the reason for the event. Second, the event is a practical example of the way the club acts as a 'community advocate, facilitator and supporter'. The organization funded and delivered the inaugural event. However, to assure the event's ongoing success and viability, the organization 'handed back' elements of the event organization and delivery to school and community partners.

(Continued)

> **Example.** Continued.
>
> This approach has resulted in the development of 'social capital', with community members developing new skills and sustainable long-term partnerships. Additionally, a sense of ownership and self-determination for stakeholders has resulted.
>
> *Source:* http://www.castlehillrsl.com.au

Themes

1. Discuss the economic and non-economic returns for organizations engaging in CSR initiatives.

2. Identify and discuss how organizations can implement CSR as part of their ongoing business strategy.

Question

1. What challenges and barriers could potentially impact on organizational achievement of CSR goals and objectives?

CSR COMPLIANCE: LEGAL VS VOLUNTARY

As previously discussed, industry and THE facilities struggle to find a clear line of distinction for what constitutes 'best practice' in terms of CSR. A further difference of opinion exists in relation to whether this practice should be compulsory, or whether it should remain the prerogative of the organization or industry concerned. Recently organizations in the THE sectors have considered strategies to audit, encourage and develop guidelines and expectations for the THE sectors' CSR activities. Overwhelmingly, in the hospitality and tourism industry these initiatives have been voluntary and include codes of conduct, best environmental practices, eco-labels, environmental management systems and environmental performance indicators (Ayuso, 2006).

To date, many THE organizations voluntarily report their CSR activities. One challenge with this approach rests with the potential tendency to overstate their involvement or, in the case of Comfort and Hillier's research on the pub industry, make 'aspirational statements that may not always be fully reflected in either strategic planning or in the everyday operations within a fiercely competitive business environment' (2006, p. 338).

One further approach to compliance is the auditing activity voluntarily undertaken by the Australian Business Events Sector (2009) as part of a project commissioned in partnership with the Australian government's Department of Tourism. The emphasis of the project was to strengthen Australia's global reputation in delivering world-class, sustainable events.

The report concluded that larger organizations were better able and more willing to engage in CSR activities. These findings illustrate the notable financial and time resources necessary to coordinate and maintain an ongoing CSR agenda. In fact, many organizations were reported to be unable to engage fully in the auditing and accreditation process because they did not have the human resources to meet the auditing administrative requirements. This was also found to be the case with the hotel and accommodation sector, with 'CSR-related performance reporting bringing logistical, technical, and attitudinal problems that need to be solved' (Bohdanowicz, 2007, p. 116). However, Bohdanowicz's (2007) research further concedes that hotel managers need to be assisted if they are to be more transparent in their operations leading to the benchmarking of performance in the sector.

In turn, the results also highlight a need to engage with smaller hospitality/tourism organizations to establish a programme of activity or support programmes and systems. Additionally, there also appears to be a lack of understanding of CSR and its potential role in the strategic and daily operations in medium to small organizations. However, this was not the case when considering Canadian tour operators: awareness was rated highly, but this was not reinforced with actionable goals and initiatives (Dodds and Kuehnel, 2010). The gap between awareness, required commitment and improvement was also identified by the Australian event sector project finding that good intentions are not always translated into practice.

Example: Trevi – the price of 'good citizenship'

Trevi Ristorante Bar and Lounge is located approximately 60 km west of Sydney's central business district. Trevi caters primarily for local residents, with some tourist trade. The local community boasts a very diverse cultural mix, and the clientele have high expectations: city quality at 'country' prices.

Recently renovated, Trevi has transformed itself to an award-winning venue. Angie Latty, Trevi's owner/manager, is the daughter of Italian immigrants and has seen both sides of her family operate businesses in the local area through her entire life. As a result, Angie developed a passion for Italian food, for commerce, a 'family' focus and a strong commitment and loyalty to the local community.

Frustrated with eating in tightly packed restaurants that seek to maximize table utilization, Angie has created a fine dining à la carte venue, where patrons have plenty of room and can spend the entire evening without any pressure to leave. Trevi keeps its prices below the local norm, without compromising quality, and creates opportunities for the local community to experience tapas and degustation evenings well below city prices.

Angie constantly seeks ways to support and work with the local community. For example, Trevi supports the local Tresillian Family Care Centre by providing families with patients staying in the Centre with discounted meals. Trevi also donates substantial gift vouchers

(Continued)

Example. Continued.

to local schools and charitable organizations, raising funds, sponsors 'opening night' functions for local theatre productions, subsidizes promotional events for new businesses starting up, and even helps advertise and promote charitable events being held at other local venues.

However, all these initiatives come at a cost. Indeed, according to Angie, Trevi could generate more revenue by 'squeezing' the tables into a smaller space and extending the (far more profitable) bar and cocktail area. Trevi could also increase its prices … but the ownership chooses not to.

Source: http://www.trevi.net.au/

Questions

1. How important is it for a small business to be a 'good citizen'?

2. Should a business like Trevi contribute to the local community, or should it simply work to maximize profits? Justify your answer.

3. What is the short-term gain and/or cost to the business of engaging in similar 'good citizen' practices? Long-term?

4. Which of the current business practices would you change? Why?

5. Do you see these practices as examples of CSR, or purely self-promotion, or some combination of both? Explain.

A further example of the movement towards a standards and accreditation approach can be seen when considering the Hotel and Catering International Management Association (HCIMA). The association is a management organization for managers in THE sectors and a registered charity with a worldwide membership covering all sectors of the industry, including hotels, restaurants, catering, pubs and clubs, as well as leisure outlets, theme parks and sports venues. Increasingly, the standards reflect aspects of CSR, including the addition of the following standard: 'a close look at "society results" – considering how a business impacts on its local environment, together with evidence of environmental responsibility'.

This CSR and environmental standards approach is further reflected in the global environmental certification programme for the travel and tourism industry, which was developed in 1996 by three international organizations: the World Travel and Tourism Council, the World Tourism Organization and the Earth Council (http://www.eyaprimo.ey.com/natlmktgaprimoey/Attachments/hospitality_insights_DF0052.pdf).

Question

1. Should it be mandatory for hospitality and/or other THE organizations to report their CSR activities?

SUMMARY

In spite of definitional debates, unclear expectations regarding the role of organizations in communities and scepticism around organizational efforts, CSR continues to grow in relevance. Consequently, THE sectors will be called on to conduct their operations in a way that acknowledges goals and objectives beyond return on investment and financial bottom lines. Consumers and employees alike are increasingly making purchase and employment decisions based on the organization's engagement with the community and business operations, which reflect heightened transparent socially acceptable moral, ethical and legal standards of practice. These community and associated stakeholder pressures have also highlighted the need to require that organizations audit and report their CSR commitment and associated activities. It is no longer business as usual; a paradigm shift is occurring in the way in which organizations and consumers expect that business be done.

Case Study

Penrith Panthers

Penrith Panthers, a National Rugby League (NRL) team located in Penrith, one of Sydney's suburbs, has been part of professional competition since 1967. The club has its own stadium; home games often attract more than 15,000 spectators. On game-days, the stadium offers a range of catering possibilities for spectators and fans. In addition, close to the stadium Penrith Panthers' licensed club features entertainment facilities and several restaurants. In the last decades, the suburb of Penrith has experienced substantial demographic changes. According to Penrith City Council (2010), in 1950, Penrith's population totalled around 15,000 residents; since then it has increased to 150,000 and it is estimated that by 2026 around 200,000 people will be living in what will probably become 'Penrith City'. Given the massive increase in population and resulting pressures on community, people and resources, the club has extended its involvement with the local community in several ways.

Shannon Donato, former Panthers athlete and currently club marketing manager, explains that a section of the club's stadium was used as a centre for individuals from the community to learn different skills. The site adjacent to one of the stadium's wings hosts a handful of members working for a community development foundation, 'Panthers on the prowl'. The foundation, established in 2002, includes class sport programmes for children identified by local school principals as potentially at risk of disengaging from school, or even from society. The site also serves as educational training for athletes who are considering professional alternatives after ending their professional playing career. 'Panthers on the prowl' is run through the club's support, as well as through external funding (grants).

(Continued)

Example. Continued.

One of the instructors mentions that the foundation's philosophy is to instil resilience, respect, as well as nurture care, strengthen personal relationships and promote excellence among children suffering from low self-esteem, lacking confidence or experiencing academic or behavioural issues.

The majority of these children will never play rugby professionally. So, why have Panthers embraced this form of CSR with no obvious gains in recruiting future players? Mr Donato points out that when a club asks for the support of the local community, the club must also be prepared to 'give' something back in return. In addition, given the popularity and importance of rugby league, and that of other professional sports, increasingly sport organizations are expected to be socially responsible in any way they can. In the case of Panthers, Mr Donato indicates that the club is seen as a leader in the suburb, even beyond its role of providing competitive sport performances and high-quality entertainment. Thus, for Panthers' management it is sensible to address such expectations in ways that are beneficial and that make a positive impact.

Despite the challenges of obtaining external funding, to date the skills programmes 'Panthers on the prowl' offers have resulted in many positive outcomes. For example, over the years the club has received letters from parents and from children showing their appreciation. Some of the instructors also explain that they have seen a deep change among many children, many of whom now display higher self-esteem, communicate better and use the word 'respect' more often as they exit the programme. With increasing needs, 'Panthers on the prowl' is broadening its scope, also offering adult literacy programmes, information technology skills to young people and adults, outdoor activities to help build social skills among both primary and secondary school children.

Source: http://www.penrithpanthers.com.au/

Questions

1. Discuss and elaborate on the implications of conducting community-based initiatives of this kind at the organization's premises, including the symbolic value in doing so.

2. Look for additional cases of other professional sport clubs, as well as THE operations that also hold these community-based programmes at their 'physical' premises.

3. Discuss the potential benefits (i.e. intangible) for Penrith Panthers in being involved in their community-based initiatives.

4. Given the current popularity or increasing endorsement of CSR initiatives, to what extent do you see hospitality, catering, event, sport and similar organizations becoming involved in such initiatives in years to come? Please discuss your answer thoroughly.

GLOSSARY OF TERMS USED IN THIS CHAPTER

Corporate philanthropy

The approach where organizations return a percentage of the firm's profits back to the community (Seifert *et al.*, 2003).

Corporate social responsibility (CSR)

'Corporate social responsibility is the commitment of business to contribute to sustainable economic development, working with employees, their families, the local community and society at large to improve their quality of life' (Holme and Watts, 2000, p. 10). Consequently, CSR sees organizations embrace business/organizational activity that focuses on accomplishments in the economic and the social sphere. In this way, organizational goals and objectives consist of financial/profit imperatives as well as social goals and programmes.

Social capital

A theoretical framework forwarded by sociologists that intellectualizes the potential positive influence that social networks can have for the betterment of the individual citizen and more broadly society at large, 'social capital stands for the ability of actors (individuals and collectives) to secure benefits by virtue of membership in social networks or other social structures' (Portes, 1998, p. 6). While historically emphasis has been placed on financial capital, more recently there has been a greater emphasis placed on the intangible social, cultural civic investments and associated outcomes.

Stakeholder

Any group or individual who is affected by or can affect the achievement of an organization's goals and objectives (Freeman, 1984).

REFERENCES AND ADDITIONAL READING

Australia's Business Events Sector (2009) National corporate social responsibility (CSR) audit for Australia's business events sector, pp. 1–20. Available at: http://www.businessevents.australia.com/Assets/Australia_National_CSR_Audit_Report_FINAL.pdf (accessed 20 July 2011).

Ayuso, S. (2006) Adoption of voluntary environmental tools for sustainable tourism: analysing the experience of Spanish hotels. *Corporate Social Responsibility and Environmental Management* 13, 207–220.

Bennett, M.A. (2005) Indigenous entrepreneurship, social capital and tourism enterprise development: lessons from Cape York. PhD thesis, La Trobe University, Victoria, Australia.

Bohdanowicz, P. (2007) A case study of the Hilton environmental reporting as a tool for corporate social responsibility. *Tourism Review International* 11, 115–131.

Branco, M. and Rodrigues, L. (2007) Positioning stakeholder theory within the debate on corporate social responsibility. *Electronic Journal of Business Ethics and Organization Studies* 12, 6–15.

Burke, L. and Logsdon, J.M. (1996) How corporate social responsibility pays off. *Long Range Planning* 29, 495–502.

Carroll, A.B. (1979) A three-dimensional conceptual model of corporate social performance. *Academy of Management Review* 4, 497–505.

Carroll, A.B. (2004) Managing ethically with global stakeholders: a present and future challenge. *Academy of Management Executive* 18, 114–120.

Clopton, A.W. and Finch, B.L. (2011) Re-conceptualizing social anchors in community development: utilizing social anchor theory to create social capital's third dimension. *Community Development* 42, 70–83.

Comfort, P. and Hillier, D. (2006) Reporting and reflecting on corporate social responsibility in the hospitality industry: a case study of pub operators in the UK. *International Journal of Contemporary Hospitality Management* 18, 329–340.

Dodds, R. and Kuehnel, J. (2010) CSR among Canadian mass tour operators: good awareness but little action. *International Journal of Contemporary Hospitality Management* 22, 221–244.

Goodsell, C.T. (1997) Public architecture as social anchor in the post-modern age. *Public Voices* 3, 89–97.

Grossman, S.J. and Stiflitz, J.E. (1977) On value maximisation and alternative objectives of the firm. *The Journal of Finance* 32, 389–402.

Freeman, R. (1984) Strategic management: a stakeholder approach. *Advances in Strategic Management* 1, 31–60.

Henderson, J.C. (2007) Corporate social responsibility and tourism: hotel companies in Phuket, Thailand, after the Indian Ocean tsunami. *Hospitality Management* 26, 228–239.

Holcomb, J.L., Upchurch, R.S. and Okumus, F. (2007) Corporate social responsibility: what are top hotel companies reporting? *International Journal of Contemporary Hospitality Management* 19, 461–475.

Holme, R. and Watts, P. (2000) Corporate social responsibility: making good business sense. Available at: http://www.wbcsd.org/web/publications/csr2000.pdf (accessed 2 August 2011).

Jackson, L. and Hua, N. (2009) Corporate social responsibility and financial performance: a snapshot from the lodging and gaming industries. *Journal of Hospitality Financial Management* 17, article 4.

Jensen, M. (2001) Value maximisation, stakeholder theory and the corporate objective function. *European Financial Management* 7, 297–314.

Jensen, M. (2002) Value maximisation, stakeholder theory, and the corporate objective function. *Business Ethics Quarterly* 12, 335–356.

Jones, P., Comfort, D. and Hillier, D. (2006) Reporting and reflecting on corporate social responsibility in the hospitality industry: a case study of pub operators in the UK. *International Journal of Contemporary Hospitality Management* 18, 329–340.

Kang, K., Lee, S. and Huh, C. (2010) Impacts of positive and negative corporate social responsibility activities on company performance in the hospitality industry. *International Journal of Hospitality Management* 29, 72–82.

Lee, S. and Heo, C. (2009) Corporate social responsibility and customer satisfaction among US publicly traded hotels and restaurants. *International Journal of Hospitality Management* 28, 635–637.

Lee, S. and Park, S. (2009) Do socially responsible activities help hotel and casino achieve their financial goals? *International Journal of Hospitality Management* 28, 105–112.

Macbeth, J., Carson, D. and Northcote, J.K. (2004) Social capital, tourism and regional development: SPCC as a basis for innovation and sustainability. *Current Issues in Tourism* 7, 502–522.

Makaros, A. and Zehavi, T. (2008) Corporate social responsibility to the community: a process-oriented model for contractual relations. *Community Development: Journal of the Community Development Society* 39, 40–50.

Margolis, J.D. and Walsh, J.P. (2001) *People and Profits? The Search for a Link between a Company's Social and Financial Performance.* Lawrence Erlbaum, Mahwah, New Jersey.

McWilliams, A. and Siegal, D. (2001) Corporate social responsibility: a theory of the firm perspective. *The Academy of Management Review* 26, 117–127.

Penrith City Council (2010) Population and household forecasts. Available at: http://forecast2.id.com.au/default.aspx?id=247&pg=5000 (accessed 20 November 2010).

Portes, A. (1998) Social capital: its origins and applications in modern sociology. *Annual Review of Sociology* 24, 1–25.

Putnam, R.D. (1995) Bowling alone: America's declining social capital. *Journal of Democracy* 6, 65–78.

Rodriguez, F.J.G. and Cruz, Y.D.M.A. (2007) Relation between social–environmental responsibility and performance in hotel firms. *International Journal of Hospitality Management* 26, 824–839.

Salzmann, O., Ionescu-Somers, A. and Steger, U. (2005) The business case for corporate sustainability: literature review and research options. *European Management Journal* 23, 27–36.

Seifert, B., Morris, S. and Bartkus, B. (2003) Comparing big givers and small givers: financial correlates of corporate philanthropy. *Journal of Business Ethics* 45, 195–211.

chapter 10

Sustainable Facilities Design and Management

Michael Conlin
Okanagan College

LEARNING OBJECTIVES

Having completed this chapter, readers should:

- have an understanding of the concept of sustainable development and how it applies to the tourism, hospitality and events (THE) sector – this understanding will include the more practical aspects of sustainable development as they impact on facilities design and management;
- have an appreciation for the relative 'newness' of sustainability to our lives generally and the THE sector specifically – this appreciation will include the ramifications of the concept's 'newness' in terms of application of its principles and practices to the sector;
- know the history of the development of sustainable development and, in particular, which the major influencers were and are on its application to the sector – this is important since they are still among the leaders in the field as it relates to the sector;
- be familiar with the principal elements and terminology of sustainable development that impact on facilities design and management;
- be aware of the future trends in sustainable facilities design and management.

INTRODUCTION

This chapter introduces what is arguably the most important factor now influencing the design and management of facilities in the THE sector, namely sustainable development. Sustainable development, notwithstanding being a fairly recent consideration for the THE sector, has now become an integral strategic factor impacting not only facilities but also all of the other functional areas of THE management, including marketing, finance and human resources. This chapter will introduce the concept of sustainable development generally and the next three chapters will focus on key areas within sustainable development and management, namely the management of the environment, corporate social responsibility and ethics, and finally energy and waste management. The four chapters combined will provide a comprehensive overview of the concept of sustainability and the key elements that developers, owners, operators and managers need to focus on with respect to sustainable design and management.

This chapter will examine sustainable development in the THE sector from the perspective of its history, imperatives and current state in three sections, which will discuss the:

- origin and growth of sustainable development in the THE sector;
- motivators for developers, owners and operators of THE facilities to adopt sustainable policies and practices;
- current state of sustainable design and management in the THE sector.

The general overview of sustainable facilities design and management in this chapter will provide the foundation for a more detailed examination of the key elements in the sustainable agenda for the THE sector in the next three chapters.

THE ORIGIN AND GROWTH OF SUSTAINABLE DEVELOPMENT IN THE THE SECTOR

The term sustainable development first gained widespread use and understanding in the late 1980s, when the United Nations World Commission on Environment and Development, more commonly known as the Brundtland Commission, published its report and discussed a wide range of issues impacting on the environment and development, and concluded that 'Sustainable development is development that meets the needs of the present without compromising the ability of future generations to meet their own needs' (Our Common Future, n.d.). In the more than 20 years since the Brundtland Commission provided this generic definition of sustainable development, the concept has evolved and been adapted and adopted by virtually all economic sectors, including the THE sector.

Activity

1. Using online secondary research, investigate the evolution of the definition of sustainable development in the THE sector since the Brundtland Commission developed its generic definition in the late 1980s.

2. Examine several major hotel company websites and identify their definition of sustainable development, usually found in their vision and mission statements or statements of commitment to sustainability. Compare and contrast several of these corporate definitions.

Sustainability is a relatively new concept for the THE sector

The pervasiveness of sustainability as an issue for virtually all aspects of contemporary life masks the fact that it is a relatively new issue for society in general and business in particular. In order to fully understand sustainability, it is important to put it into a historical context. It is only within the past 40 years that the concept has achieved any level of importance in the THE sector and indeed, it is fair to say that for the industry, it has only been a major consideration with wide-ranging impact on all areas of THE business since the early 1990s. As a result, many in the industry are still learning about the concept and how to adopt its standards and practices and how to take advantage of its opportunities and meet its challenges at a time when the concept itself is constantly evolving. It may appear that sustainable development in the THE sector is a mature concept embraced by all THE constituencies, but that would overlook the evolving nature of the concept, the rapidly changing technologies supporting sustainable design and management and the extent to which it has become an accepted component of THE facilities management.

Much of the early impetus to adopt sustainable development in the THE sector came from developers and operators in the ecotourism niche. Their early adoption reflected the initial focus of the sustainable agenda on issues directly related to environmental degradation and conservation. Ecotourism, defined in 1990 by The International Ecotourism Society (2011) as 'Responsible travel to natural areas that conserves the environment and improves the well-being of local people', was in its essence a form of tourism that depended on facilities that encompassed sustainable design. One such initiative in this regard is the Maho Bay Camps developed by Stanley Selengut in the mid 1970s. Many of the facilities design concepts now commonly seen in sustainable development were initially incorporated into Selengut's pioneering property. As the vignette below illustrates, even in the early 1990s, 15 years after the resort was founded, many of those concepts were considered to be radical departures from what was then conventional THE facilities design, construction and management. Indeed, many in the industry were sceptical of the chances for success of this type of facility and the examples of eco-resorts failing due to location, lack of market acceptance and mismanagement all seemed to support this perspective. This somewhat dubious track record continues to this day, highlighting the challenges of developing such properties and particularly challenges relating to the raising of capital (CNN, 2010).

Example: Maho Bay Camps, St John, US Virgin Islands

In 1992, the author had the pleasure of spending a few days with Stanley Selengut during a trip to the Pampas region of Venezuela. Mr Selengut described his tourism property on the US Virgin Islands, Maho Bay Camps, which he founded in 1976, and elaborated on the environmentally friendly concepts and practices that distinguished his eco-resort from other Caribbean destinations. Given the state of sustainability at that time, Stanley's property seemed somewhat strange and limited in its appeal to the travelling public. His guests stayed in tent cottages, which were structures made from recycled and renewable materials with only basic amenities. Guests shared bathrooms, had no air conditioning and the complex was connected by wooden walkways to protect the landscape from the traffic of visitors' feet.

However, Stanley's notion of an eco-resort has continued to attract a dedicated following of tourists interested in sustainability and the environment. As a result, Maho Bay Camps has become highly successful and has continued to grow and expand, all the while adhering to strict principles of sustainable development and management. The property utilizes 'site-sensitive techniques that preserve, protect, and even enhance the fragile eco-system of the island' (Maho Bay Camps, 2011), including elevated wooden walkways, recycled building materials, rainwater collection, low-flow and low-flush plumbing systems, the use of 'grey water' for irrigation, extensive composting and a very comprehensive, reduce, re-use and recycle programme for dealing with waste. The latest tent cottages operate completely on renewable technologies including, for example, hand pumps to provide water pressure in each unit.

The resort has benefited from extensive publicity since its inception and has won many awards for its pioneering work on sustainable development and operation. Its webpage lists over 70 major awards and other forms of recognition, with the first award being in 1984. And while much of the recognition of Maho Bay Camps has dated from the early 2000s, mirroring the recent rise in consciousness of the industry and travellers to environmental issues and the concept of sustainability, the property was recognized as a leader in the advancement of sustainable development in the 1990s. The United Nations Commission on Sustainable Development in 1999, in a report prepared by the World Travel and Tourism Council (WTTC) and the International Hotel and Restaurant Association, recognized a number of tourism destinations and properties as champions of sustainability, one of which was Maho Bay Camps. Importantly, the recognition was based not just on the property's sustainable facilities design, but also on the operator's involvement of the local community in the venture and its celebration of local culture, a more comprehensive adoption of the principles first put forth in the Brundtland Commission's definition of sustainable development (UN Department of Economic and Social Affairs, 1999).

Source: Maho Bay Camps (2011)

The rapid growth of interest of the general public, governments, trade associations and socially responsible companies has in the past few years moved knowledge of and commitment to sustainable development and management from what used to be considered highly specialized niches in the sector, most notably ecotourism and its specialized facilities as discussed above, into the mainstream of facilities management, albeit at varying levels of commitment. The widespread adoption by both large and small operators of sustainable practices in the management of facilities, the most ubiquitous example being the re-use of linens and towels by guests, is an indication of the industry's growing awareness of the importance of the environment for the sector. What will really signal the industry's major commitment to sustainability, however, is the extent to which new construction and major renovations of existing facilities adopt the wide range of new sustainable technology for both exterior and interior building systems.

Activity

1. There are now many eco-resorts around the world. Using the internet, identify several that adopt different and contrasting aspects of sustainability as their strategy.
2. Which of those you identify have the most impact on the environment and why?

Sustainable development in THE education and training

A measure of the growth of sustainable development can be drawn from a historical analysis of the educational and training support material for the THE sector and the extent to which it deals with the concept and its application. With respect to facilities management, the education and training of operators and managers in the sector illustrates how new the concept is. Richard Penner's book about conference centres was published over 20 years ago (1991). In his comprehensive survey of the types of conference centres and an extensive discussion of design considerations, the Cornell Hotel School professor makes no specific mention of environmental and sustainable design and management issues. Six years later in 1997, in the widely respected book on hospitality facilities management by Frank Borsenik of the University of Nevada at Las Vegas and Alan Stutts of the University of Houston, sustainability barely merits any mention (1997). Some discussion in the book's Preface mentions environmental concerns and the authors do touch on sustainable development and the opportunities presented by solar and geothermal energy in their chapter on energy management systems. They also touch briefly on concerns about the environment and the evolving nature of corporate social responsibility in the context of sustainability as well as techniques and practices such as the use of bulk dispensing of amenities in their chapter on waste and pollution management. However, in an exhaustive 40-page glossary of key terms relating to the design and management of THE facilities, not a single term relates directly to environmental or sustainable design or management.

By comparison, in the third edition of David Stipanuk's highly regarded book on hospitality facilities management published in 2006, one of the 14 chapters is titled 'Environmental and Sustainability Management'. In this chapter, Stipanuk, who is also a professor at the

Cornell Hotel School, discusses the origins of the environmental movement as it impacts on the hospitality industry and on the motivations for owners and operators to adopt design and management practices that are supportive of a sustainable agenda. Stipanuk discusses a range of ideas for managing facilities sustainably that are based, for the most part, on the WTTC's Agenda 21 for the Travel and Tourism Industry (2006, pp. 88–112).

Now, over 20 years since the publication of Penner's pioneering work on conference centre design, the present book includes four chapters focusing on sustainability, including one that discusses corporate social responsibility and ethics and the role they play in motivating operators to adopt sustainable agendas. Like sustainable development, corporate social responsibility is a relatively new concept for business generally and the THE sector in particular. Both concepts have been critical to each other's growth in importance and relevance to the THE sector.

As the above discussion illustrates, educational and training material focusing directly on THE facilities design and management has increasingly recognized the growing impact and importance of sustainability. The same, however, cannot be said for educational material for future THE departmental and general managers. These texts and other support materials have been slow to include sustainability as a key component of management curricula. For example, in the fifth edition of O'Fallon and Rutherford's text *Hotel Management and Operations* (2011), environmental design is considered only in the context of how safety and security issues impact on facilities design. The issue of sustainable design is not even mentioned. Indeed, in an extensive discussion of the hotel development process (pp. 6–14) beginning at the initial development stage and continuing through feasibility studies, determination of ownership and franchise structures, and the selection of architects and general contractors, there is not a single mention of environmental or sustainable development issues, objectives or practices. The now fairly ubiquitous 'green' influence on design, construction and management of facilities is not mentioned at all.

The emergence of sustainable development as a key issue for the THE sector traced through these important publications mirrors what can be seen in the industry. Some developers and operators outside the ecotourism niche began to adopt environmental and sustainability policies and practices in the 1990s, but it was not until the past decade that the industry began to push the sustainable development agenda in a major way. None the less, the progress of a sustainability agenda in the THE sector is dependent in part on the commitment of future leaders and managers to its principles (Barber *et al.*, 2011).

Activity

1. Examine the extent to which the programme you are enrolled in incorporates sustainability into its curriculum.
2. What sustainable topics not present currently would you recommend to be included in the curriculum?
3. How much weight should THE programmes devote to sustainable development and management?

Pioneering industry association initiatives in sustainable development

Some in the THE sector began to recognize as early as the 1970s that environmental issues were an important consideration for the future of the sector. In the early 1970s, the American Hotel and Lodging Association created a committee to examine the impact of the industry on the environment with the objective of developing policies and practices designed to ameliorate negative consequences of tourism on the environment (Stipanuk, 2006, pp. 83–84). This pioneering achievement has now grown into a comprehensive programme of policy making, certification schemes and educational programmes all designed to enhance the sustainability of the hospitality industry. In doing so, the American Hotel and Lodging Association has been both a pioneer and a major champion of sustainable development and management for the industry.

The WTTC, arguably the most important business association representing the industry on a global scale, has for the past 20 years provided leadership on environmental and sustainable management. Following the Earth Summit in Rio de Janeiro in June 1992, the WTTC in partnership with the Earth Council and the World Tourism Organization (WTO) developed Agenda 21 for the Travel and Tourism Industry. Modelled on the Earth Summit's Agenda 21, it provides a comprehensive list of issues and criteria for design, development and management of tourism facilities consistent with sustainable objectives (Wagner, n.d.). Indeed, it can be argued that this document provided the foundation for the adoption of sustainability by the industry over the past 20 years. In his chapter on environmental and sustainable development, the majority of Stipanuk's discussion focuses on the application of the Agenda to the industry and, in particular, its impact on facilities design and management (2006, pp. 88–112). As the following list demonstrates, the Agenda addresses all of the major elements in the environmental and sustainability arena and, as Stipanuk notes, they all impact on facilities design, construction and management.

Agenda 21 for the Travel and Tourism Industry

Priority Area 1: waste minimization.
Objective: to minimize resource inputs, maximize product quality, and minimize waste outputs.
Priority Area 2: energy conservation and management.
Objective: to reduce energy use and reduce potentially damaging atmospheric emissions.
Priority Area 3: management of fresh water resources.
Objective: to protect the quality of water resources and to use existing resources efficiently and equitably.
Priority Area 4: wastewater management.
Objective: to minimize wastewater outputs in order to protect the aquatic environment, to safeguard flora and fauna, and to conserve and protect the quality of fresh water resources.

(Continued)

Continued.

Priority Area 5: hazardous substances.
Objective: to replace products containing potentially hazardous substances with more environmentally benign products.
Priority Area 6: transport.
Objective: to reduce or control harmful emissions into the atmosphere and other environmental effects of transport.
Priority Area 7: land use planning and management.
Objective: to deal with the multiple demands on land in an equitable manner, ensuring that development is not visually intrusive and contributes to conserving environment and culture while generating income.
Priority Area 8: involving staff, customers and communities in environmental issues.
Objective: to protect and incorporate the interests of communities in developments and to ensure that the environmental lessons learned by staff, customers and communities are put into practice at home.
Priority Area 9: design for sustainability.
Objective: to ensure that new technologies and products are designed to be less polluting, more efficient, socially and culturally appropriate, and available worldwide.
Priority Area 10: partnerships for sustainable development.
Objective: to form partnerships to bring about long-term sustainability.

Source: Stipanuk (2006, p. 89)

Following closely on the heels of Agenda 21 for the Travel and Tourism Industry, the WTTC developed the first sustainable development and management certification programme for the industry, Green Globe, in the early 1990s. The programme enjoyed early success and by 1995 there were 350 members in 74 countries. Early adopters of the Green Globe programme introduced sustainable elements into THE properties that are now widely used, including bulk purchasing and dispensing of amenities, energy-saving technologies, comprehensive recycling programmes, and the now ubiquitous practice of giving guests the option of re-using linens and towels instead of what had been the industry standard of laundering every item after one use. One example of these early adopters was the Hotel Kurrajong in Canberra, Australia, one of the first properties in Australia to join the programme.

Example: The Hotel Kurrajong, Canberra, Australia

The Hotel Kurrajong was constructed in the 1920s, when Canberra was being developed as the new capital of Australia. Its original purpose was to house politicians during sessions of the Australian Parliament at a time when very little residential accommodation existed in the new city. As the country grew, so did Canberra and the Hotel's original purpose as

(Continued)

Example. Continued.

a dormitory for politicians changed to that of a more conventional hotel. In the decades after the Second World War, the property struggled to continue as a hotel, then as office space for the expanding Australian Federal Government. Eventually, it fell into disrepair and was essentially abandoned in the 1980s. However, as an historic protected property it could not be demolished and through a partnership between the various relevant governments and the Canberra Institute of Technology, the property was restored as a hotel and a hotel school in the early 1990s.

Part of the restoration included a commitment to sustainability, not just in terms of design or construction, but in terms of management. When the newly restored Hotel Kurrajong opened in 1995, it became one of the first hotels in Australia to earn certification from the WTTC's Green Globe. As one of the early members of the programme, the Hotel foreshadowed many of the sustainability practices that the industry now considers commonplace, including bulk packaging of toiletries, low-flow water fixtures, dual flush toilets, comprehensive recycling including a worm farm, and giving guests the option of 'recycling' towels and bed linen. It is an indication of just how far the sustainability movement has come in the past 20 years that these simple practices, which were considered quite radical in the mid-1990s, are now commonplace throughout much of the industry.

Some 20 years after the Rio Summit and the subsequent publication by the WTTC of Agenda 21 for the Travel and Tourism Industry, it is clear that sustainable design and management of THE facilities and indeed, the overall management of business in the THE sector, is now compelled by various elements of the sustainability agenda. Whether it is the marketplace, the advances in sustainable design and technology, the constraints of governments and other regulating bodies, the commitment of developers, owners, operators and managers to sustainability or what is more likely these days, a well thought-through business plan incorporating all of these elements, there is plenty of motivation for developers, owners, operators and managers to adopt a sustainable agenda.

Example: The David L. Lawrence Convention Center

The David L. Lawrence Convention Center opened in 2003 in Pittsburgh, Pennsylvania, USA and was widely recognized as the first 'green' conference and events centre. It is the only centre that has achieved Gold LEED Certification and through its sustainability programme, called 'g1', the centre incorporates virtually all large and small sustainable management practices and particularly those associated with 'green' meetings practices. Almost 10 years after its opening, the centre continues as a leader in the green meetings movement and as a platform for exhibiting sustainable management practices in the meetings and events sector.

Source: http://www.pittsburghcc.com/cc

MOTIVATION FOR ADOPTING SUSTAINABLE DESIGN AND MANAGEMENT

Developers, owners, operators and managers increasingly have a sense that sustainable facilities design and management are important to business success. The extent to which sustainable practices have become commonplace in the THE sector all attest to this. The practices that seemed non-conventional at Maho Bay Camps and at the Hotel Kurrajong some 15 and 30 years ago are now commonplace throughout the industry. Stipanuk (2006) summarized the various elements that influenced the sector to adopt sustainability into four categories: the marketplace; the legislative and regulatory environment; economic factors; and corporate social responsibility.

The next three chapters will address these motivators in varying levels of detail. However, the following discussion will focus on two overarching issues relating to motivation. The first is that no matter what the challenges are in determining what the marketplace wants and is prepared to pay for, they have now been largely superseded by the widespread adoption of a sustainable management agenda. The second is that the legislative and regulatory environment may compel rather than motivate developers and owners particularly to adopt a sustainable agenda with respect to sustainable design of facilities.

The impact of the marketplace

The degree to which people value sustainable development is influenced by a wide range of factors, including age, gender, education and wealth (Wong and Wan, 2011). Research into the factors that motivate an interest in environmental issues and a commitment to sustainability, as reviewed by Wong and Wan, confirm what many developers, owners, operators and managers have come to understand about sustainability in the past decade. Younger, well educated and relatively well-off tourists, and particularly women, appear to be more likely to be concerned about environmental issues and sustainable development. However, most of the research into consumer motivations about sustainability is generic in its perspective and simply provides some general sense of what factors are important. The challenge for developers and operators in the THE sector continues to be determining the extent to which sustainability impacts on the various source markets for THE facilities and services.

Part of that challenge for the industry is the historical impact of ecotourism and its continuing growth on sustainability. In her analysis of data relating to Americans' interest in environmental issues in general, Guber (2003) concluded that most people were concerned about sustainability but that, for the most part, they weren't actively concerned. This may have changed since then, and the marketplace may now be a more compelling factor for the industry to embrace sustainability than at any other time in recent history. In addition, a company's commitment to sustainability and its use of sustainable business practices will be critical to attracting and retaining qualified employees (Murray and Ayoun, 2011; Stephens, 2011).

Clearly, based on the growing success of properties such as the Maho Bay Camps, there is a sector that values environmentally sound and sustainably managed THE destinations and facilities.

But to what extent do these values carry over to the larger and more traditional travelling sectors? And perhaps a more compelling question is – does it matter anymore? The apparent growth of interest in the environment by the travelling public has motivated most major operators in the THE sector to incorporate varying levels of sustainable design and management into their facilities and the management of their businesses. An examination of the corporate websites of virtually any of the major international hotel companies, tour operators, and events and conference venues will find at the very least, a statement of the company's environmental and sustainability commitment. Many of them go further and actively promote themselves based on a sustainable agenda. Early adopters, such as Aitken Spence plc in Colombo, Sri Lanka, began promoting their sustainability agenda more than two decades ago. Its current sustainable agenda is an excellent example of a company that has gone beyond a superficial adoption of industry-wide sustainable practices to the point where sustainability is part of everything the company does. J.M.S. Brito, the company's CEO puts it this way:

> Our integrated sustainability policy is, in effect, a proactive long term strategy that allows us to address issues that may affect future viability, right now; ensuring that we are here today, here tomorrow. Today, all of our employees know that in the final equation, our commitment to sustainability makes strong business sense – by building long term value for our shareholders. (Aitken Spence plc, 2011)

Marriott is promoting sustainability as part of its meetings and events facilities and services. As part of this commitment, Marriott requires all of its event operations and sales managers to complete its 'Green Planners' programme (Marriott, 2011). Fairmont Hotels & Resorts was one of the first major hotel management companies to begin adopting a sustainable agenda and is now fully committed to the concept. The company fully embraces sustainability in its energy, water and waste management practices, and its 'Green Partnership Program', which is a comprehensive corporate-wide scheme of sustainable policies and practices, dates back to 1990 (Fairmont Hotels & Resorts, 2011).

Example: EC & O Venues

EC & O Venues is a major English-based conference and events centre operator. Its two signature properties are the internationally renowned Earls Court Exhibition Centre and Olympia Conference Centre, both located in London, UK. According to Nigel Nathan, the Group Managing Director, the company has pursued an increasingly aggressive policy toward sustainable development and management over the past decade and is now a leader in the field. Their properties were the first ones to receive certification to the UK BS8901 sustainable event management system and the company is involved with the formation of the international ISO20121 standard for sustainable event management.

Sources: http://www.eco.co.uk/content/uploads/files/Sustainability_Report_2011_web.pdf
http://www.bsigroup.co.uk/en/Assessment-and-Certification-services/Management-systems/Standards-and-Schemes/BS-8901

All of these companies are now committed in varying degrees to sustainable development. Many base this commitment on the marketplace, which may or may not be supportable. But the reality now is that the competitive stance of most major operators compels companies to embrace sustainability.

Activity

1. What elements in hotel property design do you feel are part of the sustainable development movement?

2. Would you be prepared to pay more for a hotel room that incorporates sustainable design elements? If yes, how much more and why? If not, why not?

The impact of the legislative and regulatory environment

Another motivator that will accelerate the adoption of sustainability in the THE sector is the extent to which legislative and regulatory factors increasingly require the inclusion of sustainable elements into THE facilities design and management. One obvious example of this is the worldwide trend on the part of governments to ban the use of incandescent light bulbs in favour of more energy efficient compact fluorescent lamps (CFLs). The impact of this for the THE sector is that operators will now be required in jurisdictions where the use of CFLs are mandated to use the more costly lamps and hopefully recoup the investment and higher initial costs through reduced energy consumption.

A more fundamental example of the impact of regulation for the THE sector is the extent to which building codes are increasingly mandating inclusion of sustainable design elements. This is best illustrated by the integration of what the United States Green Building Council (USGBC) calls 'commercial green building practices' into the building codes of states, municipalities and other jurisdictions in the USA. As of May 2011, for example, the USGBC reported that more than 40 jurisdictions in the USA had incorporated the Leadership in Energy and Environmental Design (LEED) system of building certification into their private sector building codes (USGBC, 2011, p. 6). In addition, several states and municipalities have adopted standardized building codes that now address environmental and sustainable development issues to a much greater extent than in the past. California and the City of New York are examples of this progress:

> Foreshadowing these efforts, California kicked off 2010 with the much-anticipated launch of its Green Building Standards Code. Its mandatory code will affect all new buildings in the State and, as such, is a remarkable step forward for most buildings in the state that had not previously been required to address this more holistic set of risks to human and environmental health. In New York City, the Urban Green Council (USGBC's local affiliate) released arguably the most comprehensive analysis and set of recommendations for the incremental greening of any building code. The work of NYC's Green Codes Task force, established by Mayor Michael Bloomberg and the New York City Council, mirrors a national trend of communities taking action to address today's pressing economic, environmental and community health issues. (USGBC, 2011, p. 7)

These examples illustrate the changing development perspective relating to building codes that will impact on all private sector facilities development, including the THE sector. The reality for developers, owners and operators is that sustainable facilities design will undoubtedly become an increasingly larger part of any business decision in the future regardless of their commitment to the sustainability agenda.

THE CURRENT STATE OF SUSTAINABLE DESIGN

In the 40 or so years since the THE sector began to take notice of environmental and sustainable development issues, several conclusions can be drawn. First, regardless of the challenge in identifying the exact demand on the part of the marketplace for sustainable design and management in THE facilities, the rapidly increasing adoption by companies of a sustainable agenda makes it all but inevitable that the trend will continue and become an integral part of design and management of facilities. Second, regardless of whether companies are prepared to commit to a sustainable agenda, changes in the legislative and regulatory environment will force them to adopt sustainability into their business plans. And third, as the next chapters will make clear, there will be an increasing economic imperative to adopt sustainability because of advances in sustainable technologies for facilities design and management and the rising cost of energy, water, waste management and the other elements identified in the WTTC's Agenda 21 for the Travel and Tourism Industry.

This chapter will conclude by examining two certification schemes currently available to the sector to support adoption of a sustainable design agenda, namely the LEED scheme and the Living Building Challenge. These two schemes and others like them, such as Green Globes, focusing as they do on the design and construction of facilities, represent the future of sustainable development for the THE sector and the built environment overall.

Notwithstanding that the LEED scheme only began in the late 1990s, it is now widely recognized as a leading certification programme designed to promote sustainable development in facilities design. It was developed by the USGBC, but has now become an international standard for sustainable design with LEED projects in over 30 countries as a result of partnerships within the global network of Green Building Councils (Johnston and Breech, 2010). A number of major operators, such as Starwood, Hilton, Marriott, Hyatt and Intercontinental, have all embraced the LEED scheme and the number of LEED-certified facilities is growing rapidly. It is estimated that there are as many as 7000 LEED projects certified or in progress around the world. As of 2010, there were 79 LEED-certified hotel properties and a total of 1038 properties were in the process of seeking certification. Also, there were 13 LEED-certified convention centres and 51 in the process of seeking certification (Hasek, 2010b). It is apparent to the industry that LEED certification is already an important indicator of a company's commitment to sustainability and this trend is likely to increase.

The Living Building Challenge takes the LEED scheme one step further in that it provides certification to facilities based not just on their design elements, but also on their sustainable operating performance after a minimum of 12 months of operation. Developed by the International Living Future Institute, the Challenge is a more holistic approach to building design and management than LEED. It is seen both by LEED and itself as an extension of the values and goals of LEED and has been endorsed by the USGBC. It describes its purpose as being to 'define the most advanced measure of sustainability in the build environment possible and acts to diminish the gap between current limits and ideal solutions' (International Living Future Institute, 2011). It does this by measuring building performance across seven categories: site, water, energy, health, materials, equity and beauty. The overall goal of a Living Building Challenge facility is that it will develop its own energy, only use water it captures and recycles, and process its own waste. In other words, it will have a zero carbon footprint. The Institute estimates that there are about 80 projects being designed and constructed to achieve full certification but currently none are THE facilities. Jason McLennan, the founder of the Challenge, has said of the THE sector that in terms of facilities 'This industry has extra responsibility because it interfaces with so many people. When people come to our hotels, they should leave transformed. We must go farther and faster than LEED Platinum' (Hasel, 2010a).

As the above demonstrates, sustainable development in the THE sector has come a long way in a short period of time. Notwithstanding that most operators now manage their facilities based on varying degrees of sustainable practices, the real test of commitment will be the incorporation of evolving sustainable technologies and design elements into renovated and newly constructed buildings. When this becomes commonplace, just like the recycling of linens and towels, then it will be fair to say that the industry has adopted the sustainability agenda.

Case Study

Sustainability at the Similkameen Inn

When Ben Cooper took over as the owner operator of the Similkameen Inn in Kelowna, British Columbia, Canada, he knew that he would face a number of significant challenges in renovating the old property. Having had significant experience in the property management business, he was familiar with the issues he would face regarding both exterior and interior systems related to building integrity and appearance, HVAC systems, and communications and information technology systems. But what he hadn't prepared himself for was the decision he'd have to make regarding the extent to which his property would be environmentally sustainable. Two factors impacted Ben's decision. The first was his growing awareness of the importance of sustainability throughout society in general and his growing personal commitment to doing what he could to further its cause. The second factor was more specific. The Kelowna hospitality market included properties that would be direct competitors to Ben's motel, which both embraced sustainability in their

(Continued)

Case Study. Continued.

design and management and, in one particular instance, actually promoted itself as an environmentally superior choice for guests.

The Best Western Plus Kelowna was located in the same catchment area as the Similkameen Inn and had, over the years, become a leader in the adoption of sustainable design and management. The hotel had recently received an award from the British Columbia Government recognizing its efforts to reduce its carbon footprint. In addition to the adoption of sophisticated systems such as its Solar Hybrid Heating System, the hotel was building a new wing that would be LEED certified. The property also held a 4 Key Accreditation from the Green Key Eco-Rating Program, which certifies hotel properties in Canada and the USA with respect to their sustainable practices in environmental management, housekeeping, food and beverage operations, conference and meeting facilities, and in facilities management. Indeed, Ben discovered that 17 hotel and motel properties in Kelowna had 3 or 4 Key Accreditation with Green Key, and that two of those properties, the Best Western Plus and the Delta Grand Okanagan had shown national leadership in sustainable design and management.

The Similkameen Inn was approximately 40 years old when Ben and his father purchased the property in early 2011. It sat on approximately two acres of land with 300 feet of frontage on Highway 97, the key north/south provincial highway in the British Columbia interior. It was located at the north end of Kelowna, a city of about 120,000 people and located on Okanagan Lake. Because of its location, climate and well-developed infrastructure, Kelowna had become, over the years, a major tourism destination in Western Canada. Ben had persuaded his father, a major real estate developer in the region, to purchase the motel because he believed that tourism would continue to grow and that properties like the Similkameen were well positioned to capture a segment of this business growth. At the very least, Ben's father was convinced that the potential capital appreciation of the commercially zoned land on the key transportation artery in the region would justify the investment in the first instance. Ben's father believed that if the property could become a profitable business as well, this would be 'value added' and further justify the investment.

As was the case with a lot of motels in Kelowna, the Similkameen had been neglected in terms of maintenance over the years. The previous owner had counted on capital appreciation of the property to provide him with a retirement income when he sold, a practice that was prevalent in the owner operator segment of the hospitality sector in the region. The condition of the property had been taken into consideration when the purchase was made and budgeting for the business included sufficient funding to allow for necessary renovations to be made to key building systems. With 100 guest rooms, a breakfast room and limited kitchen, and several small meeting rooms, the Similkameen offered the range of facilities that most visitors to Kelowna were seeking in the budget
(*Continued*)

Case Study. Continued.

price range. The property enjoyed an annual occupancy of approximately 68%, which was consistent with similar properties in the region. The average daily rate of CAN$83.50 produced annual revenues in the range of CAN$2 million. This could vary from year to year, but overall the trend had been consistent and recently showed signs of improving as Kelowna became more popular and the shoulder season occupancy throughout the regional industry became stronger.

Ben knew that he would have to persuade his father that the additional expense of 'greening' the property when it was renovated was justifiable. But before this, he would have to decide to what extent, if any, he should push the concept of sustainable design and management as part of the renovation. He was meeting with his father to discuss the renovation in a week and needed to resolve these issues by then.

Questions

1. What criteria should Ben use in deciding if sustainability is important to his property's clients?
2. Should Ben seek certification from Green Key or some other certification programme relating to sustainable development and management? If so, why and which one?
3. Would you advise Ben to assume a leadership role with his building renovations, for example by seeking LEED or Living Challenge certification? If so, why and which one? If not, why not?

GLOSSARY OF TERMS USED IN THIS CHAPTER

Building codes	Formal regulations propagated by municipalities and other public organizations that prescribe various aspects of building design, construction, maintenance and renovation.
Bulk dispensing of amenities	Properties provide guests with soap, shampoo and other amenities in refillable containers allowing for bulk purchasing with minimal packaging.
Compact fluorescent lamps (CFLs)	CFLs are fluorescent bulbs designed to replace incandescent lamps and are increasingly being required by building and other codes impacting building design and maintenance because of their lower power consumption and longer life span.
Corporate social responsibility	Corporate social responsibility is an approach by corporations at self-regulating their activities by expanding the traditional range of corporate stakeholders to include not just shareholders but any constituency impacted by the corporation's business activities.

Ecosystem	The term normally used to refer to biological environments and their basic elements, including organisms and the physical components making up that environment.
Ecotourism	A form of touristic activity focusing on the natural and cultural environment of destinations and designed to be low impact and sustainable.
Education and training	Courses and programmes of study focusing on various aspects of THE management provided by public and private colleges and universities as well as 'in-house' corporate education and training programmes focusing on specific topics related to the corporation's business needs.
Energy conservation	The term used to describe a range of activities, technologies and design elements in buildings with the goal of reducing the consumption of energy in the operation of buildings.
Feasibility studies	The process of determining the financial and strategic viability of a proposed course of action in a business.
Geothermal energy	An energy source derived from thermal or heat-based energy found in the earth.
Grey water	Water that is collected after use for non-human waste purposes such as dish washing and recycled for other uses such as irrigation of landscaping.
Hazardous substances	Materials in solid, liquid or gaseous form that can be harmful to humans.
Land use planning	The process, normally in the public domain, of regulating the use of land usually with the goal of rational, effective and efficient development.
Renewable technologies	Technologies designed to extract energy from renewable sources such as solar, wind and water-generated energy. Solar panels and wind turbines are the most common technologies, but the field is characterized by a high level of innovation, which results in new technologies being developed.
Reduce, re-use and recycle	Activities that form part of what is known as the waste hierarchy, designed to effectively manage waste generated by business activity.
Solar energy	An energy source derived from thermal or heat-based energy emanating from the sun.

Sustainable development	The term describes a wide range of business operations and building design, construction and management, all with the goal of reducing the impact of the business and structures on the environment.
Zero carbon footprint	The term used to describe a building that has design elements and management policies and practices that result in the building producing zero carbon emissions.

REFERENCES AND ADDITIONAL READING

Aitken Spence plc (2011) Sustainability. Available at: http://www.aitkenspence.com/sustainability/sustainability.asp (accessed September 2011).

Barber, N., Deale, C. and Goodman, R. (2011) Environmental sustainability in the hospitality management curriculum: perspectives from three groups of stakeholders. *Journal of Hospitality and Tourism Education* 23, 6–17.

Borsenik, F.D. and Stutts, A.T. (1997) *The Management of Maintenance and Engineering Systems in the Hospitality Industry*, 4th edn. Wiley, New York.

CNN (2010) Aborted Cambodian 'eco resort' leaves nothing but cleared land. CNN 27 April. Available at: http://www.cnngo.com/explorations/none/clearing-forests-failed-ecotourism-resort-548724 (accessed August 2011).

Fairmont Hotel & Resorts (2011) Green Partnership Program. Available at: http://www.fairmont.com/EN_FA/AboutFairmont/environment/GreenPartnershipProgram/Index.htm (accessed August 2011).

Guber, D.L. (2003) *The Grassroots of Green Revolution*. MIT Press, Cambridge, Massachusetts.

Hasek, G. (2010a) McLennan fascinates with living building challenge at HD Expo. *Green Lodging News* 22 May. Available at: https://ilbi.org/about/About-Docs/news-documents/pdfs/10-0522-green-lodging-mclennan-fascinates-with-living-building-challenge-at-hd-expo (accessed August 2011).

Hasek, G. (2010b) Number of LEED registered hotels hits 1,038. *Green Lodging News* 14 October. Available at: http://www.greenlodgingnews.com/blog/post/2010/10/14/Number-of-LEED-Registered-Hotels-Hits-1038.aspx (accessed August 2010).

International Living Future Institute (2011) Living building challenge. Available at: https://ilbi.org/lbc/standard (accessed September 2011).

Johnston, D. and Breech, P. (2010) An introduction to LEED certification for hotels. *Lodging Hospitality* 6 October. Available at: http://lhonline.com/green/leed/understanding_leed_1010/ (accessed August 2011).

Maho Bay Camps (2011) Available at: http://www.maho.org/ (accessed August 2011).

Marriott (2011) A deeper shade of green: EcoEvents at Marriott International. Available at: http://www.marriott.com/meetings/greenmeetingsandevents.mi (accessed September 2011).

Murray, D.W. and Ayoun, B.M. (2011) Hospitality student perceptions on the use of sustainable business practices as a means of signalling attractiveness and attracting future employees. *Journal of Human Resources in Hospitality and Tourism* 10, 60–79.

O'Fallon, M.J. and Rutherford, D.G. (2011) *Hotel Management and Operations*, 5th edn. Wiley, New York.

Our Common Future (n.d.) Available at: http://www.un-documents.net/wced-ocf.htm (accessed August 2011).

Penner, R.H. (1991) *Conference Center Planning and Design: A Guide for Architects, Designers, Meeting Planners and Facility Managers*. Restaurant/Hotel Design International, New York.

Stephens, N. (2011) Sustainability … it's good business sense. *Caterer & Hotelkeeper* 201, 4683.

Stipanuk, D.M. (2006) *Hospitality Facilities Management and Design*, 3rd edn. Educational Institute, American Hotel & Lodging Association, Lansing, Michigan.

The International Ecotourism Society (2011) Our mission. Available at: http://www.ecotourism.org/site/c.orLQKXPCLmF/b.4835251/k.FF11/Our_Mission__The_International_Ecotourism_Society.htm (accessed September 2011).

UN Department of Economic and Social Affairs (1999) *Tourism and Sustainable Development: The Global Importance of Tourism*. UN Department of Economic and Social Affairs Section 65, p. 13.

United States Green Building Council (2011) Greening the codes. Available at: http://www.usgbc.org/ShowFile.aspx?DocumentID=7403 (accessed September 2011).

Wagner, L. (n.d.) The sustainable development imperative and the travel and tourism industry. Available at: www.gppi.net/fileadmin/gppi/Wagner_Travel_Tourism.pdf (accessed September 2011).

Wong, T.K. and Wan, P. (2011) Perceptions and determinants of environmental concern: the case of Hong Kong and its implications for sustainable development. *Journal of Sustainable Development* 19, 235–249.

chapter 11

Environmental Management

Abel Duarte Alonso, Michelle O'Shea and Vlad Krajsic
University of Western Sydney

LEARNING OBJECTIVES

This chapter will critically reflect on the opportunities and challenges associated with implementing environmental management strategies, initiatives and approaches in tourism, hospitality and events (THE) facilities. Particular emphasis will be placed on the following sub-themes:

- The extent to which (how and why) human activities are placing pressure on the environment.
- Individual and organizational responsibility in relation to reductions in environmental impacts.
- How environmental sustainability can be best managed and regulated in THE-related sectors.

In addition, reference will be made to contemporary studies in THE environments, and case studies will be presented to illustrate the relevant areas of environmental management. These cases will then be extended in the form of simulations for students to reflect on, discuss and elaborate, and provide implications, suggestions/recommendations from a contemporary managerial perspective.

INTRODUCTION: THE NEED FOR INITIATIVES TO LIMIT IMPACTS ON THE ENVIRONMENT

The concerns of society, the business community and governments about the potential for natural disasters have intensified in recent years. Terms such as 'climate change' and 'global warming' have become synonymous with the devastating effects of floods or droughts, with the occurrence of these natural phenomena repeatedly being linked to human activity. Governments are considering a plurality of approaches to encourage private sector organizations to align their organizational practices with sustainable development (Font, 2001). The Australian government's proposed carbon tax scheme (World News, 2011), although neither a new nor revolutionary response, represents one of the most recent episodes where government mandate in the form of legislation is being used to persuade corporations to engage more robustly in environmental management practices.

These developments are illustrative of previously limited action by government and private organizations, and growing environmental awareness and concern among members of the public, government and non-government agencies (El Dief and Font, 2010). To an extent, pressure from these three institutions is beginning to have an impact, as environmental responsibilities are 'increasingly becoming part of the corporate agenda' (El Dief and Font, 2010, p. 157).

Example: The carbon tax proposal in Australia

Recently, the Australian government drafted a 'carbon tax' (Packham, 2011; World News, 2011) intended to curb carbon emissions among different industry 'offenders' and to instil awareness about environmental degradation. Essentially, the tax is a charge for carbon pollution through the burning of fossil fuels (World News, 2011). In a move to become a world leader in fighting pollution, Australia's current government is also planning a 'sequel' of the tax in the form of an emissions trading system that will cap the emission of pollutants such as carbon dioxide (World News, 2011). Other countries have implemented similar schemes, including Costa Rica, Denmark, Finland, India, Ireland, Norway, Sweden and Switzerland (World News, 2011) with mixed results. For example, while Denmark's per capita carbon dioxide emissions experienced close to a 15% decrease, Switzerland's greenhouse gas emissions remained stable and Norway's carbon tax did not prevent carbon emissions from increasing (World News, 2011).

Activities

Discuss the THE industry's contribution to environmental pollution. Prepare a list of the many ways in which the industry may contribute to pollution (e.g. water use, burning of fossil fuels).

(Continued)

> **Activities.** Continued.
>
> Assume the government where you live drafts and implements an emissions tax to address pollution from local companies. To what extent would such tax impact:
>
> - individual (large) THE facility operations;
> - the THE industry as a whole (in the city/region you live);
> - how would you as a hotel manager address such changes (e.g. reactive vs proactive measures)?

Overall, not only is there growing debate surrounding the necessity to minimize air pollution and water consumption, but also to avoid waste and promote alternative, cleaner and renewable energy sources. For THE facility operations, recycling materials that would otherwise continue to exert pressures on landfill space is one of the many initiatives being targeted, illustrating a desire 'to go back to basics'. Food industry waste management and food composting are receiving increasing attention, in part the result of utilization costs, such as in the case of food waste management, and because of low costs in food composting (Tronina and Bubel, 2008). The challenges of food waste management have direct implications for THE facilities, though still today most waste generated by the food industry, including food processing is not utilized (Tronina and Bubel, 2008).

While in the case of food composting and food waste management there is little involvement or proactive initiatives among some industries, in other contexts the voluntary adoption of environmental management is occurring. Non-government agencies, such as the International Organization for Standardization (ISO), have developed environmental management system (EMS) guidelines (Chan, 2008) incorporating the ISO 14000 'family' (ISO, 2011), including ISO 14000, 14001, 14004 for the business community to follow and adhere to. These guidelines represent a standard of procedures rather than of objectives or results (Viadiu *et al.*, 2006) that nevertheless can be followed in a proactive attempt to engage in environmental management.

The ISO guidelines can be beneficial for the image of organizations embracing them, including hotels and resort operators. Indeed, apart from environmental and quality improvements, following those guidelines can create positive perceptions among members of the public and organizations' stakeholders about an organization's environmental 'stewardship'. To date, very few studies have been conducted on ISO 14001 adoption in the hotel industry (Chan and Wong, 2006). Whether it is too little too late, investing resources and increasing efforts to minimize and slow the continued depletion and damage of natural resources seems to be the only way forward for society, governments and the business community.

ENVIRONMENTAL MANAGEMENT, SUSTAINABILITY AND THE BUSINESSES

Social, government and industry awareness about environmental management and sustainability are gaining in momentum. Environmental management has been referred to as efforts to minimize the negative environmental impacts of firms' products during their life cycle (Klassen and McLaughlin, 1996). A related phrase, environmental performance, measures organizational success in minimizing and reducing environmental impacts (Klassen and McLaughlin, 1996). Another associated term, environmental sustainability, refers to constraints 'on the four major activities regulating the scale of the human economic subsystem: the use of renewable and nonrenewable resources on the source side, and pollution and waste assimilation on the sink side' (Goodland, 1995, p. 10). Together, these are key elements that organizations can also refer to, and embrace, in their efforts to be more socially and environmentally responsible.

Arguably, industries such as those involved in manufacturing, oil and mineral drilling, oil refining or even transportation may cause more emissions than others. The 2010 oil spill in the Gulf of Mexico (Reuters, 2010) illustrates the devastating effects that events may have on the environment, food, tourism and hospitality industries. By comparison, the hospitality industry is neither a 'gross' pollutant nor a large consumer of non-renewable resources (Kirk, 1995). However, while the potential for mass pollution may be limited within the hospitality industry, it is also true that many hospitality operations are located in historic places, or in areas of outstanding natural beauty and delicate ecological balance (Kirk, 1995). As major tourism actors, hotels can cause significant environmental impacts (Molina-Azorín et al., 2009); furthermore, uncontrolled or unplanned hotel development can lead to significant environmental degradation (El Dief and Font, 2010).

Overall, while individually they may not largely contribute to pollution, the cumulative impact of individual operations together can affect global resources (Kirk, 1995). Thus, in geographic/physical environments there is a risk for the industry to come under public and government scrutiny. Therefore, as with other industries, today environmental management obligations have spilled over to THE-related sectors. At this juncture, it is also important to recognize that the need for environmental management in THE sectors is not a new phenomenon. As early as 1988 there were calls for the establishment of a National Tourism Strategy for the Australian tourism industry. This move was designed to address economic policy, social, environmental issues and associated infrastructure development using a collaborative and cooperative framework (Lamb, 1988).

A global view of environmental management practices in THE-related sectors

In recent decades, THE operators have greater opportunities to proactively approach the design of buildings that deliver an environmentally friendlier performance. According to McDonough et al., there is a 'need for designers to emphasize the hotel–local connection' (2001, p. 5). Moreover, this need 'will encourage the nascent environmental or "green" movement in hotel design' (2001, p. 5). Many examples exist of voluntary environmental initiatives among hotels. Enz and Siguaw (2003) refer to the Colony Hotel in Maine, USA, which involves guests in environmental education and recycling. Originally, the hotel's management went as far as employing a full-time biologist, subsequently replaced by local teachers providing educational tours. Enz and Siguaw (2003) also discussed the hotel management's plans to use recycled materials in floor coverings and soft furnishings, as well as solar-generated power. More recently, Kasavana (2008) reports that Marriott Hotels plans to install solar power in 40 of its hotel premises by 2017, and that 90% are currently involved in recycling, though very few of them recycle in-room guest litter.

Despite these proactive efforts, studies conducted in hospitality environments worldwide also provide evidence that a 'green' movement has yet to transfer from infrastructure and design to the operational aspect of hospitality operations. Some of these findings are also demonstrative of the contentious and complex nature of environmental management practices within the hospitality sector. One argument can be made that while THE operators' environmental and conservation activities are occurring across the globe, these are largely individualistic and fragmented. For example, one study that examined water consumption among hotels in Australian cities (Alonso, 2008) found that both usage and saving of water was a contentious issue among hospitality entrepreneurs. In fact, while the majority (60.6%) were concerned about the impact of future water shortages that would affect their business, only 40% agreed that authorities should pass stricter laws to oblige businesses to save water. Almost the same percentage (38.8%) were against this prospect (Alonso, 2008), and only 16.9% were prepared to pay more for their business's water consumption if prices were to increase; in contrast, 66.3% disagreed.

In a similar case, O'Neill and Alonso (2009) noted that small hospitality operators in Alabama were willing to increase their environmentally friendly involvement to limit waste produced by their businesses. However, operators identified a lack of (local town hall) support in the form of basic resources to facilitate their waste reduction and environmental impacts. Added costs and business demands that did not warrant the extra expenditure were barriers for other small hospitality and tourism entrepreneurs of Western Australia, preventing them from saving more water (Alonso and Ogle, 2010). Some of these findings support those of earlier studies (Stabler and Goodall, 1997) indicating that business strategies and practices are more likely to incorporate environmental practices if these initiatives result in lower costs or higher revenues.

More recent research on larger coastline resort operators in Australia found growing sensitivity and organizational self-commitment to environmental issues (McNamara and Gibson, 2008). However, in spite of this positive organizational example, managerial commitment and implementation of initiatives is still limited, particularly because of the legacy of inherited built environments and poor communication (McNamara and Gibson, 2008). In other environments (Hong Kong), hotel managers are still hesitant to embark on any formal environmental programme (e.g. EMS, ISO 14001), mainly due to lack of knowledge, skills, professional advice, resources and perceived costs in implementation and maintenance of pro-environmental initiatives (Chan, 2008). Wan (2007) found similar results in studying Macao hoteliers, though the major barrier in implementing environmental management initiatives was hoteliers not recognising their importance to hotel competitiveness and effectiveness.

Bohdanowicz's (2005) research conducted on hoteliers across Europe found that larger and chain-affiliated hotels were more likely to be environmentally conscious. However, such awareness appears to be symbolic rather than translated into action. As Bohdanowicz (2005) explains, other operational concerns are prioritized over environmental stewardship. Not surprisingly, Enz and Siguaw argue that while some hospitality operators may engage in environmentally friendly initiatives just because it 'is the right thing to do … others will do so because of increasing governmental regulation' (1999, p. 72). Similarly, Chan's (2008) investigation among Hong Kong hotels refers to the industry's efforts to address environmental concerns as being voluntary initiatives as well as economically motivated.

Earlier studies point at a consumer movement that to a growing extent demands 'green' facilities (Clark, 1999; Enz and Siguaw, 1999). In some cases, hotels' management implement some environmentally friendly initiatives to target a certain group of consumers. El Dief and Font's (2010) findings of pro-environmental strategies among Egyptian hoteliers to target Western tourists recognize that interests related to the hotel's image and financial returns can trigger initiatives.

Example: The Castle Hill Group

The Castle Hill Group (CHG) is a not-for-profit community club with a membership of 30,000 people. Its venue offers food and beverages, entertainment and health and fitness facilities and services.

CHG has been engaged in environmental management initiatives for 11 years. It has been involved in the practice well before 'environment' and 'environmental sustainability' became trendy buzzwords. As Allan De Paoli, building services manager explains: 'we have not just got on board … we have been self-funding initiatives for years. It is only recently that the governments have allocated grant monies for these kinds of projects and that many other organizations have come to be involved'. Mr De Paoli reflects on how the organization and its practices have evolved over this period. Initially, the club's environmental strategies were organic and reactionary; in the meantime, they have become a key component of CHG's daily activities and long-term sustainability outlook.

CHG's joining the Department of Energy, Utilities and Sustainability's 'Energy Smart Business Program' in December 2000, and its involvement in a 2004 demand management programme is illustrative of its long-term commitment. Through the project, the organization committed itself to implementing cost-effective demand- and energy-reducing strategies. These strategies continue today with the organization reporting increased power consumption of only 5% despite a membership increase of 633%. Water use has also declined, with Mr De Paoli indicating that 'despite the venue growth in size and patronage, the venue uses less water than it did 10 years ago; this is because our style and the way we run the club has changed'.

(Continued)

Example. Continued.

The substantial membership growth is the result of a 7-year building programme that has more than doubled the size of the venue. The surge in membership was also identified as an opportunity to utilize environmentally friendly architectural and operational design features. These features include, but are not limited to: reflective paint of roofs, tinted glass reducing heat loss, waterless urinals, BMS systems (TAC) on air-conditioning units, lighting upgrade, water harvesting and landscaping with 80% of plants used being native and drought-tolerant varieties.

CHG is consistently looking at strategies to reduce environmental impacts; initiatives have both tangible and intangible benefits for the organization and the community at large. CHG is engaged in environmental initiatives for two key reasons. The first reason aligns with its over-arching philosophy and mission, while the second relates to the 'business case', that is, significantly reducing operating costs associated with environmental management activities.

The organization has also pioneered some environmental management initiatives, demonstrating a leadership role within Australia's hospitality/club industry. Recently, it has invested more than AUS$530,000 in a co-generation system, in turn reducing the organization's carbon footprint by 50%. Put simplistically, co-generation is combined heat and power allowing for the simultaneous generation of usable heat and power (usually electronic) in a single process. Currently, most co-generation plant technology utilizes gas; however, the CHG is also able to use alternative and renewable fuels including biomass. CHG is one of a handful of hospitality facilities in Australia that have invested in the technology. The co-generation system will significantly reduce the energy use of the venue's health and fitness facilities; in fact, the cost-benefit analysis projects that the organization will achieve a return on investment within 4 years. CHG is also investigating the functionality of a tri-generation system for the remainder of the venue. This system would produce the energy needed to run the organization's food and beverage, gaming, entertainment and other facilities.

Source: http://www.castlehillrsl.com.au

Activities

1. Look for examples of additional environmentally friendly initiatives that other hospitality (and other THE) facilities are undertaking.
2. Provide a list of pros and cons (from the perspective of a THE facilities manager) that should be considered when further developing environmentally friendly initiatives.

Question

1. What other factors may have been considered when developing a business case for the co/tri-generation technology?

Studying hotel guests in India, Manaktola and Jauhari (2007) further underline the notion that consumers are increasingly supportive of hotels that implement environmentally friendly practices. Manaktola and Jauhari (2007) found that if service quality is not compromised, guests prefer to use those hotels; however, they are not willing to pay more for those services. Similarly, a study conducted among hotel guests in Malaysia concluded that tourists mainly choose a hotel based on attributes such as price or service quality rather than environmentally friendly organizational practices (Kasim, 2004). In addition, when presented with alternatives (air conditioning vs operable windows, or fresh towels vs reusing towels), tourists will still favour the less environmentally friendly alternatives (Kasim, 2004).

Regarding the operational/management side of hospitality facilities, Stipanuk (2006) agrees that there are three key motivators for environmental concern. First, there are economic considerations, including the opportunity to reduce energy costs through 'paybacks' from lighting conservation systems (from incandescent lamps to compact fluorescent lamps). Regulation through requirements to recycle, restrictions on water use and emissions is a second 'motivator', while the third is highlighted by market factors in the form of consumer market segments that place high value on the operation's environmental efforts/initiatives (Stipanuk, 2006).

Sloan *et al.* (2009) recognize that many hoteliers perceive limited commercial benefits and higher expense and complexity (and the potential for limited results) in adapting workers' attitude and management operations towards environmentally friendly initiatives. In comparing Estonian and German hotels, these authors found that all the studied Estonian hoteliers perceived green thinking as a way of adding value, enhancing the hotel's reputation, and acting 'as a guarantee of good service' (2009, p. 104). In contrast, German hoteliers did not express convictions as strongly, further underlining the fragmented nature of existing attitudes and perspectives among hospitality managers and the complexity of and lack of across-the-board evidence of the 'tangible' benefits associated with environmentally proactive initiatives.

Environmental management or management by the environment?

Riverside Oaks Resort Golf Course, one of the top resort courses in Australia, is set on nearly 250 hectares of natural bushland 75 minutes' drive north-west of the Sydney central business district. The resort includes function space for weddings and other events, as well as a championship-standard golf course. Currently, plans are underway for the construction of an additional 18-hole golf course.

The resort's management have a strong commitment to sound and proactive environmental management practices; however, the resort's location and setting pose unique challenges. The development and related strategies to maximize the utilization of existing facilities mean that existing environmental issues will be magnified. The resort produces its own potable water by drawing on the local river. In addition, it runs two wastewater treatment facilities with the discharge from one being treated with chlorine

(Continued)

Continued.

and the second being ultraviolet-treated. The treated effluent is passed through two large ponds before being used for golf-course irrigation.

Ground staff are constantly monitoring the use and methods of application of environmentally friendly fertilizers to prevent an impact on the water table and surrounding waterways. Waste from the clubhouse and associated facilities and accommodation is separated and collected by waste disposal companies. Cost and reliability are on-going concerns because of the relative physical isolation of the resort. The property has a large and increasing number of kangaroos on the course and surrounding bushland. The kangaroo population causes damage on fairways and greens, and while local golfers may be accustomed to the abundant droppings, there is a risk that the numerous overseas patrons may find them dirty or even offensive. In spite of these potential issues, the resort's management have made a decision not to cull the kangaroos, or disturb their presence. A commitment to minimize the impact on the terrain and larger vegetation when constructing the new course provides both challenges and opportunities to the designers.

Source: http://www.riversideoaks.com.au

Activities

Please reflect from a managerial perspective on what potential problems need to be managed if:

- there is a failure of the water or wastewater treatment facilities;
- the kangaroos on the course begin to affect patronage of the course.

Thus, unless there is a perception, particularly through 'financial' or similar tangible evidence that environmental awareness translated into practice will positively affect businesses' bottom line, many hospitality, or THE entrepreneurs for that matter, may shy away from proactive engagement/involvement in environmentally sound practices. A further aggravating issue is that the vast majority of THE operations are small to medium in size. These characteristics illustrate the vulnerability of this group, particularly in view of financial and human resource-related limitations.

Erdoğan's study among small tourism accommodation providers in Turkey illustrates this scenario, reporting a serious lack in 'understanding and practice of environmental protection and conservation' (2007, p. 1128) among operators. Moreover, normative pressures have little if any impact to encourage operators' involvement in environmental management, primarily because of a lack of 'appropriate business culture and essential financial conditions' (2007, p. 1128). These limitations, according to Erdoğan (2007), prevent operators from changing or upgrading malfunctioning equipment to newer technologies allowing for more proactive environmentally friendly practices. In contrast, Carlsen *et al.* (2001) addressed rural/family small business tourism and hospitality enterprises when evaluating their conservation ethic and implementation of sustainable management practices. Positively, these authors concluded that more than half of the owner-operated businesses they studied were engaged in sustainable and environmentally friendly business practices.

SUMMARY

The continuous growth of the world's population and rapid development in infrastructure and industries in different countries is increasing pressures on natural resources, including the impacts of pollution through emissions and/or contamination. These developments also suggest that environmental concerns will continue to be a challenge for society and governments will have to seek new ways of encouraging environmental management among industry organizations and society. However, legislation to force environmental stewardship among business entrepreneurs or rewards to become environmental guardians will not go a long way on their own. As some of the studies presented in this chapter demonstrate, there are multiple limitations and situations preventing hoteliers from being environmentally proactive, particularly, but not limited to, small hospitality operations. Impediments were also highlighted among consumers, some of whom will adhere to environmentally responsible principles as long as their comfort and overall quality of stay are not compromised.

The complexity of successfully becoming involved in environmental management calls for a systematic, strategic and long-term approach that incorporates local governments, grassroots groups and the local community, as well as THE businesses and consumers. The fundamental objective of this approach is to continue to promote awareness that continuous depletion of natural resources will inevitably lead to very serious environmental and social consequences. In the absence of any stronger encouragement, rewards or resources, education about the benefits of engaging and the consequences of not engaging in proactive environmental management initiatives could go a long way. Concerning the hospitality industry, whether its actual impact on pollution, global warming or climate change is significant or not, this sector can play an important role in encouraging awareness among different stakeholder groups. Encouragement could be in the form of education of both guests and staff about different ways to limit environmental degradation. Education could contribute to building a culture whereby stakeholders do not perceive involvement in environmentally friendly initiatives as a forceful or unpleasant process, but rather as an ethical obligation for the benefit of all.

REVIEW QUESTIONS

1. To what extent are human activities placing pressure on the environment? How and why?

2. Critically analyse the responsibility of the individual and the organization as it relates to reductions in environmental impacts.

3. Explore how environmental sustainability can be best managed and regulated in the THE industries.

Case Study

Environmental management in the context of small hospitality operations

In today's very competitive hospitality environment and economic uncertainty, to what extent can small/family hospitality operations proactively work towards environmental management practices? An interview with Angie Latty, owner of Trevi Ristorante Bar and Lounge in the outskirts of Sydney, Australia, illustrates that proactive initiatives can be a strong complement to abiding by the law.

Trevi's initiatives to minimize its impact on the environment are fundamentally based on: (a) strictly complying with local government and other legislation and standards; (b) integrating environmental concerns into the various functions of restaurant management; and (c) identifying opportunities for minimizing waste and lessening adverse environmental damage. As well as being inspected regularly by council staff, because Trevi features an 'open kitchen' its hygiene practices are additionally subject to public scrutiny on a daily basis.

Packaging waste (mainly cardboard and glass) is separated and collected by a recycling firm. Spent cooking oil is collected for recycling on a monthly basis. Food waste is minimal because supplies are purchased throughout the week (supplies for Sunday and Monday are delivered on Saturday). No food is pre-prepared, so this contributes to minimizing waste. Trevi does not keep any frozen supplies; this not only enables them to guarantee freshness, but also helps to reduce energy use. A local metal recycling business is available to collect any failed appliance that needs to be disposed of.

The restaurant has an all-gas kitchen, and has installed a 'C-Bus' – a microprocessor-based control and management system – to control lighting and all electrical services, including audio visual devices. The system enables timer-based on/off control, light dimming and sensor control in intermittent use areas such as toilets. The air-conditioning system is only switched on when required. The toilets have dual-flush cisterns, and urinal flushing is controlled by motion sensors. Sanitization equipment is serviced monthly to ensure it operates efficiently and effectively. General cleaning is outsourced to a contractor who has been providing the service for 6 years.

(Continued)

Case Study. Continued.

Trevi's management have investigated the installation of solar power; however, this alternative energy source is not viable as the restaurant is located on the ground floor of a two-storey building.

Source: http://www.trevi.net.au

Questions

1. Discuss the various initiatives Trevi is using: could they be improved? Reflect on the pros and cons of any potential improvements, especially from the perspective of a small/family hospitality and/or THE business.

2. What other initiatives could a restaurant such as Trevi implement to further reduce its environmental impact while maintaining the standards of quality and service?

THEMES FOR DISCUSSION

Refer to some of the themes discussed in this chapter, including environmental management and environmental sustainability. In addition, reflect on the number of hospitality operations located in mass-tourism destinations in both developing and developed countries, particularly on small islands. Many tourist resorts located on islands exert tremendous pressure on natural resources (see, for example, Bardolet and Sheldon, 2008; Rodríguez *et al.*, 2008). At the same time, they may provide a livelihood (jobs) to people, including local inhabitants. From a hospitality/THE manager's perspective, provide a list of reasons as to why 'voluntary' environmental management would be necessary. Also, provide a list of reasons as to why voluntary environmental management initiatives would be very difficult to implement in those environments. Finally, discuss ways to effectively develop a process and execute environmental management initiatives that may lead to short-, medium- and long-term beneficial impacts. Think of the many infrastructural and other issues that may exist in island resort environments (e.g. reduced availability and size of landfills, geographic/physical isolation and depletion/contamination of underground water reservoirs).

GLOSSARY OF TERMS USED IN THIS CHAPTER

Carbon tax	A levy imposed on companies of different industries for their carbon emissions. Definition of Parliament of Australia (2010): 'a tax on energy sources which emit carbon dioxide. It's a pollution tax…'.

Environmental management	Efforts to minimize negative environmental impacts of firms' products during their life cycle (Klassen and McLaughlin, 1996).
Environmental management system (EMS)	A management system designed to assist companies assessing and controlling the environmental impact of their activities, products and services (Standards Council of Canada, 2011).
Environmental performance measures	The level of success of firms in minimizing and reducing their impact on the environment (Klassen and McLaughlin, 1996).
Environmental sustainability	'A set of constraints on the four major activities regulating the scale of the human economic subsystem: the use of renewable and nonrenewable resources on the source side, and pollution and waste assimilation on the sink side' (Goodland, 1995, p. 10).
ISO-family	Several sets of standards (e.g. ISO 14001, 14004) that serve as guidelines, providing organizations with tools to assess and control the environmental impact of their activities, products and services rather than by prescribing environmental performance targets (Standards Council of Canada, 2011).

REFERENCES AND ADDITIONAL READING

Alonso, A.D. (2008) How Australian hospitality operations view water consumption and water conservation: an exploratory study. *Journal of Hospitality Marketing and Management* 17, 354–372.

Alonso, A.D. and Ogle, A. (2010) Tourism and hospitality small and medium enterprises and environmental sustainability. *Management Research Review* 33, 818–826.

Bardolet, E. and Sheldon, P.J. (2008) Tourism in archipelagos – Hawai'i and the Balearics. *Annals of Tourism Research* 35, 900–923.

Bohdanowicz, P. (2005) European hoteliers' environmental attitudes. *Cornell Hospitality Quarterly* 46, 188–204.

Carlsen, J., Getz, D. and Ali Knight, J. (2001) The environmental attitudes and practices of family business in the rural tourism and hospitality sectors. *Journal of Sustainable Tourism* 9, 281–297.

Chan, E.S.W. (2008) Barriers to EMS in the hotel industry. *International Journal of Hospital Management* 27, 187–196.

Chan, E.S.W. and Wong, S.C.K. (2006) Motivations for ISO 14001 in the hotel industry. *Tourism Management* 27, 481–492.

Clark, D. (1999) What drives companies to seek ISO 14000 certification? *Pollution Engineering International* 31, 14–15.

El Dief, M. and Font, X. (2010) The determinants of hotels' marketing managers' green marketing behaviour. *Journal of Sustainable Tourism* 18, 157–174.

Enz, C.A. and Siguaw, J.A. (1999) Best hotel environmental practices. *Cornell Hotel and Restaurant Administration Quarterly* 40, 72–77.

Enz, C.A. and Siguaw, J.A. (2003) Revisiting the best of the best: innovations in hotel practice. *Cornell Hotel and Restaurant Administration Quarterly* 44, 115–123.

Erdoğan, N. (2007) Environmental management of small-sized tourism accommodations in Turkey. *Journal of Applied Sciences* 7, 1124–1130.

Font, X. (2001) Environmental certification in tourism and hospitality: progress, process and prospects. *Tourism Management* 23, 197–205.

Goodland, R. (1995) The concept of environmental sustainability. *Annual Review of Ecology and Systematics* 26, 1–24.

ISO (2011) ISO 14000 essentials. Available at: http://www.iso.org/iso/iso_14000_essentials (accessed 22 July 2011).

Kasavana, M.L. (2008) Green hospitality. Hospitality upgrade. Available at: http://www.hospitalityupgrade.com/_files/File_Articles/I IUSum08_Kasavana_GreenHospitality.pdf (accessed 30 July 2011).

Kasim, A. (2004) BESR in the hotel sector. *International Journal of Hospitality and Tourism Administration* 5, 61–83.

Kirk, D. (1995) Environmental management in hotels. *International Journal of Contemporary Hospitality Management* 7, 3–8.

Klassen, R.D. and McLaughlin, C.P. (1996) The impact of environmental management on firm performance. *Management Science* 42, 1199–1214.

Lamb, A. (1988) Tourism development and planning in Australia: the need for a national strategy. *International Journal of Hospitality Management* 7, 353–361.

Manaktola, K. and Jauhari, V. (2007) Exploring consumer attitude and behaviour towards green practices in the lodging industry in India. *International Journal of Contemporary Hospitality Management* 19, 364–377.

McDonough, B., Hill, J., Glazier, R., Lindsay, W. and Sykes, T. (2001) *Building Type Basics for Hospitality Facilities*. Wiley, New York.

McNamara, K. and Gibson, C. (2008) Environmental sustainability in practice: a macro profile of tourist accommodation facilities in Australia's coastal zone. *Journal of Sustainable Tourism* 16, 85–100.

Molina-Azorín, J.F., Claver-Cortés, E., Pereira-Moliner, J. and Tarí, J.J. (2009) Environmental practices and firm performance: an empirical analysis in the Spanish hotel industry. *Journal of Cleaner Production* 17, 516–524.

O'Neill, M.A. and Alonso, A.D. (2009) Small hospitality business involvement in environmentally friendly initiatives. *Tourism Planning and Development* 6, 221–234.

Packham, B. (2011) Rate rise looms as carbon war rages. *The Australian online*. Available at: http://www.theaustralian.com.au/national-affairs/capital-circle/rate-rise-looms-as-carbon-war-rages/story-fn59nqgy-1226103190802 (accessed 28 July 2011).

Parliament of Australia (2010) Carbon taxes. Available at: http://www.aph.gov.au/library/pubs/climatechange/responses/economic/carbontax.htm (accessed 28 July 2011).

Reuters (2010) Gulf oil spill impacts fisheries, wildlife, tourism. Reuters online. Available at: http://www.reuters.com/article/2010/05/30/us-oil-rig-impact-factbox-idUSTRE64T23R20100530 (accessed 30 July 2011).

Rodríguez, J.R.O., Parra-López, E. and Yanes-Estévez, V. (2008) The sustainability of island destinations: tourism area life cycle and teleological perspectives. The case of Tenerife. *Tourism Management* 29, 53–65.

Sloan, P., Legrand, W., Tooman, H. and Fendt, J. (2009) Best practices in sustainability: German and Estonian hotels. *Advances in Hospitality and Leisure* 5, 89–107.

Stabler, M. and Goodall, B. (1997) Environmental awareness, action and performance in the Guernsey hospitality sector. *Tourism Management* 18, 19–33.

Standards Council of Canada (2011) Management system. Available at: http://www.scc.ca/en/programs-services/ms/faqs/article?classPK=faq-what-is-an-environmental-management-system (accessed 25 July 2011).

Stipanuk, D.M. (2006) *Hospitality Facilities Management and Design*, 3rd edn. Educational Institute of the American Hotel and Lodging Association, Lansing, Michigan.

Tronina, P. and Bubel, F. (2008) Food industry waste composting in a rotational reactor. *Polish Journal of Chemical Technology* 10, 37–42.

Viadiu, F.M., Fa, M.C. and Saizarbitoria, I.H. (2006) ISO 9000 and ISO 14000 standards: an international diffusion model. *International Journal of Operations and Production Management* 26, 141–165.

Wan, Y.K.P. (2007) The use of environmental management as a facilities management tool in the Macao hotel sector. *Facilities* 25, 286–295.

World News (2011) Factbox: Carbon taxes around the world. Available at: http://www.sbs.com.au/news/article/1492651/carbon-taxes-around-the-world (accessed 29 July 2011).

chapter 12

Waste and Energy Management

Işıl Özgen
Dokuz Eylül University

Kamil Yağcı
Giresun University

LEARNING OBJECTIVES

Having completed this chapter, readers should be able to:

- list basic criteria for sustainable tourism, hospitality and events (THE) site selection, design and construction;
- describe the characteristics of the waste management hierarchy;
- outline fundamental issues for THE waste and energy management programmes;
- describe several ways for improving energy efficiency in THE facilities.

INTRODUCTION

Most of the environmental problems that human beings face today are the result of waste that has not been managed properly. Nature previously had its own balance, but with a rapidly increasing population and rapidly decreasing resources placing more stress on the environment (Barrow, 2006) it does not always have the capacity to renew itself. THE, which was once seen as a 'smokeless industry' and which is highly dependent on a healthy local environment, is not smokeless anymore. THE developers today should therefore develop facilities that are not only economically viable but also environmentally responsible in the long term. This chapter will mainly focus on how energy and waste management in THE can be implemented, beginning from design, construction and operation, and its importance for saving the environment, minimizing the use of resources and decreasing operating costs.

WASTE AND ENERGY MANAGEMENT IN THE DEVELOPMENT PROCESS

THE facilities, by the very nature of their role as providers of accommodation, recreation and food service, consume large amounts of natural resources and expel large amounts of waste, which can be prevented, reduced or recycled. Prevention begins with the development process and continues with operation.

In the process of developing THE facilities, there are number of factors that should be taken into account, such as analysis of the business environment, market potential, sales forecasting, estimating and weighing prospective profitability vs risk (Gee, 1994). These factors are mainly about the economic viability of the THE facility, but in this chapter these factors will be ignored because they have little or no impact on waste and energy management issues. Instead, site selection, design and construction and their direct or indirect relationships with waste and energy management will be focused on.

Sustainability in site selection, design and construction

The impact of site selection is as important as the design and construction of the building because buildings are fixed assets and cannot be removed elsewhere. When deciding on a site, the following factors should be carefully assessed (IBLF and CI, 2005):

- Will the proposed scale of the site for the THE facility meet current and future land use regulations?
- Will local wildlife and sensitive local ecosystems be disturbed or destroyed, or an important habitat threatened significantly?
- Is the proposed site away from earthquake and hurricane zones, and will it avoid the risks of future effects of climate change such as rising sea levels, flash floods, tidal waves, increased beach and coast erosion (Holden, 2008)?
- Will the proposed site increase the amount of surface run-off?
- Is the proposed site on prime land or close to wetlands?
- Is enough natural light available for the proposed site? (Optimising natural light can be an advantage for energy efficiency and decreasing energy costs.)

In addition, choosing a location that is close to existing public transport networks, selecting a site on previously developed land and with infrastructure in place, and where possible renovating or restoring existing buildings will reduce the required input of new resources.

After these issues are carefully considered, the design and the construction stages can begin. THE facilities should be designed and constructed in a manner that:

- Protects existing landscaping, generates minimum plant disturbance and preserves species diversity (monocultures are prone to disease and insect infestation) (Garner *et al.*, 2001).
- Prepares the site for construction without completely clearing all the vegetation.
- Restores vegetation with native plants (especially drought-tolerant species because they require less water, fertilizers, pesticides and pruning, and generate less green waste), avoiding the introduction of new species.
- Considers building water reuse or capture of rainwater.
- Orientates the site on an east–west axis to provide an optimal north–south exposure for daylight, uses passive solar gain and passive cooling techniques to maximize energy efficiency (GreenSource, 2008).
- Considers wholly or partially renewable energy technologies, such as photovoltaic solar panels, solar hot water collectors, wind-generated electricity.
- Specifies minimum efficiency levels for equipment, systems, fixtures and appliances. Installs motion sensors for lighting and water use.
- Chooses local, renewable or sustainable materials appropriate to the site.
- Avoids materials that take the highest energy to produce, such as laminated beams, chipboard and hardboard that are bonded with formaldehyde, especially materials coming from far away that result in transport-generated energy costs (Sloan *et al.*, 2009).
- Removes all construction waste (concrete, stone, tiles, wood, glass, wiring, plumbing, paint containers) in a safe way, if possible arranging recycling waste bins for construction materials (brick manufacturers and concrete suppliers may accept waste returns if they are free of contamination), avoiding waste dumping anywhere on site or its neighbourhood (Sullivan and Wyndham, 2001).
- Utilizes the life cycle framework and selects sustainable construction materials that pass through a resource-efficient manufacturing process, and evaluates materials' characteristics such as recycled content, moisture resistance, zero or low air emissions, zero or low toxicity, durability, longevity and local availability.
- Installs high R-value wall and ceiling insulation in order to prevent energy loss (Calrecycle, 2011).
- Designs with adequate space to facilitate recycling collection and incorporates a solid waste management programme that prevents waste generation.

With the above sustainable building measures, THE facilities can be converted from waste producers into efficient environment conservers.

Example: Montage Beverly Hills Hotel, South California

Montage Beverly Hills is the first certified ultra-luxury hotel in Southern California for LEED for New Construction. Some of the key achievements include: recycling 83% of
(Continued)

Example. Continued.

construction site waste, limiting the amount of waste sent to landfills; sourcing 28% of the building materials from within 500 miles of the project; a location close to local infrastructure, limiting guests' need to drive to area attractions; energy-efficient systems that are 43% more efficient than a standard mixed-use building.

Source: http://www.montagebeverlyhills.com/beverly-hills-green-hotel.php

Solid waste management hierarchy

Dealing with waste is necessary in order to conserve energy, save natural resources, prolong the life span of landfills, reduce pollution, save money and help the economy by creating jobs.

Waste management requires a hierarchy (Fig. 12.1) of approaches and technologies for managing waste in order to:

1. retain as much as possible of the energy and the materials in a useful state, and
2. avoid releasing energy or matter into the environment as a pollutant (USDA, 2011).

Generally, depending on the strategy that is chosen, the upper part of the hierarchy gains more benefits in efficiency and retained economic value (USDA, 2011). Figure 12.2 demonstrates waste management hierarchy strategies relationships between costs and risks.

The top priority in the hierarchy is referred to as source reduction or waste prevention, which is an approach to minimize generation of discarded materials by not creating them in the first place, for example using ceramic cups instead of disposable ones. Source reduction or waste prevention is followed by reuse and recycling. Reuse involves putting objects back into use so that they do not enter the waste stream, such as refilling cartridges and using rechargeable batteries. With source reduction and reuse cost savings, higher productivity and quality can be achieved (Cheremisinoff, 2003). Recycling on the other hand is the process by which materials are collected, separated at source, processed and remanufactured into the same or a different product. This requires considerable effort in hotels, such as sorting the waste, providing additional storage

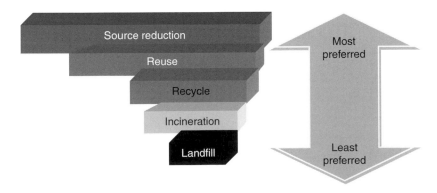

Fig. 12.1. Solid waste management hierarchy.

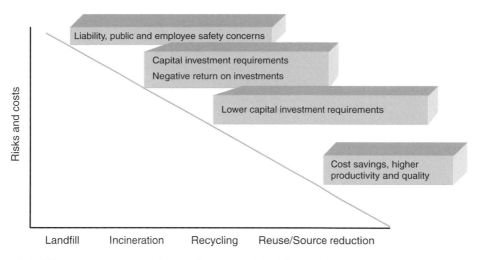

Fig. 12.2. Waste management hierarchy strategies risks and costs.

space, training employees, information for guests, and material outlay such as signs (Barrows and Powers, 2009). Recycling can be done in three ways: in process, on-site and off-site. Depending on the option chosen, recycling requires lower capital investment and partial cost recovery can be realized. Composting is another type of recycling where organic materials are biologically broken down under controlled conditions and converted into a substance that can be used as a fertilizer (Webster, 2000). Earthworm composting has become popular because unlike rubbish dumps, where organic matter produces methane, worms turn waste into stabilized organic matter, a rich black loam (humus). Earthworm (*Eisenia foetida*) compost strongly affects soil fertility by increasing the availability of nutrients, improving soil structure and its water-holding capacity (Canellas *et al.*, 2002).

Example: The Mount Nelson Hotel, Cape Town

In 2006 the Mount Nelson Hotel established an on-site worm farm as a pilot project to turn leftover food and other organic matter into vermicompost to use as fertilizer on the hotel's gardens. A third of the hotel's organic waste goes to the worms, saving a lot of money in disposal fees and fertilizer costs. The hotel aims to process 70% of their organic waste this way.

Source: http://seattletimes.nwsource.com/html/nationworld/2003330422_worms30.html

---

Incineration and landfill are the last stages in the hierarchy and the least preferred. If properly operated, incineration projects can provide energy in the form of electricity or processed steam (Eberle, 1995). However, incineration requires capital investment and there is the possibility of a negative return on investments with increasing operating costs. Among all the waste hierarchy options, landfilling has the most negative environmental consequences, such as pollution of the local environment, soil and water contamination, scavengers on the waste heaps and damage to access roads by heavy vehicles. Public and employee safety are at high risk with landfill, although modern landfills in industrialized countries are designed to collect leachate and methane gas from the decomposing organic materials and the gradual breakdown of inorganic materials and convert them into biogas (Sloan *et al.*, 2009).

THE WASTE MANAGEMENT PROGRAMME

THE facilities can minimize cost increases by determining waste reduction and recycling programmes and can eliminate much of the waste from the beginning. A successful waste management programme can be established in three phases (Fig. 12.3; Ozgen, 2005):

- preparation;
- implementation;
- evaluation.

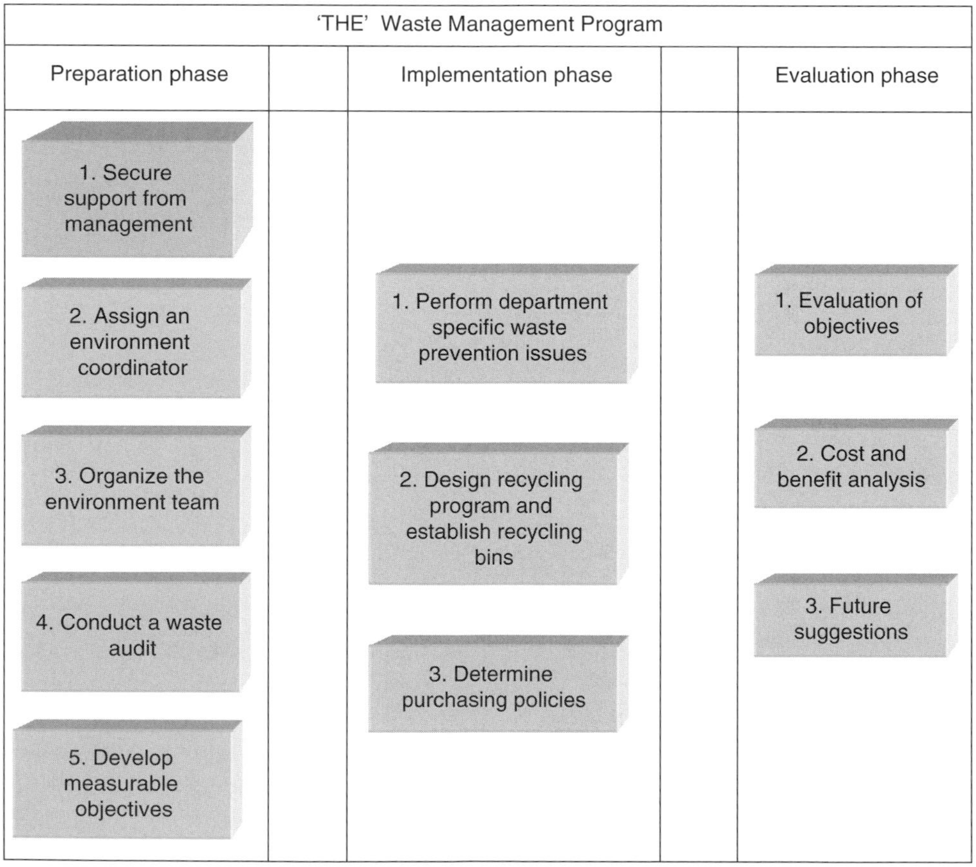

'THE' Waste Management Program				
Preparation phase		Implementation phase		Evaluation phase
1. Secure support from management				
2. Assign an environment coordinator		1. Perform department specific waste prevention issues		1. Evaluation of objectives
3. Organize the environment team		2. Design recycling program and establish recycling bins		2. Cost and benefit analysis
4. Conduct a waste audit		3. Determine purchasing policies		3. Future suggestions
5. Develop measurable objectives				

Fig. 12.3. THE waste management programme.

The first step in any waste reduction and recycling programme is to secure support and environmental commitment from the owner or top management. Without this commitment employees may be unwilling to fully implement the programme (DPPEA, 2011a). Waste reduction issues in THE facilities need considerable effort in planning, implementing and employee training, therefore someone with knowledge of the THE facility's current purchasing activities, good leadership and communication skills and a talent for organizing is needed to lead the programme. Selecting team members from every department is important to encourage employees to take ownership of the programme. Employees are likely to support a programme that they understand and have helped to design (DPPEA, 2011b).

Conducting a waste audit or assessment is necessary for waste management because it identifies the quantity and the content of materials disposed by the THE facility (Kirk, 1996), and will bring to light opportunities for waste prevention, recycling and purchasing activities. When conducting a waste assessment or audit, examining records (inventory, invoices, purchasing records), asking each employee about the types and amounts of waste generated, their willingness to participate in recycling, and their suggestions for waste prevention will provide valuable information. The baseline information gathered in the first phase will help to establish the second phase, which can be summarized as:

1. performing waste prevention issues in every department;
2. designing the recycling programme and establishing recycling bins where waste is mostly generated;
3. determining purchasing policies and practices.

Every department has different types and volumes of waste. Preparing a waste audit specific to a department also helps to establish waste prevention issues. For example, most of the waste generated by a housekeeping department is made up of soap pieces, plastic bottles and textile waste. Using refillable soap, shampoo, conditioner and hand lotion dispensers for guest rooms will eliminate soap pieces and plastic bottles.

Example: Iberotel Sarıgerme Park Resort, Turkey

Iberotel Sarıgerme Park Resort is the first ISO 14000 certified hotel in Turkey. The hotel has been recycling paper, glass, plastics, metals and oil for several years. Between 2000 and 2007 the hotel recycled 200 tonnes of glass, 204 tonnes of paper, 54 tonnes of metal, 72 tonnes of plastics and 15,356 litres of oil. It also sent 15 tonnes of bread waste and 237 tonnes of food waste to animal farms. The hotel also converts its textile waste into small carpets (woven by locals) for sale to their guests. With the sponsorship of Stuttgart University, the hotel has created its own biogas centre on site, and is using solar energy not only for heating but also for cooling.

Source: Ozgen *et al.* (2008)

First, it needs to be decided which materials are to be recycled in the THE facility's recycling programme, for example paper, glass, food waste or metals. Contracts with recycling firms then need to be made: some firms provide equipment to help recycling, for example free bins (Radwan *et al.*, 2010). A collection strategy has to be put in place, acquiring containers and locating them according to the waste-generation areas.

Careful purchasing policies can help eliminate waste from the start. When possible, items purchased should: contain recycled materials; be reusable and/or recyclable; have the minimum packaging; have a product lifespan and warranty; be repairable, reusable and safe; and be free from toxicity. Efficient waste management relies not only on careful planning, but also on everyone's participation in order to achieve a high level of success.

The third phase is the evaluation phase, in which management evaluates whether environmental objectives are being achieved. If they are not, the reasons for failure, costs and benefits of the programme and future suggestions are determined. Sometimes in this phase management may decide to discontinue one of the environmental activities. For example, a hotel may have its own composting area but because of the odour problem and complaints from hotel guests it may decide to give up composting. It is evident that in the near future all THE facilities, regardless of their size, will be forced to recover major portions of their waste. New legislation, lack of landfill space and public demand will require it.

ENERGY MANAGEMENT IN THE FACILITIES

In the World Summit on Sustainable Development 2002, where sustainable tourism, energy saving, emission control, preservation of natural resources and environmental management issues were discussed, tourism was accepted as one of the most energy-consuming sectors and countries were asked to integrate their tourism policies with energy productivity efforts (UNEP, 2003).

According to UNEP (2003, p. 6), the American lodging sector (including hotels, dormitories and other accommodation facilities) was estimated to consume 55.6 TWh of energy/year in 2000, while the corresponding figure for European facilities was 39 TWh (CHOSE, 2001). It is estimated that a typical hotel releases between 160 and 200 kg of carbon dioxide per m^2 of room floor area annually, depending on the fuel used to generate electricity, heating or cooling (Chan and Lam, 2002). There are no collective data for hotel water consumption on a global, or a European scale, but according to Davies and Cahill (2000) tourists in the American lodging sector consume approximately 174.88 million m^3 of water annually. Most of the water consumed is released in the form of sewage, requiring treatment. These discouraging figures illustrate the urgent need for more environmentally sound practices and products in THE facilities. One of the best practices is using renewable energy sources.

> **Example:** Hotel Plunhof, Italy
>
> Hotel Plunhof, a 4-star hotel in the South Tirol, consumes 800,000 kWh of electricity annually for its wellness facilities, sauna, kitchen, laundry and lighting. It has installed a photovoltaic solar power system with 386 panels, and since 2009 has produced 110,000 kWh of electricity each year, with a projected payback period of 10 years.
>
> *Source*: http://www.sunpowercorp.co.uk/commercial/success-stories/?relType=SP_Content_C&relID=1293995622328

Renewable energy use in THE facilities

As a major global economic sector with a substantial environmental impact, THE facilities can use and benefit from renewable energy systems in many ways. Renewable energy is generally the cleanest option for producing energy, eliminating greenhouse gas emissions and improving air and destination quality. Some examples of renewable energy sources are:

- passive solar design;
- solar thermal systems;
- geothermal heating systems;
- biomass systems;
- biogas;
- windpower;
- small-scale hydroelectric turbines;
- bioenergy electricity;
- solar photovoltaic cells;
- bioethanol.

While renewable energy sources are not yet a major source of energy, the future is likely to see increasing use of these sources because they are environmentally friendly.

Energy audit for THE facilities

A comprehensive energy audit examines the ways energy is currently used in the facility and identifies some alternatives for reducing energy costs. The goals of the audit are to:

- identify the types and costs of energy use, to understand how that energy is being used;
- determine and analyse alternatives such as improved operational techniques and/or new equipment that could substantially reduce energy costs;
- perform an economic analysis on those alternatives and determine which ones are cost-effective for the business (Capehart *et al.*, 2008).

Investments in more efficient energy use and improved housekeeping practices can lead to significant reductions in operating costs and energy bills within short payback periods (Talwar, 2006).

According to Lütz (2008), the biggest areas of energy consumption in most THE facilities are:

- extracting air from rooms and offices;
- open windows in rooms and offices;
- lights not being automatically switched off after guests leave their room;
- air conditioning in swimming pool areas, conference rooms, restaurants and in the lobby (including negative effects of opening doors);
- fresh air supply to the kitchen;
- hot water supply.

Lütz also proposed some methods for improving energy efficiency in hotel rooms, which are:

- fresh air reduction (better controls: air quality control, timers, presence sensors);
- volume flow reduction (electric fan energy);
- temperature reduction in certain areas (reduction of transmission loss);
- reduction in the use of, and less dependence on, conventional fossil fuels (alternative sources of energy);
- cooling reduction (better building controls, heat/cool recovery, alternative cooling systems);
- operating times (better controls, timed programmes, connection to other automation systems);
- servicing and maintenance, clean coils and replace filters regularly;
- creating a 'green' commitment.

From an environmental perspective, most tourism businesses are currently 'self-regulated'. Although the value of tourism is generally recognized, short-term financial considerations often take precedence over long-term benefits. Although, in some cases, industry practice could be improved through effective collective action, in others, additional mechanisms to improve environmental performance must be provided by external agencies. To date, renewable energy technologies have not been included in the efforts to establish environmental standards for the tourism industry. This issue needs examination by tourism agencies and other government and non-profit bodies involved in the establishment of standards and accreditation procedures.

SUMMARY

The interdependency between tourism and the physical and social environments implies that tourism's survival depends highly on its ability to reduce its negative impacts on these environments (Kasim, 2006). Such a perspective has prompted many countries to review their policies and plans and adopt a long-term vision known as sustainable tourism. Sustainable tourism aims at managing all resources in a way that enables socio-economic needs to be met, while conserving culture, environment and bio-diversity (World Tourism Organization, 2009). In this chapter, the link between water issues and corporate social responsibility has been established. This is followed by a case study on Frangipani Langkawi Resort & Spa's environmentally friendly water treatment, as well as the challenges it faces in trying to become a successful sustainable hotel. This case study should be an inspiration to all hotels to become more environmentally friendly in their operations, perhaps by addressing not just water issues, but also waste, energy and other pressing environmental issues facing the world today.

Case Study

Sustainable tourism management: wastewater treatment facility in Frangipani
Langkawi Resort & Spa, Langkawi, Malaysia

Azilah Kasim
Universiti Utara Malaysia

Anthony Wong
Managing Director, Frangipani Langkawi Resort & Spa, Malaysia

Introduction

The tremendous worldwide growth of the tourism and hospitality industry leads to ever-intensifying competition for hotels and resorts. To manage and survive competition, hotels and resorts must gain a competitive advantage. Environmental management provides an avenue for this competitive advantage, especially in the context of a developing country where the concept, though known, is still poorly embraced. Even though the greening of hotel premises is a concept that has received global acceptance and support, translating the concept into practice is not a straightforward and easy process. This case study provides a real-life example of Frangipani Langkawi Resort & Spa, Malaysia (hereafter, Frangipani) – the first hotel in Malaysia that fully embraced environmentally friendly hotel operation and management.

Malaysia is a popular tourist destination in Southeast Asia that is in its maturity stage. Langkawi is a beautiful island in the northwest of the peninsula, which is also at its maturity stage and is in need of rejuvenation if it wants to compete with more popular islands like Bali. Frangipani has thus taken the right step in reinventing itself through environmental management, thereby making it unique compared with other resorts. This case study documents one of its environmental facilities – a wetland that uses natural plants to purify its wastewater.

Frangipani is a 4-star resort on one of Langkawi's best beaches, Pantai Tengah (the resort operated under another name for several years beforehand). The resort's main function is hospitality (rooms, restaurants, spa and recreational activities) and as such is a service industry. Frangipani does not produce a product, rather it is a service provider that does not require process flows.

Langkawi's number one attraction is the waters of the Andaman Sea and protecting this tourism asset was always the highest priority when the owners took over the resort. The resort set out from its inception to offer the best accommodation it could, and with the best local service, but the priority was to establish a green resort that would reduce the resort's footprint on the environment and also be a working model for others to gain inspiration from and follow. Frangipani has received many awards recognizing its achievements in environmentally responsible tourism.

(Continued)

Case Study. Continued.

Water-related environmental facilities at Frangipani

Frangipani treats much of its waste on-site, not only to reduce the effluent that flows through the sewage treatment works and ultimately ends up in the sea, but also to keep water on-site because it is a valuable resource. Mains water is expensive to buy and the resort is making a concerted effort to lower its water consumption. Less water used means less water through the system and lost through the sewerage system.

Thus, Frangipani strives to minimize water consumption and maximize the utilization of natural rainwater. It harvests up to 80,000 gallons/40,005 litres of rainwater in over 82 water tanks and takes surface runoff through roadside drains to be used for watering purposes. Rainwater is used to flush toilets and surplus rainwater is used to wash the pool deck daily. Reclaimed water is used for irrigation around the resort. The pond containing all the rainwater and treated water (about 3000 cubic metres of water) is used to rear fish for consumption.

Frangipani has its own man-made wetland, which is used to treat the wastewater in the resort and is the first of its kind to be built in Malaysia. The wetland area is approximately 0.5855 acre (2369 m^2) with a maximum depth of 1.2–1.7 metres, depending on the season. The water in the wetland is continuously monitored with help from the local public university and private laboratories to ensure the water quality is acceptable under Malaysian standards.

Use of plants as natural water purifiers

The wetland relies on a number of perennial plant species to help purify the water. *Neptunia* spp., commonly known as water mimosa, is the main species used to treat the water. Water mimosa is a floating aquatic perennial that roots in the banks or at the bottom of water bodies. It is able to reduce total nitrogen and phosphorus values, and absorb organic compounds and suspended solids because its stems are covered with a spongy fibrous layer. Use of the plant can restrict water flow in creeks and channels, helping suspended solids to settle slowly. *Thalia geniculata*, also known as Bent Alligator-Flag, is also used in the wetland to absorb nutrients and stabilize the suspended solids.

Eichhornia crassipes, or water hyacinth, is a free-floating plant with leaves attached to a spongy, inflated petiole. Underneath the water it has a thick, heavily branched, dark fibrous root system. The use of water hyacinth actually drew on findings from NASA that showed water hyacinth can be used to treat human waste in the context of its 'environmental bubble'. It took the resort 3 years to perfect its system because water hyacinth is a very aggressive invader and can form thick mats. If these mats cover the entire surface of the pond they can cause oxygen depletion and kill fish, so it needs to be controlled. On the plus side, water hyacinth is very efficient at removing a wide range of pollutants, from

(Continued)

Case Study. Continued.

suspended materials, nutrients like nitrogen and phosphorus, to organic matter. Most importantly, it has a high capacity for taking up heavy metals like lead, chrome, cadmium, copper, aluminium, nickel and mercury, and pathogens. Water hyacinth has no known direct food value to wildlife and is considered a pest species.

Lemna minor, or common duckweed, is the smallest plant used in the wetland. It floats on the water surface in a bright green layer and has no stems and no leaves, but has tiny roots. It absorbs nitrates, phosphate, potassium, calcium, sodium and carbon. It has a useful role in controlling the growth of algae, both by removing nutrients and by shutting out sunlight by covering the water surface. Algae absorb oxygen and on decaying further reduce oxygen levels, which can severely affect aquatic life. By shading the water, *Lemna minor* keeps it cooler, allows for more dissolved oxygen and minimizes water loss through evaporation. *Lemna minor* is an important food for wild waterfowl and fish, as well as providing a source of food for small creatures that are in turn eaten by the birds and fish.

Another species used in the wetland is *Veteveria zizanioides*, also known as vetiver or miraculous grass because of its benefits and versatility. Its usefulness lies in its function in soil, water conservation and erosion control. Vetiver helps to regulate the amount of water. It has a deep, dense and penetrating root system that can reduce and prevent drainage, improve bed stability and nutrient uptake. Its stiff and erect stems can withstand high velocity flows and form a living porous barrier that can act as a very effective filter trapping both fine and coarse sediments, as well as sediment-bound contaminants (e.g. heavy metals and some pesticides residues). Vetiver is highly tolerant of adverse climatic conditions and of adverse edaphic conditions such as high soil acidity and alkalinity, and elevated levels of heavy metals such as arsenic, cadmium, copper, chromium, lead, mercury, nickel, selenium and zinc.

Nymphaea (water lilies) in the ponds remove cadmium in the water, help to reduce algae growth by shading the water and keeping it cool, and allow for more dissolved oxygen. The plant also provides hiding places for small aquatic creatures.

Ipomoea aquatica Forsskal, also known as swamp cabbage, grows wild in aquatic environments, but can also be grown in well-irrigated fields. The plant's roots hang under the water and provide a large surface area for the growth of beneficial microorganisms that can enhance nitrogen removal. Because the plants are floating, they are forced to take their nutrients and heavy metals from the water rather than from the sediments.

A few laboratories, such as University Technology Malaysia and CO2 private laboratory, are cooperating with Frangipani to test the water to ensure that the quality is maintained. The results of those tests have shown that the quality of the water is Grade A.

(Continued)

Case Study. Continued.

Being a small resort, daily checks are also easily conducted and indicators measured and recorded so that the state of the environment can be quickly gauged. Daily monitoring and data recording ensure that staff understand what environmental issues are occurring when black and grey water flow into the resort's wetland to be treated biologically. These activities are monitored by the Maintenance Department and Environmental Officer. Where necessary, resort staff consult with the local authorities to seek alternative solutions but resort staff know they can purify black and grey water using natural means to a higher standard than the local authorities can using their conventional facilities.

Frangipani has improved its wetland system by adding a paddle wheel/aerator to put more oxygen into the water to hasten the fermentation and neutralization process. The resort has also reduced water hyacinth to only one third and has added water lilies. The water from the wetland is used in the garden to water maize, pandan and vegetables. Plants absorb nutrients from the wastewater, and the remaining water returns into the water cycle.

Challenges

One of the most important challenges Frangipani faces in implementing its water-related environmental measures is staff awareness and involvement. Because there was not enough local knowledge about running a sustainable hotel, the owner had to get involved for the first three years, dealing directly with all the managers despite also having to run six or other seven companies. Younger staff often have little understanding of green measures. For example, they do not appreciate that reusing grey water for watering plants is just as good as using normal clean water, and that in the process the hotel can reduce its water consumption and wastage. As part of the solution, Frangipani ensures that money saved goes back to staff welfare by recognizing top staff and having family days that award staff with prizes.

Frangipani uses training and communication to educate its staff about its mission to be a sustainable hotel to ensure continuous staff involvement and support for all of its environmental programmes. It conducts 'Eco-walk Training' with the assistance of the Environmental Offices so that staff can become better informed about the hotel's objective to be ecofriendly. During inductions, staff are told about the resort's core values, operating procedures, vision and expectations of its employees. Each department has a set of guidelines and owns a patch in the resort grounds where they produce organically grown vegetables. Standard operation procedures and key performance indicators are given to all staff to provide proper services to the guests and the resort itself. Training programmes are planned by both the management and the staff. When a new working method is introduced, such as a new PC application, new equipment or a new operation policy, staff are given the opportunity for training.

(Continued)

Case Study. Continued.

In staff recruitment, internal promotions are preferred because this prevents high staff turnover, keeps experience in-house, and also shows appreciation for the contribution of the staff.

Internal marketing is emphasized. Frangipani has a staff notice board in the canteen that provides information on environmental matters that might be of interest to the staff. Staff are briefed regularly on the resort's environmental initiatives. At the beginning of the each shift, almost every department head will remind staff of at least one environmental initiative that is relevant to that department for them to focus on during that shift.

External marketing is through low-key marketing and PR campaigns. The resort lets its own environmental initiative and their staff's outreach into the community on environmental issues do most of the talking. Resort staff participate in activities conducted by the Malaysian Nature Society by sharing the resort's green practices with its members. Staff also cooperate with schools that are interested in going green. Frangipani staff participate in some of these school activities, such as Nature Club meetings, to share their knowledge with the schoolchildren and teachers.

A weekly flea market is held every Saturday from 6 pm to 10 pm at the Underwater World parking lot. The main idea behind this flea market is to promote the concept of the 4Rs (reduce, reuse, recycle and rethink) among the local community and foreign visitors as well. This is a place where islanders can sell and barter their secondhand goods and turn trash into treasure.

Details about how the resort became a green resort are provided on the resort's website, along with a list of over 100 green practices that have been adopted. Resort brochures also mention the resort's environmental notice board in the lobby, which has environmental news for guests to read. Throughout the resort grounds there are information signs made from recycled materials to inform guests of unique plants, flowers and animals. Resort staff also conduct regular walks around the gardens, the wetlands and recycling areas to educate guests.

Another important challenge for Frangipani is the lack of support and cooperation from its external environment. No other resorts on the island openly practice similar water-related green measures, so the resort is concerned about the lack of protection of the waters surrounding Langkawi island from inadequately treated sewage. There is a strong view that environmental stewardship is the responsibility of the government, which has led many hotels to continue directing their wastewater to the sea. In addition, government agencies do not approve of the water treatment measures taken at Frangipani because the law requires the hotel to connect a drain from the hotel to the main drain (which goes to a river to then flow into and pollute the sea). Frangipani was initially refused a

(Continued)

Case Study. Continued.

Certificate of Fitness for expanding the hotel for not being connected to the main drain, so it had to comply; however, it prevents any grey water from flowing through this drain via its closed loop system.

Clearly, without strong government support, Frangipani's effort to be green will continue to be challenging. The government has an important role in the successful implementation of water and wastewater management. The governments need to be more supportive, and implement the appropriate regulation and policy on water and wastewater management systems for the hotel industry to follow and comply with.

The third major challenge is money. As with any type of investment, Frangipani's environmental measures also required funding. All its environmental activities are funded internally from revenue generated through operating the resort and from small amounts derived from selling plants to other resorts and revenue earned from recycling activities. Millions of ringgit have been invested back into the resort for refurbishment, renovation, rebuilding and building new facilities. While only a small percentage of this has been directly related to improving environmental assets, increased return on investment has followed because better facilities mean higher rates and higher profitability.

Frangipani spends approximately RM200,000 on its corporate social responsibility programme and environmental activities each year. This does not take into account staff and owner's costs, which include employing two dedicated environmental staff, on-site input and overseas visits and lecturing. In addition, a wastewater treatment system to eliminate pollution of seawater costs another RM100,000 annually. Total capital investment is approximately RM300,000 per year.

QUESTIONS

1. Discuss within the context of your own country the importance for hotels to have water treatment systems such as the one described in this case study.

2. Do you personally believe that recycled water can and should be used to water plants, including vegetables? How else can the water be used?

3. What do you think of the local government's reaction to Frangipani's initiative?

4. With regard to question 3, how should local government react to the initiative?

5. From the marketing and communication perspective, how can Frangipani garner more support for its environmental initiatives?

6. What further information do you think is necessary in order to better understand this case study?

CASE STUDY SOURCES

Al Ayed, H.A. and Sharari, S.F. (2008) The public awareness of the citizens of the City of Ma'an of the environment and environmental law. *Mutah Journal for Research* 23, 116–149.

Ambabi, M.A. (1998) *Economy and Environment, Environmental Introduction*. Academic Bookshop, Cairo.

Atken, J. (2002) The role of events in the promotion of cities. Conference paper. Event and Place Marketing. IJTS, Sydney, 15–16 July.

Bursa Malaysia Annual Report (2009) Corporate social responsibility. Available at: http://www.bursamalaysia.com

Carlisle, Y.M. and Faulkner, D.O. (2004) Corporate social responsibility: a stages framework. *European Business Journal* 16, 143–151.

Carroll, A.B. (1999) Corporate social responsibility: the evolution of a definitional construct. *Business and Society* 38, 268–295.

Chadwick, M. (2003) Big challenge of small business for sustainability and SMEs. *Industry and Environment* 8–9.

Chetty, S. (2008) Social responsibility among SMEs in Kwazulu-Natal. Doctor of Commerce 196–199.

Csrnetwork (2009) What is corporate social responsibility? Available at: http://www.csrnetwork.com/csr.asp

Dwyer, L., Mellor, R., Mistilla, N. and Mules, T. (2000) A framework for assessing tangible and intangible impacts of events and convention. *Event Management* 6, 175–189.

Four types corporate social responsibility (n.d.) Available at: http://www.ehow.com/info_8117691_four-types-corporate-social-responsibility

Fox, T. (2005) *Small and Medium-sized Enterprises (SMEs) and Corporate Social Responsibility: A Discussion Paper*. IIED, London.

Jenkins, H. (2006) Small business champions for corporate social responsibility. *Journal of Business Ethics* 67, 241–256.

Kasim, A. (2006) The need for environmental and social responsibility in the tourism industry. *International Journal of Hospitality and Environmental Management* 7, 1–22.

Kasim, A. (2009) Towards a wider adoption of business responsibility in the hotel sector. *International Journal of Hospitality and Tourism* 8, 25–49.

Khanfar, A. and Khanfar, I. (2006) Marketing Environmental Tourism and Biodiversity. *Asyoot University* 9, 23–78.

Lepoutre, J. and Heene, A. (2006) Investigating the impact of firm size on small business social responsibility: a critical review. *Journal of Business Ethics* 67, 257–273.

Mohr, L.A., Webb, D.J. and Harris, K.E. (2001) Do consumers expect companies to be socially responsible? The impact of corporate social responsibility on buying behaviour. *Journal of Consumer Affairs* 35, 45–72.

Pacific Asia Travel Association (2002) *APEC/PATA Code for Sustainable Tourism*. Available at: http://www.pata.org

Presbury, R. and Edwards, D. (2005) Incorporating sustainability in meetings and event management education. *International Journal of Event Management Research* 1, 30–45.

Sairafi, M. (2007) *Tourism and Environment*. Dar Alfikr, Alexandria.

Sweeney, L. (2009) A study of current practice of CSR. *DIT* 80–98, 130–133.

Tajuddin, K. (2001) Consumer behaviour towards corporate social responsibility in Malaysia. *Consumer Behaviour* 1–17.

Thompson, J. and Smith, H. (1991) Social responsibility and small business: suggestions for research. *Journal of Small Business Management* 29, 30–44.

Vives, A. (2007) Responsible practices in small and medium enterprises. *CSR in SMEs* 3–8.

Yu, A.L. (2010) CSR and SMEs. *Research for Governance of Social-Ecological Systems* 1–12.

GLOSSARY OF TERMS USED IN THIS CHAPTER

Aquatic	Water environment such as lakes, rivers and oceans.
Bioethanol	A form of renewable energy that can be produced from common crops such as sugar cane, potato, manioc and maize.
Compost	Organic matter that has decomposed. Recycled as a fertilizer and soil improver.
Contamination	The presence of an unwanted constituent (contaminant) in a material, physical body, natural environment, workplace, etc.
Ecosystem	Functional units consisting of living things in a given area and the non-living chemical and physical factors of their environment, linked together through nutrient cycle and energy flow.
Energy audit	An inspection, survey and analysis of energy flows for energy conservation in a building, process or system to reduce the amount of energy input into the system without negatively affecting the output(s).
External marketing	Marketing activities targeted to the consumer or business market or both.
Grey water	Wastewater from kitchen and bathroom sinks.
Incineration	A waste treatment process that involves the combustion of substances contained in waste materials.
Internal marketing	Marketing activities targeted to the employees, usually to garner support towards a new internal policy.
Invertebrates	Species without a vertebral column.
Landfill	A site for the disposal of waste materials by burial. The oldest form of waste treatment.
LEED	Leadership in Energy and Environmental Design (LEED) is an internationally recognized green building certification system, providing third-party verification that a building or community was designed and built using strategies intended to improve performance in metrics such as energy saving, water efficiency, CO_2 emissions reduction, improved indoor environmental quality, and stewardship of resources and sensitivity to their impacts.
Natural resources	Non-renewable resources such as timber, water and minerals.
Passive cooling	A building design that attempts to integrate principles of physics into the building exterior envelope to slow heat transfer into a building and to remove unwanted heat from a building.
R-value (insulation)	A measure of thermal resistance used in the building and construction industry.
Resource consumption	The utilization of resources to produce something. For example, the utilization of electricity to produce lighting or run machines.
Sustainability	The act of harvesting or using a resource so that the resource is not depleted or permanently damaged.

Sustainable tourism The running of the tourism industry in a manner that achieves the triple bottom line of economy, environmental and social objectives.

Water plants Species of flora that live within the aquatic environment.

REFERENCES AND ADDITIONAL READING

Barrow, C. (2006) *Environmental Management for Sustainable Development*. Routledge, New York.

Barrows, C.W. and Powers, T. (2009) *Introduction to Hospitality Industry*. Wiley, Hoboken, New Jersey.

Calrecycle (2011) *Sustainable Green Building Basics*. Available at: http://www.calrecycle.ca.gov/green-building/Basics.htm#Energy (accessed 8 June 2011).

Canellas, L.P., Olivares, F.L., Okorokova-Facanha, A.L. and Rocha Facanha, A. (2002) Humic acids isolated from earthworm compost enhance root elongation, lateral root emergence, and plasma membrane H+-ATPase activity in maize roots. *Plant Physiology* 130, 1951–1957.

Capehart, B., Turner, W.C. and Kennedy, W.J. (2008) *Guide to Energy Management*, 5th edn. Fairmont Press, Lilburn, Georgia.

Chan, W.W. and Lam, J.C. (2002) Prediction of pollutant emission through electricity consumption by the hotel industry in Hong Kong. *International Journal of Hospitality Management* 21, 381–391.

Cheremisinoff, N.P. (2003) *Handbook of Solid Waste Management and Waste Minimization Techniques*. Butterworth-Heinemann, Oxford.

CHOSE (2001) Energy savings by combined heat cooling and power plants (CHCP) in the hotel sector. *Report of the Commission of the European Communities*. Directorate General for Energy, Stockholm, Sweden.

Davies, T. and Cahill, S. (2000) *Environmental Implications of the Tourism Industry*. Resources for the Future, Washington, DC.

DPPEA (2011a) *Restaurant Waste Reduction Manual: A Step-by-Step Approach to Developing a Waste Reduction Campaign*. North California Division of Pollution Prevention and Environmental Assistance. Available at: http://www.p2pays.org/ref/03/02368.pdf (accessed 10 June 2011).

DPPEA (2011b) *Waste Reduction in Hotels and Motels*. North California Division of Pollution Prevention and Environmental Assistance. Available at: http://www.p2pays.org/ref/04/03266.pdf (accessed 10 June 2011).

Eberle, W.M. (1995) *Integrated Waste Management*. Kansas State University Document Number: EP-19. Available at: http://www.ksre.ksu.edu/library/solw2/ep19.pdf (accessed 9 June 2011).

Garner, A., Stevely, J., Smith, H., Hoppe, M., Floyd, T. and Hinchcliff, P. (2001) *A Guide to Environmentally Friendly Landscaping: Florida Yards and Neighborhoods Handbook*. Florida Cooperative Extension Service, Institute of Agriculture Sciences, University of Florida Document Number: SP 191. Available at: http://hillsborough_fyn.ifas.ufl.edu/FYN%20PDF%20Files/FYN%20Handbook.pdf (accessed 8 June 2011).

Gee, C.Y. (1994) *International Hotel Management*. Educational Institute of AH&MA, East Lansing, Michigan.

GreenSource (2008) *Emerald Architecture Case Studies in Green Building*. McGraw-Hill, Columbus, Ohio.

Holden, A. (2008) *Environment and Tourism*. Routledge, New York.

IBLF & CI (2005) *Sustainable Hotel: Siting, Design and Construction*. IBLF & CI Publishing, London.

Kasim, A. (2006) The need for environmental and social responsibility in the tourism industry. *International Journal of Hospitality and Environmental Management* 7, 1–22.

Kirk, D. (1996) *Environmental Management for Hotels: A Student's Handbook*. Butterworth-Heinemann, Oxford.

Lütz, H. (2008) Energy efficiency in hotels. Available at: http://www.buildingexperts.info/en/english/paper/title/energy-efficiency-in-hotels-1.html (accessed 8 July 2011).

Ozgen, I. (2005) Waste management in large scale hotel establishments and a case study at Iber Hotel Sarıgerme Park Resort. PhD thesis. Dokuz Eylül University Social Sciences Institute, Izmir, Turkey.

Ozgen, I., Tükeltürk Aydın, Ş. and Perçin Şahin, N. (2008) Management issues concerning environment: a hotel best practice. *Tourism Today* 8, 145–153.

Radwan, H.R.I., Jones, E. and Minoli, D. (2010) Managing solid waste in small hotels. *Journal of Sustainable Tourism* 18, 175–190.

Sloan, P., Legrand, W. and Chen, J. (2009) *Sustainability in the Hospitality Industry*. Butterworth-Heinemann, Oxford.

Sullivan, R. and Wyndham, H. (2001) *Effective Environmental Management: Principles & Case Studies*. Allen & Unwin, Crows Nest, Australia.

Talwar, R. (2006) *Travel and Tourism Management*. Gyan Books, Delhi, India.

UNEP (2003) *Switched On: Renewable Energy Opportunities in the Tourism Industry*. Available at: http://www.unep.fr/shared/publications/pdf/3258-SwitchedOn.pdf (accessed 14 July 2011).

USDA (2011) *Integrated Solid Waste Management for Rural Areas. A Planning Toolkit for Solid Waste Managers*. US Department of Agriculture, Rural Utilities Service. Available at: http://www.usda.gov/rus/water/docs/swmgmt.pdf (accessed 8 July 2011).

Webster, K. (2000) *Environmental Management in the Hospitality Industry: A Guide for Students and Managers*. Cassell, London.

World Tourism Organization (2009) *Confidence in Tourism Sector Gradually Picking Up*. World Tourism Organization, Madrid, Spain.

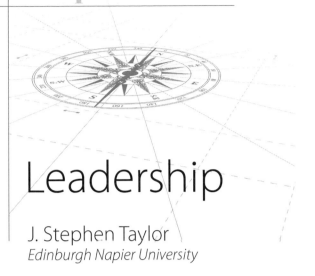

chapter 13

Leadership

J. Stephen Taylor
Edinburgh Napier University

LEARNING OBJECTIVES

Having completed this chapter, readers should be able to:

- identify a number of key leadership theories from the 1940s through to the present day;
- outline the characteristics associated with effective leaders;
- understand the nature of effective leadership behaviours;
- evaluate the role of leadership within organizations and its importance.

INTRODUCTION

This chapter is concerned with the topic of leadership. As will become clear, despite the fact that leadership is probably one of the most extensively researched topics in the field of management, we appear to be some considerable distance from a single definitive theory of leadership. Instead, we have a rich tapestry of theories and research on leadership stretching back over a century. The focus in this chapter is to introduce you to some of this richness and to highlight some of the key theories and contributions on the topic of leadership.

Leadership is closely related to the topic of innovation because both are concerned with transformation and change within organizations – that is, going beyond the status quo. They are about creativity and building something new, something better – both are concerned with vision. Thus leadership is all about providing a direction and focus for organizational members and securing their commitment towards achieving the associated objectives

© CAB International 2013. *Facilities Management and Development for Tourism* (eds. A. Hassanien and C. Dale)

and goals. The need for this capacity in all forms of organizational activity within society is vital (see the Ritz Carlton example below for coverage of this importance and its potential impact).

However, what *exactly* is leadership? The preceding paragraph is rather vague and lacks precision. Most of us probably have the feeling that we are familiar with the concept and can attach our own meaning to it (in much the same way as we can with concepts such as 'love' or 'happiness'), but we need to develop a shared meaning if we are to usefully progress in our exploration of the topic here. That said, a review by Fleishman *et al.* (1991) identified that 65 different classification systems to define dimensions of leadership had been developed in the preceding 60 years, highlighting the diversity of thought and understanding associated with leadership. None the less, it is possible to broadly group these classifications. Leadership has been variously seen as: (i) the focus of group process; (ii) a personality perspective; (iii) an act or behaviour; (iv) the power relationship between leaders and followers; (v) a transformational perspective; and (vi) a skills perspective (capabilities).

As such, one is reminded of John Godfrey Saxe's (1816–1887) famous poem of the 'six men of Indostan' who, all being blind, attempting to describe what an elephant is from touching only one different part of the elephant each (e.g. the trunk, the tail, the ear and so on). All come to very different conclusions as to what an elephant is (i.e. a tree, a rope, a fan and so on). In the Indian religion of Jainism, this story is used to illustrate its philosophy of demonstrating tolerance towards different viewpoints, with the blind men arguing between themselves about the nature of an elephant until they are told by a wise man:

> All of you are right. The reason every one of you is telling it differently is because each one of you touched the different part of the elephant. So, actually the elephant has all the features you mentioned.

As we will see, in many ways the various theories of leadership (and their associated theorists!) are very similar in that they all seem to describe different parts of leadership and never quite the entire thing!

Defining leadership

As always, it is useful to develop a working definition of the topic at hand. Northouse offers a succinct definition that: 'leadership is a process whereby an individual influences a group of individuals to achieve a common goal' (2007, p. 3). Despite its brevity, we can identify four central components of the leadership phenomenon here:

- leadership is a process;
- leadership involves influence;
- leadership takes place in a group context;
- leadership involves goal attainment.

The process aspect places emphasis on a transactional (interactive) event between leaders and followers and not on leadership traits or characteristics. Process implies that a leader affects and is affected by followers. The role of leader is not necessarily fixed within a given group. With regards to influence the concern here is with how the leader affects followers – influence is *the* defining characteristic of leadership – it cannot exist without it! With reference to groups, this recognizes that leadership takes place in the context of groups. It is in this social context in which influence within and on groups towards a common purpose is the focus of leadership upon achieving goals – that is directing a group of individuals to achieve some defined task or end.

Is leadership the same as management?

In some aspects yes, as both involve influence, working with people and goal attainment, but leadership is also different from management. We can trace leadership back to at least the Ancient Greeks, but management, by comparison, is essentially a 20th-century phenomenon that arose from the industrial revolution. The primary functions of management were first described and formalized by Henri Fayol (1916) as being concerned with planning, organizing, staffing and controlling. One of the best attempts to clarify the differences between leadership and management is offered by Kotter (1990). He identifies that management's primary function is to provide order and consistency to organizations, whereas leadership is concerned with producing change and movement within organizations.

Thus leadership is concerned with establishing direction and creating a vision. It involves clarifying the big picture and setting strategies, then aligning people through communicating goals, seeking commitment and building teams and coalitions. It involves motivating and inspiring followers, to energize and empower subordinates, helping them to satisfy unmet needs. By comparison, management's concern is with producing order and consistency. Thus the management task of planning and budgeting involves establishing agendas, setting timetables and allocating resources. With regard to organizing and staffing associated with management, this is concerned with providing structure, making job placements and establishing rules and procedures. Finally, management's focus on controlling and problem solving involves developing incentives, generating creative solutions and where necessary taking corrective action.

SOME KEY DIMENSIONS OF LEADERSHIP

Trait vs process perspectives of leadership

The trait perspective sees leadership being based on innate or inbred characteristics; it supports the idea that 'leaders are born not made'. Here leadership is seen to be based on physical characteristics such as a person's height, personality, abilities and so on. A very large body of research based on this perspective exists and the earliest theories of leadership reflect this perspective. The process perspective sees leadership as something that everyone can learn to perform and not restricted to a small elite. Here leadership is seen to exist in a set of behaviours. It is this perspective that is given the greater emphasis in this chapter. Thus the stance taken here is that we can all learn to perform a leadership role within both our professional and personal contributions to society.

Assigned vs emergent leadership

Here we recognize that a given individual might be formally designated as a 'leader' by their position in their organization (what we call assigned leadership) or be accorded that position by the responses to them by other group members (what we call emergent leadership). This recognizes the possibility that in reality the assigned leader may not be the actual leader in a given context. If group members perceive another individual as exhibiting leadership behaviours and respond to this accordingly, then that individual becomes the *de facto* leader (i.e. emergent leadership). This might occur in a specific situation where an individual has particular experiences or skills that the group depends on for direction.

Leadership and power

As leadership involves influence, this links to the issue of power, which is the capacity or potential to influence others. French and Raven (1959) identified five important and common bases of power: reward, coercive, legitimate, referent and expert. It is possible to group these to identify the two major sources of power in organizations: position power (which incorporates legitimate, reward and coercive bases of power), which is based on an individual's office or rank, and personal power, which is based on the remaining two bases of power in the form of perceived likeability (referent) and knowledge (expert).

> **Example:** The Ritz-Carlton and the importance of leadership
>
> The Ritz-Carlton motto 'We are Ladies and Gentlemen serving Ladies and Gentlemen' is widely known and quoted. What is less well known is the wider context in which this phrase is actually situated with regards to the organization's legendary commitment to service excellence underpinned by excellent leadership. The Ritz-Carlton hotel chain has a world-class reputation for service excellence, which is recognized and reflected in the creation of the award winning training facility 'The Ritz-Carlton Leadership Centre' (which has attracted tens of thousands of managers from across the full spectrum of business activity since its launch in 2000) and more recently in the publication of the book *The New Gold Standard* (Michelli, 2008), which outlines the leadership principles that underpin The Ritz-Carlton's enduring success.
>
> The modern Ritz-Carlton Hotel Company originates from The Ritz-Carlton Boston, whose own legacy goes back to the famous hotelier Cesar Ritz. Today, The Ritz-Carlton Hotel
>
> *(Continued)*

Example. Continued.

Company is an independently operated division of Marriott International. It manages 73 hotels across 24 different countries and employs 38,000 people. A key element of The Ritz-Carlton's success resides in the effectiveness of the leadership role played by its upper-management team.

Since 1983, initially under the direction of Horst Schulze, the senior management team has assumed direct responsibility for managing quality because they believe this is not something they can delegate. The success of this approach is evidenced by the fact that The Ritz-Carlton has won the Malcolm Baldrige National Quality Award, widely recognized as the premier quality certification scheme in the USA, in 1992 and 1999 respectively, the only service organization ever to do so twice (http://www.nist.gov/baldrige/). In 2003, The Ritz-Carlton was named 'Highest in Guest Satisfaction Among Luxury Hotels' by global marketing information services firm J.D. Power and Associates. On that occasion the company's press release quoted the then President and Chief Operating Officer Simon F. Cooper, stating that this was 'a validation of The Ritz-Carlton vision to grow and extend its brand, without sacrificing our long-standing commitment to providing the finest service and surroundings to our guests.'

In July 2010, once again The Ritz-Carlton was recognized by J.D. Power and Associates by being named winner of the 'North America Hotel Guest Satisfaction Index', scoring 861 points out of a total of 1000 with a sector average score of 822. In addition, The Ritz-Carlton has received the J.D. Power and Associates rating 'Among the Best' for the past five years. In August 2010, Robert J. McCarthy, Marriott International Group President, announced that Herve Humler was to be appointed as President and Chief Operations Officer of The Ritz-Carlton brand. McCarthy highlighted the importance of this leadership role and its focus, stating that 'Herve is a true international hotelier with more than 35 years in the luxury lodging business and has helped to build The Ritz-Carlton into a world-class brand. We feel most fortunate to have Herve in this position of increased responsibility where he can continue to provide his strong leadership to this iconic brand'.

Herve Humler now occupies the leadership role, initiated by Horst Schulze 30 years ago, that marked the start of The Ritz-Carlton's obsessive focus on service quality excellence. As it is often quipped, it is more accurate to think of achieving service quality as a journey rather than a destination. The Ritz-Carlton story exemplifies this metaphor with a journey that can be traced back to the very first steps towards quality under Horst Schulze's leadership in 1983.

Sources: http://www.baldrige.nist.gov/PDF_files/RCHC_Application_Summary.pdf
The Ritz-Carlton Hotel Company press releases 27 July, 12 August 2010
J.D. Power and Associates Company press release 27 July 2010

Question

1. What does this case tell us about the role of leadership within organizations?

LEADERSHIP THEORIES 1940s–1970s

In this section we will focus on the development of leadership theories during a period approximately spanning the 1940s and 1970s. We examine five approaches or theories of leadership that emerged during this period:

- trait approach;
- skills approach;
- style approach;
- situational approach;
- contingency theory.

In the final part of the chapter we will look at what has been broadly called 'The New Leadership Approach', which essentially covers the period from the 1980s through to the present day.

Our first theory, the trait approach, represents the first systematic approach to the study of leadership. At the outset it is useful to compare and contrast the trait approach to leadership with that of the process approach to leadership. The trait perspective sees leadership being based on innate or inbred characteristics, thus the phrase 'leaders are born not made'. This body of research sees leadership based on physical characteristics (e.g. height), personality, abilities etc. A large body of research is based on this perspective and is outlined below. By contrast, the process perspective sees leadership as something that everyone can learn to perform, that is it resides in a set of behaviours. It is this perspective that is emphasized in this chapter because the concern is with identifying how we, as individuals, might learn to become more effective leaders in organizations of which we are members.

Trait approach

Here the focus is on understanding the personal traits that are associated with effective leadership. This area is sometimes referred to as 'great man theories' because the original research focus was on famous political and military leaders. This approach sought to answer the question: 'what are the innate qualities that appear to separate leaders from their followers?' The assumed universality of leadership traits was questioned by Stogdill (1948). He analysed the findings of some 124 previous trait studies covering the period 1904 through to 1947. He identified that leaders differed from average group members in terms of their intelligence, alertness, insight, responsibility, initiative, persistence, self-confidence and sociability. However, possessing these traits is not enough and they must be relevant to the situation.

Thus leadership is not a passive state but a working relationship between the leader and other group members. This insight marked the start of a research focus on leadership behaviours *and* leadership situations.

In a second survey in 1974, Stogdill reviewed a further 163 studies of leadership (1948–1970) that had taken place since his first survey. While the findings of his first survey suggested that situational factors determined leadership not personality factors, the findings of the second survey suggested that *both* personality and situational factors determine leadership. This lends some support to trait theory, namely that leadership characteristics are part of leadership. In his second survey Stogdill identified 10 key leadership characteristics.

Additional reviews of trait studies

Mann (1959) looked at 1400 findings. He gave less emphasis to situational factors, with the leadership personality traits being identified as: intelligence, masculinity, adjustment, dominance, extraversion and conservatism. A subsequent study by Lord *et al.* (1986) re-examined Mann's findings and identified intelligence, masculinity and dominance as being traits associated with leadership across all situations. A more recent study by Kirkpatrick and Locke (1991) further supported the existence of leadership traits. Table 13.1 below summarizes the key traits identified by the various trait researchers.

Critique

With 100 years of research into leadership traits, findings suggest that the key traits are intelligence, self-confidence, determination, integrity and sociability. Here the focus is on the leader, not the followers and/or situation. The trait approach sees effective leadership residing in individuals having certain personality traits. Consequently, adopting this approach would suggest that organizations should recruit people with these traits for leadership roles.

Table 13.1. Leadership characteristics identified by trait research studies.

Stogdill (1948)	Mann (1959)	Stogdill (1974)	Lord *et al.* (1986)	Kirkpatrick and Locke (1991)
Intelligence	Intelligence	Achievement	Intelligence	Drive
Alertness	Masculinity	Persistence	Masculinity	Motivation
Insight	Adjustment	Insight	Dominance	Integrity
Responsibility	Dominance	Initiative		Confidence
Initiative	Extroversion	Self-confidence		Cognitive ability
Persistence	Conservatism	Responsibility		Task knowledge
Self-confidence		Cooperativeness		
Sociability		Tolerance		
		Influence		
		Sociability		

Trait theory is seen as being intuitively appealing because it accords with popular beliefs about leaders and leadership. It has 100 years of research behind it and is the most developed area of leadership research. It has a sole focus on just the leader element not followers or situations. However, this is also potentially a weakness, but it has allowed for a real depth of focus on a specific area. It provides benchmarks for the traits required to be a leader and thus provides us with a basis for assessing individuals and their likely leadership effectiveness.

Despite 100 years of research, a definitive list of traits has not been produced. Situational factors, the leadership context that is central to most of the leadership theories we examine below, is excluded. The leadership traits that have been identified are considered to be highly subjective. The studies undertaken have not sought to link traits of particular leaders to actual leadership outcomes, with the emphasis being on leadership emergence and not on employee or organizational performance. Trait theory is not viewed as being useful for training and developing because it is not easy to teach new traits since these are seen as being largely fixed in individuals.

Skills approach

Our second leadership theory is similar to the trait approach in that it is a leader-centred perspective of leadership. The focus here, however, is on the skills required to be an effective leader not the personality traits associated with leadership. It suggests that in addition to certain traits, effective leaders need particular skills and that these can be developed, unlike the personality traits.

It is generally acknowledged that the key shift towards the skills approach was marked by the publication of the *Harvard Business Review* article by Robert Katz (1955) entitled 'Skills of an effective administrator'. Here Katz argued that effective administration (i.e. leadership) is based on three basic personal skills: technical skills (know-how relevant to a particular type of work or activity), human skills (knowledge about and ability to work with people) and conceptual skills (ability to work with ideas and concepts). Thus skills are the knowledge and competencies leaders can use to accomplish a set of goals/objectives. Unlike the naturally acquired traits in trait theory, here leadership is viewed as a set of skills that can be learned and developed. Katz suggested that the relative importance of these skills varied by the level of organizational position involved (see Table 13.2).

Table 13.2. Katz's skills of an effective administrator. (From Katz, 1955.)

Management level	Technical skills level	Human skills level	Conceptual skills level
Top	Low	High	High
Middle	Medium	High	Medium
Supervisory	High	High	Low

Skills model

A major piece of research by Mumford *et al.* (2000) involved 1800 subjects and was commissioned by the US military. This research subsequently developed a skills-based model of leadership consisting of five components: (i) individual attributes (general cognitive ability, crystallized cognitive ability, motivation, personality); (ii) competencies (problem-solving skills, social judgement skills and knowledge); (iii) leadership outcomes (effective problem solving and performance); (iv) career experiences (which impact on components (i) and (ii)); and (v) environmental influences (which impact on components (i), (ii) and (iii)). It implies that leadership is not the provenance of a small elite, but that in the correct circumstances, many people can acquire the necessary know-how.

Critique

It is a descriptive approach that offers a structure for understanding effective leadership in terms of the skills required. While Katz (1955) suggested that the required leadership skills required vary by management level, subsequent research by Mumford *et al.* (2000) offers a more complex and sophisticated take on this approach. Overall, the skills approach offers a basis for understanding how leaders can become more effective in terms of the necessary leadership skills and capabilities.

As a leader-centred model, it emphasizes the need to develop certain leadership skills. It implies that being skills-based, effective leadership is something open to all – unlike trait theory. The Mumford *et al.* (2000) skills model provides a detailed, comprehensive basis for conceiving of, and researching in, leadership skills. Importantly, the skills approach is compatible with a general approach to leadership education.

The breadth of skills and variables covered by the skills model of leadership is very wide and arguably goes beyond just leadership and is therefore too general. It is seen to have weak predictive value and does not explain how skills lead to effective leadership performance. While claiming not to be a trait model, a major component of the model concerns personal traits. As the model is based on research undertaken entirely within the US Army, the question arises as to how applicable is it to other contexts. More research is required on this aspect of the model.

Style approach

The style approach places the emphasis on the behaviour of leaders. It is thus very different from both the trait approach and skills approach, which refer to the leader's personal dimension. Consequently, it expands the study of leadership to include a leader's actions to subordinates in different contexts. There have been two general behaviours identified: task behaviours (those behaviours that facilitate goal achievement) and relationship behaviours (those behaviours that focus on subordinates).

The Ohio State studies

Referred to as the 'Ohio State studies' because they took place at Ohio State University, this research expands across three decades between the 1940s through until the 1970s, and is based on Stogdill's original (1948) work. Rather than looking at traits, the emphasis was on the behaviour of leaders. The research used a questionnaire that was completed by subordinates who were asked to identify how often their organizational leader engaged in certain specified behaviours. This was originally a 150-item questionnaire (Hemphill and Coons, 1957) known as the Leadership Behaviour Description Questionnaire (LBDQ), but Stogdill (1963) published a shortened version containing only 12 items (known as the LBDQ-XII) and this is the version most widely used in the research.

It was found that the responses of subordinates tended to cluster around two general types of leadership behaviour: (i) initiating structure and (ii) consideration (Stogdill, 1974). With the initiating structure behaviours the focus was on *task* behaviours such as organizing work, structuring work context, defining work roles and scheduling activities. In terms of the consideration behaviours the focus was on *relationship* behaviours such as building groups, respect, trust and mutual respect between leaders and followers. Thus the LBDQ-XII identifies two types of behaviours that are the basis of the style approach. Here these are seen as two distinct behaviours and not as two different points on a single continuum. Consequently, an individual leader could exhibit high or low in either or both behaviours. An obvious key question is which leadership style is most effective? The answer would appear to be it all depends. Findings suggested that in particular contexts one or both behaviours can be more, or less, important. A key area of research thus concerns identifying the optimal mix of behaviours for a given context.

The University of Michigan studies

Here the focus was on leadership behaviour in the context of small groups. It identified two types of leadership behaviours: (i) those with an employee orientation and (ii) those with a production orientation (Bowers and Seashore, 1966). As such, these findings can be seen to closely parallel the findings of the Ohio State research. A key difference is the two types of leadership behaviours were originally conceived as being at opposite ends of a single continuum. This was later treated as two separate and independent orientations and thus brought into line with the treatment of the two types of behaviours identified in the Ohio State research.

Through the 1950s and 1960s both Ohio State and Michigan conducted studies with a view to establishing how leaders might combine both behaviour types to maximize followers' satisfaction and performance levels. The goal was a universal theory of leadership that provided an explanation of leadership effectiveness in every situation. The results, however, were contradictory and unclear (Yukl, 1994), with some indication that a high task and a high relationship orientation is best in all leadership situations (Misumi, 1985).

Blake and Mouton's Leadership Grid

Probably one of the best known and most widely used variants of the style approach is the Leadership Grid, developed by Blake and Mouton in the 1960s and subsequently revised several times in the intervening decades. It offers a practical model of leadership that reflects the style approach with two separate behaviours, *task* and *relationship* oriented. Blake and Mouton

(1985) claim that individuals usually have a dominant grid style plus a back-up style that is used when the dominant style fails or the individual is under pressure. Their model is widely used in consulting and in organizational development.

The grid has two dimensions: (i) concern for results and (ii) concern for people, with each running from one through to nine (i.e. low to high). Thus a leader with a style that has the lowest concern for results and the highest concern for people would be scored a '1, 9' on the grid, a style of leadership labelled as 'country club'. The complete opposite style (highest concern for results, lowest concern for people) scores '9, 1' and is labelled as 'authoritarian'. Other labels exist for different scores on the grid, i.e. the low/low score of '1, 1' is 'impoverished management'; while the high/high score of '9, 9' is 'team leaders' and the medium/medium score of '5, 5' is labelled as 'middle of the road' as a style of leadership.

Critique

The style approach does not represent a refined theory or set of prescriptions on effective leadership, but offers a framework for assessing leadership in broad terms in the form of describing a leader's task and relationship behaviours. It highlights that two types of behaviour are involved in leadership, task and relationship oriented, and that the particular emphasis on each for effective leadership will depend on the specific leadership context.

The style approach marked a shift away from leadership being seen exclusively as a personality trait and broadened the focus to include leadership behaviours. It is supported by a wide range of research studies and can be considered as a viable basis on which to examine the leadership process. It makes clear that from a conceptual basis *both* task and relationship behaviours form the core of the leadership process. It provides a powerful lens through which to view leadership and to assess leadership effectiveness.

The research undertaken has not shown the links between styles and performance outcomes (e.g. morale, job satisfaction and productivity). The only strong finding is that considerate leaders have more satisfied followers (Yukl, 1994). Consequently, it fails to provide a universal style of effective leadership (Northouse, 2007). Some researchers have implied that a 'high task–high relationship' style is most effective overall, but this is only weakly supported by the actual research findings (Yukl, 1994).

Situational approach

Probably one of the more widely recognized approaches to leadership is that developed by Hersey and Blanchard (1969). They argue that different types of situations require different types of leadership and that to be effective, leaders need to adapt their style to the specific context they face. Their theory emphasizes that effective leadership has two dimensions: a directive (task) and a supportive (relationship) one. Here a key task is for a leader to assess subordinates in terms of their competence (skills) and commitment (motivation) for a given task at a particular point in time. This will determine whether the appropriate leadership style should be oriented more or less towards the directive or supportive dimensions.

Critique

The concept of 'situation' refers to where employees are on a developmental continuum – this is represented by their relative level of competence (skills level) and commitment (motivation level) in respect of a given task. Thus the leader is required to identify this level and to match this to the appropriate management style. Although there is arguably a tension here – does the leader match to the needs of the individual or the work group? This raises questions about how practical this prescription of adjusting leadership style to the situation where this might involve varying needs across a group of people. None the less, the broad implication of the situational approach is that leaders need to adjust their leadership style to fit the different contexts (situations) that regularly arise within the organization.

The situational approach is well recognized and accepted across many organizations as a basis for leadership training purposes. It is easily understood and applied by practitioners and is perceived to be useful across a wide range of contexts. As a leadership theory it offers a set of clear prescriptions, for example: competent but low in confidence employees require a supporting style and so on. It places an emphasis on leadership flexibility and the need to adapt leadership style to be effective. In addition, it reminds leaders that subordinates need to be treated as individuals.

The theory is based on a very limited number of published research studies, which does raise questions about its theoretical basis (Vecchio and Boatwright, 2002). With regard to the development level of subordinates – their commitment and competence – the conceptualization of this is considered to be weak (Yukl, 1994). In addition, the validity of the prescriptions of the model has been questioned (Vecchio, 1987; Fernandez and Vecchio, 1997). Finally, the theory ignores the impact of demographic influences on employees' preferences, e.g. age, gender, experience (Vecchio and Boatwright, 2002).

Contingency theory

There are a number of approaches that could be labelled 'contingency theory', but best known is Fiedler's (1964) contingency theory. This theory attempts to match leaders to appropriate situations (this is the contingency) because it is believed that leadership effectiveness depends on how well a leader's style fits a given context. Fiedler and his colleagues assessed many different leaders in many different contexts in terms of their effectiveness. Contingency theory is concerned with styles and situations. The focus here is on providing a framework for matching the leader and the situation to one another.

The key elements of Fiedler's model are leadership styles and situational variables. With regard to leadership style, Fiedler devised a method to measure a leader's style when seeking to achieve a goal using the Least Preferred Coworker (LPC) scale. This was seen to effectively identify whether a leader was either task (= low LPC) or relationship (= high LPC) motivated. The key situational variables are: (i) leader–member relations – refers to the group atmosphere, the degree of confidence, loyalty and attraction workers feel towards leader; (ii) task structure – which concerns how well structured and clear work tasks are – the more this is the case, the more control leader has over subordinates; and finally (iii) position power – which is the leader's authority to reward or punish – this is strong when a leader can hire and fire!

Critique

Fiedler's model suggests that task-motivated leaders (low LPC) will be effective in situations which are *both* favourable (high structure, strong power and good relations) and unfavourable (low structure, weak power and poor relations). Conversely, those relationship-motivated leaders (high LPC) do better in between these extremes. However, it is not clear why this should be the case. There is some suggestion that a mismatched style leads to stress and poor decision making. A number of questions remain as to how the theory really works.

Contingency theory is grounded in extensive research and it has broadened our understanding of leadership by including the impact of situations on leaders. It is predictive in that, based on the LPC score achieved, it indicates the probability of success for a given individual in a given situation. Additionally, it does not demand or suggest that a leader fit with every organizational situation that might arise and it also provides data (LPC scores) to help support personnel and organizational development.

Fiedler's theory fails to explain *why* certain leadership styles are more effective than others in certain situations. Perhaps the biggest criticisms surround the LPC aspect of the theory, which has been questioned as to its validity. What is the logic of evaluating yourself by focusing on another person? What is the actual method for selecting your LPC? From a practical perspective, the theory is not easily applied in the real world due to the number of variables that have to be considered.

SUMMARY

We have gone from a sole focus on leadership traits to a focus on leadership as a process involving specific behaviours within particular situations. This has provided us with a much more complex picture of leadership. It suggests that personality traits do not in themselves explain effective leadership. While both leadership skills and behaviours are important, these should be matched to the specific leadership context or situation.

According to Bryman (1999) it is possible to identify four distinct stages of leadership theory, with each subsequent stage marking a change in emphasis rather than the demise of the previous stage(s):

1. until the late 1940s: the trait approach;
2. until the late 1960s: the style approach;
3. until the early 1980s: the contingency approach;
4. from the early 1980s: the new leadership approach.

The first three stages we have already discussed and it is to Bryman's fourth stage of the new leadership approach that we now turn.

Example: Festivals and events – the importance of cultural leadership

Many, if not most, festivals and events are celebrations of the cultural dimension of human existence. The importance of effective leadership here is being increasingly recognized and in 2006 the Arts Council England launched a cultural leadership programme which, supported by £12 million of central government funding, aimed to provide leadership training for 2000 individuals in the cultural sector during 2006–2008. Its purpose was to develop dynamic, diverse and genuinely world-class leadership within the sector. Below are a series of quotes from those occupying cultural leadership roles, which provide some interesting perspectives on an activity traditionally seen as being alien to this sector and which highlight the characteristics of both effective leaders and of effective leadership.

Cultural leaders are as different in style and background as the organisations they serve. And that's as it should be, particularly in a world as diverse as the creative sector. However, in my experience, all successful cultural leaders have a few qualities in common. For one, they display clarity of vision coupled with a steely determination to deliver. They resist the temptation to get caught up in detail. Instead, they are able to identify – and then concentrate on – the few issues that really matter to any organisation at any given time. Cultural leaders invariably identify with the success of their organisations in an entirely personal way; whatever is good for the organisation is good for them. At the same time, they are aware that the converse is not necessarily true. Their ability to empathise and engage with people at every level of their organisation is integral to generating the excitement and enthusiasm that are essential for success in the creative world. Yet much as they identify with the people they lead, they can also detach their own intellects from their emotions. This enables them to make the often difficult – and sometimes even painful – decisions that are the price of true leadership.

(Peter Hewitt, Chief Executive, Arts Council England)

At heart, a great cultural leader is passionate with a huge respect for artistic talent and the vision to push that talent to its limits. Sometimes there is an element of saving creative people from themselves. You need grit, determination, and an ability to make your team have one vision.

(Robin Millar, Producer, Hon. Patron, Music Producers Guild)

To be a great cultural leader, the range of skills needed to come together in one human being is immense: entrepreneurial, logistical, visionary, curatorial, political and strategic. But all of those are as nothing, if you do not have the most important skill: the ability to really listen.

(Augustus Casely-Hayford, Director, inIVA)

Cultural leaders have the capacity to ask questions other people didn't think of, turn these questions into a dynamic vision, and drive the vision forward through all the problems. The confidence to discover dynamic models and ideas from a range of places, apply them, but to throw them out again once they start to get in the way.

(John McGrath, Artistic Director, Contact Theatre)

Source: Arts Council England (2006) *Introducing the Cultural Leadership Programme.* Arts Council England.

Question

1. From the quotes above, to what extent do the theories covered in this chapter appear relevant to leadership in the cultural sector?

THE NEW LEADERSHIP APPROACH

The 'new leadership' term is used to describe a number of approaches to leadership that emerged in the 1980s. While these approaches share a number of common themes, they also display some differences. Consequently, a number of different terms have been used to describe this new turn in leadership research, ranging from transformational leadership (Bass, 1985; Tichy and Devanna, 1986); to charismatic leadership (House, 1976; Conger, 1989), visionary leadership (Sashkin, 1988; Westley and Mintzberg, 1989) and more recently just plain leadership (Bennis and Nanus, 1985; Kotter, 1990).

What's new about 'new leadership'?

A common thread that runs through the so-called new leadership approach is an emphasis on 'leaders as managers of meaning rather than in terms of an influence process' (Bryman, 1999, 30). A key contribution is the study by Burns (1978) of political leadership, which outlined the dichotomy of transactional leadership, based on the process of exchange between parties and the offer of rewards to followers (shown to be ultimately ineffective), and what he called transforming leadership in which the leader raises, and creates shared, followers' aspirations and morality (which was seen to be more effective). Another important influence was the best-selling book by former McKinsey & Co. consultants Peters and Waterman (1982), *In Search of Excellence*, which emphasized and demonstrated through a series of high-profile success case studies the importance of transforming leadership and vision. This later emphasis on the link between leadership and vision saw the term changed from transform*ing* to transform*ational*.

Transformational leadership and charisma

The House (1976) theory of charismatic leadership is often seen and treated as synonymous with transformational leadership. Here charisma is seen as a special gift that enables individuals to achieve extraordinary things, to be able to act in ways that will have positive effects on followers. According to House (1976), these personal characteristics include being dominant, a strong desire to influence others, self-confidence and having strong values. Thus charismatic leaders display certain behaviours and have certain effects on their followers (see Table 13.3).

Bass's (1985) model of transformational leadership

The early of work of Burns (1978) and House (1976) was developed and extended by Bass (1985), who conceived of a single continuum for transactional and transformational leadership. It is argued that this style of leadership motivates followers to achieve a higher level of performance by: (i) increasing their awareness of the importance and value of the set goals; (ii) transcending their self-interest for that of the collective; and (iii) making them address higher level needs. The Bass model identifies seven different factors: four transformational factors (known as the 4 'I's'), two transactional factors and a single non-leader/non-transactional factor. These are shown below in Table 13.4.

The transformational leadership factors

The first of these is idealized influence or charisma. This factor describes leaders who act as strong role models for followers. Followers identify with leaders and seek to emulate them. Such leaders are seen to have high standards of ethical and moral conduct. Their followers deeply respect and trust their leadership, which provides a clear vision and sense of mission.

The second of the transformational factors is inspirational motivation. This involves leaders who communicate high expectations to followers and then subsequently inspire and motivate followers to a commitment and engagement in a shared vision of the organization. Here transformational leaders use symbols and emotional appeals to focus the group members to achieve more than just self-interest and to ensure that team spirit is promoted.

Table 13.3. House's charismatic leadership. (From House, 1976.)

Personality characteristics	Behaviours	Effects on followers
Dominant	Sets strong role model	Trust in leader's ideology
Desire to influence	Shows competence	Belief similarity between
Confident	Articulates goals	leader and follower
Strong values	Communicates high	Unquestioning acceptance
	expectations	Affection toward leader
	Expresses confidence	Obedience
	Arouses motives	Identification with leader
		Emotional involvement
		Heightened goals
		Increased confidence

Table 13.4. Bass's model of transformational leadership. (From Bass, 1985.)

Transformational leadership	Transactional leadership	Laissez-faire leadership
Factor 1: Idealized influence (charisma)	Factor 5: Contingent reward (constructive transactions)	Factor 7: Laissez-faire (non-transactional)
Factor 2: Inspirational motivation	Factor 6: Management-by-exception; active and passive (corrective transactions)	
Factor 3: Intellectual stimulation		
Factor 4: Individualized consideration		

The third factor is intellectual stimulation through which leaders motivate followers to be creative and innovative. The emphasis is on encouraging followers to challenge their own beliefs and values and those of the leader and the organization. The leader supports followers to try new approaches and develop innovative ways of dealing with organizational issues. Quite simply, that is to challenge the 'status quo'.

The fourth and final transformational factor is individualized consideration. This refers to the behaviour whereby leaders provide a supportive climate in which they listen carefully to the needs of followers, viewing them and treating them as unique individuals and responding to them in a personal manner. Here the leader acts as both a coach and an advisor, encouraging and supporting self-actualization among followers.

The transactional leadership factors

In the case of transactional leadership, leaders do not individualize the needs of subordinates nor focus on their personal development. Instead the emphasis is on exchanging things of value with subordinates to further both the leader's and the followers' agendas. The first factor is known as contingent reward or constructive transactions. This involves an exchange process between leaders and followers in which effort by followers is exchanged for specified rewards. The second transactional factor consists of corrective transactions and takes the form of management-by-exception, which involves corrective criticism, negative feedback and negative reinforcement. This can take two forms: an active one whereby the leader watches followers closely to identify mistakes/rule violations; and a passive one whereby the leader intervenes only after standards have not been met or problems have arisen.

The laissez-faire leadership factor

The seventh and final factor in the Bass (1985) model is a 'non-leadership' factor and denotes the absence of leadership. This involves behaviours that fall at the extreme right of the transformational–transactional leadership continuum. It is characterized by a 'hands-off' approach and refers to leaders who abdicate responsibility, delay decisions, give no feedback and make little effort to help followers to satisfy their needs. In short, the total absence of the behaviours identified under the transformational leadership factors.

Critique

Providing a general way of thinking about leadership that stresses ideals, inspiration, innovations and individual concerns, transformational leadership has been broadly and widely researched, including a large body of qualitative research centring on prominent leaders and CEOs in major firms. It has an intuitive appeal; people are attracted to transformational leadership because it makes sense to them. It is process-focused because it treats leadership as a process occurring between followers and leaders. Transformational leadership provides a broader view of leadership that usefully augments other leadership models. The emphasis is on followers, emphasizing their needs, values and morals. Finally, available evidence (see Yukl, 1999) supports the view that it is an effective form of leadership.

There is some criticism that the Bass (1985) model lacks conceptual clarity because its dimensions are not clearly delimited, with a significant overlap between each of the transformational factors (Tracey and Hinkin, 1998). The parameters of transformational leadership are seen to overlap with similar conceptualizations of leadership (Bryman, 1992). Other criticisms concern how transformational leadership is actually measured and the validity of the main research instrument – the Multifactor Leadership Questionnaire (MLQ) – has been challenged and there is some concern that the transformational factors are not unique to the transformational model (Tejeda *et al.*, 2001). As Bryman (1992) has noted, this approach treats leadership more as a personality trait or predisposition than a behaviour that can be taught. Relatedly, it is an approach that is seen as being elitist and antidemocratic (Avolio, 1999) and as suffering from a heroic leadership bias (Yukl, 1999). Both aspects hint at the potential for transformational leadership to be abused.

SUMMARY

This chapter has provided an overview and introduction to the main leadership theories developed since the 1940s. Starting with the earliest, this involved coverage of the so-called trait theories, which focused on the characteristics of leaders and those concerned with leadership skills. This later emphasis marks the shift towards those theories more associated with the leadership process, such as the style and situational approaches and contingency theory. Rather than replacing earlier theories, each subsequent theory overlaps and builds on early theories to a greater or lesser extent.

The final part of the chapter introduced transformational leadership as a representative theory of the approaches that have developed from the mid-1970s, collectively referred to as the new leadership approach. Again, while clear echoes of the early leadership theories can be seen here, the distinctive contribution is the focus on managing meaning rather than the traditional focus on leadership as an influence process (Bryman, 1999). The reference at the start of the chapter comparing leadership theory to the 'six men of Indostan' would appear apposite! To paraphrase the wise man:

> All of you leadership theorists are right. The reason every one of you is telling it differently is because each one of you touched a different part of leadership. So, actually leadership has all the features you mentioned.

REVIEW QUESTIONS

1. Define the concept of leadership and explore its dimensions within the context of the tourism, hospitality and events industries.
2. Discuss the similarities and differences between management and leadership.
3. Explain what you understand by the following approaches to leadership: trait approach; skills approach; style approach; situational approach; contingency theory.

Case Study

Leadership lessons from Mickey Mouse

Walt Disney, the founder of the Disney organization, is widely recognized as being an example of an excellent leader. Today this is reflected in the Disney Institute's offer of a programme on leadership excellence based on the leadership approach of the founder, which it claims continues to shape its own leadership practices. The essence of this leadership programme is summarized below.

A key element of the Disney approach is drawing on what it sees as the legacy of Walt Disney, which involved providing a clear direction (underpinned with a commitment to proactive change) for the efforts of organizational members based on his own core values, which were subsequently shared by those leaders who followed in his footsteps.

The need to develop a clear vision that springs from the organization's core values is seen as crucial. The next step is the importance of being able to share this vision with organizational members and getting them to 'buy in' to it. Here Disney claims to draw on its 'decades of storytelling heritage' to create the required level of emotional engagement necessary to underpin effective action.

Having developed and sold the vision, the next key task for leadership is to ensure that the key operational elements are in place to enable the achievement of the vision. In many ways this can be seen as the overlap between leadership and management mentioned at the beginning of the chapter. It involves the planning, organizing and resourcing elements that are critical to any effective operation.

Employees at Disney are referred to as 'cast members' a clear reminder of the nature of their roles. The importance of team work is stressed and the vital need to ensure that team members are motivated and allocated appropriate levels of responsibility with the necessary inputs and resources they require to attain the set performance targets. Here the emphasis is on the enabling role of organizational leadership.

The importance of leaders to ensure that day-to-day activities are seen to be tangible steps towards the achievement of the overall organizational vision is stressed. Thus a key leadership task is linking short-term operational actions and gains to the overall strategic level and major outcomes over the longer term within the organization.

Finally, Disney emphasize the need to 'leave a legacy' in that holding to the organization's core values is a critical dimension of effective leadership and the characters of those occupying leadership roles. It is this aspect that more than anything that will have a lasting positive impact on the organization.

To see details of the actual Disney leadership excellence programme go to: http://www.disneyinstitute.com

Question

1. Which leadership theories seem to be reflected in 'Disney's leadership excellence programme'?

GLOSSARY OF TERMS USED IN THIS CHAPTER

Contingency theory	A leadership theory that attempts to match leaders to appropriate situations (this is the contingency) because it is believed that leadership effectiveness depends on how well a leader's style fits a given context.
Leadership	Leadership is concerned with establishing direction and creating a vision. It involves clarifying the big picture and setting strategies, then aligning people through communicating goals, seeking commitment and building teams and coalitions. It involves motivating and inspiring followers, to energize and empower subordinates, helping them to satisfy unmet needs.
Management	Management is concerned with producing order and consistency. Thus the management task of planning and budgeting involves establishing agendas, setting timetables and allocating resources. With regard to organizing and staffing associated with management, this is concerned with providing structure, making job placements and establishing rules and procedures. Finally, management's focus on controlling and problem solving involves developing incentives, generating creative solutions and where necessary taking corrective action.
Relationship behaviours	Those behaviours that focus on subordinates.
Situational approach	A leadership theory that argues that different types of situations require different types of leadership and that in order to be effective leaders need to adapt their style to the specific context they face. Their theory emphasizes that effective leadership has two dimensions: directive (task) and supportive (relationship). Here a key task is for a leader is to assess subordinates in terms of their competence (skills) and commitment (motivation) for a given task at a particular point in time.
Skills approach	A leadership theory that is similar to the trait approach in that it is a leader-centred perspective of leadership. It focuses on the skills required to be an effective leader not the personality traits associated with leadership. It suggests that in addition to certain traits, effective leaders need particular skills and that these can be developed, unlike the personality traits.

Style approach	A leadership theory that places emphasis on the behaviour of leaders. It is thus very different from both the trait approach and skills approach, which refer to the leader's personal dimension. Consequently, it expands the study of leadership to include a leader's actions to subordinates in different contexts.
Task behaviours	Those behaviours that facilitate goal achievement.
Trait approach	A leadership theory that focuses on understanding the personal traits associated with effective leadership. This area is sometimes referred to as 'great man theories' because the original research focus was on famous political and military leaders. This approach sought to answer the question: 'what are the innate qualities that appear to separate leaders from their followers?'

REFERENCES AND ADDITIONAL READING

Avolio, B.J. (1999) *Full Leadership Development: Building the Vital Forces in Organizations*. Sage, Thousand Oaks, California.

Bass, B.M. (1985) *Leadership and Performance Beyond Expectations*. Free Press, New York.

Bennis, W.G. and Nanus, B. (1985) *Leaders: The Strategies for Taking Charge*. Harper & Row, New York.

Blake, R.R. and Mouton, J.S. (1985) *The Managerial Grid III*. Gulf Publishing Company, Houston, Texas.

Bowers, D.G. and Seashore, S.E. (1966) Predicting organizational effectiveness with a four-factor theory of leadership. *Administrative Science Quarterly* 11, 238–263.

Bryman, A. (1992) *Charisma and Leadership in Organizations*. Sage, London.

Bryman, A. (1999) Leadership in organizations. In: Clegg, S.R., Hardy, C. and Nord, W.R. (eds) *Managing Organizations: Current Issues*. Sage, London, pp. 26–42.

Burns, J.M. (1978) *Leadership*. Harper & Row, New York.

Conger, J.A. (1989) *The Charismatic Leader: Behind the Mystique of Exceptional Leadership*. Jossey-Bass, San Francisco, California.

Fayol, H. (1916) *General and Industrial Management*. Pitman, London.

Fernandez, C.F. and Vecchio, R.P. (1997) Situational leadership theory revisited: a test of an across-jobs perspective. *Leadership Quarterly* 8, 67–84.

Fiedler, F.E. (1964) A contingency model of leadership effectiveness. In: Berkowitz, L (ed.) *Advances in Experimental Social Psychology*. Academic Press, New York.

Fleishman, E.A., Mumford, M.D., Zaccaro, S.J., Levin, K.Y., Korotkin, A.L. and Hein, M.B. (1991) Taxonomic efforts in the description of leader behaviour: a synthesis and functional interpretation. *Leadership Quarterly* 2, 245–287.

French, J.R. and Raven, B. (1959) The bases of social power. In: Cartwright, D. (ed.) *Studies in Social Power*. Institute for Social Research, Ann Arbor, Michigan.

Hemphill, J.K. and Coons, A.E. (1957) Development of the Leader Behavior Description Questionnaire. In: Stogdill, R.M. and Coons, A.E. (eds) *Leader Behavior: Its Description and Measurement* (Research Monograph No. 88). Ohio State University, Bureau of Business Research, Columbus, Ohio.

Hersey, P. and Blanchard, K.H. (1969) Life-cycle theory of leadership. *Training and Development Journal* 23, 26–34.

Hogg, M.A. (2001) A social identity theory of leadership. *Personality and Social Psychology Review* 5, 184–200.

House, R.J. (1976) A 1976 theory of charismatic leadership. In: Hunt, J.G. and Larson, L.L. (eds) *Leadership: The Cutting Edge*. Southern Illinois University Press, Carbondale, Illinois, pp. 189–207.

Katz, R. (1955) Skills of an effective administrator. *Harvard Business Review* 33, 33–42.

Kirkpatrick, S.A. and Locke, E.A. (1991) Leadership: do traits matter? *The Executive* 5, 48–60.

Kotter, J.P. (1990) *A Force for Change: How Leadership Differs from Management*. Free Press, New York.

Lord, R.G., Devader, C.L. and Alliger, G.M. (1986) A meta-analysis of the relation between personality traits and leadership perceptions: an application of validity generalization procedures. *Journal of Applied Psychology* 71, 402–410.

Mann, R.D. (1959) A review of the relationship between personality and performance in small groups. *Psychological Bulletin* 56, 241–270.

Michelli, J. (2008) *The New Gold Standard*. McGraw-Hill, New York.

Misumi, J. (1985) *The Behavioral Science of Leadership: An Interdisciplinary Japanese Research Program*. University of Michigan Press, Ann Arbor, Michigan.

Mumford, M.D., Zaccaro, S.J., Connelly, M.S. and Marks, M.A. (2000) Leadership skills: conclusions and future directions. *Leadership Quarterly* 2, 289–315.

Northouse, P.G. (2007) *Leadership: Theory and Practice*, 4th edn. Sage, Thousand Oaks, California.

Peters, T. and Waterman, R.H. (1982) *In Search of Excellence: Lessons from America's Best-run Companies*. Harper & Row, New York.

Sashkin, M. (1988) The visionary leader. In: Conger, J.A. and Kanungo, R.N. (eds) *Charismatic Leadership: The Elusive Factor in Organizational Effectiveness*. Jossey-Bass, San Francisco, California.

Smith, J.A. and Foti, R.J. (1998) A pattern approach to the study of leader emergence. *Leadership Quarterly* 9, 147–160.

Stogdill, R.M. (1948) Personal factors associated with leadership: a survey of the literature. *Journal of Psychology* 25, 35–71.

Stogdill, R.M. (1963) *Manual for the Leader Behavior Description Questionnaire Form XII*. Ohio State University, Bureau of Business Research, Columbus, Ohio.

Stogdill, R.M. (1974) *Handbook of Leadership: A Survey of Theory and Research*. Free Press, New York.

Tejeda, M.J., Scandura, T.A. and Pillai, R. (2001) The MLQ revisited: psychometric properties and recommendations. *Leadership Quarterly* 12, 31–52.

Tichy, N.M. and Devanna, M.A. (1986) *The Transformational Leader*. Wiley, New York.

Tracey, J.B. and Hinkin, T.R. (1998) Transformational leadership or effective managerial practices? *Group and Organization Management* 23, 220–236.

Vecchio, R.P. (1987) Situational leadership theory: an examination of a prescriptive theory. *Journal of Applied Psychology* 72, 444–451.

Vecchio, R.P. and Boatwright, K.J. (2002) Preferences for idealized style of supervision. *Leadership Quarterly* 13, 327–342.

Watson, C. and Hoffman, L.R. (2004) The role of task-related behaviour in the emergence of leaders. *Group & Organization Management* 29, 659–685.

Westley, F.R. and Mintzberg, H. (1989) Visionary leadership and strategic management. *Strategic Management Journal* 10, 17–32.

Yukl, G. (1994) *Leadership in Organizations*, 3rd edn. Prentice Hall, Englewood Cliffs, New Jersey.

Yukl, G. (1999) An evaluation of conceptual weaknesses in transformational and charismatic leadership theories. *Leadership Quarterly* 10, 285–305.

chapter 14

Innovation

Ahmed Hassanien, Pauline Gordon
Edinburgh Napier University

Crispin Dale
University of Wolverhampton

LEARNING OBJECTIVES

Having completed this chapter, readers should be able to:

- define and explore the concept and scope of innovation;
- discuss the key motives and drivers of innovation within tourism, hospitality and events (THE) facilities;
- understand the different types of innovation;
- evaluate the different categories of measuring innovation management.

INTRODUCTION

There is a strong relationship between innovation and business success, sustainability, competitive advantage and growth in the THE industries. Therefore, it is essential to develop the skills and core competencies of organizations in order to become more innovative. Despite its vital importance, innovation is still a vague concept, challenging activity and risky task for many THE organizations because of different types of external and internal factors. This chapter will initially outline what is meant by innovation and its significance to THE facilities. The chapter will then move on to a discussion of the different types and levels of innovation and their influence over decision making by the THE facilities manager.

DEFINITION

An examination of the literature uncovers the fact that the concept of innovation has been defined and described in a variety of ways. Some definitions (Table 14.1) have emerged, however, which are useful for understanding the concept and scope of facilities management.

So, what can we understand about innovation from the above definitions? From a general perspective we can deduce the following:

- There are many definitions of 'innovation', but the concept is closely linked to various business activities and can be applied to new product development (NPD), new service development (NSD), new or improved products, processes or business models.

Table 14.1. Definitions of innovation.

Definition
Schumpeter (1934, p. 66) has developed a holistic approach to define innovation. He defines innovation as a multi-dimensional process which includes: introducing new products; applying new production methods; opening new markets; using new supply sources; implementing new forms of organizational structure.
Crawford (1994, p. 26) defines innovation as 'the act of creating a new product or process'.
Kanter (1988, p. 170) defines innovation as 'organization's ability to promote both process and product innovation, regardless of an immediate need for change'.
According to Mulgan and Albury (2003, p. 3) 'Successful innovation is the creation and implementation of new processes, products, services and methods of delivery which result in significant improvements in outcomes efficiency, effectiveness or quality'.
'Innovation is the multi-stage process whereby organizations transform ideas into new/ improved products, services or processes, in order to advance, compete and differentiate themselves successfully in their marketplace' (Baregheh *et al.*, 2009, p. 1325).
The *Oslo Manual* (OECD, 2005, p. 46) defines innovation as the implementation of a new or significantly improved product (good or service), or process, a new marketing method, or a new organizational method in business practices, workplace organization or external relations.
Tushman and Nadler (1986, p. 74) suggested that innovation is the creation of any product, service or process that is new to the business unit.

- In the modern business environment it is widely accepted that the competitiveness of any organization is highly dependent on the ability to be innovative, challenge competitors and constantly exceed customer expectations. Innovation is therefore about a business making specific and significant changes to products or services in order to make improvements.

- 'Innovation is generally understood as the introduction of a new thing or method and is the embodiment, combination or synthesis of knowledge in original, relevant, valued new products, processes or services' (Luecke and Katz, 2003, p. 2).

- There are different types of innovation, such as product, process, market and organizational.

- The main aim of innovation is to help organizations to achieve their goals in terms of competitive advantage, sustainability, profitability and flexibility.

- While most of these definitions may differ, a common thread emerges regarding the criteria that can be used to explore innovation within THE facilities. These criteria can include: what is new (e.g. product, service, process, market, partnership), new to whom (e.g. company, customer, market), and the target of innovation (e.g. competitiveness, leadership and effectiveness), degree of newness (e.g. radical vs incremental innovations) and impact of newness (e.g. sustaining vs discontinuous innovations). These criteria can help us to understand the different types, levels, degrees and impact of innovation on THE facilities.

Why innovation? Drivers and motives

The changing business environment, in addition to the desire of organizations to improve their image, is the main driving force behind innovation in the THE industries. That is because the changing business environment has forced THE facilities to reconsider the way in which they approach their tasks to achieve their goals. For example, consumer tastes, wants and needs are changing from time to time and new competitive patterns are emerging. Also, the economic recession has been another key driver of cost reduction and innovation. The importance of political, legal and regulatory drivers has amplified in the past few decades. In addition, contemporary issues such as environmental management and corporate social responsibility have motivated organizations to improve their image through more green practice and sustainable development innovations. Therefore, it has become essential for an organization to innovate to survive in the market and to cope with the dynamic and changing business environment (Kotler *et al.*, 2002; Trott, 2008; Hassanien *et al.*, 2010). Accordingly, THE facilities should have strategies that enable them to carry on innovation and to develop solid innovation competencies. The main drivers of innovation in THE facilities can include:

- financial pressures to reduce operational costs;
- improving quality and increasing value;
- increasing customer expectations;

- industry and community stakeholders requests for sustainable development;
- intense competition;
- managerial urge for sustainability, growth and development;
- shorter product life cycles (e.g. e-travel agents and traditional travel agents);
- socio-cultural and market changes;
- strict rules and regulations;
- the availability and applications of new technologies;
- the changing economic environment.

As a result, innovation can be regarded as one of the main sources of competitive advantage for organizations. For example, organizations can apply innovation to their businesses through the use of new technologies and new approaches to carry out their activities (Porter, 1990). However, Chesbrough argues that 'most innovations fail and companies that don't innovate die' (2003, p. XVII). Therefore, THE facilities need to be aware of the imperative significance of innovation and also should know how to do it successfully. That is because innovation is the only option for any organization to maintain its viability (Tidd *et al.*, 2001).

Along the same lines, there are many different reasons that explain the role played by innovation in the success of THE facilities. These reasons might be classified as strategic, operational or functional objectives to be achieved by innovation. Key authors list many different reasons that make innovation and product development essential for THE operations (Booz Allen Hamilton, 1991; Kuczmarski, 1992; Wheelwright and Clark, 1992; Cooper and Edgett, 2003; Hart *et al.*, 2003; Owens, 2004, 2007; Gerwin and Ferris, 2004; Jena, 2007; Crawford and Di Benedetto, 2008; Lantos *et al.*, 2009; Hassanien *et al.*, 2010). These reasons include:

- achieving financial goals such as profitability and income generation;
- balancing a product mix (e.g. developing a holistic product);
- complying with new technology in the market;
- complying with new trends in the market (e.g. new customer lifestyle, wants or needs);
- coping with governmental or industry requirements;
- business growth and development;
- business sustainability;
- customer attraction, retention, loyalty, trust and/or satisfaction;
- rising costs of operations;
- entering new markets;
- gaining competitive advantages through differentiation and uniqueness;
- improving corporate brand, image, position or standards (e.g. upgrading the organization to a higher category);
- keeping up with the competition;
- maintaining or increasing the company's market share;
- maximizing capacity (e.g. utilization of excess or off-season capacity, unused resources).

TYPES OF INNOVATION

As mentioned before, innovations can be explored through identifying what is being changed or what is the innovated object or aspect of the business. This innovation typology can include four types of innovations (Schumpeter, 1934; OECD, 2005). Each type of innovation may be different in terms of the levels of novelty (incremental or radical) and its effect on the market (sustaining or discontinuous):

- product/service innovation;
- process innovation;
- marketing innovation;
- organizational innovation.

However, most innovation that takes place in organizations is a mix of more than one of the above mentioned types of innovation. Thus, it is challenging to delineate between these different innovation types because they often overlap and are closely interrelated. For example, a successful provision of services by an external contractor for a THE facility (i.e. outsourcing) can be described as an organizational innovation and/or a process innovation. Table 14.2 provides an example regarding the innovation practices of easyJet to further explore these points.

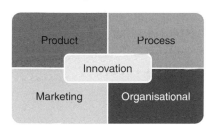

Fig. 14.1. Types of innovation.

Product/service innovation refers to changes in the offerings of an organization, while process innovation is related to changes in the methods through which these offerings are produced and delivered (Tidd *et al.*, 2001). These are the most common types of innovation in the literature. Product/service innovation focuses mainly on NPD and/or NSD. Examples of new products include new to the world products (new products that create an entirely new market); new product lines (new products that allow a company to enter an established market for the first time); additions to existing product lines (new products that supplement a company's established product lines); and improvements to existing products (new products that provide increased performance or greater perceived value and replaced existing products). Along the same lines, services marketing scholars suggest similar classification. For example, Lovelock and Wirtz (2004, pp. 116–117) and Zeithaml *et al.* (2006, p. 256) state that there are different categories of NSD as follows:

- major or radical innovations, which includes services for completely new markets;
- start-up businesses and services for an existing market with existing products;
- new services for markets that are currently being provided for by existing products that meet the same common needs;
- new services for the currently served market that have not been available previously;
- service line extensions to the current service offerings;
- service improvements to those lines currently offered;
- style changes that are clearly apparent within the service offering.

Table 14.2. Examples of easyJet's innovation practices.

2012	Organizational/ service innovation	New partnership with TripAdvisor	easyJet announces a pan-European partnership with TripAdvisor, which shows independent hotel reviews from the world's largest travel community featured on the easyJetHotels.com website.
2011	Organizational/ process innovation	easyJet announces plans for 'easyJet ecoJet' to cut CO_2 emissions by 50% by 2015	The aircraft incorporates the latest research by airframe and engine manufacturers around the world: The projection for the 50% CO_2 reduction is based on the findings from the latest research by industry leaders and will come from the engines (25%), the lightweight airframe (15%) and improvements to air traffic control technology and design (10%).
2011	Organizational/ process innovation	easyJet introduces nano-technology coating used on military airplanes	Coating reduces friction and drag on the surface of the aircraft, resulting in fuel efficiency.
2011	Organizational/ marketing innovation	easyJet became a redemption partner with the loyalty programme Nectar in the UK. Nectar is the leading coalition programme in the UK, co-founded by Sainsbury's	The 17 million members of Nectar are able to redeem their points for free seats on easyJet. While the revenue impact may be minimal from being reimbursed for the redemptions, easyJet benefits from more marketing, especially from instore marketing in Sainsbury's and TV advertising.
2011	Marketing innovation	Introduced Memory maker application via Facebook	By uploading pictures, consumers are able to produce a short film, which they can share with their Facebook friends, and there is also the opportunity to win a holiday.

(Continued)

Table 14.2. Continued.

2011	Marketing/ organizational innovation	easyJet and Low-cost Travel Group announce a strategic agreement	Consumers are able to book an impressive range of flexible holidays through a single website, easyJet.com, supported by a state of the art call centre.
2010	Process innovation	easyJet introduced Airborne Volcanic Object Identifier and Detector (AVOID)	A pioneering technology designed by Norway's Institute for Air Research which might make large-scale disruption from volcanic ash history. The ash detector will enable aircraft to see and avoid the ash cloud, just like airborne weather radars and weather maps make thunderstorms visible.
2009	Marketing innovation	easyJet becomes the first major European low-cost airline to distribute through GDS – global distribution systems	This innovative business development enables corporate travel agencies to view and book easyJet flights within their preferred GDS environment alongside other carriers to make easy comparisons and bookings. Rewarded with the innovative award in air travel.
2008	Marketing innovation	easyJet launches virtual customer community	The easyJet Community provides a two-way discussion platform between the airline and a selected group of passengers who have travelled with the company over the past 12 months.
2008	Marketing innovation	easyJet joins Twitter	Benefits include: (i) enables easyJet to reach massive, targeted audiences for a low-cost; (ii) provides greater favourable perceptions of a brand and a better understanding of the customer's brand perceptions; (iii) consumers can book flights via Facebook as well as being updated with the latest news and can be part of competitions; (iv) very cost-effective to conduct market/consumer research; and (v) provides free source of constant information.
2008	Marketing innovation	easyJet joins Facebook	

(Continued)

Table 14.2. Continued.

2008	Organizational/ marketing innovation	easyJet launches a co-branded MasterCard with Citibank	Cardholders enjoy three great extras with the easyJet MasterCard offer, which lasts for the first 90 days from activating their card. These are: one free easyJet flight worth up to £40 (including taxes) when they spend £250 or more in the first 3 months; 10% back on all easyJet flights booked within the first 3 months.
2007	Process/product innovation	easyJet introduce Speedy-Boarding Plus	The new fast check-in option offers a dedicated check-in desk for the customers who have made additional payments to be among the first passengers to board a flight but still have luggage to check-in. Gives customer more choice and flexibility.
2006	Process/product innovation	easyJet becomes first European airline to offer online check-in	Online check-in reduces costs and minimizes the time for the passenger to check-in.
2005	Product/service/ process innovation	easyJet uses customer-relationship-management (CRM) in its online distribution	Features a knowledge base that refines and grows the more it is used, allowing easy and timelier access to booking information.
2005	Organizational innovation	First low-cost airline that cooperates with leading travel management company Business Travel International	Business Travel International's corporate customers, including large corporations such as Bank of Scotland, able to view and buy easyJet's inventory through their own systems and alongside the inventory of other airlines. Facilitated through an Application Programming Interface (API) and, in addition to seat purchasing, automatically fulfils various administrative functions such as billing, providing management information and notification in the event of flight disruptions.

(Continued)

Table 14.2. Continued.

2005	Product/service innovation	easyJet introduces easyJet Lounges	Lounges offered free drinks, snacks and magazines as well as the standard flight information and access to phone, internet and email.
2005	Organizational innovation	easyJet opens new world-class training academy	The centre for learning and development at London Luton Airport is the heart of the airline's recruitment and training. The centre, based at Luton Airport, is used for recruitment, training, development and cultural activities.
2005	Process/service innovation	Upgrade of its software system: fares online include taxes and charges	easyJet's as well as Ryanair's web bookings stated the complete fare only in the last stages of making a booking.
2004	Product/service innovation	easyJet starts flights to newly-enlarged European Union	First airline to take advantage of the newly-enlarged European Union.
2003	Product/process innovation	easyJet launched easyJet.com/b2b	A simplified version of its internet site for use by corporations.
2001	Product/process innovation	Improving the quality of online booking	First airline to allow customer to view and change their booking details.

Sources: Jones (2007); Minkova (2009); Euromonitor International (2010); Financial Times Ltd (2010), easyJet plc (2011); Preuss (2011); *The Economist* (2011).

All of these new product or new service classes are common in the THE industries.

Process innovation is about the use of novel or highly enhanced methods of production or delivery. This comprises major alteration in techniques, equipment and/or software. Cost reductions and improving the efficiency and effectiveness of production and delivery are always the main intention of process innovations (OECD, 2005). A common example of process innovation in THE facilities nowadays is the automated front and back office services. As mentioned before, it is difficult to separate product innovation from process innovation because of the inseparable nature of services (see Chapter 2, this volume). This is because it is not easy to change the services offerings without changing elements of the production or delivery process. For example, in order for a conference centre to attract and fulfil the requirements of a new target market, it might need to add new products or services (product/service innovation) and improve further the quality of its service.

Marketing innovation refers to the implementation of novel marketing approaches, such as attracting a new market segment, entering a new market, using new channels of distribution, new communication/promotional tools and pricing techniques. Organizational innovation refers to the application of innovative organizational ways with regard to the practices of the business (e.g. environmental management and corporate social responsibility), the organization of the workplace (e.g. human resources development or organizational restructure) or external relations (e.g. outsourcing, partnerships, sponsorship or strategic alliances). For example, CSR has been one of the most common innovation tools in the THE industries in the past two decades.

Corporate social responsibility (CSR) can be described as the process through which 'companies integrate social and environmental concerns to their business operations and in their interactions with stakeholders on a voluntary basis' (Commission of the European Communities, 2001, p. 6). An exploration of the literature reveals that CSR can equip organizations with great opportunities to encourage and practice innovation (Porter and Kramer, 2006; Husted and Allen, 2007). Similarly, Nidumolu *et al.* argue that CSR and sustainability can be regarded as 'key drivers for innovation' (2009, p. 57). There are two main types of CSR, responsive and strategic (Porter and Kramer, 2006). Responsive CSR refers to 'acting as a good corporate citizen, attuned to the evolving social concerns of stakeholders, and mitigating existing or anticipated adverse effects from business activities' (Porter and Kramer, 2006, p. 85). In other words, it refers to a restricted and reactive level of CSR practices. This kind of responsive CSR can help an organization to enhance its image in the market and to build up positive relations with the stakeholders. Nevertheless, it has a limited impact on the incremental innovation practices of the organizations because of its restricted reactive nature. On the contrary, the other type of CSR rises above the execution of best practices. The strategic CSR practices enable organizations to occupy a unique position in the market through distinguishing them from their competitors. Consequently, the strong positive correlation between incremental/radical innovations and CSR practices is deep-rooted (Bocquet *et al.*, 2011).

Example: CSR innovation practices of Manchester International Festival

Manchester International Festival (MIF) is committed to developing a festival that benefits the local economy, is engaging for local communities and tries to minimize its environmental impact. These principles guide all of their sustainable development activities, from ensuring their offices are welcoming and resource efficient to sourcing and creating their productions responsibly and working with partner venues and suppliers to reduce the environmental impact of MIF events.

(Continued)

Example. Continued.

Some of their sustainable actions during MIF 2011 included:

- keeping approximately a third of the Festival's Programme free – including the family-friendly interactive Music Boxes at MediaCityUK and John Gerrard's Infinite Freedom Exercise just off Albert Square;
- continuing with their compostable cutlery and tableware at Festival Square and expanding their recycling facilities, which resulted in them saving 79% of their waste from going to landfill – with over 90,000 visitors across the 18 days, that's a lot of waste…;
- working with Manchester City Council to supply Festival Square with electricity, negating the use of external generators – this not only benefited MIF but will continue to benefit all other temporary activities held in Albert Square in the future;
- re-using, hiring or recycling all of their production sets;
- introducing three Festival bikes for staff to get round the city;
- turning their Festival banners into bags – stylish, practical and 'green'.

Source: http://mif.co.uk/about-us/

Activity

1. Select a THE facility of your choice. Profile the different types of innovation that the facility has undertaken.

2. Evaluate the reasons why these innovations have been used.

3. Make further suggestions on innovations that the facility could pursue.

MEASURING INNOVATION MANAGEMENT

According to Albury, 'Successful innovation is the creation and implementation of new processes, products, services and methods of delivery which result in significant improvements in outcomes, efficiency, effectiveness or quality' (2005, p. 2). However, current experts suggest that in order to gain competitive success, businesses need to be able to effectively implement, monitor and measure the innovation process.

Although innovation involves small, incremental changes to products, services and processes, it does involve all managers in every department from finance to customer services. It therefore needs to be planned and managed as a core business process covering all parts of a business (Eveleens, 2010, p. 3). Consequently, businesses need to encourage employees to be creative and give them the opportunity to convert ideas into plans of action in order for innovation to be effective. Indeed, it is important to reinforce that in order for innovation to be successful there needs to be a democratic style of management, because an authoritative style would oppress innovation and the flow of ideas within an organization.

Accordingly, employees should feel that the work environment is secure and allows them to develop ideas and be recognized for their efforts.

While innovation is not a new phenomenon, many authors argue that it is crucial for the survival of an organization to innovate (Mulgan and Albury, 2003; Tidd *et al.*, 2005), regardless of whether it is a public- or private-sector business (Cooper, 2005). If businesses are not engaged in innovation, then business is likely to decrease as more innovative products and services are introduced into the market (Eveleens, 2010). Many organizations can become so involved in what they are good at (i.e. their core competencies) that they forget to develop or diversify their product or service and they become complacent. Therefore, organizations must adapt to environmental changes in order for them to survive in their markets (Leonard-Barton, 1992; Benner and Tushman, 2000).

The literature on innovation management has grown considerably over the past 20 years. However, it is widely accepted that there are significant problems with the literature; it can be quite confusing because of the use of a wide variety of approaches and practices, as well as the increasing number of different models of innovation processes and measurement (Eveleens, 2010). In fact, in the literature related to innovation, it is widely recognised that there is no holistic framework that can be utilized to measure the activities that are necessary to convert innovative ideas into successful products or services.

According to Frenkel *et al.*, 'Quantifying, evaluating and benchmarking innovation competence and practice is a significant and complex issue for many contemporary organisations' (2000, p. 429). Indeed, it is widely accepted that it is just as important for a business to develop innovative products and services that can be monitored and measured. Interestingly, many researchers have studied and identified the key activities that are related to the innovation management process, and presented them in the form of innovation process models. However, from a measurement perspective these models are inadequate because they do not take into account the uniqueness or the individual demands of different organizations. In their research, Adams *et al.* (2006) developed an 'innovation measurement model' that consists of seven categories that they believe are important factors in the measurement of innovation. These include 'inputs, knowledge management, strategy, organization and culture, portfolio management and project management commercialization' (Eveleens, 2010, p. 3).

INPUTS

Inputs management is largely related to the availability of resources for innovation tasks and comprises a wide variety of aspects such as finance, employee and physical assets and the generation of new ideas. However, many organizations measure innovation by using a metrics system to measure areas such as research and development, product development and the research and development budget, along with the number of people employed and the output. It is important to stress that the outputs are difficult to classify until the process is complete because it is quite difficult to predict what the outputs will be. Although this measurement tool can be useful, it does offer a limited view of an organization's innovativeness because research and development is not the only input in the innovation process. Furthermore, it is not a particularly suitable measure for small and medium-sized enterprises or service firms, which do not necessarily have enormous research and development activities (Hipp and Grupp, 2005).

Activity

- Make suggestions on the appropriateness of input measures for small and medium-sized THE facilities.

KNOWLEDGE MANAGEMENT

'Knowledge absorption is an organisation's ability to identify, acquire and utilise external knowledge, and it can be critical to a firm's successful operation' (Zahra and George, 2002, p. 219). For example, innovation cannot occur 'without an understanding of the resources, tools, technologies, materials, markets, and needs within a particular situation' (Kim and Wilemon, 2002, p. 28). It is therefore quite common for organizations to spend significant amounts of resources on participating in research and the acquisition of knowledge. However, just because organizations can invest in research does not necessarily mean that they will be successful in developing a profitable innovation. According to Stone *et al.*, it is important to highlight that 'whatever the outputs of innovation may be it does incorporate an organization's current knowledge, every tangible and intangible (process and product) output reflects the firm's knowledge of the resources, technologies, markets and consumers' (2008, p. II-7).

Knowledge management is therefore focused on gaining and communicating the ideas and knowledge that support innovation activities (Zahra and George, 2002). The problem with the innovation process is how organizations can successfully measure the output of knowledge. Generally there are three areas of importance within knowledge management, which include idea generation, knowledge repository and information flows. It is important to stress that the initial stages of the innovation process tend to be fast, quantitative and low cost. However, as the process develops, the 'measurement approaches become both increasingly qualitative and more costly and time-consuming' (Adams *et al.*, 2006, p. 29). Although it is notoriously difficult to measure, it is crucial for organizations to implement processes in order to measure the accumulated knowledge because of its vital significance to innovation.

Activity

- Identify and evaluate different quantitative and qualitative approaches to the measurement of knowledge and innovation.

INNOVATION STRATEGY

Innovation strategy focuses on the development of a firm through new products or services, production and delivery processes or novel business models. In simple terms, it is a strategy that assists a business to plan, monitor and meet their objectives (Adams *et al.*, 2006). However, the activities must be consistent with the organizational strategy. Innovation strategy is about making future plans for an organization:

- what kind of products and services will the organization deliver;
- to what markets;
- how does the organization get there;
- how will the organization innovate;
- will the organization innovate radically or incrementally;
- will the organization create an internal climate for innovation and hire the best designers, researchers and engineers;
- does the organization strive for patents and other intellectual property?

A key basis for innovation strategy should be the delivery of 'co-creation experiences' (Prahalad and Ramaswamy, 2004) and how this can generate further value for the THE facility. Indeed, the inseparable nature of the THE experience and the direct customer interaction that occurs often enable a value-enhancing experience. For example, themed environments, such as Disney, ensure customers are central to co-creating their experience with them. THE facilities should seek to develop dialogic exchanges with their customers that enable new innovations to occur.

The main challenge of the innovation strategy is making decisions about a future that has not occurred. The only way to effectively deal with this challenge is to design several scenarios, so there is a range of possible outcomes. The difficulty with this situation is that organizations will not know which scenario is the right one until it actually happens, thus having implications on how organizations can measure this innovation process.

Activity

- Develop possible scenarios for a THE facility of your choice. What should be the innovation strategy for the facility based on the scenarios you have proposed?

ORGANIZATION AND CULTURE

According to Poskiene, organizational culture 'refers to the complex set of ideologies, traditions, commitments, and values that are shared throughout the organisation and that influence how the organisation conducts its whole performance becoming a potential source of innovation, advance and advantage' (2006, p. 47). As such, inevitably 'it is not the values individuals bring to the organisation that count, but the values the organisation brings to the individual' (2006, p. 47). Various scholars suggest that it is a necessity for organizations to create a culture that encourages employees to generate ideas that produce innovative products and/or strategies. However, in order for it to be successful the culture must be perceived by employees to be a desired and supported organizational objective (Vyakarnam and Adams, 2001). Organizations must therefore allow employees to explore creative possibilities, but at the same time maintain sufficient control in order to manage innovation in an effective and efficient manner (Ernst, 2002). However, it is important to stress that innovating organizations need to adopt a more structured climate when they move from the initiation to the implementation stages of innovation (Ernst, 2002).

Activity

• Suggest techniques for measuring the structural shift of THE facilities towards an innovative culture.

PORTFOLIO MANAGEMENT

Portfolio management concentrates on 'making strategic, technological and resource choices that govern project selection and the future shape of the organization' (Adams *et al.*, 2006, p. 35). Portfolio management for new products should involve a vigorous decision making and monitoring process in which new products and research and developments projects are prioritized, evaluated and selected. However, it is important to mention that if the research and development portfolio is not managed effectively, it can have a detrimental impact on the organization's competitive advantage (Adams *et al.*, 2006). That said, most organizations do have issues related to producing and maintaining leading-edge products and portfolio management has been identified as an extremely fragile area in product innovation management (Adams *et al.*, 2006). Furthermore, it is believed that businesses that do not effectively measure the output of their product portfolio put themselves at risk. Problems associated with NPD include: inefficient and unprofitable projects, projects not reflecting the overall strategy, poor management of ranking projects and a poor balance of projects. Currently, many models of portfolio management innovation are useful in devising a system to help secure resources to enhance the product development portfolio. However, some experts suggest that a systematic process that measures output could help further enhance an organization's competitive position.

Activity

• Propose methods for measuring the output of portfolio management.

PROJECT MANAGEMENT

The main focus of project management is the process that enables firms to turn ideas into a viable innovation through the use of organizational resources and capabilities. It is a multi-dimensional process that is full of continuous activities and events, which need to run concurrently, on time and to budget (Adams *et al.*, 2006). This can be extremely challenging, particularly if businesses aim to manage projects on time and to budget. It is therefore crucial that organizations have an effective project plan that enables them to deal with innovation uncertainties because of the change and dynamic nature of the innovation process. 'The best approach is to embrace the idea that innovation will continue to change, and that organizations that seek to profit from innovation must take on the challenge of changing with it' (Adams *et al.*, 2006, p. 71). The most common tools used to measure project management success include project management efficiency in terms of project costs, time, speed, revenue, forecasting, quality, customer satisfaction and performance (Adams *et al.*, 2006, p. 71).

Activity

- Evaluate the strengths and weaknesses of the different techniques for measuring project management.

COMMERCIALIZATION

Commercialization involves 'making the innovative process or product a commercial success and includes areas such as marketing, sales, distribution and joint ventures' (Adams *et al.*, 2006, p. 721). Developing new products and new services for markets is vital for the growth of any business. However, the journey of actually taking an idea from concept to market involves organizations adopting a series of new techniques in which there are many obstacles and possible entry and exit points. Marketing activities are essential for commercialization. These activities include market planning, reaching the customer and market analysis and monitoring. However, in terms of innovation management, the area of commercialization seems to be the least developed and measuring tools appear to be rather unsophisticated. In fact, 'measures are frequently restricted to numbers of products launched in a given period, market analysis and monitoring' (Adams *et al.*, 2006, p. 72). This is a huge gap because without measuring the input, the output will not have a successful outcome for the firm. 'This area of innovation is therefore in urgent need of further development, from both theory and measurement perspectives' (Adams *et al.*, 2006, p. 72).

Activity

- Analyse the different commercialization techniques used by THE facilities. Provide rationales for which you believe are the most appropriate measurement tools.

SUMMARY

This chapter has contained a comprehensive discussion of the concept of innovation in the THE facilities literature. The chapter has also dealt with various aspects of innovation in the hospitality industry. It includes discussion of the definition, importance, motives, drivers, types, process and measurement of innovation. It starts with clarifying the significance of innovation and identifying the relationship between business success and innovation in the THE industries. Finally, the chapter has concluded with an analysis of the measurement categories of innovation management. These include inputs, knowledge management, strategy, organization and culture, portfolio management and project management commercialization.

REVIEW QUESTIONS

1. Define the concept of innovation and explore its significance within the context of the THE industries.
2. Explain what you understand by the following types of innovation: product/service innovation; process innovation; marketing innovation; organizational innovation.
3. Choose a THE facility. How could the facility become more innovative? Propose how these innovations could be measured.

Case Study

Product innovation in the Scottish event venue sector

This case study explores the reasons, barriers, process and evaluation of product innovation and development in different types of event venues, based on qualitative research using a sample of seven venues selected from event venues in the UK. Events venue type, age and recent NPD experience were the main criteria for the selection of venues. The following sections discuss the main findings of this research study.

Venue description and NPD aim

Table 14.3 gives details of the generic characteristics of the seven participating venues, together with a designator letter (A to G) by which they will be identified.

NPD reasons

Managers were asked to identify the main reasons for developing new products for their venues (Table 14.4). The main reasons for product development in each case study include revenue generation, competition, customer demand, improving standards and quality, technology, environmental efficiency, maximizing capacity and space flexibility.

(Continued)

Case Study. Continued.

Table 14.3. Venue characteristics.

Venue	Focus	Revenue	Year of operation	Purpose built or renovation	Target groups	Accommodation provision
				Characteristics		
A	Religious	Not for profit	2003	Renovation	Community	No
B	Local authority	Not for profit	1995	Purpose built	Corporate and associations	No
C	Visitor attraction	Charitable trust	1999	Purpose built	Schools, families and corporate clientele	No
D	Higher education	Profit	1990	Purpose built	Corporate and associations	Yes
E	Hotel	Profit	1988	Purpose built	Executive clientele	Yes
F	Historic house	Charitable trust	1970	Renovation	Corporate incentive and gala dinner markets	No
G	Local authority	Charitable trust	Various	Purpose built	Community	No

(*Continued*)

Case Study. Continued.

Table 14.4. Reasons for NPD.

Venue A	Venue B	Venue C	Venue D	Venue E	Venue F	Venue G
• Diversification • Revenue generation • Generate flexibility of the facility • Consumer demand • Keep up with competitors	• Gain environmental efficiencies • Maximize capacity during tough periods • To remain competitive • Generate flexibility of the facility • To develop an holistic product • Technological innovations • Profitability • Market leadership	• Technological innovations • Consumer demand • Competitors • Revenue generation	• Technological innovations • Generate flexibility of the facility • To develop an holistic product • Profitability • Consumer demand	• Maximize capacity during tough periods • Updating the facility • Gain environmental efficiencies • Competition • Revenue • Market leader	• Development of ancillary services • More financial income • Reuse of existing facilities • Competition	• Encouraging participation • Revenue generation • Consumer demand • Competition

(*Continued*)

Case Study. Continued.

It can be seen from the above tables that all the venues under study had different reasons for their product development projects. 'Competition from other venues' and 'revenue generation' were found to be the two main reasons in most of the venues. 'Generate flexibility of the facility' was the main reason in cases A, B, D and E. 'Consumer demand' was another main reason in case A and particularly in cases C and F. Overall, these reasons indicate that NPD is an essential activity for firms that desire to face competition on the basis of quality and suitability of purpose.

Other remarkable insights can be drawn from the research findings. First, all of the venues (profit and non-profit organizations) are aware of the high levels of competition in their markets. Second, the non-profit organizations (e.g. cases A, E and F) are deeply concerned with this intense competition and they develop new products to maximize their capacity and utilize their resources to generate further revenue to overcome the decreasing funding challenges they face.

The new (changing) image and role of non-profit organizations is towards income/revenue generation initiatives. This is based on adapting the facilities' resources to accommodate new market opportunities. Indeed, under-utilization of a facility provides scope for adding additional value to the existing resource base.

NPD barriers

The main barriers to NPD in the studied event venues are shown in Table 14.5, which shows that NPD within event venues are usually affected by various barriers or challenges. These barriers can be classified as:

- organizational barriers (e.g. lack of resources, knowledge or capabilities and the power and interest of stakeholders);
- external and market barriers (e.g. customer/competition-related barriers, political, economic, social, technological, environmental and legal factors);
- NPD process barriers (e.g. the risk associated with NPD and time constraints).

In all cases, there were significant barriers to NPD. Resource limitations are a key factor in this respect. Overall, financial resources and the cost of development were found to be the most important constraints to NPD in all the venues. In most cases, financial constraints and limited budget were significant barriers to NPD in venues, as explored by the following statement:

> There are limited funds. Physical changes are limited by the listed Grade B building. The venue is limited by location and space. Running costs are very high because of the historic nature of the building (venue A).

All managers indicated that they are trying to overcome such financial challenges through prioritizing and phasing their NPD plans.

(Continued)

Case Study. Continued.

Table 14.5. Barriers to NPD.

Barrier	Venue A	Venue B	Venue C	Venue D	Venue E	Venue F	Venue G
Corporate governance	Yes	Yes	No	Yes	No	Yes	Yes
Resistance to change in the company	Yes	Yes	No	No	No	No	No
Stakeholders	Yes	No	No	Yes	No	Yes	Yes
Physical limitations	Yes	Yes	Yes	Yes	No	Yes	Yes
Financial constraints	Yes	Yes	Yes	Yes	Yes	Yes	Yes
External and competitive factors	Yes	No	Yes	Yes	No	No	Yes
Time constraints	Yes	No	No	No	No	Yes	Yes
Lack of skilled personnel to develop NP	No	No	No	Yes	No	No	No
Lack of information on technologies	Yes	No	No	No	No	No	No
Lack of information on markets and external opportunities	Yes	No	No	No	No	No	No
Lack of customer responsiveness to NPD	No	Yes	Yes	No	Yes	Yes	Yes
Bureaucracy	Yes	No	Yes	Yes	No	Yes	Yes
High costs of NPD	Yes	Yes	Yes	Yes	Yes	Yes	Yes
NPD is risky	Yes	No	No	No	Yes	Yes	Yes
New products are easy to copy	Yes	No	Yes	Yes	No	No	Yes
Lack of top management support	No	No	No	No	No	No	No
Lack of leadership skills	No	No	No	No	No	No	No
Lack of project management skills	No	No	No	No	No	No	No
Industry regulations	No	No	No	No	No	No	No

(*Continued*)

Case Study. Continued.

Physical limitation (e.g. lack of space or physical resources – listed buildings) was an important barrier to product development in cases A, D and F. This was reflected in the following statement by the manager of venue A:

> This is a Grade B listed building, so you are limited by what the public authorities (Historic Scotland) will or won't approve to be done to the building. You are limited by how the building is constructed and where it is. We would have loved an outdoor space but there is no way of creating one here so there were all kinds of barriers during the refit (venue A).

A lack of accommodation was seen as a significant barrier to adding value to the physical resources of venues. This is in terms of not only generating additional revenue but also providing a holistic venue experience. Indeed the development of accommodation is seen by some venue managers as a means to change the 'rules of the game' among fellow event providers. Venues B, D and F all stated that a specific advantage could be gained by affiliating the event facilities with accommodation. The following comment emphasizes this point:

> That is why the accommodation is important. This would take us from being a conference centre with accommodation to more of an accommodation facility with a conference centre. That is where we see ourselves going (venue B).

Stakeholders and corporate governance were found to be two of the main barriers to renovation in event venues regardless of the venue category or the venue operation type. It is also worth noting that in most of the cases investigated, all NPD programmes were altered and delayed because of resistance from stakeholders (e.g. community, owners, employees). Most managers stated that stakeholders in the events industry are now powerful enough to impede innovation and product development. This power and interest is further determined by the corporate governance and ownership of the venue. The findings suggest that the influence of key stakeholder players is significant in terms of venue development. Where the venues are limited companies, shareholders play an influential role in the goals of the organization. Return on investment is the driving factor in terms of venue development. This is in contrast to venues that are governed by community interests and are underpinned with a social ethos.

NPD process

Respondents were asked to underline the significance of various stages of the NPD process. The findings revealed that events venues do not entirely follow all the stages of the NPD model. The results show that venue management appears to draw more attention to the idea generation and screening stages of the development process of venue services. On the other hand, 'test marketing' was found to be the least important stage of the NPD process. Accordingly, this disregard of some NPD activities in events venues might be attributed to a couple of reasons: (i) the nature of product innovation

(Continued)

Case Study. Continued.

or NPD in most of these venues, which is mainly product modifications and (ii) 'me too' competition or copying competitors.

Furthermore, influencing factors are based on who, and what, drives the NPD process. Differences among the venues are apparent in whether NPD is driven 'top down' or 'bottom up'. Indeed, who drives the process influences the priority that is given to the different stages of the NPD process. Though the emphasis is predominately on the former, the collation of ideas from the bottom up is encouraged. The top sources of new product ideas for most venues were competition, customer feedback, suppliers, staff and other stakeholders. Interestingly, most venues stated that they encourage staff to put forward innovative ideas.

NPD evaluation and performance measurement

Table 14.6 summarizes the main new product performance indicators for venues. As can be seen in this table, managers considered that they use different types of methods to evaluate the performance of their venue products. The results revealed that the most widespread NPD evaluation methods among venues were: (i) income generation and

Table 14.6. Key performance measurement indicators.

- Income generation
- Profitability
- Occupancy levels
- Sales volumes
- Social responsibilities
- Benchmarking against other venues
- Accommodation rates, average spend
- Professional bodies e.g. environmental awards – CUBO report, which is published annually to compare various universities)
- Budget assessment
- Customer satisfaction
- Questionnaires in bedrooms
- Website feedback
- In-house feedback (e.g. guest comment cards – customer survey or questionnaire – customer complaints – post visit feedback)
- Clients feedback (i.e. event organizers)
- Verbal feedback from event organizers and customers
- Market share
- Industry standards
- Industry accreditations

(Continued)

Case Study. Continued.

profitability; (ii) benchmarking against other venues; (iii) customer and client feedback; (iv) market share; (v) professional bodies; (vi) industry and government standards; (vii) industry accreditation and (viii) corporate social responsibilities. This result confirms that quantitative evaluation methods are used in events venues more than qualitative ones. Is this because quality-related issues are difficult to measure? There could be other reasons. This could provide an interesting starting point for further research. Also, financial indicators such as income generation and profitability were the top measures in most venues. This is not surprising bearing in mind the costly resources that have been invested in the venue development and the negative impact of the economic downturn on the event industry. As a result, venue organizations look ahead to a financial reward to survive in their markets. Certainly this was a point confirmed by the manager of venue E who, in response to the question of what evaluation methods are used, replied, 'Profitability is the most important measure but also market share, customer satisfaction and repeat business.' However, the term profitability was replaced by income generation in venues A and G due to the nature of these venues being non-profit organizations.

Indeed, for non-profit organizations, social responsibility was a significant indicator of performance. Venue A's primary focus was as a place of religious practice. However, with declining parishioner numbers the facility adopted, from a strategic perspective, a method of diversification into a new but related area (Ansoff, 1988). By staging events the venue was able to generate revenue, in addition to fulfilling its social objective of contributing to the community. This is in terms of encouraging community volunteerism and staging events that acknowledge the primary values of the facility. In this respect, the facility also has the opportunity of encouraging active participation as a parishioner. Similar findings were also found for venue G, the other non-profit organization sampled, where increasing participation rates among unrepresented community groups was seen as a key measure of performance. For both venues A and G, and in keeping with their social objective, any income generated is reinvested back into the organization.

As a performance indicator, increasing participation can be influenced by government standards, as was the case for venue G, though this is not unusual where funding arrangements influence the objectives of the facility. Contrasting findings were revealed for the importance of government and industry standards for performance measurement. Indeed, venues B and E challenged the importance of the industry standards because they exceed them. For a number of venues, benchmarking against competition is seen as a more significant indicator of performance. As Table 14.6 outlines, and as highlighted previously, this is predominately based on quantitative rather than qualitative information, including customer numbers, repeat business, market share and so on. The venue operators view competitor replication of another's business advantage as a major threat. Protecting this

(Continued)

Case Study. Continued.

advantage from competitors, therefore, becomes an objective, as the following comment from venue B highlights: 'we are going to be quite unique because we will have a lot of features that other venues potentially will not have and we will be a leading light for anything in the future. If they want to copy us, they can do but we will already have it in place and the marketplace is always competitive'. What is surprising is the increasing role of technology (e.g. website and social networks) in most cases.

Conclusions

This case study has reviewed the reasons, barriers, process and evaluation of NPD and innovation in event venues. The case study has revealed a number of key findings in NPD.

In terms of reasons, the research has found that the entry of non-profit making organizations into the event venues sector is becoming more profound. Though the core business of these organizations is not as an events venue, their rationale for entry is primarily based on the need to generate additional revenue streams. This revenue can then support other aspects of the organization's business, whether this is, for example, as a religious house or an educational institution. In terms of barriers to NPD and product innovation, managers believe that many exist within their event venue operations. The main barrier is the lack of resources, especially the financial and physical resources and the perceived risks of NPD. Also, lack of intellectual resources is seen with regard to leadership and project management skills in some venues. Most venue managers claim to have adequate knowledge regarding their customers, competitors and markets. Similarly, they do not view regulation as a barrier to product innovation within their venues.

In terms of NPD process, event venue operations do not fully follow all of the different stages of the NPD process because of the nature of their product development or lack of resources. The level of risk becomes a major factor influencing the decision making process in NPD and, maybe unsurprisingly, finance acts as the key driver. This is in terms of access to finance and the resources required to fund potential innovation. These resources are generated through reinvestment or external sources such as bank loans or private equity. As part of this process importance is given to the preparation of a business plan and feasibility study, which is a standard requirement for obtaining external funding.

In terms of NPD evaluation, quantitative measures are predominately used. These are driven by financial performance, with revenue and profitability acting as the key indicators of performance in the majority of events venues. In this respect, the 'bottom line' of financial viability is essential whether you are a profit or not for profit event venue. Nevertheless, the research reveals that for non-profit making events venues, social responsibility is a key focus of their day-to-day activity. Increasing participation rates enables the events venue to develop the well-being of the community and to further reinvest income generated into the facility.

(Continued)

Case Study. Continued.

The research suggests that product innovation has the potential to improve performance in events venues, though product innovation tends to be reactive in nature, because events venues strive to match developmental solutions to problems as they arise. Issues concerning the cost, time and risk implications of new developments are factors that confront events venues in being able to incorporate a systematic product innovation process in their development strategies.

Source: Adapted from Hassanien and Dale (2012, 2013)

Questions

1. Identify and discuss the main driving forces of product innovation in the events venues sector of the Scottish events industry. To what extent do you agree that product innovation in this sector is market driven? Why?

2. Explore the main barriers to product innovation in the Scottish events venues sector.

3. One of the main conclusions of this case study is that the entry of non-profit making organizations into the event venues sector is becoming more profound. Discuss.

4. Why are quantitative evaluation methods used more than qualitative ones in events venues?

GLOSSARY OF TERMS USED IN THIS CHAPTER

Corporate social responsibility	The process through which companies integrate social and environmental concerns into their business operations and into their interactions with stakeholders on a voluntary basis.
Innovation	A multi-stage process whereby organizations transform ideas into new/improved products, services or processes, in order to advance, compete and differentiate themselves successfully in their marketplace.
Innovation measurement model	Seven factors believed to be important in the measurement of innovation: inputs, knowledge management, strategy, organization and culture, portfolio management, project management commercialization.
Marketing innovation	The implementation of novel marketing approaches such as attracting a new market segment, entering a new market, using new channels of distribution, new communication/promotional tools and pricing techniques.
Organizational innovation	The application of innovative organizational ways with regards to the practices of the business (e.g. environmental management and corporate social responsibility),

the organization of the workplace (e.g. human resources development or organizational restructure) or external relations (e.g. outsourcing, partnerships, sponsorship or strategic alliances).

Process innovation   Changes in the methods through which an organization's offerings are produced and delivered.

Product/service innovation   Changes in the offerings of an organization.

REFERENCES AND ADDITIONAL READING

Adams, R., Bessant, J. and Phelps, R. (2006) Innovation management measurements: a review. *International Journal of Management Reviews* 8, 21–47.

Albury, D. (2005) Fostering innovation in public services. *Public Money and Management* 25 January, 51–56.

Ansoff, I. (1988) *New Corporate Strategy*. Wiley. New York.

Baregheh, A., Rowley, J. and Sambrook, S. (2009) Towards a multidisciplinary definition of innovation. *Management Decision* 47, 1323–1339.

Bassanini, A. and Ernst, E. (2002) Labour market institutions, product market regulation, and innovation: cross-country evidence. OECD Economics Department Working Papers, No. 316.

Benner, M. and Tushman, M. (2000) Process management and organizational adaption: the productivity dilemma revisited. Working paper. Harvard Business School Press, Boston, Massachusetts.

Bocquet, R., Le Bas, C., Mothe, C. and Poussing, N. (2011) CSR firm profiles and innovation: an empirical exploration with survey data. Available at: ftp://ftp.gate.cnrs.fr/RePEc/2011/1117.pdf

Booz Allen Hamilton (1991) *New Product Management*. Booz Allen Hamilton, New York.

Bowie, R. and Buttle, F. (2004) *Hospitality Marketing: An Introduction*. Butterworth-Heinemann, Burlington, Massachusetts.

Chesbrough, H. (2003) *Open Innovation: The New Imperative for Creating and Profiting from Technology*. Harvard Business School Press, Boston, Massachusetts.

Commission of the European Communities (2001) Green Paper 'Promoting a European Framework for Corporate Social Responsibility'. COM 366 final. Commission of the European Communities, Brussels, Belgium.

Cooper, R.G. (2005) *Product Leadership*. Basic Books, New York.

Cooper, R.G. and Edgett, S.J. (2003) Overcoming the crunch in resources for new product development. *Research Technology Management* 46, 48–59.

Cordero, R. (1990) The measurement of innovation performance in the firm: an overview. *Research Policy* 19, 185–192.

Crawford, C.M. (1994) *New Product Management*. Richard D. Irwin, Homewood, Illinois.

Crawford, M. and Di Benedetto, A. (2008) *New Products Management*, 9th edn. McGraw-Hill Irwin, Boston, Massachusetts.

easyJet plc (2011) Annual report and accounts 2010. Available at: http://2010annualreport.easyjet.com/files/pdf/Full_Report_easyJet_AR10.pdf

easyJet plc (2011) Chief Executive's statement. Available at: http://2010annualreport.easyjet.com/chief-executives-statement.asp

easyJet plc (2011) Do you care about the environment? We do too! Available at: http://www.easyjet.com/EN/About/information/infopack_environmentalpolicy.html

easyJet plc (2011) Quick facts. Available at: http://corporate.easyjet.com/media.aspx?sc_lang=en

Ernst, D. (2002) Global production networks and the changing geography of innovation systems: implications for developing countries. *Economics of Innovation and New Technology* 11, 497–523.

Euromonitor International (2010) easyGroup Ltd in Travel and Tourism (World). Available at: https://www.portal.euromonitor.com/Portal/Pages/Search/SearchResultsList.aspx

Eveleens, C. (2010) Innovation management; a literature review of innovation process models and their implications. Lectoraate Innovatie Publieke Sector 1–16. Available at: http://www.lectora-atinnovatie.nl/wp-content/uploads/2011/01/Innovation-management-literature-review.pdf

Financial Times Ltd (2010) EasyJet to test ash detector on aircraft. Available at: http://www.ft.com/cms/s/0/0f6140d2-703a-11df-8698-00144feabdc0.html#axzz1f83bKrYd

Frenkel, A., Maital, S. and Grupp, H. (2000) Measuring dynamic technical change: a technometric approach. *International Journal of Technology Management* 20, 429–441.

Gerwin, D. and Ferris, S.J. (2004) Organising new product development projects in strategic alliances. *Organisation Science* 15, 22–38.

Hart, S.J., Hutlink, E., Tzokas, N. and Commandeur, H. (2003) Industrial companies' evaluation criteria in new product development gates. *Journal of Product Innovation Management* 20, 22–36.

Hartley, J. (2005) Innovation in governance and public services: past and present. *Public Money and Management* 25, 27–34.

Hassanien, A. and Dale, C. (2012) Drivers and barriers of new product development and innovation in events venues: a multiple case study. *Journal of Facilities Management* 10, 75–92.

Hassanien, A. and Dale, C. (2013) Product innovation in events venues: directions, process and evaluation. *Journal of Facilities Management*, in press.

Hassanien, A., Dale, C. and Clarke, A. (2010) *Hospitality Business Development*. Elsevier, Oxford.

Hipp, C. and Grupp, H. (2005) Innovation in the service sector: the demand for service-specific innovation measurement concepts and typologies. *Research Policy* 34, 517–535.

http://corporate.easyjet.com/media/latest-news/news-year-2012.aspx

http://corporate.easyjet.com/media/latest-news/news-year-2012/27-06-2012-en.aspx

http://corporate.easyjet.com/sustainability/charity.aspx

http://www.easyjet.com/en/news/academy_opening.html

Husted, B.W. and Allen, D.B. (2007) Strategic corporate social responsibility and value creation among large companies. *Long Range Planning* 40, 594–610.

Jena, R. (2007) The innovation backlash. Available at: http://www.businessweek.com/innovate/content/feb2007/id20070212_728732.htm

Johnson, G., Scholes, K. and Whittington, R. (2008) *Exploring Corporate Strategy*. Pearson, Harlow, UK.

Jones, L. (2007) *easyJet – The Story of Britain's Biggest Low-cost Airline*. Aurum Press, London.

Kanter, R.M. (1988) When a thousand flowers bloom: structural, collective, and social conditions for innovation in organization. *Research in Organizational Behavior* 10, 169–211.

Keegan, W.J., Moritary, S., Duncan, R.T. and Paliwoda, S. (1995) *Marketing*. Prentice-Hall Canada, Canadian Edition, Ontario.

Kim, J. and Wilemon, D. (2002) Focusing the fuzzy front-end in new product development. *R&D Management* 32, 269–279.

Kotler, P. and Armstrong, G. (2004) *Principles of Marketing*, 10th edn. Prentice-Hall, Englewood Cliffs, New Jersey.

Kotler, P., Armstrong, G., Saunders, J. and Wong, V. (2002) *Principles of Marketing*, 3rd European Edition. Prentice-Hall, Harlow, UK.

Kuczmarski, T.D. (1992) *Managing New Products*, 2nd edn. Prentice-Hall, Englewood Cliffs, New Jersey.

Lantos, G.P., Brady, D. and McCaskey, P.H. (2009) New product development: an overlooked but critical course. *Journal of Product & Brand Management* 18, 425–436.

Leonard-Barton, D. (1992) Core capabilities and core rigidities: a paradox in managing new product development. *Strategic Management Journal* 13, 111–126.

Lovelock, C. and Wirtz, J. (2004) *Services Marketing: People, Technology and Strategy*, 5th edn. Pearson Prentice-Hall, Englewood Cliffs, New Jersey.

Lovelock, C. and Wirtz, J. (2007) *Services Marketing: People, Technology and Strategy*, 6th edn. Pearson Prentice-Hall, New Jersey.

Luecke, R. and Katz, R. (2003) *Managing Creativity and Innovation.* Harvard Business School Press, Boston, Massachusetts.

Minkova, V. (2009) *Low Cost Carriers – Business Model, Impacts of its Expansion and Challenges.* GRIN Verlag, Norderstedt, Germany.

Mulgan, G. and Albury, D. (2003) *Innovation in the Public Sector.* Strategy Unit, Cabinet Office, London.

Nada, N., Turkyilmaz, A. and El-Badawy, A. (2011) *SMEs Innovation Management Framework.* Available at: http://tiec.gov.eg/SiteCollectionDocuments/SMEs_Innovation_%20Management%20 Framework.pdf

Nidumolu, R., Prahalad, C.K. and Rangaswami, M.R. (2009) Why sustainability is now the key driver of innovation. *Harvard Business Review* September, 56–64.

OECD (2005) *The Measurement of Scientific and Technological Activities: Guidelines for Collecting and Interpreting Innovation Data: Oslo Manual*, 3rd edn. Prepared by the Working Party of National Experts on Scientific and Technology Indicators. OECD, Paris, para. 163.

Owens, J.D. (2004) An evaluation of organisational groundwork and learning objectives for new product development. *Journal of Enterprising Culture* 12, 303–325.

Owens, J.D. (2007) Why do some UK SMEs still find the implementation of a new product development process problematical? An exploratory investigation. *Management Decision* 45, 235–251.

Porter, M. (1990) *The Competitive Advantage of Nations.* Macmillan, London.

Porter, M.E. and Kramer, M.R. (2006) Strategy and society. *Harvard Business Review* December, 77–92.

Poskiene, A. (2006) Organizational culture and innovations. *Engineering Economics* 46, 45–50.

Prahalad, C.K. and Ramaswamy, V. (2004) *The Future of Competition: Co-creating Unique Value with Customers.* Harvard Business School Press, Boston, Massachusetts.

Preuss, R. (2011) An investigation of innovation at Easyjet. Unpublished BA (Hons) report, Edinburgh Napier University, Scotland, UK.

Schumpeter, J.A. (1934) *The Theory of Economic Development.* Harvard University Press, Cambridge, Massachusetts.

Stone, A., Rose, S., Lal, B. and Shipp, S. (2008) Measuring innovation and intangibles: a business perspective. Science and Technology Policy Institute. IDA Document D-3704. http://www.athena-alliance.org/pdf/MeasuringInnovationandIntangibles-STPI-BEA.pdf

The Economist (2011) Changes in the air. Available at: http://www.economist.com/node/21527035

Tidd, J., Bessant, J. and Pavitt, K. (2001) *Managing Innovation: Integrating Technological, Market and Organisational Change*, 2nd edn. Wiley, New York.

Tidd, J., Bessant, J. and Pavitt, K. (2005) *Managing Innovation: Integrating Technological, Market and Organisational Change*, 3rd edn. Wiley, Chichester, UK.

Trott, P. (2008) *Innovation Management and New Product Development.* Pearson Education, Harlow, UK.

Tushman, M. and Nadler, D. (1986) Organizing for innovation. *California Management Review* 28, 74–92.

Verworn, B. and Herstatt, C. (2002) The innovation process: an introduction to process models. Working Paper No. 12, TU Harburg, Germany. http://www.tu-harburg.de/tim/downloads/ arbeitspapiere/

Vyakarnam, S. and Adams, R. (2001) Institutional barriers to enterprise support: an empirical study. *Environment and Planning C: Government and Policy* 19, 335–353.

Wheelwright, S.C. and Clark, K.B. (1992) *Revolutionising Product Development.* The Free Press/ Macmillan, New York.

Zahra, S. and George, G. (2002) Absorptive capacity: a review, reconceptualization and extension. *Academy of Management Review* 27, 213–240.

Zeithaml, V.A., Bitner, M.J. and Gremler, D.D. (2006) *Services Marketing: Integrating Customer Focus Across the Firm*, 4th edn. McGraw-Hill, Boston, Massachusetts.

chapter 15

Entrepreneurship and Facilities Management

Dimitri Tassiopoulos
SAHARA, Human Sciences Research Council, South Africa

LEARNING OBJECTIVES

Having completed this chapter, readers should be able to:

- discuss the entrepreneurial nature of facilities management functions and practice;
- evaluate entrepreneurship (and intrapreneurship) within the context of facilities management;
- apply entrepreneurial skills for facilities management business development.

INTRODUCTION

Facilities management is about managing people and places to achieve best value for money by balancing user needs with tourism, hospitality and events (THE) business needs to achieve optimum organizational effectiveness. This chapter investigates the theory and practice of entrepreneurship within the context of facilities management. Elements of entrepreneurship and facilities management will be discussed in the context of facilities management business development and management.

> Entrepreneurship is first and foremost a mindset. It covers an individual's motivation and capacity, independently or within organisations, to identify an opportunity and to pursue it in order to produce new value or economic success. It takes creativity or innovation to enter and compete in an existing market, to change or even create a new market. To turn a business idea into success requires the ability to blend creativity or innovation with sound management and to adapt a

business to optimise its development during all phases of its life cycle. This goes beyond daily management: it concerns a business' ambition and strategy. (European Commission, 2003, p. 5)

Entrepreneurship can be defined, without repeating an already extensive debate, as 'a way of thinking, reasoning and acting that is opportunity obsessed, holistic in approach and leadership balanced. It results in the creation, enhancement, realisation and renewal of value, not just for the owners, but also for all the participants and stakeholders' (Timmons, 1999, cited in Jordaan, 2000, p. 2).

Creativity, innovation and unique value are the key elements of entrepreneurial businesses that distinguish entrepreneurs from business owners. Increasingly, state Timmons and Spinelli (2003, p. 274), research indicates that new ventures that flourish and grow to become sustainable businesses are headed by entrepreneurs that are also effective managers.

THE businesses create value through entrepreneurially bringing together resources and processes in a way that constitutes a viable 'business model'. A business model is the system that transforms an intangible business idea into products and offerings that have value in the THE market place. It is how a THE entrepreneur exploits an opportunity, by combining resources and facilities in a particular way so that products and offerings can be delivered that THE customers need (Stokes and Wilson, 2010).

Example: Kensington Stadium, New Zealand

The redeveloped Kensington Stadium in Northland, New Zealand, which reopened in May 2002, is now a true multipurpose facility, with a huge variety of events held annually. With a floor area in excess of 1700 m², the design of the new stadium also allows for drop-down curtains to divide the floor space, providing opportunities for many smaller community groups to afford to use the floor space. Up to three different user groups can now access the floor simultaneously.

Northland's premiere indoor sports stadium has a:

- seating capacity of 800 people;
- total floor available space 57 m × 30 m (1710 m²), which can be divided up into smaller areas by drop-down divider curtains (e.g. for basketball, netball, volleyball, badminton, indoor soccer);
- location on Kensington Park, with user friendly flow from outdoor to indoor;
- Sutherland Security 'Rock wall' – Northland's only commercial indoor climbing wall;
- two canteens (indoor and outdoor);
- four spacious changing rooms (indoor and outdoor);
- one office;
- public toilets (indoor and outdoor);

(Continued)

Example. **Continued.**

- first aid room;
- disabled access to facilities;
- free parking for 350 cars.

The stadium has hosted the following high-profile events:

- Whangarei Boys High School Jubilee – 2006
- Young Farmer of the Year – 2005
- Northland Home Show – Annual
- Northland Sports Awards Dinners – Annual
- Dunkleys Craft Show – Annual
- New Zealand Cheer Leading Competition – 2006
- Indoor Bowls Tournament – 2006
- House of Travel Expo
- Maori Golf Association Tournament – 2007
- Force vs Fiji International Netball Game – 2004
- Waitangi Cultural Kapa Haka – Annual

In addition, the stadium is home to a variety of local sporting groups and users including:

- local basketball leagues (junior/senior);
- indoor social netball;
- volleyball;
- fencing;
- karate tournaments;
- indoor climbing wall sessions;
- unihoc (indoor hockey) league;
- indoor soccer league;
- over 50s short tennis/badminton;
- primary, intermediate and secondary school sports tournaments.

The Stadium is available for hire on a casual or regular basis and is ideal for sports tournaments and events (indoor and outdoor), trade shows, concerts, exhibitions, shows and as a home for any size community sports group.

Source: Sport Northland (2011)

ENTREPRENEURIAL NATURE OF FACILITIES MANAGEMENT FUNCTIONS AND PRACTICE

Entrepreneurial approaches in destinations leads to changes in the nature of planning and urban development. Cotts *et al.* (2010) indicate that facility managers are increasingly required to think entrepreneurially 'outside-the-box', with outsourcing, quality management, customer orientation, sustainability and security/emergency management having such an organizational tailwind that, if managed properly, will put them at the forefront of THE facility management practices. In order to reduce costs, some THE facilities are operating extended hours to maximize the use of their existing facilities rather than building or leasing new ones. In some cases, that could actually mean 24/7 operations within the facilities. At the same time, some THE facilities' major functions may have been outsourced to providers that may be a dozen time zones away and this may require extended hours in portions of the home operation for continuity. This can reduce the time that these facilities are available for operations and maintenance that may, in fact, require adjusting entire operations and maintenance schedules to accommodate customers. The key skills identified by Cotts *et al.* (2010, p. 543) for facility managers are:

- be a change agent;
- be a decision maker;
- be a people leader;
- be an entrepreneur;
- set and follow through on priorities;
- develop and maintain a network;
- be visible, be open to criticism and manage by walking around;
- be the type of person whom other people trust;
- be flexible.

Contrary to popular belief, good facilities management does not just maintain the status quo; it assists the workplace on a daily basis. Facilities that are functional, well maintained and eye-pleasing add property value. In addition, when a THE customer walks through or drives into the parking lot, the facilities advertise the business. Additionally, the morale and productivity of employees rise in accordance with the respect shown to them and comfort given to them in the form of quality facilities (Nathan, 2008). The scope of a facility's facilities management varies based on the size of a facility. A small THE facility will have few facilities management concerns, while government projects, public sectors, universities and major THE businesses often have huge complexes requiring separate facilities management departments (Nathan, 2008).

Example: Polana Serena Hotel, Maputo, Mozambique

Built in 1922 along sweepingly splendid lines, the magnificent Polana Serena Hotel has long been considered one of Africa's finest hotels. Located on the leafy boulevards of one of Maputo's most exclusive residential districts, the Polana Serena Hotel belongs to an elite class of world-famous hotels, which includes such timeless legends as Raffles Hotel in Singapore, The Dorchester in London and The Ritz in Paris.

(Continued)

Example. Continued.

As part of the Serena Group's commitment towards showcasing the best of local architecture, culture and heritage, the Polana has recently emerged from an extensive renovation programme, which has resulted in the presentation of a landmark historic building whose classic charm has been fused with the ultimate in world-class amenities.

Offering 142 rooms, many of which are spacious suites, the 'Grande Dame' of Maputo now also offers a choice of three restaurants: the all-day dining Varanda Restaurant, the Delagoa fine-dining experience in the French style, the Aquarius Sushi Bar and the Polana Bar. The hotel also offers the 'Maisha' Mind Body and Spirit Health Club and Spa, a stunning swimming pool, extensive gardens, an exclusive residents' lounge, a business centre, a beauty salon and three gift shops.

At the forefront of Maputo's business venues, the hotel also offers its own conference and social events suite, which features a majestic ballroom.

Source: Serena Group of Hotels (2011)

Entrepreneurship and destination facility development

Cities have invested in flagship projects to spur economic development efforts with a bricks and mortar approach by bringing visitors to downtown areas and by generating publicity for what are perceived to be dour, in decline, formerly industrial cities (Barghchi *et al.*, 2009). It originated in the late 1980s in developed economies when several cities used property and enterprise-led development policies to build prestigious sports-led development to promote regional and economic development. This led to changes in the nature of planning and urban development, with a series of large-scale urban redevelopment projects, introducing the use of the entrepreneurial approach to local development. Re-invention, indicate Bycroft *et al.* (n.d.), is based on entrepreneurial governance and commenced with the publication in 1992 of David Osborne and Ted Gaebler's book, *Reinventing Government*, and formalized the move from input to outcome thinking and funding. It also introduced the notion that the public sector could be entrepreneurial and use multiple methods of service delivery.

Barghchi *et al.* (2009, pp. 185–195) state that this shift in the approach of urban governments towards development-oriented activities can be characterized as a movement from managerialism to entrepreneurialism, or even 'municipal capitalism'. In this new era, the public sector has evolved from a facilitator of development to 'active capitalist development'. THE facilities could be seen as catalytic facilities that receive public support in order to spur development in the immediate surrounding area. 'Catalytic facilities – usually buildings – can be described as those that generate urban development in their immediate surroundings, thereby meriting community support, possibly in the form of public subsidies' (Sternberg, cited in Barghchi *et al.*, 2009).

Entrepreneurship and opportunity recognition

Entrepreneurial strategy, according to Shane (2003, p. 194), is the intersection between all strategic actions and all activity to exploit opportunities. Opportunity has become a central concept in the study of entrepreneurship, indicates Tassiopoulos (2010b), and the discovery, exploration and exploitation of opportunities are recognized as fundamentally important processes in entrepreneurial activity. They propose that opportunity recognition is a learning process in which individuals make sense of their world through scanning, interpretation and action, and term this the *enactment perspective*, where opportunities are the result of what individuals do, rather than what they see. Opportunity can thus be defined as a gap or discontinuity between current, perceived reality and future possibility. This can, for instance, include an unmet market need; a mismatch between supply and demand; the potential for applying a solution to a problem; an introduction of a new technology; or transferring a product or process from one situation to another. This requires the imagination or perception of what could be, and the action to realize the possibility. If opportunities do not exist as objective facts but rather are recognized and created by people in their subjective perception, then they form part of that person's learning process. The same opportunities are not apparent to everyone because of the myriad of differences in context, experience and perception; some people perceive the same opportunity more quickly than others through imagination and foresight. It is posited that this may be a result of superior learning ability.

Example: Cape Town Stadium, Cape Town, South Africa

The Cape Town Stadium is a newly built stadium that was used for the 2010 FIFA World Cup. During the planning stage, it was known as the Green Point Stadium, which was the name of the previous stadium on the site, and this name was also used frequently during World Cup media coverage.

A consortium consisting of South Africa's Sail Group and French-based Stade de France were awarded the service contract to operate the stadium and ensure that it remained a sustainable multi-purpose venue after the 2010 FIFA World Cup. The consortium, called Business Venture Investments 1317, was involved in the management of the stadium from January 2009 onwards. The city municipality paid the consortium to manage the stadium up to and during the World Cup, after which the consortium will lease the stadium from the city for a period of not less than 10 years and not more than 30 years.

Following the World Cup, the stadium capacity has been reduced to 55,000, enabling it to cater for all types of sports, including rugby, as well as music concerts and other major events. The stadium features corporate hospitality suites, medical, training, conferencing and banqueting facilities. The consortium was to operate the stadium as well as manage and maintain the defined areas of the surrounding urban park and sport precinct on the 85-hectare Greenpoint Common from stadium revenue.

Source: Wikipedia (2011)

Example: Company withdraws from taking over lease of World Cup stadium

Cape Town ratepayers will have to pay for the operating costs of the Cape Town World Cup stadium after a company that had agreed to take over a 30-year lease withdrew.

A joint venture between a South African company and the company that runs the 1998 World Cup final venue, the Stade de France, had earlier agreed to operate the Cape Town World Cup stadium.

The South African Press Association reported Thursday that the chief executive of Sail Stadefrance Operating Company (SSOC), Morne du Plessis, said they had withdrawn due to 'unresolved matters and severe operating constraints', which would have led to 'substantial losses'.

'The operating cost was surprising. The maintenance costs were way above expectations,' the former Springbok rugby player is quoted as saying.

> In the light of unresolved matters that materially affected the viability of the lease and severe operating constraints, we have advised the city that SSOC would not be in a position to enter the lease on 1 November 2010, as the shareholders were not prepared to enter the lease under circumstances that projected substantial losses.

Du Plessis said that high costs of maintaining the stadium, the failure to secure anchor tenants and 'business constraints' had been behind their decision.

Acting Cape Town Mayor Ian Neilson said that they did not know at this stage what it would cost local ratepayers. 'In the end it will be up to the citizens of Cape Town on whether they come to the stadium to support the teams and events'.

Neilson called on the national government to take over some of the financial responsibility and said that football's controlling body FIFA had insisted on the stadium being built at Greenpoint.

> 'We had cheaper sites at Athlone and Newlands, but these were not suitable to FIFA,' he said. 'It was Greenpoint or don't be involved in the World Cup.'

The acting mayor said that, for the foreseeable future, the city would have to take over the management of the stadium, but that they did not want this to be permanent.

Earlier an official told parliament that the operational and maintenance of the stadium would be some ZAR 46.5 million (or USD 6.77 million).

Source: M & C (2010)

FACILITIES MANAGEMENT AND THE ENTREPRENEURIAL SPECTRUM

Maas (1996, pp. 53–54) distinguishes between owner-managers and entrepreneurs and quotes D'Ambiose and Muldoney (1984):

> An entrepreneur is an individual who establishes and manages a business for the principal purpose of profit and growth. The entrepreneur is characterised principally by innovative behaviour and will employ strategic management practices in the business. A small business owner is an individual who establishes and manages a business for the principal purpose of furthering personal goals. The business must be the primary source of income and will consume the majority of one's time and resources. The owner perceives the business as an extension of his or her own personality, intricately bound with family needs and desires.

An entrepreneur, continues Maas (1996, p. 55), symbolizes a person who aims for growth and development, while an owner-manager displays a maintenance role in the operation of a business. The six dimensions of business practice identified by Chell (2001, p. 283) are: strategic orientation; commitment to opportunity; commitment to resources; control of resources; management structure; and reward philosophy. Visser (2003, p. 133) consolidates entrepreneurial attributes into six dominant themes: commitment and determination; leadership; opportunity obsession; tolerance of risk, ambiguity and uncertainty; creativity and self reliance and the ability to adapt; and motivation to excel.

Rogers refers to an 'entrepreneurial spectrum that at its respective poles has *independent entrepreneurship* and *intrapreneurship*' (2003, cited in Tassiopoulos, 2010a, p. 153). The development of new sustainable THE business ventures by individuals, according to Geneste, 'falls within the domain of independent entrepreneurship' (2010, p. 118). Independent entrepreneurship refers to 'the process whereby individuals or group of individuals, acting independently of any association with an existing organisation, create a new organisation' (Tassiopoulos, 2010). However, individuals and small teams too, can form entrepreneurial groups within a facility capable of altering the behaviour of others in the organization to create new resources for the facility. This is the domain of intrapreneurship (or corporate entrepreneurship). Once the innovative start-up THE facility is established in the community, has a regular income and is surviving and operating successfully, how can the facility continue to be innovative? A key success factor of innovative facilities is the ability to create entrepreneurs within the facility. These corporate entrepreneurs or 'intrapreneurs' are the facility's employees and managers or, as will be seen later, even the members of a community. The entrepreneurial firm clearly needs to evolve when it moves from a new start-up venture to an independent entrepreneurial firm to one that eventually relies on its personnel to continue to create innovations, new and improved offerings. This is where intrapreneurship comes in – the creation of new entrepreneurs within the THE facility.

Intrapreneurship can be described as the process of developing new products, services and lines of business within an existing THE facility. It is perhaps best understood as a form of internal entrepreneurship that takes place with the encouragement and support of management.

An employee who takes responsibility for developing an innovative idea into a marketable product is known as an intrapreneur. Intrapreneurship, according to Geneste, 'is the creation of new ventures within (THE) organisations and the renewal of key organisational ideas and strategies. While the focus of intrapreneurship has been predominantly on large organisations, it is equally important in small to medium sized tourism enterprises particularly in industries undergoing turbulent change' (2010, p. 118). Motivating factors that assist the emergence and development of intrapreneurship

> include the demands and constraints of the external environment and includes the desire to penetrate new markets, increase an existing competitive advantage or develop new ones. These are also referred to as external triggers some of which can be hostile such as declining fortunes and actions of competitors. Dynamic, turbulent and constantly changing industry environments also are triggers for industry growth and increased demand for new products also are external motivators to intrapreneurship. In the era of hyper-competition and industry dynamism, organisations are now more dependent on the knowledge and skills of innovative, opportunity seeking intrapreneurial employees than ever before. (Geneste, 2010, pp. 122–123)

Drucker (1985), according to Arslan and Cevher (n.d., p. 73), has stated that 'today's businesses, especially the large ones, simply will not survive in this period of rapid change and innovation unless they acquire entrepreneurial competence'. Today, especially, large-size companies are turning to intrapreneurship because they are not getting the continual innovation, development and value creation that they previously had. The term intrapreneurship refers to a process that goes on within a founded firm, regardless of its size, and leads not only to new business ventures but also to other innovative activities and orientations such as development of new products, services, technologies, managerial techniques, strategies and competitive postures. Another motivating factor that contributes to the emergence of intrapreneurship is the growth orientation of the business. In Carrier's (1996) research:

> all of the entrepreneurial founders of the firms in her study had clear growth objectives in mind. Intuitively, it makes sense that firms that are intrapreneurial are likely to be aiming for growth. Without this aim, it is unlikely that the owner/founders and senior management of the firm will be supporting the development of entrepreneurial individuals within the firm. A final motivator that facilitates the emergence of intrapreneurship is related to the internal management, production or marketing problems that exist within the firm. A willingness to assist complex operations and avoid organisational problems leads to the development of intrapreneurial mindsets. (Geneste, 2010, p. 123)

THE facilities need to create a culture that provides employees with both freedom and encouragement to develop new ideas. Support for intrapreneurship must start with top executives of THE facilities and work its way down in the form of policies, programmes and reward systems. THE facilities have to learn how to leverage the competencies and the assets that they already have within by encouraging employees to form competing teams that function like small businesses or internal vendors. This could happen through the creation of formal innovation programmes to ensure that every new idea receives a fair hearing with upper management of THE facilities behaving like a venture capital firm, evaluating and providing financial support for promising new ideas.

> **Example:** New dining option at Shelley Point Hotel, South Africa
>
> Shelley Point Hotel, Spa & Country Club in the Western Cape has added the Cattle Baron Grill and Bistro to its hospitality offering. The restaurant aims to expand the hotel's facilities to the local community while providing guests with another specialized dining option.
>
> Food and beverage manager, Kathy Matthee, says: 'It's important for us to not only offer our hotel guests an alternative eatery, but also that we offer the local market a choice, tried-and-tested steakhouse-cum-bistro. Visitors to St Helena Bay are not spoilt for choice when it comes to places to eat and we hope to fill a gap in the market with our variety of restaurant options.'
>
> The Cattle Baron offers a range of steaks, including the Green Pepper Fillet Madagascar, brandied Flaming Chateaubriand and the pan-fried Pepper Fillet. Old-fashioned charcoal grills with firebrick are used, enabling steaks to be grilled at an optimal temperature.
>
> Shelley Point Hotel, Spa & Country Club launched its new wing this month and now offers 86 suites, a choice of two restaurants, a deli and alfresco bistro, conferencing facilities for up to 80 delegates, wellness centre and spa, golf, gymnasium, two swimming pools and a Kids' Club.
>
> *Source:* Now Media (Pty) Ltd (2011a)

STRATEGY AND GROWTH: RATIONALE AND MOTIVATION

THE business development, according to Nieman *et al.* (2003, pp. 220–222), has been identified as a priority by governments because of the potential to create jobs and provide a solution to unemployment. The lack of an entrepreneurial mindset or desire to grow is seen as a major hurdle to growth experienced by many business owners. The potential to grow distinguishes an entrepreneurial business from a small business and in order for growth to be achieved there must be a long-term or 'strategic plan'. Strategic growth, argue Nieman *et al.* (2003, p. 237), is the change that takes place in the way the business interacts with the environment and it is the technique that the business develops for it to exploit a presence in the THE marketplace. It is underscored that strategic objectives change as THE businesses move through the stages of their life cycle: in the start-up and early growth stages, the strategy is mostly aimed at survival, in the following stage the focus is on building a customer base, maintaining profit and obtaining resources.

Structure, according to Nieman *et al.* (2003, p. 237), follows strategy because structural growth is related to the changes that have taken place in the way the THE business organized its internal systems, roles and responsibilities, reporting relationships, communication and control systems. THE facilities are required to develop and change their structure to meet the requirements of change and growth and with each strategic phase are required to adapt their structure and processes. The structure of THE facility business is representative of a response to the contingencies of size (the larger the THE business, the more complex this will be), technology (the way the THE business does its business will determine the complexity of the operational technology required), strategy (the manner by which the THE business competes for business) and environment (this impacts on the structure and strategy, offering resources and/or challenges to the THE business).

The strategic process is utilized to reassess the organizational system in order to determine any contradictions to the business's goals and objectives involving internal resources, capabilities and systems. External strategies position THE businesses in relation to their place in the THE industry value chain and this may include a strategy of integration, which could be vertical, horizontal or lateral. Internal strategies focus on an increase in market share, developing new products and service and/or entering new markets (Nieman *et al.*, 2003, p. 255).

The research findings of Szivas (2001, p. 164) indicate that there are two aspects to THE businesses that need to be noted: the relative ease of entry into the THE industry because many of the (particularly, small) entrants into the THE industry come from a wide range of industries, and the 'way of life' motives for entrepreneurial entry into THE reveal that the industry is seen as offering a better lifestyle and a better standard of living while promising a pleasant work environment and high levels of human interaction. Lewis (2004, p. 2) and George (2007, p. 190) propose that the growth potential of THE businesses is influenced by the attitude to growth held by the owner. There is a distinct difference between growth- and profit-orientated THE business owners entrepreneurs and autonomy, lifestyle or capped-growth entrepreneurs to the extent that autonomy- and lifestyle-orientated entrepreneurs are usually regarded as owner-managers, rather than entrepreneurs.

Example: New owners announce big plans for V&A Waterfront, Cape Town, South Africa

The new owners of Cape Town's V&A Waterfront have wasted no time in confirming their commitment to the ongoing expansion of the South African landmark, with the announcement of a ZAR500 million redevelopment programme of the Clock Tower precinct over the next four years.

All conditions of the Government Employees Pension Fund (GEPF) and Growthpoint's purchase of the V&A Waterfront have been met and redevelopment is already under way. The major Clock Tower Precinct development will establish a new professional business district at the heart of the V&A Waterfront, while maintaining the heritage credentials of one of the oldest sites in and around Cape Town.

In addition to the refurbishment of the existing Clock Tower retail facility, the other areas earmarked for development include the unused grain silo building, and the collier jetty alongside the Clock Tower retail centre.

(Continued)

Example. Continued.

V&A Waterfront CEO, David Green, says the V&A Waterfront management team is extremely positive about the transaction. 'We pride ourselves on being a benchmark for international waterfront developments and the change of ownership bodes well for long-term development and sustainability. The new owners have shared their immediate plans for the property and we are looking forward to working closely with them to bring these plans to fruition.'

Norbert Sasse, CEO of Growthpoint Properties Limited, explains that the V&A Waterfront, with its established record of performance, represents an opportunity for growth, which will come from the future development of the undeveloped bulk of this prize property asset. 'Our investment in the V&A Waterfront is driven by the existing performance and future potential,' says Sasse. 'More than being the premier property asset in Africa, the V&A Waterfront has all the performance fundamentals in place. It enjoys robust demand across all sectors with lower vacancy rates than anywhere else in the country and benefits from significant nett income growth.'

Source: Now Media (Pty) Ltd (2011b)

STRATEGIC FACILITIES MANAGEMENT

As mentioned in Chapter 1, facilities management has developed a strong practice around providing a supportive framework for businesses and organizations based on the physical facilities. According to Hoffmann *et al.*, 'Newer definitions of facilities management however communicates a broader ambition of facilities management to become a strategically integrated approach to maintaining, improving, and adapting the buildings and supporting services of an organization in order to create an environment that strongly supports the primary objectives of that organisation' (2010, pp. 2–3). Facilities management is described by BIFM as 'the integration of processes within an organisation to maintain and develop the agreed services which support and improve the effectiveness of its primary activities' (2011, n.p.). Facilities management reduces costs, increases productivity and aids competitiveness. Facilities management encompasses multidisciplinary activities within the built environment and the management of their impact on people and the workplace. Effective facilities management, combining resources and activities, is vital to the success of any THE business. At a corporate level, it contributes to the delivery of strategic and operational objectives. On a day-to-day level, effective facilities management provides a safe and efficient working environment, which is essential to the performance of any THE business – whatever its size and scope. Within this fast-growing professional discipline, facilities managers have extensive responsibilities for providing, maintaining and developing myriad services. These range from property strategy, space management and communications infrastructure to building maintenance, administration and contract management.

Example: Burj Khalifa, UAE – the world's tallest tower

World's tallest building. A living wonder. Stunning work of art. Incomparable feat of engineering. Burj Khalifa is all that. In concept and execution, Burj Khalifa has no peer.

More than just the world's tallest building, Burj Khalifa is an unprecedented example of international cooperation, symbolic beacon of progress, and an emblem of the new, dynamic and prosperous Middle East.

It is also tangible proof of Dubai's growing role in a changing world. In fewer than 30 years, this city has transformed itself from a regional centre to a global one. This success was not based on oil reserves, but on reserves of human talent, ingenuity and initiative. Burj Khalifa embodies that vision.

Mr Mohamed Alabbar, Chairman, Emaar Properties, said: 'Burj Khalifa goes beyond its imposing physical specifications. In Burj Khalifa, we see the triumph of Dubai's vision of attaining the seemingly impossible and setting new benchmarks. It is a source of inspiration for every one of us in Emaar. The project is a declaration of the emirate's capabilities and of the resolve of its leaders and people to work hand in hand on truly awe-inspiring projects.

At The Top, Burj Khalifa experience

Your At The Top, Burj Khalifa visit begins in the reception area on the lower ground level of The Dubai Mall. Here and throughout your journey, you will be entertained and informed by a multi-media presentation that chronicles Dubai's exotic history and the fascinating story of Burj Khalifa.

Leave the reception area aboard the 65-metre-long travelator on a trip that transports you through time, from the earliest days of Dubai to the present. Pause briefly at a unique viewing point for your first close-up view of the soaring Burj Khalifa, seen through a skylight framing its awe-inspiring height.

Begin your vertical ascent to the observation deck in a high-speed elevator, travelling at 10 metres per second. As the doors open, floor-to-ceiling glass walls provide a breathtaking unobstructed 360-degree view of the city, desert and ocean. By night, sparkling lights and stars compete for your attention.

Special telescopes provide virtual time-travel visions of the scenes beyond and below. You'll see close-up real-time views as well as the past and the future, by day and by night. You can also walk the entire perimeter for the most comprehensive views. If you wish, adventure outside onto the open-air terrace to enjoy another perspective of the sweeping views below.

You can even shop At The Top, Burj Khalifa and take home a truly unique souvenir of your visit. The At The Top, Burj Khalifa tour typically lasts 1 hour. However, you can linger as long

(Continued)

Example. Continued.

as you like before making the return journey to the base of Burj Khalifa. You'll be taking with you a fuller appreciation of this architectural wonder and a deeper understanding of Dubai's remarkable vision.

Stay with Armani

Soaring high above Downtown Dubai in the iconic Burj Khalifa, the world's tallest building, Armani Hotel Dubai is the world's first hotel designed and developed by Giorgio Armani. Reflecting the pure elegance, simplicity and sophisticated comfort that define Armani's signature style, the hotel is the realization of the designer's long-held dream to bring his sophisticated style to life in the most complete way and offer his customers a Stay with Armani experience. Every detail in the hotel bears the Armani signature, beginning with the warm Italian-style hospitality and moving to each element of the design from the Eramosa stone floors to the zebrawood panels, bespoke furnishings and personally designed hotel amenities. Sophisticated colours, clean lines and unique textures blend together seamlessly with the tower's stunning architecture and natural light to create an atmosphere of calm serenity where guests can retreat into a world of minimalist elegance. Nestled in the world's tallest tower, occupying the concourse level to level 8 and levels 38 and 39, Armani Hotel Dubai offers sweeping views of the city. With its own dedicated entrance to the tower, it is easily accessible within walking distance to the world's largest mall and some of the region's most exclusive leisure and business outlets.

The hotel features:

- 24 Armani Studio rooms
- 54 Armani Classic rooms
- 26 Armani Premiere rooms
- 4 Armani Premiere rooms with Balcony
- 26 Armani Suites
- 2 Armani Suites with Balcony
- 12 Armani Executive Suites
- 3 Armani Ambassador Suites
- 3 Armani Ambassador Suites with Balcony
- 5 Armani Signature Suites
- 1 Armani Dubai Suite.

Dine: Armani Hotel features eight restaurants offering a wide choice of world cuisines ranging from Japanese and Indian to Mediterranean and authentic fine-dining Italian. The impressive culinary options reflect the cosmopolitan nature of the city.

Shop: Armani Hotel guests can take home part of the Armani lifestyle experience with carefully selected products from the designers' unique in-house retail outlets.

(Continued)

Example. Continued.

ARMANI/DOLCI: Armani/Dolci offers a sweet selection of biscuits and chocolates, petits fours, biscotti and more, all bearing the unmistakable Armani signature.

ARMANI/FIORI: Armani/Fiori features fresh flower arrangements and exclusively designed vases by Giorgio Armani. The vases' quintessential designs follow the fluid shapes of the flowers themselves. Delight in the signature flower: a simple yet elegant white rose.

ARMANI/Galleria: Armani/Galleria presents haute-couture fashion accessories from the Giorgio Armani Privé collection. It's the first and only place in Dubai where the exclusive collection is available.

Relax: An oasis of peace and tranquillity in the heart of a bustling city, the 12,000 square feet Armani/SPA reflects the Armani lifestyle and design philosophies, offering beautiful unique spaces and outstanding service for individually personalized treatments, personal fitness, sequential thermal bathing, creative spa cuisine, or simply private and social relaxation.

ARMANI/Events: Whether a once-in-a-lifetime occasion or high-profile business conference, events at the Armani Hotel provide an elegant and tasteful setting. The hotel offers a luxurious ballroom seating up to 450 people; a stunning outdoor pavilion area overlooking The Dubai Fountain; a charming Majlis offering an Arabic style meeting room, and several meeting lounges and boardrooms.

Source: Emaar Properties PJSC (2011)

VALUE CREATING DIVERSIFICATION

Although business-unit managers are concerned with optimizing their internal value-creating chains of relationships (by forging effective competitive strategies), corporate-level managers are responsible for arranging (and monitoring) the best system of value creating relationships among sister business units, as well as with outsiders – which may include international suppliers (and distributors), locally competent suppliers (and distributors) within each site of international operations, competitors, local governments that build and support local infrastructures, and customers, among others. Doing so requires THE facilities to maintain strategic flexibility, since strategy implementation may involve cross-licensing (or other forms of information exchange), joint ventures (or other forms of equity participation) or direct investments through acquisition.

Within flexible organizations, corporate-level strategy initiates and audits competitive advantages based on organizational attributes. In particular, effective vertical strategies require a continuous process of redesigning task responsibilities (in collaboration with suppliers and customers) to create more value-added opportunities internally while continually weeding-out activities (and customers) that do not fit the firm's choice regarding what businesses it wants to be in (vertical integration), hence what competencies it wants to develop to sustain its competitive advantage. Vertical relationships can be secured through contractual ties, strategic alliances or equity ownership, depending on the competitive environments where transactions must occur. Disinvestment (or the severing of vendor–customer relationships) must occur when necessary, even where the same corporate parents own both business units. Thus, corporate-level oversight is mandatory – especially where sister business units are linked in such buyer–supplier relationships – to avoid perverting the firm's strategic vision (Malonis, 2006).

Strategic flexibility requires organizations to gain new capabilities – through acquisition or internal development, depending on the timing requirements of effective implementation – before competitors reach similar conclusions. Strategic flexibility may require facilities to relocate stages of their value chain where national cost advantages in factors of production are short-lived. Where easy international flows of information make competitive imitation inevitable and timing advantages based on proprietary information are increasingly short-lived, flexible organizations need a corporate strategy that moves them from less-competitive businesses to those where opportunities to prosper are greater and success requirements are more compatible with the strengths they have developed internally (Malonis, 2006).

Example: Nelson Mandela Bay Stadium, Port Elizabeth, South Africa

Initial fears that the Nelson Mandela Bay Stadium would become a white elephant have been allayed, with the stadium generating ZAR11 million in revenue since the FIFA World Cup – believed to be more than any other South African stadium purpose-built for last year's soccer extravaganza.

The facility – which cost ZAR2.4 billion to build – costs ratepayers R21 million to operate each year. However, an investigation into the feasibility of the world-class stadium has revealed that Access Management, appointed as the official operator in 2009, has helped generate R11 million in revenue since then, more than halving the running costs for the municipality. Next year, revenue is expected to increase to ZAR17 million and by 2013 it is expected to start breaking even and even turn a profit.

Meanwhile, some other World Cup stadiums have yet to even leave the starting blocks. The Cape Town Stadium, which cost ZAR4.5 billion to build and costs ZAR57 million a year to operate, does not even have an operator yet and city officials were unable to give projections this week as to when the stadium would become sustainable. However, the promise of Super Rugby in the Eastern Cape and the prospect of further Test matches involving the Springboks have resulted in all 49 of the Nelson Mandela Bay Stadium's hospitality suites being sold out for rugby for the next three years. That, coupled with the success of recent concerts, soccer matches, music festivals and the provision of cleaning, security and food and beverages has ensured the stadium is the most viable of all those built for the World Cup.

(Continued)

Example. Continued.

Access Management chief executive Stephan Pretorius said the company, of which former SARU chief executive Rian Oberholzer is managing director and a shareholder, was satisfied with its progress. 'So our long-term plan is to develop or get a soccer team that is a Port Elizabeth-based side that can play all their matches here. I think getting Maritzburg and Cosmos to play here is a lead-up to that'. Asked which events generated the most income, Access Management marketing and communications manager Buli Ngomane said they were reluctant to give exact figures because they were competing with all the new stadiums.

'Our ability to attract the large events to our metro depends partly on structuring attractive packages for the event organisers to lure them away from those venues and consider us instead. Each quote is tailored to each client's needs,' Ngomane said.

Source: Reeves and Mthetho Ndoni (2011)

Case Study

Moses Mabhida Stadium, Durban, South Africa

The Moses Mabhida Stadium has a range of retail, sport, cultural and leisure facilities and is the heart of the King's Park Sporting Precinct in Durban, South Africa. The stadium was constructed as one of the key points for the 2010 FIFA World Cup. The design of the stadium centred on creating 'a state-of-the-art landmark sports facility with excellent amenities, and a sustainable recreational and multi-disciplinary sporting venue'. The stadium is designed with the 'arch of triumph' that spans the width of the stadium. This enabled the stadium to have comparisons with other major city landmarks such as the Sydney Opera House and The London Eye. The SkyCar is utilized as a key tourist attraction at the stadium. This is a single car which runs along steel tracks on top of the north arch and can transport up to twenty visitors to its highest point. The south part of the arch provides an Adventure Walk where visitors, with the assistance of safety equipment, can go to the top via a walk of 550 steps.

The stadium was designed with flexibility in mind. This would enable the facility to cater for a range of leisure events so it could compete effectively in the international stadia marketplace. In particular, the indoor seating arrangement provides visitors and spectators with continuous sight of the sporting or cultural event they have come to see. The stadium has repositioned the concept of sporting venues in South Africa; from venues where a range of sport, leisure and cultural events can take place.

Broader to the stadium is the King's Park Precinct. The precinct offers walkways, parks, retail and eating facilities that cater to a range of consumer not just those whose primary interest is 'sport' related. Though, the precinct was designed to ensure the efficient and safe transit of attendees during major sporting events. To the south of the stadium is

(Continued)

Case Study. Continued.

the 'People's Park' which provides green space for relaxing, picnicking and cycling. To the north of the stadium is Imbizo Place which provides shops, restaurants and an outdoor amphitheatre. The area also has others features including; Heroes' Walk, Moses Mabhida Square, People's Park restaurant, two training fields and a 1km circular track for walking, jogging and cycling.

Source: Moses Mabhida Stadium Durban (2011)

Questions

1. Evaluate the primary catalyst for the construction of the stadium and its associated facilities.
2. What entrepreneurial opportunities arose as an outcome of the construction of the stadium?
3. What are the challenges entrepreneurs would be presented with when wanting to gain a presence in the King's Park Sporting Precinct?

SUMMARY

In this chapter, various theoretical concepts were discussed related to the entrepreneurship spectrum within the context of facilities management. THE facilities often obtain a new role as catalytic buildings and spur development in destinations. In an ever-increasing competitive global tourism market, THE facilities are seeking novel ways to gain a competitive advantage over their peers; entrepreneurial facilities management has come into the limelight as one of the major resources on which to rely.

REVIEW QUESTIONS

1. Identify a number of important roles played by entrepreneurship within THE facilities.
2. Discuss examples of the different types of entrepreneurship within THE facilities.
3. Describe intrapreneurship and its role in the overall business strategy of a THE facility, and state some of the principal measures facilities managers can take to enhance and manage intrapreneurship.

GLOSSARY OF TERMS USED IN THIS CHAPTER

Business model   The system that transforms an intangible business idea into products and offerings that have value in the THE market place.

Catalytic facilities   Usually buildings, they can be described as those that generate urban development in their immediate surroundings, thereby meriting community support, possibly in the form of public subsidies.

Corporate entrepreneurs or 'intrapreneurs'	The facility's employees and managers or even the members of a community.
Entrepreneur	An individual who establishes and manages a business for the principal purpose of profit and growth. The entrepreneur is characterized principally by innovative behaviour and will employ strategic management practices in the business. A small business owner is an individual who establishes and manages a business for the principal purpose of furthering personal goals (D'Ambiose and Muldoney, 1984).
Entrepreneurship	A way of thinking, reasoning and acting that is opportunity obsessed, holistic in approach and leadership balanced. It results in the creation, enhancement, realization and renewal of value, not just for the owners, but also for all the participants and stakeholders (Timmons, 1999).
Intrapreneurship	The process of developing new products, services and lines of business within an existing THE facility. It is perhaps best understood as a form of internal entrepreneurship that takes place with the encouragement and support of management.

REFERENCES AND ADDITIONAL READING

Arslan, E.T. and Cevher, E. (n.d.) Intrapreneurship enabling organizations to drive innovation. Available at: http://ces.epoka.edu.al/icme/a7.pdf (accessed 12 July 2011).
Barghchi, M., bt. Omar, D. and Aman, M.S. (2009) Cities, sports facilities development, and hosting events. *European Journal of Social Sciences* 10, 185–195.
BIFM (British Institute of Facilities Management) (2011) Facilities management introduction. Available at: http://www.bifm.org.uk/bifm/about/facilities (accessed 12 July 2011).
Bycroft, P., Fajak, A. and Renda, M. (n.d.) Alliances, partnerships and mergers: lessons for facilities managers about the three major new directions in outsourcing and partnering. Available at: http://www.wintercomms.com.au/files/.../PeterBycrof_FajakRenda.pdf
Chell, E. (2001) *Entrepreneurship: Globalisation, Innovation and Development.* Thomson Learning, London.
Cotts, P.G., Roper, K.O. and Payant, R.P. (2010) *The Facility Management Handbook*, 3rd edn. AMACOM, New York.
Emaar Properties PJSC (2011) Burj Khalifa – the world's tallest tower. Available at: http://www.burjkhalifa.ae/language/en-us/the-tower.aspx (accessed 12 July 2011).
European Commission (2003) *Entrepreneurship in Europe.* Green Paper. COM (2003) 27: final. European Commission, Brussels, Belgium.
Osborne, D. and Gaebler, T. (1992) *Reinventing Government: How the Entrepreneurial Spirit is Transforming the Public Sector.* Addison-Wesley, Reading, Massachusetts.
Geneste, L. (2010) Intrapreneurship in the venture: evolution, hurdles, leadership. In: Tassiopoulos, D. (ed.) *New Tourism Ventures: An Entrepreneurial and Managerial Approach*, 2nd edn. Juta (Pty) Ltd, Cape Town, South Africa, pp. 117–131.
George, R. (2007) *Managing Tourism in South Africa.* Oxford University Press, Cape Town, South Africa.
Hitt, M.A., Duane Ireland, M.R. and Hoskisson, R.E. (2010) *Strategic Management: Competitiveness & Globalization, Concepts*, 9th edn. South-Western Cengage Learning, Independence, Kentucky.

Hoffmann, B., Munthe-Kaas, P., Larsen, J.L. and Elle, M. (2010) Facilitating creative environments – when the winds of creativity hit FM. *Proceedings of the 9th EuroFM Research Symposium – EFMC2010*, Madrid, Spain.

IFMA (International Facility Management Association) (2011) Views from the top: executives evaluate the FM function. Research Report #17. Available at: http://ifma.org/resources/research/reports/pages/views-from-top.htm (accessed 12 July 2011).

Jordaan, J.W. (2000) The challenge of integrating entrepreneurship in tertiary agricultural education: a South African experience. *Proceedings of the Conference Internationalising Entrepreneurship Education and Training*. Tampere, Finland, 10–12 July.

Lewis, K. (2004) New Zealand SME owners: in it for 'lifestyle' or 'freestyle'? Conference proceedings of the Institute of Small Business Affairs, 27th National Conference. ISBA, Newcastle, Gateshead, UK.

M & C (Monsters and Critics) (2010) Company withdraws from taking over lease of World Cup stadium (Oct 7). Available at: http://www.monstersandcritics.com/news/africa/news/article_1589737.php/Company-withdraws-from-taking-over-lease-of-World-Cup-stadium (accessed 12 July 2011).

Maas, G.P.J. (1996) Kreatiwiteit in Suid-Afrikaanse Klein- en Mediumgroot Ondernemings. Thesis, University of Stellenbosch, South Africa.

Malonis, J.A. (2006) Strategy. In: *Encyclopedia of Business*. eNotes.com, Gale Cengage. Available at: http://www.enotes.com/biz-encyclopedia/strategy (accessed 12 July 2011).

Moses Mabhida Stadium Durban (2011) Welcome to the Moses Mabhida Stadium. Available at: http://www.mosesmabhidastadium.co.za (accessed 12 July 2011).

Nathan, B.R. (2008) Facility management minimizes the cost. *Businessgyan*. Available at: http://www.businessgyan.com/node/4107 (accessed 12 July 2011).

Nieman, G., Hough, J. and Nieuwenhuizen, C. (2003) *Entrepreneurship: A South African Perspective*. Van Schaik, Pretoria, South Africa.

Now Media (Pty) Ltd (2011a) New dining option at Shelley Point Hotel. *Tourism Update*. Available at: http://www.tourismupdate.co.za/NewsDetails.aspx?newsId=59698 (accessed 12 July 2011).

Now Media (Pty) Ltd (2011b) New owners announce big plans for V&A Waterfront. *Tourism Update*. Available at: http://www.tourismupdate.co.za/NewsDetails.aspx?newsId=59475 (accessed 12 July 2011).

Reeves, A. and Mthetho Ndoni, M. (2011) Bay's new stadium 'profitable by 2013'. *PE Herald*. Available at: http://www.peherald.com/news/article/248018 (accessed 12 July 2011).

Serena Group of Hotels (2011) About The Polana Serena Hotel. Available at: http://www.serenahotels.com/serenapolana/default-en.html (accessed 12 July 2011).

Shane, S. (2003) *A General Theory of Entrepreneurship*. Edgar Elgar, Cheltenham, UK.

Sport Northland (2011) Multi purpose stadium: Kensington Stadium – our multi-purpose stadium. Available at: http://www.sportnorthland.co.nz/default.asp?PageID=5728 (accessed 12 July 2011).

Stokes, D. and Wilson, N. (2010) *Small Business Management and Entrepreneurship*, 6th edn. South Western Cengage Learning EMEA, Andover, UK.

Szivas, E. (2001) Entrance into tourism entrepreneurship: a UK case study. *Tourism and Hospitality Research* 3, 163–172.

Tassiopoulos, D. (ed.) (2010a) *New Tourism Ventures: An Entrepreneurial and Managerial Approach*, 2nd edn. Juta (Pty) Ltd, Cape Town, South Africa.

Tassiopoulos, D. (2010b) An investigation into the co-producers of preferred strategic behaviour in small, micro and medium tourism enterprises in South Africa. DPhil. thesis, University of Stellenbosch, South Africa.

Timmons, J.A. and Spinelli, S. (2003) *New Venture Creation: Entrepreneurship in the 21st Century*, 6th edn. McGraw-Hill, Boston, Massachusetts.

Visser, D.J. (2003) An investigation into the aspects of transformational leadership in South African small to medium sizes enterprises (SMEs). Thesis, University of Stellenbosch, South Africa.

Wikipedia (2011) Cape Town Stadium. Available at: http://en.wikipedia.org/wiki/Cape_Town_Stadium (accessed 12 July 2011).

chapter 16

The Role of Work Process Knowledge in Managing Facilities

Shuna Marr
Edinburgh Napier University

LEARNING OBJECTIVES

Having completed this chapter, readers should be able to:

- introduce the concept of work process knowledge (WPK);
- explore what drives the need for WPK in staff in tourism, hospitality and events (THE) service industries;
- understand how WPK underpins the delivery of excellent customer service;
- identify the factors that affect WPK and how best to support its growth in staff.

INTRODUCTION

This book has been written on the assumption that it will be read by people who are either managing a facility in the THE industries, or studying to be in management in the future. The other chapters of this book give you, as a current or aspiring manager, lots of excellent practical and theoretical advice about what you need to know to effectively run a facility. However, using industry examples to illustrate the points, this chapter will try to convince you that underpinning everything else you do, you need to recognize and understand why supporting and expanding the WPK of your staff is so important.

This chapter begins by defining what is meant by WPK. It will show how modern business structures and multi-tasking ways of working, employees themselves and most importantly customers all drive the need for WPK. Examples are given throughout that show how workers with well-developed WPK can deliver better customer service and conversely how lack of WPK contributes to customer service failure. Finally, the chapter explores the factors that affect WPK and how managers can help encourage the development of WPK in their staff.

DEFINING WORK PROCESS KNOWLEDGE

Modern working conditions are changing what knowledge workers need to have. In a place where workers have little responsibility and perform narrow, closely prescribed tasks, they only need a bare minimum of underpinning knowledge. However, increasingly businesses are expecting their employees to be problem solvers, work within non-hierarchical organizational structures, flexible working systems and information sharing cultures (Marr, 2007). The concept of WPK emerged within the vocational education community. The impact of globalization and changing work practices has challenged researchers across Europe to understand how vocational education and training can support and prepare apprentices and the existing workforce in meeting these challenges.

Flexible work systems require employees at all levels to understand the work process in the organization as a whole. Knowledge, therefore, has become a valuable commodity in modern business. It is one of the organization's most important resources and all levels of employees need to be able to generate and share knowledge freely with their colleagues (Boreham, 2002a). However, it is important not just to see WPK as a 'label' (Boreham, 2002a). Instead it should be viewed as 'a way of representing the kind of expertise needed under modern working conditions' (Norros and Nuutinen, 2002, p. 25) and a 'key construct for explaining success in the highly competitive marketplace of today' (Mariani, 2002, p. 15).

Wilfried Kruse was the first person to coin the phrase 'work process knowledge' in 1986, although, because he was German, he actually described it as 'Arbeitsprozeßwissen', which was originally translated as 'labour process knowledge' (Boreham, 2002b; Fischer and Boreham, 2004). Kruse was being funded at the time by the European Commission to promote economic development in the Mediterranean. As one of a series of projects, he was involved in studying how to improve the performance of a small group of hotels in Mallorca (Boreham, 2002a). In an attempt to improve the quality of in-house service, a Japanese 'quality circle' approach was adopted. This quickly uncovered that many of the problems arising within one department frequently arose from actions or inactions of colleagues in other departments, which highlighted the interdependency of the different departments and the interconnectedness of workers' roles.

Later research by Boreham (2004) and Fischer (2005) further expanded the definition of the concept of WPK into a number of different contexts such as car manufacturing, chemical plants, oil platforms and medical services. However, it wasn't until 2007 that the concept of 'work process knowledge' was applied to a sector where customer service is of such great importance. Much of this chapter relates to a comparative case study of six visitor attractions in Scotland, which had a specific remit to study the nature of WPK in visitor attractions, what factors affected it and what relationship WPK had to customer service (Marr, 2007). This was the first time since Kruse's initial study that this sector had been investigated through the lens of WPK.

Visitor attractions serve as a microcosm of the THE industries. They are obviously part of the tourism industry and draw and attract a lot of visitors to view whatever exhibit is on offer (in this case the sites were a castle, a historic house, a canal attraction with visitor centre, a science centre, a historic village and a mountain visitor centre). However, because visitors need to be fed and watered and otherwise accommodated, each of these sites offers hospitality in the shape of cafés, restaurants and even on-site hotels. Furthermore, the demand for unusual venues and the pressure to widen their revenue streams meant that all of the visitor attractions are very heavily event driven, all relying on events from weddings to product launches, to supplement their income. Therefore, this study offers an excellent opportunity to draw from examples covering these different aspects of the THE industry.

So what is WPK?

For the purposes of this chapter, the following definition (by Marr, 2007) will be used, which has been adapted slightly to broaden the context to incorporate hospitality and events, as well as tourism facilities.

Figure 16.1 shows a diagram illustrating that WPK in THE contexts includes the following vital aspects.

1. How the company works. This includes work processes within the framework of a company's work organization, such as the labour, production and business processes.
2. The specific peculiarities of the process relating to the organization's unique selling proposition, i.e. those particular aspects of knowledge that are specific to that organization.
3. The concrete consequences that can be derived from specific actions. This means that an employee with well-developed WPK will understand that what they do will have a knock on effect in another department.
4. How the organization inter-relates with internal and external partners and the associations to which they belong. For example, many organizations or events rely on external catering or wedding event providers to deliver part of the service on their behalf and it is important that both parties understand the work processes of the other.
5. Knowledge of the local area, the microenvironment in which the organization operates and how the organization relates to the rest of the destination. For example, visitors to THE facilities may wish to know what there is to see and do in the area surrounding the facility, where the local walks are, bus routes, restaurants etc.

Hence we can see that 'WPK is set within a context of complex factors, including amongst others: flexible working practices, teamwork, non-hierarchical organisational structures and information sharing cultures' (Marr, 2011, p. 153). However, what does that actually mean in practice? Perhaps the best way to understand what WPK involves is to show it to you in action.

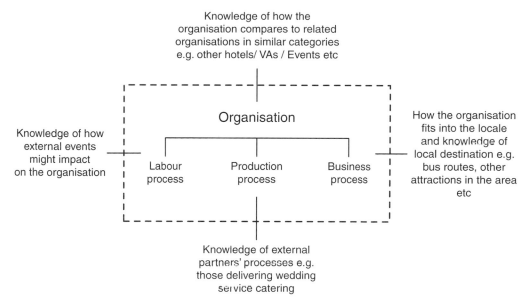

Fig. 16.1. Diagram of what work process knowledge entails in the THE context.

Example: An example of WPK in action

The following account illustrates how the WPK of colleagues at a visitor attraction in central Scotland helped them to deal effectively with a potentially problematic situation. Late one morning, a coach party of 19 visitors arrived with their guide at the visitor attraction entrance for a booked tour. This group had also reserved a table for lunch at the visitor attraction bistro café at 12.15 pm.

However, the visitor attraction employee at the reception desk who received them realized that the group was mistakenly booked in for the *à la carte* menu and not, as coach parties usually were, for the *table d'hôte*. This, she recognized, would have consequences for the kitchen staff; if 20 people arrived in the restaurant and ordered different items from the *à la carte* menu, the kitchen would require considerable time to prepare for them. This would not only put a lot of pressure on kitchen and waiting staff, but would also seriously compromise the speed of their service for the group and other diners.

However, the visitor attraction staff member did not inform the customer of this, but sent them off on their tour with a smile. Meanwhile, she phoned down to inform the café manager and advise her that she had sent the tour guide down to the café to discuss the lunch booking.

(Continued)

> **Example.** Continued.
>
> Pre-warned, the café manager suggested to the guide that the group pre-order, selling the benefits of saving time for the customer. As the tour had been held up at a previous attraction and was running a little late, the guide was very grateful at this wonderful accommodation of her group's needs and went away extremely happy, unaware that there had been any potential problem. The visitor attraction kitchen staff now had time to prepare and get menus printed up for them. When the group arrived for lunch, it was promptly served.
>
> This example, typical of the simple incidents staff deal with daily, clearly demonstrates the importance of workers having an overview of the whole organization and an understanding of the needs of other departments, to be able to maintain the smooth operation of daily business. It also reveals the importance of working collectively and sharing communication with colleagues. The kitchen staff who would have been most inconvenienced by this problem were not instrumental in solving it; instead it was through the recognition by reception staff of the needs of the kitchen staff that the potential problem was averted. The WPK of the visitor attraction employee enabled her to anticipate the potential problem for another department and set in motion the communication chain necessary to prevent it, thus ensuring smooth service was maintained. It was the WPK of the staff, i.e. their understanding of the consequences of actions at a systems level, which empowered them to deliver better customer service, through anticipating and preventing the problem.
>
> *Source:* Marr (2008, pp. 230)

WHY WPK IS NEEDED IN THE ORGANIZATIONS

> The biggest single factor in visitor satisfaction and loyalty is the perceived responsiveness of employees … the role of the server, the employee, cannot be over emphasised. (Buissink-Smith and McIntosh, 2001, pp. 80–81)

In the THE industries, in a world where so many organizations are competing for the tourists' pound, dollar or yen, excellent customer service is recognized as a key way in which an organization can differentiate itself from the rest. And yet, customer service is inseparable from the person who delivers it. Therefore, the crucial and central importance of the individual front-line worker in delivering excellent customer service is becoming increasingly recognised (Marr, 2011). However, it might surprise you to discover that the ability of an employee to deliver excellent customer service is almost certainly more dependent on their WPK than on any customer service training they may have received (Marr, 2008).

This section of the chapter explores how modern business structures and multi-tasking ways of working, employees themselves and most importantly customers all drive the need for WPK.

Three main drivers of WPK have been recognized: the organization, the individual worker and the customer. This is shown in Fig. 16.2.

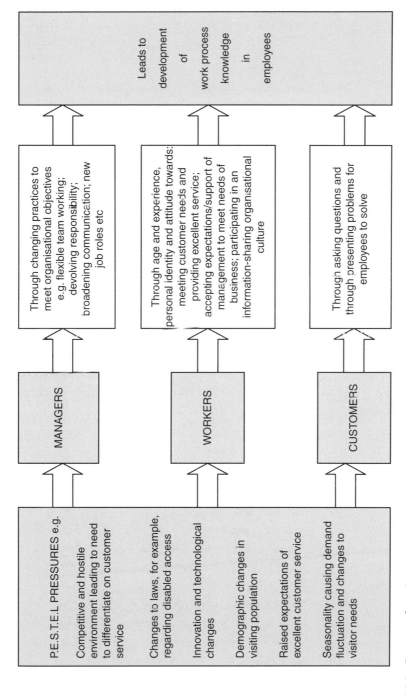

Fig. 16.2. Drivers of work process knowledge.

The organization as a driver

An increasingly vital component of modern organizations in the service industries is in developing the functional flexibility of their staff. For many organizations this is primarily to do with satisfying the business needs of the business, such as allowing the organization to deploy staff where needed, give more rapid response to change and have a larger pool of people to draw upon.

However, Oliveira *et al.* (2002) has shown that the need for organizational flexibility drives the necessity for WPK. Encouraging this versatility not only offers the organization functional flexibility, it also has the effect of broadening and developing the WPK of staff, enabling them to anticipate the needs of other areas more effectively and better understand how the process integrates. Therefore, an organization shifting from segregated departments to integrated multi-functional team working can rapidly lead to cohorts of employees with highly developed WPK as a result.

The individual as a driver

Personal attitudes towards work and personal qualities of workers have been found to be a second important driver of WPK development. As Jones and Haven-Tang (2005) have observed, there has been a recent tendency in the tourism industry to move away from recruiting people with craft skills to recruiting and training individuals with what employers consider is the 'right' attitude, enthusiasm and interest. Although no doubt companies have always focused on recruiting employees with the 'right skills and attitudes for the job', what they consider to be the 'right skills' has undergone a significant change in recent years.

Many organizations are moving away from having employees with 'subject specialist skills' to having 'customer service skills' (Marr, 2007). For example, where in the past a science centre might have employed a scientist, or a castle might have employed a historian, many have since found that the best scientist or best historian might not necessarily have the best attitude towards customers. As the depth of science or history required by the average tourist is not extensive, some organizations have changed their recruitment focus to employ people who have good customer service skills and are good communicators, rather than necessarily with a specific subject specialism, because these skills are more highly useful. Consequently, 'having the right skills' now means 'having good customer service skills' and the 'right attitude' means an enthusiastic interest in customer service and a willingness and ability to answer customers' questions about things that extend well beyond obvious job roles. Employees who have this type of attitude are driving themselves to satisfy customer expectations. They are keen to provide good customer service and so actively work at building up their WPK to be able to do so effectively. In a visitor attraction this might include finding out what events or activities are happening in other parts of the site during the day, anticipating what customers might ask them. In a hotel it might be a receptionist who finds out what the soup of the day is. At a festival it might be to know what the local bus times are.

Willingness to share knowledge is also a key aspect of enabling workers in THE industries to rapidly enhance and expand their WPK in the day-to-day running of the business. Therefore WPK is not just about knowledge but incorporates an attitudinal component: that of possessing a collegial attitude, a willingness to share information and work collaboratively.

The customer as a driver

A third and very important driver of WPK development is the customer themselves. Often the product offering within THE industries is made up of disparate elements, for example, exhibits, catering and room facilities, and also interactions with staff. However, it has been found that all these individual parts and the interactions that customers have with employees are viewed by the customer as a collective whole (Leighton, 2006). Therefore, the way the customer interacts with staff forms a crucial part of the work process.

Through aiming to provide good customer service, workers with the 'right attitude' to customer service find themselves responding to what the customer wants and trying to deliver it. In THE industries, the end user is a major and constant focus of workers' days. The majority of employees who deal directly with the customer are compelled on a daily basis to be often minutely aware of what their customers want. This constant interaction compels employees to look at their own work process from the customers' viewpoint, which causes them very rapidly to gain a strategic overview of the site, whether this is a festival, hotel or visitor attraction.

This is because customers arriving on site for the first time may not be fully aware of the detail of the site and so they themselves have a strategic overview. They arrive with a general idea of what they want to achieve from the experience of the visit and come armed with questions that they expect employees to be able to answer to help them get the best out of their time there. These questions might be about the event or site itself, for example, what is going on in different areas at different times and what is the best order to see things? They come with an expectation that employees will be able to help them get the best out of their visit.

Employees who are customer-focused try to deliver what visitors want. Consequently, employees learn very quickly that what visitors to their site want is for all staff members to have an overview of the site (and beyond) and be able to advise them how to make the most of their visit, whatever that entails. To be able to deliver good customer service, it is essential that employees have a well-developed overview of everything that goes on in the organization and how it all inter-relates. In turn, employees with the 'right attitude' push themselves to meet and deliver these expectations. This close employee–customer relationship consequently has a profound effect on workers' WPK and thus visitors very strongly push employees to develop WPK.

WPK AND THE DELIVERY OF CUSTOMER SERVICE

The better-developed WPK the worker has, the better able they are to deliver excellent customer service. This is because, if an employee understands the organization they work in at the strategic level, how all the departments fit and work together, their own importance in the overall scheme of things and the goals of the organization, then they have good WPK. Workers with good WPK are better problem solvers, better strategic thinkers, are more empowered and flexible workers and are better able to respond to the unusual. Workers with this broad range of skills are more capable of handling the unexpected situations customers pose daily. An employee who can judge, anticipate and deliver what the customer wants is providing good customer service. WPK thus empowers workers to deliver the best customer service through helping them to anticipate problems and prevent them from occurring, and understanding the consequences of their actions.

This section of the chapter provides some examples that demonstrate how a developed knowledge of the work process can improve customer service and, conversely, how a lack of WPK can lead to service failure. We will start with how customer service is enhanced by workers with well-developed WPK.

When things go right

The example above has already shown how the team collectively handling the potential problem of the group of visitors booked in for the wrong lunch. The example below shows how an understanding of the work process of another department and a willingness to use this knowledge can enhance customer service.

Example: How understanding of the work process can enhance customer service

This visitor attraction has two reception points. One is the public ticket desk at the front entrance, which is the first point of contact for visitors entering the building. Most business visitors will arrive and announce themselves and their intentions at this desk. They are then usually directed along the corridor to the second reception, which doubles as both the business guest reception and as the call centre for handling bookings. This is a minute or two's walk along the corridor. Employees on the ticket desk, who have also worked in the call centre, know that if they direct a business guest along to the second reception, it is useful to call and let reception staff know that the business visitor is on their way. Having been in the position themselves, they know this gives the receptionist time to contact the member of staff the guest wishes to see. If this information is communicated promptly, then, when the guest arrives at the second reception, the receptionist can greet the guest by name and advise them that the person they are there to see has already been informed and is on their way.

(Continued)

Example. Continued.

As the receptionist explained: 'I work at both the reception desk and the ticket desk ... If someone is expecting visitors or someone for an interview, then I let the receptionist know – this gives a better impression ... If I'm working at the ticket desk then I can ask the customer who they're here to see and I'll phone along to reception and give the receptionist advance warning and give them time to phone the person. It gives them an extra minute to locate the person and be prepared – it makes it seem more seamless ... it's not part of the set requirements, but I do it because I know it's helpful because I work on reception too.'

Source: Marr (2007, pp. 159–160)

This simple example demonstrates how WPK can help an employee to anticipate a colleague's needs and how simple communication can ensure a smoother customer service. The customer is likely to get a better first impression and feel more welcome than if he had arrived unannounced, had to introduce himself for a second time and then wait while the receptionist located the person. This shows how good customer service relies on effective communication and the collegial sharing of WPK.

Another good example of how WPK can enhance customer service is shown below, describing how a visitor attraction managed to improve customer progression through their restaurant when they began to integrate their internal partner into the daily and ongoing communication networks. Changing the way this subcontracted arm was incorporated into the business positively affected communication and WPK within the different teams within the organization.

Example: Improving customer service through understanding the WPK of internal partners

One particular visitor attraction subcontracts the catering aspect of their business to an external firm. The location of the restaurant is physically distant from the main part of the visitor attraction and the restaurant is run and manned by independent staff. Since opening, the physical distance and the different ownership had resulted in the two teams being completely separate.

However, a change in attitude came about because one young man, John, was the first person to make the transition from working in the restaurant to becoming a member of the visitor attraction customer service team. John brought with him a unique perspective of how the restaurant and the visitor attraction fit together, which enabled him immediately to begin sharing the restaurant perspective at daily briefing sessions. Many problems caused by lack of understanding of the work process in each area were resolved as a result.

(Continued)

Example. Continued.

For example, it had long been a complaint of visitor attraction staff that although they only get a half-hour for lunch, they often spent 15 minutes in a queue to buy food at the restaurant. John knew that it would not be possible to have a separate till for employees, but was able to suggest that visitor attraction personnel could negotiate payment in advance or later so they do not waste their break time. Once John was able to share the different perspectives with both teams, the channel of communication was opened and the benefits of sharing information between the two teams became more obvious. Consequently, all restaurant employees are now invited to morning briefing meetings.

However, this improved communication has benefited both parties. Management in the restaurant told of another communication failure that had caused problems, but has since been resolved. This was where visitor attraction staff responsible for booking school visits failed to advise groups how to pay for pre-ordered lunches. They should have advised the teacher to collect the money and make one payment at the till. Failure to pass this message on, however, meant that on one occasion 31 school children each paid £4.70 individually, each presenting a £5 note, requiring 31 lots of 30 pence change. Inevitably, this held up the queue for other customers.

Now the restaurant manager attends the morning daily meetings, he knows if school visits are expected and does not have to rely on this being passed on. He is also in a better position to ensure that students are asked in advance what they want, so the kitchen can prepare. Visitor attraction staff who meet groups arriving by bus also now know to ask if the group are going to buy lunch so they can pre-warn the restaurant. These examples shows how effective communication with internal partners has helped expand the WPK of staff within the centre. The unique knowledge of the restaurant that John brought with him to the visitor attraction team was the catalyst that enabled them to bridge a gap that had existed between these two parties and having been brought together, and information on both sides shared, long-standing problems have been resolved.

Source: Marr (2007, pp. 162)

This example was a restaurant in a visitor attraction, but it could just as easily have been a restaurant within a hotel or a catering facility at a festival. Having an understanding of different areas of an organization enables workers to have the 'systems-level' view of the organization they need in order to have well-developed WPK.

The final example in this section shows how the attitudinal component is such an important aspect of WPK in the THE service industries: a willingness to share information, to anticipate colleagues' needs, to answer customer questions and to see oneself as part of the whole organization. This view of oneself as an important part of the whole organization demonstrates the significance of attitude towards delivering good customer service and is an integral part of WPK in this service sector. The following quotes show that these employees understand the importance of their individual contribution to the overall customer service experience.

Example: The importance of attitude as part of WPK

The following two quotes were given by members of staff at two different organizations.

> It may seem that I'm only working in a shop, but I love what I do – it's such an open management style here and that makes a difference to feeling being a worthwhile part of the workplace … I'm not just selling a pencil or a thimble – I feel that I'm selling memories.

> [We are] selling memories of a wonderful day and want that whole experience to be nice – and that includes the interaction they have with the staff.

Source: Marr (2007, pp. 206–207)

An important aspect of the WPK, therefore, is the reliance on the collegiality of workers; their ability and willingness to share information among themselves to ensure that smooth service is maintained. Employees have to be aware of what is going on in and around the business and have to be willing to update and share that information with colleagues on a continual basis.

However, it is important to highlight that attitude in respect of being positive to developing WPK is not restricted solely to an individual but is an important aspect of the culture of the entire organization. One hotel manager explained that although an employee's attitude is important, it is also management's duty to convey to staff how important they are to the success of the business, saying 'If I didn't turn up for work tomorrow no one would miss me in the short term but if the kitchen porter didn't turn up for work, the whole thing would grind to a halt!' If an organization wishes to imbue good customer service in its staff, then they must establish a culture that leads by example and supports the individual.

When things go wrong

Now we come to the converse of this. The following examples show how a lack of or ineffective communication between colleagues causes problems. There are numerous examples of when this occurs and it often appears that the root cause of the communication failure is based on a lack of understanding of the work process of the other area, which can adversely affect the customer experience. Below is an example of customer service problems caused by a lack of understanding of work processes in another department.

Example: Where lack of understanding of the work process of another department causes service failure

A visitor attraction has a popular ride that many visitors enjoy. Advance bookings for this ride are handled by a separate booking department. Problems sometimes arise because of a lack of understanding of the work process by the booking staff, about the problems that may be caused by taking bookings too close together or that might be faced in handling different types of customers. The ride staff explained about one particularly traumatic example. The ride involves capsule seats suspended from an overhead rail with a simple retainer bar across the front to keep customers in their seat. Staff load two passengers into each capsule and it slowly follows a convoluted, but ultimately circular track through the exhibit to the exit point, where customers leave. The empty capsules then continue to be refilled for the next circuit. Two ride technicians are needed to operate this ride at any time. One technician is needed to oversee the safe loading and another oversees the safe unloading of the capsules. When a customer is less mobile, the rest of the ride has to be held up while the customer takes time to climb into the capsule. Child buggies or wheelchairs have then to be conveyed round to the unloading area. All this takes time and holds up the ride. The occasional wheelchair or buggy does not interrupt service too much. However, one particular day, the booking office staff were called down to the ride to witness for themselves the chaos that had ensued from them accepting a booking for the ride where 17 of the party were customers in wheelchairs, with a party of 50 school children booked in immediately behind them.

Source: Marr (2007, p. 158)

This incident shows that when workers lack an understanding of the needs and work processes of another area of the organization, then they are not always aware of the consequences of their actions (or inactions). Through not understanding how the ride had to adapt for wheelchair users, the booking staff did not anticipate the disastrous consequences that would occur through booking parties too close together. This lack of WPK meant long queues and delays and customer service suffered as a result.

Below is another example of how customer service can be compromised when two different arms of the organization do not understand the work process requirements of the other and consequently fail to communicate vital information.

Example: Where lack of understanding of the work processes and lack of communication contribute to service failure

This particular visitor attraction is a canal attraction and has boat rides that are sold through the visitor centre. The boat rides are run by canal staff and the tickets are sold by the customer service team. The boat master has the final say about when the boat departs, but if this information is not communicated to the staff selling tickets, then customer service can obviously suffer. One of the visitor team complained how this affected them: 'People sometimes hold on to information and don't share it … for example, if I'm selling tickets for a sailing, the boat crew say 'ok, keep them coming' … but then the boat goes without warning us and people who have bought a ticket don't get on and the next boat is full, so people get held up. This is especially a problem if the next trip isn't for an hour.'

However, this lack of understanding of the work processes of the two areas evidently works both ways. On the same day as the previous example was heard, the boat master explained that operational difficulties also occur if the numbers of passengers booked by the ticket desk is not communicated in time. He explained that within the canal apparatus, which conveys the boats between the two canals 'the water level discrepancy has only a 75 mm tolerance. If we are out by more than that, there can be as much as a 3 tonne discrepancy in weight. We have to pump water in and out to bring it back into tolerance. If people book late or more people come on board than the desk have communicated, then it can hold up the sailing while water levels are changed.'

These two examples by members of two different teams in the one organization show that a lack of understanding of the work process of another area can lead to necessary information not being communicated in time, thus causing customer service to suffer while the ensuing problems are resolved.

Source: Marr (2007, p. 157)

The final example in this section refers again to the importance of the attitude of workers towards developing WPK. The example refers to a castle in Scotland that welcomes visitors during the summer. After many years of having separate teams for reception and guiding, the castle had decided to introduce more 'multi-functional' working practices. During an interview with the chief guide, he explained the difficulties that he had had in dealing with the resistant attitude of existing workers to developing cross-functional skills compared with the attitude of the new 'customer service-oriented' guides that they had recruited for the first time that summer.

Example: The desire to develop WPK relies on the worker's attitude towards collegial sharing

For the first time, the reception team and the guiding team have been required to overlap some of their duties. Previously these two teams have been severely demarcated, with physical lines on the floor over which one team could not cross to 'invade' the other's territory. The change to their working practice as an amalgamated team has proven problematical for some. The new guiding staff taken on for the first time this year have apparently been very willing to adopt this way of working, whereas staff in the reception team, who have returned from previous years, have shown some resistance.

The chief guide explained 'Five out of the six [reception staff this year] have worked here before and there's still a wee bit of the old concept yet. "We do our bit and what happens after they leave reception is not our problem." But in fact this attitude is a problem – for the rest of the castle'.

He explained about the problems with this changeover of culture 'I am struggling to get some of the reception team to buy into [cross-functional working]. Some of them have been here two or three years and have got a little bit of what we'd call the "seasonal staff ethic" – "I'll come and work and do my job and go home at night" sort of attitude – not particularly wanting to expand their role. The guides we have brought in are much keener on this – they are dying to do other things. So I've got one side dying to do other things and the other side just happy to plod through the day'.

This example highlights a trade-off that sites can face between having staff with established skills and having staff with a good customer service attitude. In re-recruiting staff from previous years, the castle gains technical knowledge, employees that are well up the learning curve of specific work skills. However, because these particular employees lack real customer service drive, they are not really interested in widening their base of WPK; they want to focus only on their own job and are uninterested in what goes on in other departments and how the system fits together as a whole. On the other hand, although new staff coming in with a positive and enthusiastic attitude may require more initial technical training, the expectation and experience of sites is that they are more likely to acquire and develop WPK far quicker than their more experienced, but resistant, counterparts.

Source: Marr (2007, pp. 204–205)

The first four examples thus show that where workers understand the work processes of other departments and possess a collegial attitude, the organizations are able to enhance their customer service both at an individual level and an organizational level. Conversely, the three examples that followed demonstrated how a lack of understanding of the work processes within the organization, and an attitude closed to learning about other areas, can often lead to service failure.

How WPK underpins excellent customer service

We thus come to the crux of the argument of this chapter, which is an understanding of the relationship between customer service and WPK (abridged from Marr, 2007, pp. 272–274).

It has already been established that the importance of attitude and personal qualities of employees are recognized as central factors in customer service excellence. However, the personal attitudes of an individual worker towards work, and especially openness to change at work, are also recognized as important factors in developing WPK. What studies in this area have found is that the attitude and personal qualities required by an individual worker to deliver the desired level of customer service and those necessary to develop WPK, do not simply have common characteristics but virtually overlie one another.

Managers would invariably describe what they meant by having 'good customer service skills' and 'the right attitude' as workers who were customer focused, able and willing to communicate with customers, answer their questions and be willing to sort out their problems. They also would be a team player, open to changes in the workplace, willing to work within a flexible framework and multi-task. In addition, they were willing to take personal responsibility for all aspects of the customer experience, even down to picking up litter.

In other words, the qualities they described are those required for WPK development: someone who is willing to work in an environment incorporating problem-solving situations, willing to participate in an information-sharing culture, accepts devolved authority and who can interact organically in a flexible, multi-skilled, team-working environment. Accordingly, in the view of the managers, the best workers are those who have well-developed WPK. Table 16.1 outlines these traits.

Table 16.1. Personal qualities required for excellent customer service and WPK development.

Personal qualities required for excellent customer service	Personal qualities required for WPK development
Customer focused	Willing to work in an environment
Willing and able to answer questions, sort out problems	incorporating problem-solving situations
Team player	Participates in an information-sharing culture
Flexible worker and open to change	Can interact organically in a flexible, multi-skilled, team-working environment
Multi-skilled	Will accept devolved authority
Take personal responsibility for the customer experience	

Therefore, having good WPK enables a worker to deliver excellent customer service. The way the front-line staff member interacts with the customer is increasingly of vital importance, as employee behaviour is by far the most influential factor in shaping customers' perceptions. To perform their job and meet the demands of the customer, workers must be able to answer customer questions and meet customer needs in a countless variety of forms; they have to offer a seamless service. In addition, because the customer's definition of quality does not remain static and customers' concept of quality excellence is continually rising (Kandampully, 1997), it is necessary to have workers who can adapt and develop their skills to meet those changing needs and exceed their expectations.

The workers capable of doing that are those with a wider understanding of how the organization operates; with enough knowledge to be able to anticipate and handle customer problems; who can answer customer questions because they know what is going on in other parts of the organization and beyond; and recognize their individual importance in delivering quality service. Thus, it can be seen that what underpins good customer service, in this industry at least, is WPK.

HOW TO SUPPORT AND DEVELOP WPK IN YOUR STAFF

Having hopefully convinced you, the manager or potential THE manager, that WPK is a vital component to underpin the service your staff will deliver, you may be wondering how to go about making sure you develop the WPK of your workers. This section will therefore outline the various factors that affect WPK and discuss various ways other managers have used to develop the WPK of their staff. After describing different aspects of each factor, there is a key message for you to 'take home'.

Factors that affect WPK

There are six main factors found to affect WPK development (Marr, 2007). These are:

1. the degree of systems-level communication shared with workers;
2. how multi-skilled workers need to be (their functional flexibility);
3. the size and complexity of the site and operations;
4. the individual attitudes the workers bring to the job;
5. how running an event affects the WPK workers need to have;
6. how seasonality changes the WPK workers need to have.

It is important to first establish what is meant by 'communication' in this context. It incorporates both formal and informal methods of transmitting information between people. The information may be written, spoken or through action, such as showing or demonstrating something physically.

Formal methods of communication involve channels that have been set up by the organization and are often characterized by written rules and procedures. Formal communication methods include daily or periodical meetings and written or computerized booking information. These methods of communication are the channels through which the company tends to give information to, and receive information from, its employees. These channels also tend to be vertical through the chain of command. An important point to note is that while staff may not see these channels as 'formal', in that conversations or meetings may be quite relaxed and do not follow rigid procedures, they are none the less channels set up by the company to exchange information.

Informal channels of communication, on the other hand, usually have no written rules or set procedures, but colleagues still use these channels to share information that is pertinent to their job. Informal methods usually involve face-to-face and verbal communication such as in an office or staff room, in the activities of their job or through media like telephone, email or walkie-talkie radios. The sharing of information typically takes place between colleagues or with line managers in an informal setting that has not been officially organized by the company. Organizations may, however, still facilitate informal communication by providing the means to make it possible, for example providing radios or staff rooms for their employees to use.

There are many methods through which formal communication can take place with and between staff; for example, daily booking sheets, handover diaries, team meetings and intranets. Information can be 'cascaded' down from the office, through the managers of the different departments to the customer-facing staff, or it can be communicated with them directly in an inclusive way.

The degree of systems-level communication that is shared with staff

It is clear that sites that develop an extensive, information-sharing culture are more likely to create the type of environments conducive to learning in work contexts identified by Rolo (1996, cited in Oliveira *et al.*, 2002) than sites where a lesser amount of information sharing is evident.

Sites that hold daily meetings, have intranets and give wide access to long-term organizational plans and other systems-level knowledge have workers who demonstrate the most well-developed WPK. Workers at those sites were more likely to report feeling involved. The sites with the most open and inclusive formal methods and those actively supporting informal communication were the ones where employees had access to a wider overview of the business. This better equipped workers to develop WPK and also made them feel more valued. Employees interviewed across all sites in the study appear to have a good understanding of the importance of having an overview of what is happening both within and around their site on a daily basis. They were able to provide numerous examples of how this daily overview gives them the WPK they need to ensure the smooth day-to-day running of the service. The way a site facilitates communication or contributes to lack of communication appears to have a direct effect on the culture within the site, on how valued employees feel and how much WPK development is supported.

Take home message 1

An important task for a company trying to create an environment suitable for improving WPK is to establish a culture of information sharing, especially of systems-level information.

Example: An exercise to stimulate thought and discussion on methods of communication that support WPK development

Below are three quotes from employees discussing methods their organizations use to communicate information. Which methods do you think are most and least likely to support WPK development?

> There is a 'Magic Circle' held every Wednesday, where all staff on duty come in early to attend these sessions. These sessions might be used for 'tool box talks', such as how to use particular goggles or binoculars, and to convey ecology training about the mountain or company information about budgets. However, this is not the only method for staff to gain information about the mountain's business. As well as the daily and weekly meetings held, there is also a staff communication folder, which contains a wide range of company business and is available to all employees.

> Daily team meetings can convey information about the business from wider perspectives. At the meetings … we get an overview of what's going on that day, and in the future, and a general view of how it affects us … They tell us about our 5-year plan … we can hear about what's going on in other departments and how this affects us. For example, [colleague name] and [colleague name] gave us a presentation this morning about our new exhibition 'Alice through the Looking Glass', about what it was and what its aim is – this was first mentioned 6 months ago.

> Every time something doesn't work we think 'well, what did we do wrong there?' and one of our snags is the fact that we cannot get the whole team together, ever, on the same day during the season … Our manager tries to do a monthly staff meeting … in fact we had one last week, but we were all far too busy – none of the seasonal were staff were at it … I wasn't at it, because we had 25 coaches that day, no one could be spared to go to a meeting. … However, having meetings that many staff cannot attend is counterproductive, as it adversely affects staff's perception of the organization. We are thinking of changing that because, if you aren't at the meeting, all sorts of things go through people's minds like 'Was I excluded intentionally? What's happening? How will it affect me?' It's actually quite a routine, boring meeting about simple things, and anything that generally affects the seasonal staff, they'd hear about through me, but there's still this feeling that there's something going on that [they] are excluded from…

Source: drawn from Marr (2007, pp. 144–167)

Flexibility

The dynamic nature of the THE industries and the constant need to react to the changing demands of the customer and business makes flexibility an essential aspect of modern organizations. There are various ways in which an organization can introduce flexibility, including numerical flexibility (changing numbers of employees), product flexibility and flexibility through outsourcing some services. Some aspects of flexibility involve fundamental business requirements, such as flexible shifts to suit changing patterns of business. However, an increasingly vital component of businesses is in developing the *functional flexibility* of employees (Marr, 2007). There has been a noticeable trend in recent years to move away from having separate teams performing distinct duties and more towards having highly flexible, multi-functional teams. Developing employees' multi-functionality also has the effect of broadening and developing the WPK of staff, enabling them to anticipate the needs of other areas more effectively and better understand how the process integrates.

There are a variety of ways in which organizations support and develop multi-functionality, some of which are outlined below.

JOB ROTATION. Job rotation within a multi-functional team is an extremely effective way of developing knowledge and understanding of the work process. Job rotation systems can broaden employees' perspective of the work process by giving a better perception of what another area does. This enables them to perform their job better and to provide improved information and service to their customers, because they have worked in multiple areas of the business and have a better overview of how they interact. This broader perspective can help encourage more tolerance and awareness of the needs of other departments because they have a common ground of understanding. Some organizations actively support and encourage staff to widen their skills range by financially rewarding training for different areas within the site. Those employees with a high degree of job rotation seem to build up expanded WPK far more quickly than employees whose job roles are more demarcated.

However, it is important to recognize that in multi-functional team working many of the crossover activities are at a low skill level. Most sites have specialized areas that are not regularly incorporated into the job rotation of the multi-functional team roles. Mostly this is because specialized skills or qualifications are required, such as catering, which demands hygiene training, and technical and skilled trades, for example, technicians and electricians. These higher and more specialized skills make it more difficult, not only to get people to cover these jobs, but also for others to have the same intimate understanding of this aspect of the work process as they might otherwise do if they performed the job themselves.

MOVING FROM PART-TIME TO FULL-TIME STAFF. Some organizations have moved from employing largely part-time staff, to fewer full-time staff with a multi-skill base, because they have found that full-time workers had a 'full-time attitude and commitment' and it enabled them to spread the workload and deploy staff more effectively.

FAMILIARIZATION VISITS.   Another way used by several sites to encourage employees to have a broader and more objective perspective of the organization is to get them to look at their own work practices through the lens of comparison with others. Familiarization visits to other similar organizations help to increase their product knowledge and get a different perspective of a similar organization. In discussion after the visit, employees can then identify good and bad points and reflect on their own service. Familiarization visits can give staff more objectivity of their own practices from the customer's viewpoint.

REPOSITORIES OF KNOWLEDGE.   Some key job roles have been identified that seem to rapidly accelerate WPK development. An organization may have a few key employees to perform specific job roles that have a huge impact on their development of WPK. These positions tend to involve reception and problem-solving duties and require an extensive overview of the workplace to be able to solve the problems presented to them by customers and staff alike. These key members of staff become, in effect, 'repositories of WPK' within the work place, with knowledge that can be tapped into by other staff. However, there may be a danger in relying too heavily on the strengths of individual staff members. In the same way staff can be specialized by their qualification and skills, employees can become specialized by their WPK. Although having 'repositories of WPK' is useful for staff to draw on, it is important to consider succession management or other ways of managing collective competence to ensure this knowledge is not lost due to unforeseen changes.

RENAMING OF TEAMS.   A way to promote changes in attitudes is the renaming of roles to reflect the change in focus from being employed for a specific job task to being employed for customer service and flexibility. The Science Centre in the study, for example, has a 'Customer Service' team, which covers the functions of sales, reception, IMAX, welcome host, education bookings and accounts, the science floors, workshops and planetarium. Changing to a generic job title for multi-skilled teams has been found to forestall problems with job demarcations and boundaries, change an employee's perception of their individual role and encourage personal responsibility for customer service (Evans-Platt, 1991; Kelliher and Riley, 2002). However, as Norros and Nuutinen (2002) have previously shown, the development of identity is inseparable from the development of knowledge and skills, and Fischer and Röben (2002) have noted that an individual worker's WPK includes the importance of knowing how his or her role fits into the company as a whole. Hence, having a team identity focused on customer service is not only clearly helpful for an organization wishing to promote a customer service culture, but it also contributes to development of WPK. Changing a team name helps workers focus on customer service as their main job and identify with the whole site rather than a specific job specialism. Where specialism is unavoidable, it is important for the worker to understand their role in the overall picture to counteract a silo attitude.

None the less an organization may find that multi-functionality may introduce conflict within teams, depending on the existing site culture. For example, prevailing attitudes towards demarcation of roles may lead to unwillingness on the part of some employees to change their established contracts.

Take home message 2

As teams build up WPK it becomes of vital importance to consider succession management and managing collective competence in the WPK of their teams. Organizations working actively to develop this aspect of their staff must also incorporate ways to protect it.

Size and complexity of the site and operations

There are various measures of size, whether the physical size of the site or the numbers of employees or visitors. For example, size may relate to one hotel or to a chain of hotels across a geographic area, or across continents. The complexity of operations relates to the range of departments each site has, the range of different services they provide and whether they have internal or external partners delivering part of the main service.

Although size can increase complexity or make communication more complex, the physical size of a site itself has been found to have relatively little impact on WPK. Both the size of an organization and its complexity of structure tend to have some impact on the development of WPK, mainly where these affect other factors such as communication or flexible working. The far more important factor in creating WPK is in the breadth, depth and frequency of communication that occurs. As long as communication systems inform staff of systems- and business-level information and provide means to gain an overview of the site, then it is possible to counteract most problems posed by size. However, informal communication, as well as the formal structure, is an important consideration for management/leadership to consider, because the cultural information-sharing dimension is so essential to WPK in this context.

Complexity of site operations can be problematic to WPK development. There are various types of complexity, but the aspect of complexity most adversely affecting WPK development is job specialism. Many of the sites are moving towards simplifying the workforce and reducing job specialism through creating multi-functional teams. Sites also renamed their multi-functional teams with a customer service name.

Employee profile

A most desired skill or quality in employees in THE industries is excellent customer service skills. A key aspect of customer service skills is perceived to be the possession of WPK. Employers and employees may not use this term, but none the less recognise that someone who knows the work process and possesses knowledge extending across the whole site and beyond will be able to answer questions, anticipate needs and solve problems more effectively. An employee with well-developed WPK is recognized as being undoubtedly more able to serve the customer.

A number of different factors have been found to affect the way in which an individual can accumulate WPK.

AGE AND EXPERIENCE.   As might be expected, various aspects of an employee's biography have an impact on the level of WPK they may possess. These aspects include the length of service and the level of staff turnover within the site. This makes a difference not only to the individual amount of WPK a staff member may accumulate over time, but also to the collective competence of the staff within the site, and how available this knowledge is for new employees to draw on. The age of the employee and whether they are drawn from the local or foreign market can also make a difference to the amount of local, historical, geographical and cultural knowledge they may have about their site, the local area and the industry in general.

SPEED OF DEVELOPING WPK.   Sites with long-serving employees and a low staff turnover have an obvious advantage in developing a collective competence. This is important to them because a collective body of WPK is something that can be accessed by other staff members. However, these are not emphatic requirements. What is perhaps surprising is the number of occurrences where employees with none of this profile still achieve high levels of WPK very quickly. It is possible for someone quite young and inexperienced to pick up a fair amount of WPK quite fast, which means its development is not necessarily tied to age or experience. Some employees accumulate a lot of WPK in a short space of time because the company has supported them or they have felt driven to do so for themselves.

If accumulation of WPK is desirable, then a variety of methods are available to allow workers to rapidly accumulate it. The main methods identified supporting WPK acquisition include: job roles involving an overview of the organization, intensity of work, job rotation encouraged by financial and other rewards, and formal training providing an overview of the company and/or a wider perspective.

COLLEGIAL ATTITUDE.   The evidence suggests, however, that it is possible for a long-term employee actively to resist developing WPK, whereas someone keen to learn and supported by their employer can accumulate a substantial amount of WPK within a few months. Although WPK is cognitive, it also incorporates an attitudinal component: that of possessing a collegial attitude, a willingness to share information and work collaboratively. Although WPK is embodied within individual workers, it is also embedded within the organizational culture and held in patterns of social relationships with others.

Consequently, both a positive individual and cultural attitude to working collaboratively and sharing information are seen as essential to the successful operation of these sites and are thus an important aspect of the WPK of workers in this industry. The most important single factor, therefore, thought by employers to influence whether workers in these sites effectively develop WPK, is for employees to have the 'right attitude'. Willingness to share knowledge is an essential precondition in this industry to enable workers to enhance and expand their WPK.

COLLECTIVE COMPETENCE.   Tapping into a collective body of knowledge enables new staff to widen their own knowledge base quickly, as well as enhance the customer service experience they are able to deliver. However, high staff turnover (a problem in organizations with seasonal employees or in teams that come together for the first time to run an event or festival) causes problems in maintaining a body of staff with a developed level of WPK. To counteract the consequent loss of group knowledge caused by a mass departure of seasonal staff, some organizations write down the procedures to make up for the lack of 'collective competence' or 'group knowledge' caused by high turnover of staff.

TRAINING TO SUPPORT WPK.   In THE organizations, where seasonality, high staff turnover and transitional teams are an issue, employees are often expected to have a good working knowledge within a few months or even weeks and are therefore put under pressure to develop WPK in short spaces of time.

It is possible to support WPK development through incorporating WPK into the formal training programme, for example by, in addition to providing the basic types of training, such as product knowledge or hygiene training, also including an overview of the organization to give the new employee a systems-level overview of the organization. Helping a new employee understand their role and how they fit into the wider organization and actively encouraging employees to look at their business as a whole and extend their knowledge to include a wider perspective will go a long way towards supporting and developing their WPK.

Take home message 3

The customer–employee relationship is central to WPK because it is a central dimension of the work process. The best employees are, unsurprisingly, those possessing good task skills, customer service skills and developed WPK.

Events

Events incorporate a diverse range of different activities, from birthday parties to corporate functions, from weddings to product launches, from banquets to large music festivals. What is the same for all events, however, is that they are usually a one-off, finite process within a specified space of time, as opposed a continuous process. There are two factors that distinguish an event from the other types of structure and business processes previously discussed in this chapter: first, it is a relatively short burst of activity and second, it involves groups of teams and individuals, quite often from different organizations, who have to pull together to deliver it. This section looks at the various factors that affect WPK in the context of events.

COMMUNICATION.   Communication between the different departments and knowledge of what needs to be done for this different type of service is vital to ensure the smooth running of the event. All employees on duty must know what event is happening on the day and their role in delivering the service.

IMPACT OF THE EVENT ON THE WORK PROCESS.   Some functions are very small and held in designated private facilities, which have little impact on the rest of the site. Likewise, if the event is being held in a purpose built event space, such as a hotel function room or a conference centre, or in a space such as a visitor attraction that does relatively few weddings or large functions in a year, and where these do not interfere much with normal service, the impact on the WPK of internal employees is limited. However, other events that are larger and incorporate more aspects of the site, including areas or amenities that may normally feature as part of, for example, a visitor attraction experience, do have an impact on the work process. The impact on WPK is more obvious where a site handles several weddings or functions per week, using entirely in-house employees, or where the wedding or function involves major changes to the times of operation and/or purpose of space within the site. Furthermore, the way each site handles functions and the main business priorities evident from them, undoubtedly influences, albeit sometimes inadvertently, the cultural attitude within the site towards different customer groups.

CHANGEOVER OF SPACE.   The impact on a site brought about by a wedding or function depends partly on the type and size of the function being held and the facilities available on site. This will differ depending on what the site is normally used for. Hotels and conference centres, for example, have dedicated function suites and therefore have the relative luxury of having time to set up in advance. However, a visitor attraction or a venue that serves another purpose adds a different dimension – that of having to change the venue's purpose in a short space of time.

There are interesting differences in the way sites handle this overlap of service between visitor attraction and function venue. Most of the sites tend to try to maintain their regular opening times and cause as little disruption as possible to the tourism visitor, although some will close specific areas of the site a bit earlier to allow preparation to take place. However, all sites try to maintain normal service for as long as possible, usually leaving only an hour in which to convert the space from one purpose to the other. As these changeovers are sometimes extreme, it is vital that everyone knows exactly what to do to effect this rapid transformation.

The additional WPK they need includes:

- how to transform spaces from one purpose to another;
- how to adapt service to account for the changes that a wedding or event brings;
- what communication and information needs to be exchanged and with whom;
- how to handle tensions caused by an overlap of service between the two purposes, and which groups take priority.

THE COMBINATION OF INTERNAL AND EXTERNAL PARTNERS.   There is undoubtedly an impact on WPK when internal and external partners have to come together to deliver the service. For example, there has to be an understanding by internal staff of the needs of the external catering company or company delivering the service on their behalf. Although internal employees may not deliver the event service themselves, they still have to know what preparations are required to bring the site into readiness for the event staff who will come in.

This is the second major impact on a site brought about by involving external partners: the bringing together all of the different aspects of the event and yet still presenting a united front. The events team thus have to liaise very closely with, and there has to be complete understanding between, the site and the suppliers that they use, of what is required. All sites have a corporate image that they wish to maintain and the external companies used also become responsible for presenting that image on behalf of their client. There needs to be a dovetailing of the cultural attitude between the external supplier and the site, and a crossover of knowledge of the internal work process by the external supplier, for this alliance to be successful. An understanding of internal work processes and corporate image is thus an important part of the external partner's remit. Both the site and their external and internal partners have to come together, work closely, share information and communicate effectively in order to work as one to deliver the service.

CLASHES OF CULTURE.   A large event tends to be a combination of location, staffing, catering and entertainment. Where these are handled in-house by a single organization, the WPK of staff must incorporate the additional duties a wedding or function brings into their routine. The knowledge of employees grows to incorporate the addition of the altered work processes. There is also a continuation of culture and standard of service; the same people responsible for delivering the usual service bring with them the same values and standards that are part of the site's existing culture. The event organizer thus remains more in control of the service provided. However, where external parties provide a large part of the service, there must be close sharing of communication between the various parties and a sharing of culture, information and expectations to achieve the same end.

Take home message 4

The more aspects of an event that are handled in-house, and the more that regular staff have to incorporate these added duties into their work, the greater the impact on their WPK. Where external partners are involved there has to be a close understanding of the work processes and aligning of cultural attitude to maintain consistent service.

SUMMARY

This chapter has shown that when organizations move away from fragmented departmental structures towards organic, flexible organizational structures, multi-functional working practices and information-sharing cultures, these lead to WPK development. The sections above have shown how WPK helps employees to deliver better customer service and itemized the factors that affect development and how you, as current or aspiring THE managers, can support WPK development in your staff.

The final factor that has been found to affect WPK in THE organizations is seasonality. However, rather than summarize what these impacts are, a case study has been provided for you to read and identify these for yourself. Read the following case study and answer the questions at the end, drawing from the discussion in this chapter to help you.

REVIEW QUESTIONS

1. What is WPK and what drives the need for WPK in staff in THE service industries?
2. How does WPK underpin the delivery of excellent customer service within THE facilities?
3. What factors affect WPK and how can its growth in staff be supported?

Case Study

The impact of seasonality on WPK

Cairngorm Mountain is a year-round Scottish tourism attraction; however, seasonal changes between winter and summer dramatically affect business operations, and consequently the WPK of employees. The nature of the business and the facilities offered changes between the winter and summer seasons. In virtually every aspect of the business, there are major changes to how Cairngorm Mountain operates, affecting the work process and hence what an employee needs to know. These changes include the types of visitors who come, their purpose for visiting and which areas of the site are accessible to the public, the operation of the funicular railway, the retail and catering arrangements, aspects of communication and the main duties of staff.

Changes to visitor groups between seasons
From Easter to October, Cairngorm Mountain attracts a changing kaleidoscope of visitor groups who come for a variety of reasons. During Easter and summer school holidays, mainly families come to visit the shop, travel up the mountain on the funicular railway and enjoy the spectacular mountain views. During May to July, their main customers are older people on coach tours who make good use of the lower site café. Coach tours of the area continue to include Cairngorm Mountain as part of their itinerary during July to September. However, the summer months and better weather also bring walkers to the site, as there are several designated walks and footpath trails in the area. High summer sees locals and holidaymakers alike coming to travel up the funicular railway to the upper restaurant to enjoy fine dining and regular ceilidh dances. Families and foreign visitors also come in large numbers during high summer, tailing off as the holidays end, to enjoy a brief resurgence during the October school holiday week. November tends to be very quiet and is when most essential

(Continued)

Case Study. Continued.

maintenance and training is done because there are usually very few visitors unless there is a very early fall of snow; summer is over and winter has not quite begun.

However, the first fall of snow brings quite different sorts of clientele: the skier, the snowboarder and the rock and winter climbers. These visitors come with quite a different purpose and their arrival brings major changes to the way the site operates. In summer, access to the external slopes from the upper site is restricted for ecological conservation purposes, as the mountain terrain is very fragile. However, the protective covering of snow now allows it to be traversed. The ski tows, unused all summer, open for business, as does the ski hire shop where repairs and waxing are also done. When the snow is good, 2000 skiers can be hitting the slopes between 8 and 10 am.

Funicular railway – changes to operation

A sudden massive influx of people wanting quick access to the slopes affects many aspects of how the business operates, not least the funicular railway. During the summer months, these trains are fitted with seats and carry up to 60 people on a leisurely 8-minute journey up the mountain, with a commentary on the history, the area and the spectacular views. During the snow sport season, these seats are removed to allow easier access for up to 120 people and their equipment. The train doubles its speed from 4.9 metres per second to 9 metres per second to make the journey in a rapid 3–4 minutes. In winter, no one watches the views; they just want to hit the slopes as quickly as possible. Trains also run on demand, rather than the timetable they run to in summer. In winter they carry about 2000–2500 passengers per day, running at speed as skiers turn up. In summer and less busy times, the turnaround is every half-hour.

The trains also stop at different stations and stops. In summer the restricted access to the slopes means that the central station is not used, but in winter this gives access to the nursery slopes. In summer the exit points for the train are different too. As summer visitors are restricted to the restaurant, shop, exhibition and viewing terrace, the train stops at the entrance to these areas. However, in winter the primary purpose is to allow easier access to the slopes, therefore the train stops higher up, right at the exit door. The earlier winter darkness also brings the last train down at 4.30 pm rather than 5.15 pm. Funicular train drivers consequently need to make significant adjustments to their work process between these two seasons.

Catering – changes to service

However, other areas of the site are equally altered by this change in clientele and purpose. In the upper catering site, the entire mode of service changes between the two seasons. During the summer, the restaurant operates a waitress service and food is cooked to order. Visitors, often older people, want to sit and dine in a leisurely way, looking out over the wonderful vista. In winter, the restaurant operates as a canteen, offering hot drinks, soups

(Continued)

Case Study. Continued.

and sandwiches, and big pots of chilli to skiers and snowboarders, who come in with their skis and boots and trail lots of water in with them.

As a result, most of the restaurant service equipment is on wheels, so that it can be moved around to accommodate the different uses of the space. The type of tables and chairs used are different too, with more robust versions being used during the ski season and better equipment stored away until it is needed again in the summer months. Large numbers of winter skiers also affects how the catering manager operates her rota system and manages her staff because they have rushes for service.

Therefore, it can be seen that for catering at this site there is a stark contrast in the work process between the two seasons. In winter their work process operates along the lines of a frantic cafeteria, whereas in summer they function as a restaurant, catering for more sedate fine dining, weddings and corporate functions, which require elegant table service skills. Consequently, the knowledge required by staff to operate between the two seasons differs substantially.

Retail – changes to facilities offered

The retail side of the business also has to make significant adjustments to their operation between the two seasons. The stock each shop carries is different and the levels of business change. In winter, skiers just want to buy things like water or gloves. They come in with their skis and boots and things get grubby, meaning the shop has to be repainted every spring. In summer the shop is much busier with coach tourists, families with children and walkers. Therefore, in summer the shop stocks walking items, things like maps or poles and lots of gift items.

Retail workers at Cairngorm Mountain incorporate more peripheral multi-tasking during the winter season, when the shop is a lot quieter; they may be called on to work in other areas like the restaurant or ski hire. In summer, when the site offers evening dining and weddings, the shop stays open on wedding and function evenings until 8 or 9 pm, and they help out the catering department by serving Pimms to the wedding guests.

Seasonal weather changes

Aside from catering and retail, employees working in other customer service areas at Cairngorm Mountain also have quite different duties to perform in different seasons. For example, the working day of an employee who primarily drives the funicular train during the summer months changes significantly during the skiing season, when duties then include communicating weather and snow conditions to the public. During the skiing season, information about snow conditions and skiing reports needs to be continually updated on radio bulletins and the Ski Scotland website, so this information generation and distribution often takes place in the morning and train operation returned to in the afternoon.

(Continued)

Case Study. Continued.

This change in the work process shifts the knowledge employees need to have to include the names of the runs on the 38 km of pisted runs. There is more radio communication with ski patrols. The amount of snow determines which lifts are operating and so determines the prices that are charged, so those working in the ticket office have to be aware of which runs are operating and what prices should be charged.

All year round, the work processes of staff at Cairngorm Mountain revolve to a great extent around the weather and the changes this can make to customer demand. During both summer and winter, staff have to be extremely aware of the weather conditions on the mountain because their daily routines depend, and must be responsive to, sometimes extreme and rapidly changeable weather conditions. For example, if there is no snow then there is little demand, but a sudden snowfall can result in the operation having to go from nothing to fully operational literally overnight.

However, sometimes the weather can become extreme, with high winds, torrential rain, heavy fog or really driving snow, which can necessitate everyone leaving Cairngorm Mountain for safety reasons. Employees at Cairngorm Mountain call this being 'stormed off'. When this happens, the snow gates are closed and everyone is evacuated from the hill, sometimes with only 5 minutes' warning. Everyone has to know what procedures to follow and work together to get everyone off the mountain in time.

Multi-functionality

Changes in seasons also bring about changes in the multi-functionality of staff at the site. Employees at this site are expected to be extremely multi-functional and be deployed wherever the business needs them most. An example of the need for multi-functionality and ability to respond rapidly to changing conditions was when Cairngorm Mountain was faced with an unprecedented fall of snow on a weekend in March, making it much more likely that snow sports enthusiasts would come in large numbers. Their close attention to approaching weather fronts had given site staff some indication that this might occur and they had taken some measures to prepare. For example, they had turned a counter in the lower shop into an extra catering counter, one ticket counter had been turned into a cash-only booth for speedier operation and all employees had been called to turn up. However, even so, they were quite overwhelmed. Several thousand people were attracted to 'hit the slopes' and the facility struggled to cope. There were too many vehicles in the car park, cars were queuing on the road and the gates had to be closed. Their response was to pull together as a team and the operation was adapted as best they could; the train was speeded up, everyone worked at full stretch and even senior management cleared tables in the café.

These rather extreme conditions obviously required rather extreme changes to the work process. However, this example illustrates an important point about the WPK at this site. WPK is strategic and at this site a strategic view includes being aware of

(Continued)

> **Case Study.** Continued.
>
> the constantly changing weather conditions and being aware of how this will affect their work process. Their close proximity to the sometimes dangerous nature of the changing weather conditions and the direct impact on their work processes as a result mean that constant awareness of the weather is an essential aspect of their WPK.

Questions

The highly seasonal nature of many parts of the THE industry means that sites attract, at different times and in varying numbers, different types of clients who visit with a different purpose.

1. Draw up a table and summarize how the work processes of this organization changed between the different seasons. How did this organization have to change their staff, their service delivery and the function and purpose of space and equipment?

2. What impact did these changes to the work processes have on the knowledge the staff needed to know?

3. If you were a manager here, how might you support your employees to manage the change in knowledge they needed to have between seasons?

4. What other seasonal operations in THE industries might involve a significant change in the WPK that workers would need to have between seasons?

GLOSSARY OF TERMS USED IN THIS CHAPTER

Collective competence	Tapping into a collective body of knowledge enables new staff to widen their own knowledge base quickly, as well as to enhance the customer service experience they are able to deliver.
Complexity of operations	Relates to the range of departments each site has, the range of different services they provide and whether they have internal or external partners delivering part of the main service.
Flexibility	Flexibility includes numerical flexibility (changing numbers of employees), product flexibility and flexibility through outsourcing some services. Some aspects of flexibility involve fundamental business requirements, such as flexible shifts to suit changing patterns of business. However, an increasingly vital component of businesses is in developing the functional flexibility of employees (Marr, 2007).

Formal channels of communication	Often characterized by written rules and procedures; include daily or periodical meetings and written or computerized booking information.
Informal channels of communication	Usually have no written rules or set procedures, but colleagues still use these channels to share information that is pertinent to their job.
Work process knowledge (WPK)	Incorporates: (i) how the company works; (ii) the specific peculiarities of the process relating to the organization's unique selling proposition; (iii) the concrete consequences that can be derived from specific actions; (iv) how the organization inter-relates with internal and external partners and the associations to which they belong; and (v) knowledge of the local area, the microenvironment in which the organization operates and how the organization relates to the rest of the destination.

REFERENCES AND FURTHER READING

Boreham, N. (2002a) Work process knowledge in technological and organizational development. In: Boreham, N., Samurçay, R. and Fischer, M. (eds) *Work Process Knowledge*. Routledge, London, pp. 1–14.

Boreham, N. (2002b) Professionalization and work process knowledge in the UK's National Health Service. In: Boreham, N., Samurçay, R. and Fischer, M. (eds) *Work Process Knowledge*. Routledge, London, pp. 171–182.

Boreham, N. (2004) Collective competence and work process knowledge. *European Conference on Educational Research*, University of Crete, September.

Buissink-Smith, N. and McIntosh, A. (2001) Conceptualizing the 'spirit of service' in tourism education and training: a case study from New Zealand. *Journal of Teaching in Travel and Tourism* 1, 79–96.

Evans Platt, C. (1991) Guest care culture: an approach for the leisure industry. *Leisure Manager* 9, 7–8.

Fischer, M. (2005) The integration of work process knowledge into human resources development. *Human Factors and Ergonomics in Manufacturing* 15, 369–384.

Fischer, M. and Boreham, N. (2004) Work process knowledge: origins of the concept and current developments. In: Fischer, M., Boreham, N. and Nyhan, B. (eds) *European Perspectives on Learning at Work: The Acquisition of Work Process Knowledge*. Cedefop, Luxembourg, pp. 12–53.

Fischer, M. and Röben, P. (2002) The work process knowledge of chemical laboratory assistants. In: Boreham, N., Samurçay, R. and Fischer, M. (eds) *Work Process Knowledge*. Routledge, London, pp. 40–54.

Jones, E. and Haven-Tang, C. (2005) Tourism SMEs, service quality and destination competitiveness. In: Jones, E. and Haven-Tang, C. (eds) *Tourism SMEs, Service Quality and Destination Competitiveness*. CAB International, Wallingford, UK, pp. 1–24.

Kandampully, J. (1997) Quality service in tourism. In: Foley, M., Lennon, J.J. and Maxwell, G. (eds) *Hospitality, Tourism and Leisure Management*. Cassell, London, pp. 3–20.

Kelliher, C. and Riley, M. (2002) Making functional flexibility stick: an assessment of the outcomes for stakeholders. *International Journal of Contemporary Hospitality Management* 14, 237–242.

Kruse, W. (1986) On the necessity of labour process knowledge. In: Schweitzer, J. (ed.) *Training for a Human Future*. Weinheim, Basle, pp. 188–193.

Leighton, D. (2006) 'Step back in time and live the legend': experiential marketing and the heritage sector. *International Journal of Nonprofit and Voluntary Sector Marketing* 12, 117–125.

Mariani, M. (2002) Work process knowledge in a chemical company. In: Boreham, N., Samurçay, R. and Fischer, M. (eds) *Work Process Knowledge*. Routledge, London, pp. 15–24.

Marr, S. (2007) Work process knowledge in Scottish visitor attractions. PhD thesis, University of Stirling. Available at: http://hdl.handle.net/1893/254

Marr, S. (2008) Work process knowledge and customer service excellence: lessons from the Scottish visitor attraction industry. *Managing Leisure* 13, 227–241.

Marr, S. (2011) Applying 'work process knowledge' to visitor attraction venues. *International Journal of Event and Festival Management* 2, 151–169.

Norros, L. and Nuutinen, M. (2002) The concept of the core task and the analysis of working practices. In: Boreham, N., Samurçay, R. and Fischer, M. (eds) *Work Process Knowledge*. Routledge, London, pp. 25–39.

Oliveira, M.T., Oliveira Pires, A.L. and Gaio Alves, M. (2002) Dimensions of work process knowledge. In: Boreham, N., Samurçay, R. and Fischer, M. (eds) *Work Process Knowledge*. Routledge, London, pp. 106–118.

chapter 17

Knowledge Management

Mohamed F. Hawela
Greenwich School of Management

Ahmed Hassanien
Edinburgh Napier University

Crispin Dale
University of Wolverhampton

LEARNING OBJECTIVES

After reading this chapter, readers should be able to:

- understand the importance of knowledge to tourism, hospitality and events (THE) facilities;
- distinguish between different types of knowledge;
- understand the concept of knowledge management;
- explain the knowledge management processes.

INTRODUCTION

As a future manager in the THE industries, it is essential that you have a sound basic knowledge and understanding of acquiring, managing, developing (and sometimes discarding) a bundle of resources (assets). As Enz (2010) suggests, most of these resources can be generally categorized as: financial, physical, human, knowledge and learning, and general organizational resources (for example, reputation, brand name and management contracts). Knowledge is one of the most important assets; it is considered to be one of the main sources of competitive advantage (Teece, 1998; Hallin and Marnburg, 2008). Despite the importance of knowledge and its management, there has been little practical research on knowledge management in THE industries (Bouncken and Pyo, 2002; Yang and Wan, 2004; Cooper, 2006; Hawela *et al.*, 2007a; Pizam, 2007; Hallin and Marnburg, 2008; Cope *et al.*, 2011; Hawela, 2011). This motivated us to write this chapter to bridge part of this gap and to help you to gain an understanding of the notion of knowledge management.

THE IMPORTANCE OF KNOWLEDGE

The starting point of the knowledge management process is the recognition of the importance of knowledge (Kianto and Ritala, 2010). In this part we will highlight the importance of knowledge and in the next part we will illustrate where you can locate knowledge outside and inside your THE facility.

We will start with the dynamic knowledge-based view of the company to highlight the importance of knowledge. The dynamic knowledge-based view of the company (Nonaka, 1994; Nonaka and Takeuchi, 1995; Nonaka *et al.*, 2008) provides a lens for understanding the importance of knowledge to any organization. According to this view, a company is an entity that continuously creates knowledge. Nonaka *et al.* note that 'The raison d'être of a firm is to continuously create knowledge' (2000, p. 2). The dynamic knowledge-based view of the company argues that knowledge and the capability to create and utilize such knowledge are the most important sources of a company's sustainable competitive advantage (Nonaka and Takeuchi, 1995; Nonaka and Toyama, 2003; Nonaka *et al.*, 2008). Knowledge and skills give a firm a competitive advantage. It is through this set of knowledge and skills a firm is able to innovate, to create new products/processes/services, or improve existing ones more efficiently and/or effectively.

Figure 17.1 provides a summary of the importance and benefits of knowledge for the THE facilities. In the left box in Fig. 17.1 we show knowledge as a source of wealth creation through facilitating innovation (Bessant and Venables, 2008; Quintane *et al.*, 2011). Innovation here is defined as the application of new ideas in creating new products, services and/or processes, or the improvement of existing ones. These products, services and processes are expected to create value for the THE facilities. In the second box in the middle of Fig. 17.1, knowledge is considered as an intermediary asset (Harrison, 2003; Enz, 2010) that can be used to develop other assets, for example, financial, physical, human and general organizational assets. Creating new knowledge about how to manage these assets effectively and efficiently will help in the renewal and development of these assets. The third box in the right side of Fig. 17.1 shows that one of the reasons for existence of any company is to continuously create knowledge. Let us assume that there is a start up THE facility that began with the founder's knowledge. This facility will not be able to survive if it does not continue to create new knowledge. This new knowledge will help the THE facility to survive and to cope with the changes in the external environment.

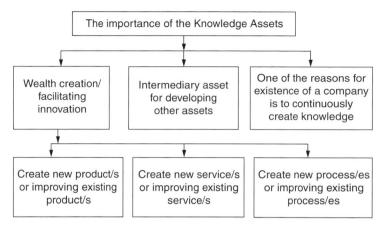

Fig. 17.1. The importance of the knowledge assets for THE facilities.

SOURCES OF KNOWLEDGE: INSIDE AND OUTSIDE THE FACILITIES

The identification of the strategically significant knowledge within and outside the organization is the second step in knowledge management. Our focus here will be on answering the question of where can knowledge be found? Knowledge can be found inside and outside THE facilities. As depicted in Fig. 17.2, knowledge can be found in three places in THE facilities: in databases and standard operating procedures manuals, in employees and in practice.

Examples of knowledge that might be found outside THE facilities are: knowledge in universities (Pertuzé *et al.*, 2010); knowledge in governmental agencies; knowledge that resides in competitors; knowledge in suppliers (Wigg, 2004) and knowledge in customers (Garcia-Murillo and Annabi, 2002; Gebert *et al.*, 2003; Sigala, 2012). An example of how to manage customer knowledge can be found at http://www.mystarbucksidea.com. You do not need to be limited by this list of knowledge sources. Any other sources of knowledge can be added to this list. You need to devise your knowledge management approach in each of the external sources of knowledge (illustrated in Fig. 17.2 by a knowledge management circle that connects the knowledge in the external sources with the knowledge that resides inside THE facilities). You need to identify which of these sources of knowledge is important to your THE facility. You might focus on one or more of these sources, depending on your circumstances.

Each of the internal and external sources of knowledge can be considered as a context and a place of learning for individual, group and organization as well. The case study at the end of the chapter is about how a facility may locate and facilitate the capturing and usage of employees' knowledge (internal knowledge), based on the Innovaccor initiatives of the Accor Hotel Company (more information about the company can be found at http://www.accor.com).

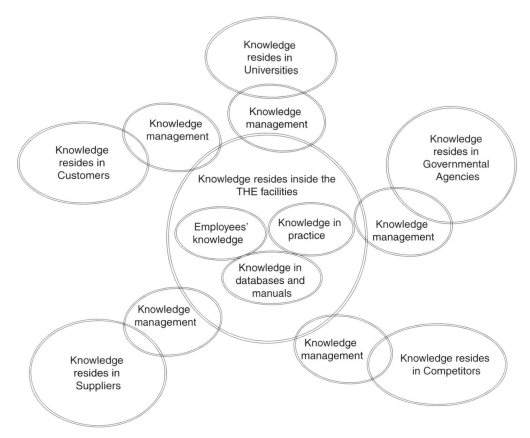

Fig. 17.2. Locations of knowledge inside and outside the firm.

TYPES OF KNOWLEDGE

Kianto and Ritala (2010) argue that an important factor in managing knowledge for renewal is the comprehension of the different types of knowledge assets. Therefore, you need to be aware of the different types of knowledge that can be found in any company.

According to Nonaka and Konno (1998), knowledge takes two forms, 'explicit and tacit'. Explicit knowledge is codified and is transmittable in formal, systematic language. It can take the form of words, numbers, specifications, manual, books, electronic databases, articulated online information and courses. For example, when you are reading this chapter, you are collecting explicit knowledge.

Tacit knowledge, on the other hand, is highly personal and not formalized. It is deeply rooted in an individual's actions and experience, as well as in the ideals, values or emotions he/she embraces (Nonaka, 1994; Nonaka and Takeuchi, 1995). Subjective insights, intuitions and hunches fall into this category of knowledge (deep knowledge, insights, expertise). Nonaka and Knonno (1998) highlight that there are two dimensions of tacit knowledge: the technical dimension, (know how) which encompasses such things as informational personal skills or crafts, and the cognitive dimension, which consists of beliefs, ideas, values and mental models that are deeply ingrained in us and that we often take for granted. The cognitive dimension of tacit knowledge shapes the way we perceive the world (Nonaka and Takeuchi, 1995; Nonaka and Knonno, 1998; Nonaka and Toyama, 2003).

An example of tacit knowledge is when you have two chefs and you provide them with a standard recipe; however, they produce two dishes with two different tastes. In this case they have used their tacit knowledge. Each chef has added his/her own experience. You will never be able to capture what they did and how they did it (their tacit knowledge) unless you talk to them or try to observe and ask them during the preparation process. Tacit and explicit knowledge can be found in many places inside and outside THE facilities. See the interaction between tacit and explicit knowledge in Fig. 17.4.

KNOWLEDGE MANAGEMENT PROCESSES

Knowledge management deals with all processes or features of knowledge in the THE facility. These include knowledge acquisition/creation; identification/refinement; codification and storage in repositories (organizational memory); dissemination/sharing/retrieval; and leverage/usage (Davenport and Prusak, 2000; Probst *et al.*, 2000; Gupta *et al.*, 2004). Figure 17.3 shows these processes and how they interact with each other. There is no particular sequence for these processes of knowledge management inside the organization. It is an enduring spiral process that can take the form of a web connecting knowledge processes to one another.

As mentioned, knowledge provides the basis for improvements and innovation in organizations. Each of the knowledge management processes will be discussed in detail, starting with the process of knowledge creation.

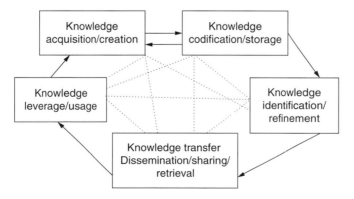

Fig. 17.3. Knowledge management processes. (Hawela (2011) and adapted from Probst et al, 2000; p. 30)

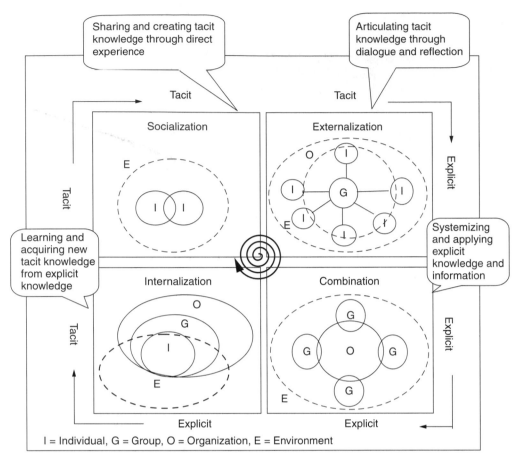

Fig. 17.4. The SECI model for knowledge creation. (Sources: adapted from Nonaka et al. 2008; Nonaka & Toyama, 2003)

The process of knowledge creation/acquisition

One of the most cited models of knowledge creation is the SECI model by Nonaka (1994) and Nonaka and Takeuchi (1995). At the core of the model is the distinction between tacit and explicit knowledge, and the analysis of the dynamics of knowledge creation through cycles of socialization, externalization, combination and internalization (SECI cycles) that engage tacit and explicit knowledge across organizational levels.

In order to harness individualized tacit knowledge to create new organizational knowledge, a firm needs to manage the process. Knowledge management requires a firm to transform individual tacit knowledge into explicit knowledge through codification, to store it in a repository, to disseminate it throughout the organization (see Fig. 17.5, the example of Innovaccor) and make it easily retrievable by employees so that it can be exploited and applied (Yang and Wan, 2004).

Therefore, it is vital to develop an understanding of how the process of knowledge creation takes place in the firm. Nonaka and colleagues have developed the SECI model of knowledge creation,

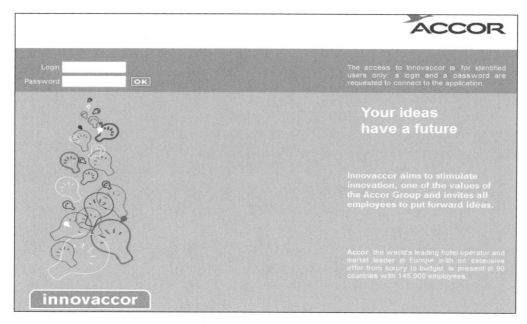

Fig. 17.5. Innovaccor homepage. (Sources: adapted from Nonaka et al. 2008; Nonaka & Toyama, 2003)

which argues that new organizational knowledge from which innovations arise occurs when tacit individual knowledge is transformed into explicit organizational knowledge (Nonaka, 1994; Nonaka and Takeuchi, 1995; Nonaka and Knonno, 1998; Nonaka *et al.*, 2000; Nonaka and Toyama, 2003).

As mentioned before, SECI refers to the socialization, externalization, combination and internalization processes involved in knowledge creation, as depicted in Fig. 17.4. The process of knowledge creation is manifested as a continuous spiral process where an individual, group and/or organization 'transcend the boundary of the old self into a new self by acquiring a new context, a new view of the world, and new knowledge; in short it is a journey from being to becoming' (Nonaka *et al.*, 2000, p. 3).

In Fig. 17.4 the interaction between tacit and explicit knowledge is referred to as 'knowledge conversion' and leads to the creation of new knowledge (Nonaka *et al.*, 2000). The combination of the two categories makes it possible to conceptualize four conversion patterns:

1. Socialization: from tacit to tacit knowledge. Employees gather information from internal/ external sources and direct experience and others acquire it through observation and other non-formalized means.

2. Externalization: from tacit to explicit knowledge. Knowledge can be shared by others and become the basis of new knowledge such as concepts, images, ideas and written documents. Dialogue is an effective tool to articulate one's tacit knowledge and to share the articulated knowledge with others. To ensure that the knowledge remains explicit it is wise for it to be codified (Gupta *et al.*, 2004).

3. Combination: from explicit to explicit knowledge. The new explicit knowledge is synthesized and disseminated among members of the THE facility. The creative use of networks and large-scale databases can facilitate this mode of conversion. This phase relies on four organizational processes: capturing, integrating, disseminating and editing.

4. Internalization: from explicit to tacit knowledge. Training programmes, if properly conducted, help trainees understand the THE facility and themselves. Employees can internalize the explicit knowledge gained from the training programme and convert it into tacit knowledge with the potential of creating new knowledge.

Knowledge storage, identification, sharing and retrieval processes

In this stage (process) the THE facility deals with what it knows (Drew, 1999). Figure 17.3 shows that after knowledge is created or acquired, it should be stored and codified. Therefore, it is not only after knowledge is created but also during the process of knowledge creation (learning) or acquirement that knowledge should be stored. These dynamic processes are depicted as two-way arrows between knowledge creation and storage (see Fig. 17.3). To avoid losing or forgetting the created or acquired knowledge, it must be easily stored, organized and retrieved (Walsh and Ungson, 1991; Alavi and Leidner, 2001; Fiedler and Welpe, 2010; Rowlinson *et al.*, 2010).

Knowledge storage, codification, identification and retrieval also refer to the development of the THE facility's memory or knowledge stocks, and the ways for accessing its content (Walsh and Ungson, 1991; Anand *et al.*, 1998; Moorman and Miner, 1998). Many authors have highlighted the importance of developing an organizational memory. Huber (1991) emphasized the vital role played by organizational memory in organizational learning, and Anand *et al.* (1998) noted the important role of organizational memory in decision making. Further, Huber (1991) explained that the usability of what has been learned by the organizations depends, on a greater extent, on the effectiveness of managing the organization's memory. Weick noted 'If an organization is to learn anything, then the distribution of its memory, the accuracy of that memory, and the conditions under which that memory is treated as a constraint become crucial characteristics of organizing' (1979a, p. 206, cited in Walsh and Ungson, 1991, p. 57).

It is salient for the THE facility to consider its memories as dynamic rather than static. At the organizational level, memory may lead to keeping the status quo. This could in turn lead to resistance to learning and change (Argyris and Schon, 1996; Alavi and Leidner, 2001).

There are many views about the nature and types of organizational memory (Rowlinson *et al.*, 2010). A THE facility's memory could be viewed as being on three levels. These levels are individual, group and organizational stocks of knowledge. For individuals and groups to be able to access the explicit knowledge from organizational memory, they will need first to be able to locate the knowledge they need (Anand *et al.*, 1998). Individuals and groups can identify/locate the required tacit knowledge using several approaches. They can search the organization directories and intranet for the holder of the required knowledge (for example, if the organization created a list of the subject area experts and what they know). Individuals and groups can make a request for the required knowledge using the organization's intranet

(Anand *et al.*, 1998; Alavi and Leidner, 2001). Other examples include expert interviews, best practice cases, knowledge brokering (third parties connecting knowledge seekers to knowledge sources), experience reports (documenting positive and negative experiences on projects), databases and professional research services.

Advancements in web information and communication technologies have played an important role in improving storage, codification, identification and retrieval processes and in building organizational memory (Alavi and Leidner, 2001; Hustad and Teigland, 2008; Fiedler and Welpe, 2010). The final processes of knowledge management that will be discussed here are knowledge transfer, sharing and utilization.

Knowledge sharing, transfer and utilization

Kogut and Zander point out that 'What firms do better than markets is the sharing and transfer of the knowledge of individuals and groups within an organization' (1992, p. 383). Therefore, the THE facilities need to nurture the process of knowledge sharing and transfer between individuals, groups and organizational levels. The processes of knowledge sharing and transfer are inseparable (Tsai, 2001). They are related to the flow of knowledge between different levels: individuals, groups and organizations. All teams (including virtual teams) must develop mechanisms for sharing knowledge, experiences, and insights critical for accomplishing their missions. Knowledge sharing includes the transfer of existing knowledge among team members and bringing new knowledge into the team (Rosen *et al.*, 2007, p. 260).

There are two approaches to knowledge sharing and transfer in the extant literature. One approach is knowledge sharing and transfer by codification and storage where there is no interpersonal exchange. The second is the sharing and transfer of knowledge through storage, codification, communications and interpersonal exchange (Hansen *et al.*, 1999; Haas and Hansen, 2007). The first approach can be called human to computer or database interaction. When you use your computer or mobile phone to search the web to get some information, this is an example of the first type of knowledge sharing and transfer (there is no interpersonal exchange).

The second approach to knowledge sharing depends on the interpersonal exchange of knowledge in knowledge sharing networks. The facilitation of knowledge sharing and learning requires understanding of various types of knowledge networks (Hansen, 2002; Ganley and Lampe, 2009; Foss *et al.*, 2010). Verburg and Andriessen (2011) suggest four types of knowledge networks: (i) informal networks (an example of this is your network with your friend on Facebook, where you share and transfer knowledge and information); (ii) question and answer networks; (iii) strategic networks; and (iv) online strategic networks. It is important to note that there are no clear boundaries between these types of knowledge networks. Further, they are not necessarily stable – they might shift in purpose and membership (Verburg and Andriessen, 2011).

The value and purpose of these different types of network, as suggested by Andriessen *et al.* (2004), are as follows: solving an immediate individual problem in a work situation; building a wider perspective in the practices of a group work; developing guidelines, best practices, standard operating procedures for the organization; and developing innovative product, services and work practices for the organization.

There are many enablers and barriers to knowledge sharing and transfer (O'Deli and Grayson, 1998; Tsai, 2001; Lee and Choi, 2003; Yang and Chu Chen, 2007; Anantatmula and Kanungo, 2010; Foss *et al.*, 2010; Lilleoere and Hansen, 2011). Encouraging reciprocity and sustaining knowledge exchange by using motivators is one of the enablers (King and Marks, 2008). For example, managers should develop strategies or mechanisms that encourage the interaction and strength of the relationships among members (Min Chiu *et al.*, 2006). Sharing a common language between individuals and groups is another enabler to knowledge sharing and transfer. Here, 'language' is not used in the traditional sense, as in a language like German, Arabic or English. A common language in this context means sharing assumptions, goals, vision and vocabulary. Sharing a common language will help in encouraging knowledge exchange activities and improve the quality of the shared knowledge (Nahapiet and Ghoshal, 1998; Tsai and Ghoshal, 1998; Min Chiu *et al.*, 2006). Swap *et al.* (2001) claim that mentoring and storytelling are effective ways for enabling sharing and transferring knowledge, and informal ways of learning. Brink (2001) explained that there are three conditions that help in enabling knowledge sharing. These are social conditions, organizational conditions and technological conditions (for more information see Brink, 2001). Wellman *et al.* (2001) suggest that internet technologies help in increasing knowledge sharing. Technology can support the two approaches of knowledge sharing; codification and storage (repositories) and interpersonal exchange. Brink (2001) suggests that sharing explicit knowledge can be supported by knowledge repositories, sharing explicit and tacit knowledge can be supported by a knowledge route map and sharing tacit knowledge can be supported by using a collaboration platform. Knowledge repository, knowledge route map and collaboration platform are described by Brink as follows:

> Knowledge repository: Knowledge repositories hold collections of knowledge components that have a structured content like information from business applications, manuals, reports and articles, or customer related databases. A content classification scheme or taxonomy is used to organize the knowledge repositories to facilitate grouping, sorting, visualization, searching, publication, manipulation, refinement, and navigation.

> Knowledge route map: Knowledge route maps are guides, directories, or pointers to an organization's internal and external information and knowledge sources – both tacit and explicit. Knowledge route maps provide pointers to sources of knowledge that can include people with a special expertise or may offer links to documents that describe research results, best practices, lessons learned, diagnostics tools, or list frequently asked questions. Another functionality that knowledge route maps offer is that of online learning (computer based training), in which access to – possible interactive, multimedia – educational material is given.

> Collaborative platform: A collaborative platform is a functionality of information and communication technology that – electronically – facilitates group or teamwork and collaboration. It is a distributed virtual environment that may encourage debate, dialogue, interaction, creativity, innovation, and sharing … that otherwise would have been constrained by barriers of time and place. (Brink, 2001, pp. 4–5)

In particular, Web 2.0 can help in enabling knowledge sharing and management. Web 2.0 can be a knowledge repository, route map and collaboration platform, depending on how Web 2.0 technologies are being utilized by the THE facility (Hawela *et al.*, 2007b; Ganley and Lampe, 2009). Some example of Web 2.0 technologies are Twitter, Facebook, Weblog and Wiki.

The barriers to knowledge sharing/transfer are the opposite of the enablers (Lilleoere and Hansen, 2011). A misfit between technology and task or between technology and the type of knowledge that needs to be shared can be a barrier to knowledge sharing/transfer. Another barrier to knowledge sharing/transfer is not providing the motivational and conducive factors that support knowledge sharing (discussed above).

An additional barrier to knowledge sharing and transfer is when knowledge is sticky (Von Hippel, 1994; Szulanski, 1996, 2000). The transfer of knowledge is not a simple process. Szulanski states 'Even though intra-firm transfers of knowledge are often laborious, time consuming, and difficult, current conceptions continue to treat them as costless and instantaneous' (2000, p. 23). The stickiness of knowledge may be defined in relation to costs. It can be defined as the 'incremental expenditure required to transfer [a] unit of information to a specified locus in a form usable by a given information seeker. When this cost is low, information stickiness is low; when it is high, stickiness is high' (Von Hippel, 1994, p. 430).

Szulanski (1996, 2000) has identified several 'origins of stickiness' or barriers to the transfer and sharing of knowledge – the characteristics of: the knowledge transferred, the source, the recipient and the context in which the transfer takes place. Barriers related to characteristics of the knowledge transferred are (i) causal ambiguity and (ii) un-proven-ness (knowledge with a proven record of past usefulness is less difficult to transfer). Barriers related to the source are: (i) lack of motivation and (ii) not perceived as reliable. Barriers related to the recipient are: (i) lack of motivation; (ii) lack of absorptive capacity (recipients might be unable to exploit outside sources of knowledge; that is, they may lack absorptive capacity. Such capacity is largely a function of their preexisting stock of knowledge and it becomes manifest in their ability to value, assimilate and apply new knowledge successfully to commercial ends (Szulanski, 1996, 2000)); and (iii) lack of retention capacity (a transfer of knowledge is effective only when the knowledge transferred is retained). Barriers related to the last factor, the context in which the transfer takes place, are: (i) a barren organizational context and (ii) an arduous relationship.

Szulanski (1996, 2000) found that these factors vary in importance over the stages of the transfer process. The transfer stages are the: initiation stage, implementation stage, ramp-up stage ('The ramp-up stage offers a relatively brief window of opportunity to rectify unexpected problems where the recipient is likely to begin using new knowledge ineffectively, ramping-up gradually toward a satisfactory level of performance, often with external assistance'; Szulanski, 2000, p. 15) and the integration stage.

> Knowledge transfer should be regarded as a process of reconstruction rather than a mere act of transmission and reception. (Szulanski, 2000, p. 23)

SUMMARY

This chapter has explored the concept of knowledge management and explored its significance and types within the context of THE facilities. The chapter has looked at the internal and external sources of knowledge within organizations. Finally, it has explained the processes of knowledge creation/acquisition; knowledge storage, identification, sharing and retrieval processes; knowledge sharing, transfer and utilization.

REVIEW QUESTIONS

1. Define the concept of knowledge management and explore its significance within the context of THE facilities.
2. Define the different stages of the knowledge management processes.
3. Discuss the enablers and barriers of knowledge sharing. Illustrate your answer with industry-related examples.

Case Study

Innovaccor (https://www.innovaccor.com)

Innovaccor was developed by the corporate human resource department in Paris and was launched at the end of the year 2001 and beginning of 2002. Innovaccor is a project aimed at promoting innovation among the Accor Group's employees. It takes the form of an intranet tool that enables Accor employees to suggest ideas to improve the operation of their own hotel or department. Nearly 30,000 employees from all continents at that time participated in the project. The second international Innovactors (the people in charge of establishing Innovaccor) meeting was held at the Académie Accor and was attended by Innovaccor managers from all countries and businesses where the programme is already established. At that time (2003) there were 11,000 proposed ideas and 3844 have been implemented. This means that 35% of the proposed ideas have been utilized by the company. In the year 2011, Accor Company reported the implementation of 2000 ideas during that year.

Innovaccor is an online tool that enables staff to propose ideas, demonstrate creativity and take initiative, and managers to organize challenges and problems for staff to experience and to become aware of best practices so that they can apply them within their organization.

All employees can present their ideas by either going to Innovaccor online or filling in a paper-based form; then the idea is reviewed by the hotel general manager or

(Continued)

Case Study. Continued.

Innovactor (the person who is in charge of Innovaccor in a specific hotel). The idea is evaluated according to its originality, impact and ease of implementation. If the idea is refused, a full explanation is provided to the employee who suggested it. If the idea is accepted, it will be rated according to a rating system of 1 bulb to 4 bulbs. This rating system works as follows: 1 bulb = 1 to 5 points; 2 bulbs = 6 to 15 points; 3 bulbs = 16 to 30 points; 4 bulbs = 31 to 60 points. When the hotel general manager accepts the idea, s/he implements it and rewards the employee who suggested it. If the idea can benefit more than one hotel, then the hotel general manager will suggest it to be added to the best practice database.

Below are few examples of the simple and efficient ideas that were suggested and implemented.

Simple ideas that are having a commercial impact
- Novotel Melbourne St Kilda makes forms available to all team members in order to record information on the preferences of regular guests (reading, football club, drinks, sport, etc.). This information is then collected by the Customer Relations Manager and recorded in the hotel's database. In this manner, the team becomes more aware of the habits of regular guests, who are delighted to find a personal welcome in their bedroom, rather than a standard complimentary gift.
- How to create the surprise for Accor's guests? Mercure Hotels in Portugal created a database indicating the birthdays of their guests. Then, a special 'Mercure Portugal' birthday card was printed and sent to guests on their birthday.
- How to boost sales of the Accor Favorite Guest Card? Ibis in Germany prints a sales slogan on all customer bills explaining the advantages of the card. For example: 'Using an AFGC, you would have saved 10% on the total amount of your bill! Please enquire with reception for further information.'
- Novotel Lyon Nord systematically sends an SMS to clients having made a booking to remind them of their reservation or of the automatic cancellation of their room at 6 pm. In this manner, all bookings are confirmed by 6 pm. Customers feel reassured. This quick and modern process has considerably reduced the number of 'no shows' and enables easier management of 'overbooking'.

Simple ideas that makes a difference for guests
- It is quite common for guests to leave their spectacles at home; hence they have difficulty in reading the menu. Swiss hotels propose a range of spectacles/magnifying glasses for use by their guests.
- Guests often need practical information, such as the nearest cash dispenser or the opening hours of different shops. Ibis Portsmouth has created a map of such information, which can be copied whenever a customer needs it.

(Continued)

Case Study. Continued.

- The front office team at Novotel Birmingham Centre automatically ask guests when checking in whether they need a taxi for the following morning. In this manner, the guest does not have to wait for his taxi and can leave on time without feeling frustrated.

- In addition to their usual luggage, many guests arrive with their clothes on a hanger. This is quite problematic during check-in procedures since they have nowhere to temporarily hang their clothes. Ibis Berlin Dreilinden has found a solution: hooks are discretely placed near to the reception desk.

- Ibis Den Haag Centre has bedrooms catering for people with disabilities. However, staff were not familiar with the facilities in these rooms. The solution was to create an information sheet containing written information and photographs. Hence, when a customer calls to book a room asking, for example, whether a wheelchair can pass through the door, the receptionist can respond precisely and immediately.

Simple ideas that make a difference to staff's daily routine

- How to prevent wall plugs from being ripped out by the vacuum cleaners in the bedroom corridors? Ibis Lourdes has found the solution: a mini-extension lead measuring approximately 40 centimetres has been fitted onto the plug of each vacuum cleaner. When the main lead of the cleaner becomes taught, rather than ripping out the wall plug, the mini-lead becomes unplugged instead.

- The distribution of bedrooms for housekeepers was rather time-consuming and was not always very clear. Ibis Paris Versailles Parly II created an Excel table that has resolved the problem: before, it took at least 20 minutes to work out the room allocation when the hotel was full. By using this document, it now takes less than 5 minutes.

- How to make sure the correct products are used for cleaning the bedrooms in Ibis, while ensuring optimum hygiene? By using a cloth that is the same colour as the packaging of the cleaning product.

- The new Novotel bedrooms have a complimentary tray providing a kettle for making a cup of tea or coffee in the room, in addition to a selection of welcome products. Corinne Julien from Novotel Caen Côte de Nacre invented and manufactured a wooden compartment box that can be fixed onto the Novotel trolley. This box makes it easier to properly sort out the welcome products on the trolley and protects their packaging.

Questions

1. To what extent has Innovaccor been successful in promoting innovation among the Accor Group's employees?

2. Using the above SECI Model for Knowledge Creation (Fig. 17.4), discuss the process of knowledge creation in Innovaccor.

GLOSSARY OF TERMS USED IN THIS CHAPTER

Explicit knowledge   Codified and transmittable in formal, systematic language. It can take the form of words, numbers, specifications, manual, books, electronic databases, articulated online information and courses.

Knowledge management   Deals with all processes or features of knowledge in the THE facility. These include knowledge acquisition/creation; identification/refinement; codification and storage in repositories (organizational memory); dissemination/sharing/retrieval; and leverage/usage.

Tacit knowledge   Highly personal and not formalized. It is deeply rooted in an individual's actions and experience as well as in the ideals, values or emotions he/she embraces. Subjective insights, intuitions and hunches fall into this category of knowledge (deep knowledge, insights, expertise).

REFERENCES AND ADDITIONAL READING

Alavi, M. and Leidner, D. (2001) Review: Knowledge management and knowledge management systems: conceptual foundations and research issues. *MIS Quarterly* 25, 107–136.

Anand, V., Manz, C. and Glick, W. (1998) An organizational memory approach to information management. *Academy of Management Review* 23, 796–899.

Anantatmula, V. and Kanungo, S. (2010) Modeling enablers for successful KM implementation. *Journal of Knowledge Management* 14, 100–113.

Andriessen, E., Huis, M. and Soekijad, M. (2004) Communities of practice for knowledge sharing. In: Andriessen, E. and Fahlbruch, B. (eds) *How to Manage Experience Sharing: From Organizational Surprises to Organizational Knowledge*. Elsevier, Oxford, pp. 173–194.

Argyris, C. (1976) Single-loop and double-loop models in research on decision making. *Administrative Science Quarterly* 21, 363–376.

Argyris, C. and Schon, D. (1996) *Organizational Learning II: Theory, Method and Practice*. Addison-Wesley, Reading, Massachusetts.

Bessant, J. and Venables, T. (2008) Introduction. In: Bessant, J. and Venables, T. (eds) *Creating Wealth from Knowledge: Meeting the Innovation Challenge*. Edward Elgar, Cheltenham, UK.

Bouncken, R. and Pyo, S. (2002) Achieving competitiveness through knowledge management. In: Bouncken, R. and Pyo, S. (eds) *Knowledge Management in Hospitality and Tourism*. The Haworth Hospitality Press, New York, pp. 1–4.

Brink, P. (2001) Measurement of conditions for knowledge sharing. *Second European Conference on Knowledge Management*, Bled, Slovenia.

Cooper, C. (2006) Knowledge management and tourism. *Annals of Tourism Research* 33, 47–64.

Cope, R., Cope III, R., Bass, A. and Syrdal, H. (2011) Innovative knowledge management at Disney: human capital and queuing solutions for services. *Journal of Service Science* 4, 13–20.

Davenport, T. and Prusak, L. (2000) *Working Knowledge: How Organizations Manage What They Know*. Harvard Business School Press, Boston, Massachusetts.

Drew, S. (1999) Building knowledge management into strategy: making sense of a new perspective. *Long Range Planning* 32, 130–136.

Enz. C. (2010) *Hospitality Strategic Management: Concepts and Cases*, 2nd edn. Wiley, New York.

Fiedler, M. and Welpe, I. (2010) How do organizations remember? The influence of organizational structure on organizational memory. *Organization Studies* 31, 381–407.

Foss, N., Husted, K. and Michailova, S. (2010) Governing knowledge sharing in organizations: levels of analysis, governance mechanisms, and research directions. *Journal of Management Studies* 47, 455–482.

Ganley, D. and Lampe, C. (2009) The ties that bind: social network principles in online communities. *Decision Support Systems* 47, 266–274.

Garcia-Murillo, M.A. and Annabi, H. (2002) Customer knowledge management. *Journal of the Operational Research Society* 53, 875–884.

Gausemeier, J., Fink, A. and Schlake, O. (1998) Scenario management: an approach to develop future potentials. *Technological Forecasting and Social Change* 59, 111–130.

Gebert, H., Geib, M., Kolbe, L. and Brenner, W. (2003) Knowledge-enabled customer relationship management: integrating customer relationship management and knowledge management concepts [1]. *Journal of Knowledge Management* 7, 107–123.

Gupta, N., Sharma, K. and Hsu, J. (2004) An overview of knowledge management. In: Gupta, J.N.D. and Sharma, S.K. (eds) *Creating Knowledge Based Organizations*. Idea Group, New York, pp. 1–28.

Haas, M. and Hansen, M. (2007) Different knowledge, different benefits: toward a productivity perspective on knowledge sharing in organizations. *Strategic Management Journal* 28, 1133–1153.

Hallin, C. and Marnburg, E. (2008) Knowledge management in the hospitality industry: a review of empirical research. *Tourism Management* 29, 366–381.

Hansen, M. (2002) Knowledge networks: explaining effective knowledge sharing in multiunit companies. *Organization Science* 13, 232–248.

Hansen, T., Nohria, N. and Tierney, T. (1999) What's your strategy for managing knowledge? *Harvard Business Review* 77, 106–116.

Harrison, J. (2003) Strategic analysis for the hospitality industry. *Cornell Hotel and Restaurant Administration Quarterly* April.

Hawela, M. (2011) E-learning as a tool for organizational learning and knowledge management in international hotel companies. PhD thesis, University of Ulster, UK.

Hawela, M., Boyle, E. and Murray, A. (2007a) E-learning as a tool for knowledge creation in international hotel companies. In: Sigala, M., Mich, L. and Murphy, J. (eds) *Proceedings of the 14th International Conference Information and Communication Technologies in Tourism*, Ljubljana, Slovenia. Springer, Vienna, Austria.

Hawela, M., Boyle, E., Murray, A. and Connolly, M. (2007b) Web-Logs and Wikis: tools for organisational learning, collaboration and knowledge management in international hotel companies. EuroCHRIE; Conference '25 years of Showcasing Innovation in Education, Training and Research through Tourism, Hospitality and Events', Leeds, UK, 25–27 October.

http://www.accor.com/fileadmin/user_upload/Contenus_Accor/Hotellerie/img/Developpement_Hotelier/PDF/EN/Development_made_in_Accor_EN.PDF (accessed 17 July 2012).

Huber, G.P. (1991) Organizational learning: the contributing processes and the literatures. *Organization Science* 2, 88–115.

Hustad, E. and Teigland, R. (2008) Implementing social networking media and Web 2.0 in multinationals: implications for knowledge management. *Proceedings of the European Conference on Knowledge Management*, Southampton, UK, pp. 323–331.

Kianto, A. and Ritala, P. (2010) Knowledge-based perspective on dynamic capabilities. In: Wall, S., Zimmermann, C., Klingebiel, R. and Lange, D. (eds) *Strategic Reconfigurations: Building Dynamic Capabilities in Rapid Innovation-based Industries*. Edward Elgar, Cheltenham, UK, pp. 86–104.

King, W. and Marks, P. (2008) Motivating knowledge sharing through a knowledge management system. *Omega: The International Journal of Management Science* 36, 131–146.

Kogut, B. and Zander, U. (1992) Knowledge of the firm, combinative capabilities, and the replication of technology. *Organization Science* 3, 383–397.

Lee, H. and Choi, B. (2003) Knowledge management enablers, processes, and organizational performance. *Journal of Management Information Systems* 20, 179–228.

Lilleoere, A. and Hansen, H. (2011) Knowledge-sharing enablers and barriers in pharmaceutical research and development. *Journal of Knowledge Management* 15, 53–70.

Min Chiu, C., Hsu, M. and Wang, E. (2006) Understanding knowledge sharing in virtual communities: an integration of social capital and social cognitive theories. *Decision Support Systems* 42, 1872–1888.

Moorman, C. and Miner, A. (1998) Organizational improvisation and organizational memory. *Academy of Management Review* 23, 698–723.

Nahapiet, J. and Ghoshal, S. (1998) Social capital, intellectual capital, and the organizational advantage. *Academy of Management Review* 23, 242–266.

Nonaka, I. (1994) A dynamic theory of organizational knowledge creation. *Organization Science* 5, 14–37.

Nonaka, I. and Konno, N. (1998) The concept of 'Ba': building a foundation for knowledge creation. *California Management Review* 40(3), 40–54.

Nonaka, I. and Takeuchi, H. (1995) *The Knowledge-Creating Company: How Japanese Companies Create the Dynamics of Innovation*. Oxford University Press, New York.

Nonaka, I. and Toyama, R. (2003) The knowledge-creating theory revisited: knowledge creation as a synthesizing process. *Knowledge Management Research & Practice* 1, 2–10.

Nonaka, I., Toyama, R. and Hirata, T. (2008) *Managing Flow: A Process Theory of the Knowledge-based Firm*. Palgrave-Macmillan, Basingstoke.

Nonaka, I., Toyama, R. and Nagata, A. (2000) A firm as a knowledge-creating entity: a new perspective on the theory of the firm. *Industrial and Corporate Change* 9, 1–20.

O'Deli, C. and Grayson, J. (1998) If only we knew what we know: identification and transfer of internal best practices. *California Management Review* 40, 154–174.

Pertuzé, J., Calder, E., Greitzer, E. and Lucas, W. (2010) Best practices for industry–university collaboration. *MIT Sloan Management Review* Summer, 83–90.

Pizam, A. (2007) Does the tourism/hospitality industry possess the characteristics of a knowledge-based industry? *International Journal of Hospitality Management* 26, 759–763.

Probst, G., Raub, S. and Romhardt, K. (2000) *Managing Knowledge: Building Blocks for Success*. Wiley, Chichester, UK.

Quintane, E., Casselman, M., Reiche, S. and Nylund, P. (2011) Innovation as a knowledge-based outcome. *Journal of Knowledge Management* 15, 928–947.

Rosen, B., Furst, S. and Blackburn, R. (2007) Overcoming barriers to knowledge sharing in virtual teams. *Organizational Dynamics* 36, 259–273.

Rowlinson, M., Booth, C., Clark, P., Delahaye, A. and Procter, S. (2010) Social remembering and organizational memory. *Organization Studies* 31, 69–87.

Sigala, M. (2012) Social networks and customer involvement in New Service Development (NSD): the case of www.mystarbucksidea.com. *International Journal of Contemporary Hospitality Management* 24, 966–990.

Swap, W., Leonard, D., Shields, M. and Abrams, L. (2001) Using mentoring and storytelling to transfer knowledge. *Journal of Management Information Systems* 18, 95–114.

Szulanski, G. (1996) Exploring stickiness: impediments to the transfer of best practice within the firm. *Strategic Management Journal* 17, 27–43.

Szulanski, G. (2000) The process of knowledge transfer: a diachronic analysis of stickiness. *Organizational Behavior and Human Decision Processes* 82, 9–27.

Teece, D. (1998) Capturing value from knowledge assets: the new economy, markets for know-how, and intangible assets. *California Management Review* 40, 55–79.

Tsai, W. (2001) Knowledge transfer in intraorganizational networks: effects of network position and absorptive capacity on business unit innovation and performance. *Academy of Management Journal* 44, 996–1004.

Tsai, W. and Ghoshal, S. (1998) Social capital and value creation: an empirical study of intra-firm networks. *Academy of Management Journal* 41, 464–476.

Verburg, R. and Andriessen, E. (2011) A typology of knowledge sharing networks in practice. *Knowledge and Process Management* 18, 34–44.

Von Hippel, E. (1994) Sticky information and the locus of problem solving: implications for innovation. *Management Science* 40, 590–607.

Walsh, J. and Ungson, G. (1991) Organizational memory. *Academy of Management Review* 16, 57–91.

Wellman, B., Quan-Haase, A., Witte, J. and Hampton, N. (2001) Does the Internet increase, decrease, or supplement social capital? Social networks, participation, and community commitment. *American Behavioral Scientist* 45, 437–456.

Wigg, K. (2004) *People-Focused Knowledge Management: How Effective Decision Making Leads to Corporate Success*. Elsevier, Amsterdam, The Netherlands.

Yang, C. and Chu Chen, L. (2007) Can organizational knowledge capabilities affect knowledge sharing behavior? *Journal of Information Science* 33, 95–109.

Yang, J. and Wan, C. (2004) Advancing organizational effectiveness and knowledge management implementation. *Tourism Management* 25, 593–601.

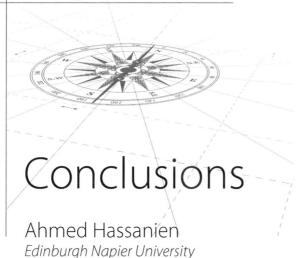

chapter 18

Conclusions

Ahmed Hassanien
Edinburgh Napier University

Crispin Dale
University of Wolverhampton

LEARNING OBJECTIVES

Having completed this chapter, readers should be able to:

- review the contribution of this book;
- explore the issues surrounding the development, operation and management of tourism, hospitality and events (THE) facilities;
- propose future directions for facilities management in THE.

Having come to the end of this book, it is necessary to reflect on the contents of the preceding chapters, appraise the key issues that have emerged and propose future directions for facilities management in THE. It is evitable that whether facilities management is an academic subject will continue to be debated. Facilities management comprises a number of different areas and this book has gone some way to bringing together the key themes that are emerging in THE. Indeed, management of facilities is essential for the THE industries to function effectively.

The first section of the book (Chapters 1 and 2) provides an initial understanding of what facilities are and their scope in the context of THE. Chapter 1 provides an overview of THE facilities and explored the concept, significance, evolution and scope of facilities management. It should be acknowledged that THE facilities are varied in scope. This is compounded further by the size, nature and characteristics that can be associated with the THE industries. Furthermore, the composite sectors that make up the THE industries are disparate. Bringing together the different aspects of facilities management can be challenging and in some respects conflicting. The term 'facilities manager' is not commonly used in THE premises, but it amalgamates the functional and operational aspects of other roles in the organization. Yet what is key is that facilities management is fundamental to the day-to-day performance of the THE facility. It combines a holistic view that enables the overall success of the business.

The evolution of facilities management has come about as a consequence of competitive pressures and businesses needing to generate further value. Facilities management has therefore evolved from a property-focused to a strategic discipline incorporating issues concerning outsourcing and value creation. This has been bought about by a number of external and internal factors, as highlighted in Table 18.1. These factors reinforce the need to embrace facilities management in the context of THE, and managers need to be aware of the implication they may pose for their businesses.

Table 18.1. External and internal factors influencing the evolution of facilities management.

External factors	Internal factors
• Globalization	• Effective management of an organization's resources
• Business continuity	• Improving staff skills
• Workforce protection	• Enabling new working styles and processes
• Security improvement	• Helping integration processes associated with change, post-merger and acquisition
• Changes in legislation and government policy	• Enhancing an organization's identity and image
• Development of information and communication technologies	• 'Sweat the assets'
• Increasingly mature and competitive markets	• Enabling future change in use of space
• Fluctuating land and property prices	• Delivering effective and responsive services
• Changing consumer demands and expectations	• Providing competitive advantage to the core business
	• Need for leaner and more efficient organizational structures
	• Need for greater flexibility in use of space and working environments
	• Tighter operating margins and cost/revenue-driven strategies

Chapter 2 looked at the concept and environment of THE facilities. It investigated the different levels of THE facilities and scanned the scope of THE facilities. Finally, the chapter evaluated the characteristics of services and their impact on THE facilities.

The second section this book (Chapters 3–8) continued to explore the different services that facilities management can cover within the context of THE facilities. Chapter 3 introduced the concept and purpose of project management. It explored project management and its application within the THE sectors. Chapter 4 explored the definition and function of feasibility studies in THE facilities. It analysed the key components of a feasibility study and discussed its limitations. Chapter 5 discussed the concept and dimensions of physical evidence. It explored services by function and nature for physical evidence. Also, it investigated how physical evidence might work in terms of its role and impact in the service setting. Chapter 6 considered the historical context of information technology and explored its role in THE facilities and examined the different types of technologies in THE facilities. Chapter 7 looked at the concept and scope of outsourcing in THE facilities. It highlighted the importance of outsourcing for THE facilities and outlined its advantages and disadvantages. Then, it analysed the outsourcing decision criteria. Chapter 8 explained project cost management principles, concepts and terms. It analysed cost management in the contemporary THE facilities context. It critically discussed and applied cost management principles including opportunity costs, revenue management and other principles relevant to THE operations' bottom line.

The third section (Chapters 9–12) of this book focused on the sustainable development and management of THE facilities. Chapter 9 conceptualized and defined corporate social responsibility (CSR) from the perspectives of a range of stakeholder interests. It critically reflected on CSR as part of the THE organizations' business and marketing philosophy. The chapter went on to discuss the financial (tangible) and engagement/outreach (intangible) outcomes of organizational CSR initiatives. It reflected on the nature and value of community engagement initiatives incorporating industry, market, government, joint government–industry and educational initiatives. In addition, it helped readers to develop a philosophical view of CSR in the context of THE organizational operations. Chapter 10 explored different dimensions of sustainable development and how it applies to the THE sector. It comprised many practical aspects of sustainable development as they impact on facilities design and management. The chapter investigated the relative 'newness' of sustainability to our lives generally and the THE sector specifically. This included the ramifications of the concept's 'newness' in terms of application of its principles and practices to the sector. The chapter discussed the history of sustainable development and, in particular, what the major influencers were and continue to be on its application in the sector. It familiarized the readers with the principal elements and terminology of sustainable development and the future trends that impact on facilities design and management. Chapter 11 reflected on the opportunities and challenges associated with the implementation of environmental management strategies, initiatives and approaches in THE facilities. It placed particular emphasis on the extent to which (how and why) human activities are placing pressure on the environment. It discussed the responsibility of the individual and the organization as it relates to reductions in environmental impacts. The chapter went on to explore how environmental sustainability can be best managed and regulated in the THE industries. Chapter 12 examined basic criteria for sustainable THE site selection, design and construction. It described the characteristics of the waste management hierarchy and outlined fundamental issues for THE waste and energy management programmes. Also, the chapter looked at several ways for improving energy efficiency in THE.

The fourth section (Chapters 13–17) explored various key competencies or functions required for effective facilities management and development. Chapter 13 identified a number of key leadership theories from the 1940s through to the present day. It outlined the characteristics associated with effective leaders. It helped readers to understand the nature of effective leadership behaviours. Finally, the chapter evaluated the role of leadership within organizations and its importance. Chapter 14 defined and explored the concept and scope of innovation. It discussed the key motives and drivers of innovation within THE facilities. It looked at the different types of innovation and evaluated the different categories of measuring innovation management. Chapter 15 emphasized that facilities management is about managing people and places to achieve best value for money by balancing user-needs with THE business needs to achieve optimum organizational effectiveness. This chapter investigated the theory and practice of entrepreneurship within the context of facilities management. Elements of entrepreneurship and facilities management were discussed in the context of facilities management business development and management. It investigated the entrepreneurial nature of facilities management functions and practice. Also, the chapter evaluated entrepreneurship (and intrapreneurship) within the context of facilities management and applied entrepreneurial skills for facilities management business development. Chapter 16 introduced the concept of work process knowledge (WPK) and explored what drives the need for WPK in staff in THE service industries. The chapter explored how WPK underpins the delivery of excellent customer service and discussed the factors that affect WPK and how best to support its growth in staff. Chapter 17 discussed the concept of knowledge management and explored its importance, types and process within the context of THE facilities.

From summarizing the individual chapters, some final concluding thoughts can be proposed. First, the breadth of THE facilities is significant. This can make it challenging to address all the issues that may be relevant across all THE facilities. What is apparent is that their uniqueness enlivens the vitality of the THE industries to which they belong. This book has provided a range of global examples that enable an understanding of the key facility management issues. It is also acknowledged that different country contexts will influence the management of facilities. Nevertheless, generic issues relating to sustainable design and management are relevant for all THE facilities. This book has also illustrated how facilities management cuts across both operational and strategic aspects, including, for example, design issues involving the servicescape of the facility through to decisions about outsourcing parts of the facility to an external provider.

Second, customers should be central to the management and development of a facility. This may sound obvious, but facility managers and operators can become blinkered to what is occurring around them. It is crucial, therefore, that any development decisions and projects are based on a sound appraisal of the market and competitors. If customers are not satisfied with the facility offer then, they will make the decision to use an alternative provider that can more effectively deliver what they want.

Third, acknowledging the hard and soft approaches to the management and development of THE facilities is crucial. This book has noted factors concerning the coordination and planning of facilities in respect of the financial bottom line and project management. Yet there are a host of psychological and behavioural factors that influence the design of the facility and its day-to-day operations. This includes encouraging an enterprising and intrapreneurial culture that enables innovation and creativity to be engendered in the facility.

Fourth, for the purposes of longevity, the sustainability of THE facilities should not be underestimated. Corporate social responsibility and environmental and waste management practices should be deeply embedded in how any THE facility operates and how it visualizes its way forward. Such practices can enable the facility to gain an advantage through not only cost efficiencies in the long term, but also as a means for differentiating the facility from others.

There may be aspects of facilities management and development that this book has not been able to address. Nevertheless, facilities management is a dynamic area of study and this book has gone some way to addressing the key issues that are central to the topic in the THE industries.

To sum up, this book showed the richness and complexity of the facilities that make up the THE industries. We have attempted to develop a systematic and grounded business approach to the understanding of the development and management of these facilities through the introduction of the literature on THE facilities and also through the examination of case studies that have explored actual developments and management in the industry. We believe that linking the academic and the practical is the only way to obtain a full understanding of the forces that shape THE facilities planning and development. The future of the THE industries lies in the hands of the people reading this book, as you will become the key players in the industry in the not too distant future. We have not supplied all the answers; in fact, if you read the book carefully we have not provided you with any answers. What we have attempted to do is to highlight the principles that underpin sound business processes and to demonstrate why and how they can help develop successful THE facilities. Our models are theoretical, but they are grounded in practice and the rigorous application of them within the context of specific THE facilities planning and developments can only help to guide the direction of the business towards success.

We hope you have enjoyed this book and will find the challenge of developing and managing THE facilities sufficiently interesting to become the next generation of THE entrepreneurs. Enjoy the journey!

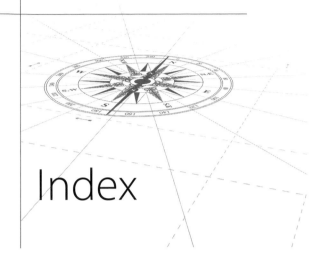

Index